TIN PAN
ALLEY

TIN PAN ALLEY

❦

The Composers, the Songs, The Performers and their Times

❦

THE GOLDEN AGE OF AMERICAN POPULAR MUSIC FROM 1886 TO 1956

❦

DAVID A. JASEN

Primus

DONALD I. FINE, INC.
NEW YORK

Library of Congress Cataloging-in-Publication Data

Jasen, David A.
  Tin pan alley / by David Jasen.
    p.   cm.
  Includes index.
  ISBN 1-55611-168-1
  1. Popular music—United States—History and criticism.
I. Title
ML3477.J34   1989   89-45549
781.64'0973—dc20   CIP

Manufactured in the United States of America

10   9   8   7   6   5   4   3   2   1

All photographs used in book belong to the National Academy
of Popular Music Archives, ASCAP, and the personal collection of the author, and are
used by permission.

The photograph of Harms' Broadway location in 1891 Courtesy
of New York Historical Society, New York City.

Design by Stanley S. Drate/Folio Graphics Co. Inc.

To my parents
Gertrude and Barnet Jasen
and to my wife Susan
and son Raymond
for giving me love and happiness

You write in the morning, you write at night. You write in a taxi, in the bathtub, or in an elevator. And after the song is all finished it may turn out to be very bad, but you sharpen your pencil and try again. A professional songwriter has his mind on his job all the time.

IRVING BERLIN

Jerome H. Remick & Company, at 45 West 28th Street in New York City, the largest publisher in Tin Pan Alley, around 1905.

C · O · N · T · E · N · T · S

A · C · K · N · O · W · L · E · D · G · M · E · N · T · S

Writing this book was first suggested to me by former ASCAP Director of Public Relations, Walter Wager. Randy Poe, General Manager of Leiber & Stoller, offered practical assistance, as did good friends Tim Brooks, Jane Cole, Lois Cordrey, Solomon Goodman, Randolph Herr, Jerome Karpf, Jr., Miles Kreuger, Bob Lachmann, Connie Newell, Bill Simon, Donald J. Stubblebine, Steve Suskin, Trebor Tichenor, Howard Wolverton, Ronnie and Larry Zimmerman, and Dick Zimmerman. My wife, Susan Jasen, helped with the last two chapters specifically, and with my life generally.

The following dealers in sheet music, records and piano rolls have not only helped me to assemble my collections, but with their expertise, they all encouraged me with their keen interest and by going out of their ways to bring facts and information to my attention: Bob Altshuler, Wayland Bunnell, Beverly Hamer, Herb Hurwitz, Lillian and Dulcina McNeill, Helen and Joel Markowitz, Mike Schwimmer (who plays washboard and sings "Peoria" like nobody's business), and Les Zieger.

I am grateful to the following composers, lyricists, publishers, arrangers, pluggers and publicists who, through the years, have taken the time to speak with me about our favorite subject—Tin Pan Alley: Lee Adams, Stanley Adams, Mickey Addy, Richard Adler, Lewis Allan, Louis Alter, Maxine Andrews, Bennie Benjamin, Roy Bennett, Walter Bishop, Eubie Blake, Oscar Brand, Leon Brettler, Irving Caesar, Sammy Cahn, Sam Coslow, Hal David, Ervin Drake, Milton Drake, Edward Eliscu, Sammy Fain, Leonard Feist, Milt Gabler, Don George, Otto Harbach, Sheldon Harnick, Sammy Kaye, Michael Kerker, Helmy Kresa, Burton Lane, Jack Lawrence, Alan Jay Lerner, Lou Levy, Sid Lippman, Bob Lissauer, Gerald Marks, Johnny Marks, Jack O'Brien, Abe Olman, Mitchell Parish, Buddy Robbins, Harold Rome, Russell Sanjek, George Simon, Lou Singer, Herman Steiger, Gary Stevens, Dana Suesse, Kay Swift, Arthur Tracy, Richard Voltter, George David Weiss, and P. G. Wodehouse.

I should like to thank the National Academy of Popular Music Archives and ASCAP for the use of their photographs, and the New York Historical Society for one photograph. All others and the sheet music illustrated are from the personal collection of the author.

Special thanks to Gene Jones for his wise counsel and for taking the time to make me readable.

While there have been studies of Tin Pan Alley and of songwriters, this book, for the first time, places the songwriters, publishers and performers into context with the popular dances and different media of the changing times. This is also the first book to detail the history of the major publishers, their sometimes confusing and short-lived partnerships, and their peripatetic journey from the Bowery to the Brill Building in New York City. Through the Alley's seventy turbulent years, changes in writing, marketing and performing styles took place, and this book hopes to make clear the process involved in getting the songs not only to attract immediate public acceptance (hits), but also to establish them as durable pieces of American life (standards).

Each major publisher's and composer's career is dealt with as one entry, usually in the decade of his first success, occasionally in the decade of his greatest importance. Birth and death dates, when known, are given at first mention, or at the time the person is most fully discussed. Popular dance, musical theatre, and performers are considered in each decade, along with the outstanding individual songs of that decade. Unless otherwise stated, the dates given for songs are the years they were copyrighted and published, and the dates for musical shows are for the opening nights on Broadway.

The history of Tin Pan Alley is the history of the United States as seen by its tunesmiths. We find an incredible variety of materials documented in songs which do, indeed, seem to have mirrored every aspect of American life from the beginning of Tin Pan Alley in the 1890's to the latest laser technology in the 1980's. We can chronicle the changing musical tastes of Americans, along with our social, economic and political concerns, by the kinds of popular music we bought, played and listened to—from the tear-jerker to the latest rock song.

Just what is Tin Pan Alley and where is it to be found? In an era before Elvis Presley made a song's performance more important than its publication, when a song's popularity was determined not by the number of records it sold but by the number of copies of sheet music it sold, Tin Pan Alley was the name given to the publishing business that hired composers and lyricists on a permanent basis to create popular songs. The publishers would market these songs in sheet music form with attractive covers to the general public by means of extensive promotion campaigns. Originally, Tin Pan Alley was a nickname given the actual street (West Twenty-eighth Street between Broadway and Sixth Avenue) in Manhattan where many of the fledgling popular music publishers had their offices. In time, it became the generic term for all publishers of popular American sheet music, regardless of their geographic locations.

The pop music scene today consists almost entirely of music video-tapes, audio tape cassettes, compact discs and flat disc recordings of both 45-rpm single and LP. Pop music itself is called rock, featuring high-powered electronic machines which create a multitude of layered sounds. The music is primarily marketed to the teenaged audience and the songs have very simple messages.

Today's approach to pop music is a far cry from the beginning of mass-marketed popular music, which started toward the end of the nineteenth century and ended in the middle of the nineteen fifties. Throughout the Alley's seventy years, popular music was developed in a variety of forms—love ballads, syncopated tunes, Latin American music, nonsense songs, show tunes—and marketed for adults. The music was presented and promoted in sheet music form for voice and piano. The public was induced to purchase the music sheets when they saw and heard their favorite performers incorporate the songs in their acts, first in the theater and in vaudeville, then through recordings (first on cylinders, then on flat discs which turned at 78 revolutions per minute), later on radio and then in films, and finally on television. Throughout most of the life of Tin Pan Alley, sheet music publishers dominated the popular music business, with the greatest part of their profits coming from the sale of sheet music.

What was this "popular" American sheet music business and how does it differ from the development and selling of martial music, children's music, folk music, religious music and classical music? Surely, each of these kinds of music contains representative pieces, vocal and instrumental, which were and are truly popular.

Before the 1890's, such occupations as composers, lyricists, and even publishers of popular music did not exist. This is not to say that popular songs were not written and published, but that nobody was hired expressly to compose and write them on demand. That demand came later, after the Alley was firmly established, either from the stars who wanted songs suited to their personalities or else from the publishers who demanded songs of a type which a rival publisher had and which the public was currently buying.

Pre-1890's music publishers were either classical publishers, music store owners, or local printers, who, along with such commodities as stationery, books, broadsides, magazines, advertisements and posters, printed sheet music. Popular sheet music from these printing houses and stationers across America was sold in their own stores, with larger firms getting salesmen of other goods to handle this product as a sideline. As these early printers could not afford their own full-time sales forces, they hired salesmen of clothing, notions and supplies to carry sample cases of music with them when they made their rounds throughout their territories. (One thinks of Meredith Willson's Professor Harold Hill in THE MUSIC MAN as a humorous caricature of these early music publishers.) These regional salesmen would get commissions from the orders sent in by local music store owners.

In a short while, these salesmen not only knew the likely customers for music among these local store owners, but also which songs were selling best in which areas. Some of these salesmen began to think that they could write better songs than those they were selling on commission. For less than a thousand dollars worth of printing credit, a salesman could write, publish, and go on the road to sell his own songs. From these roots, Tin Pan Alley was born. The first of these "salesman-composer-publisher" firms were Charles K. Harris in Milwaukee, Will

Rossiter and Victor Kremer in Chicago, Jerome Remick in Detroit, John Stark in St. Louis, Vandersloot in Williamsport, Pennsylvania, Walter Jacobs in Boston, and the Witmarks, Joseph Stern, Maurice Shapiro, F. A. Mills, Howley, Haviland & Company, T. B. Harms, Leo Feist, and Harry Von Tilzer in New York City.

Many famous publishing names got into the business as an afterthought. Full-line music stores like Sherman, Clay & Company of San Francisco, Lyon and Healy of Chicago, Oliver Ditson of Boston, Grinnell Bros. of Detroit, Carl Hoffman and J. W. Jenkins' Sons, both of Kansas City, began their own publishing imprints, although music publishing was always incidental to their main store operations. Men like Edward P. Little and Elmer Grant Ege, who founded and ran Sherman, Clay and J. W. Jenkins' Sons publishing departments, respectively, deserve the billing of publishers as much as Jerome H. Remick, Leo Feist and Edward B. Marks do, for they initiated and developed their businesses with the same care and attention as did those who had their names on their publishing firms. However, it took Little and Ege a long time before they were made directors of their firms.

These young, dynamic publishers had a common goal: to get enough potential sheet music customers to hear the music so they would then go out and buy it. The new wrinkle for this new business was song promotion. Anywhere and everywhere people congregated was fair game: vaudeville, bars, lobster palaces, beer gardens, theatres, brothels, nickelodeons. In the beginning, the publisher himself made the rounds of the entertainment centers, some publishers visiting as many as sixty places a week. These publishers also printed what they called "Professional Copies"—cheap newsprint editions without fancy illustrated covers—to give away free of charge to orchestra leaders and singers to induce them to perform their numbers, often sealing the deal with free drinks. These energetic publisher-salesmen then started offering star performers gifts and, later, money to feature their songs in their acts.

As business picked up, the publishers' promotional efforts became more sophisticated. They hired scores of men known as "pluggers" to perform all the songs in the publishers' catalogs. Pluggers, who reported to the firms' professional managers, were men of great personal charm and contacts, who could sell the songs by demonstrating them in music stores (and in the music sections of department stores) during the daytime, and by making the rounds of theatres, beer halls and vaudeville houses during the evening. The best pluggers concentrated on getting vaudeville headliners to sing their songs, sometimes singing along with them from the audience the first time the song was introduced. To get the leading performers to sing the songs whenever they appeared was always the goal of the plugger, so that favorite performers could put the songs over to the audiences, who would then go and buy the sheet music so they could learn and perform the songs themselves.

As the Alley developed, plugging remained essentially the same, but the methods changed with technology. After the vaudeville era, when radio captured audiences, airtime became a precious commodity, and pluggers (now sometimes called "contact men") concentrated on those orchestra leaders who had their own programs. It didn't matter to the plugger how famous or obscure the performer was. If he had airtime and could perform a song during that time, he became a target of the plugger. While getting the song recorded by as many performers as possible was desirable, the main thrust of plugging before the Presley era was to sell copies of sheet music.

During the 1890's, a publisher spent approximately $1,300 to create a hit song. In the 1950's, the figure rose to over $30,000 for a single song to be turned into a hit.

Along with getting a star to use a song in the act or on the air, publishers discovered early in the history of Tin Pan Alley that the song's cover played a most important role in the selling of the popular music sheet. Although fancy-lettered, engraved black-and-white covers were issued prior to the birth of Tin Pan Alley, and black-and-white lithographs of scenes illustrating the titles of songs were also common, it wasn't until "After the Ball," which featured the photograph of its popularizer, James Aldrich Libbey, prominently on the cover, that the appeal of catchy cover art was recognized as a link in the success of selling sheet music.

From the mid-1890's on, publishers took great care with their covers. Sometimes a combination of photograph and art illustration was used, other times just artwork or a photograph. Occasionally, famous illustrators of books, magazines and posters created sheet music artwork or allowed their previous work to be used as cover art: James Montgomery Flagg, Archie Gunn, Maxfield Parrish, Grace G. Drayton, Edward Windsor Kemble, Charles Dana Gibson, Henry Hutt, Raeburn Van Buren, Howard Chandler Christy, Rose O'Neill, Russell Patterson, John Held, Jr., Alberto Vargas, and Norman Rockwell.

Famous cartoonists also illustrated cover sheets: Richard Outcault, Palmer Cox, Rudolph Dirks, Bud Fisher, Frederick Opper, Winsor

McCay, George McManus, Rube Goldberg, George Herriman, Billy DeBeck, Frank King, Sidney Smith, Carl Ed, Milt Gross, Al Hirshfeld, Ham Fisher, Walt Disney, Edwina, Charles Schulz, Stan Mac Govern, Hank Ketcham, and Al Capp.

Several commercial artists made sheet music covers their life work: Fred W. Starmer, Bert Cobb, Edgar Keller, John Frew, Edward Henry Pfeiffer, Andre DeTakacs, and Albert Barbelle.

Edward Taylor Paull (1858–1924) was the first and only publisher who regularly used five-color lithography for his covers. He started publishing (mostly marches) in 1894 and continued publishing his highly collectible sheets until his death.

A publisher sometimes used a performer's photograph on the cover as an incentive for the performer to retain the song in his repertoire. A photograph also served as a reminder of the time the potential purchaser saw and heard the performer sing the song, and encouraged the customer to buy the sheet as a souvenir. Whatever the motivation, by the turn of the century, cover art was a significant element in helping to sell copies of sheet music. Today, these covers often comprise the only extant photographs of some of the places and people of this era, giving the covers added desirability, importance, and value.

The artwork of each era in Tin Pan Alley's history is distinctive. As many people collect sheet music today as collect postcards, posters and other works of popular art.

Sheet music wholesalers, otherwise known as jobbers, were very much a part of the publishing and plugging business. The major jobbers were Col. A. H. Goetting in Springfield, Massachusetts (who also owned Coupon Music Company in Boston and Enterprise Music Supply Company in New York); Plaza Music and Crown Music in New York City; Oliver Ditson in Boston; F. J. A. Forster and McKinley in Chicago; and Sherman, Clay in San Francisco. They did more than just fill orders. They acted as selling agents for the smaller publishers. They also undertook to plug certain numbers on their own. When Jack Robbins worked for the Enterprise Music Supply Company, he noticed a tune languishing on their shelves. He thought it could be a hit, so he pushed it. The tune was "Smiles," published by its composer Lee S. Roberts in Chicago. Robbins was so successful that Remick bought the song from Roberts, and Mose Gumble, Remick's professional manager, turned it into a three-million seller. Plugging independently was such a natural for these go-getters that jobbers like Maurice Richmond (who worked for

Goetting), Jack Robbins (who later worked for Richmond), Jerry Vogel (who worked for Plaza), and Henry Waterson (who worked for Crown), all eventually became full-time music publishers themselves.

Between 1900 and 1910, one hundred songs were said to have sold more than one million copies each—and this to a national population of just over ninety million. The songs sold for an average of fifty cents apiece (5&10-cent stores selling them for a dime), when the average take-home wage of a family of four was $12.75 a week. The expenditure was justified, however, for in the era before radio, there wasn't very much to do after work except gather round the family piano in the evening to sing songs. Many more girls than boys took piano lessons, perhaps because boys thought playing piano was sissy-stuff. Therefore, many of the jobs, such as demonstrating music in stores, accompanying performers and playing at nickelodeons, became the preserves of women.

Men took the jobs playing in saloons and whorehouses, where having a good ear, not reading music, was essential. The best of the male piano players would be found in sporting houses, where tips frequently amounted to over $100 an evening. It was in these sporting houses that a revolutionary form of popular instrumental music emerged at the turn of the century. This new music form was called ragtime. Its first million-selling hit, and the piece that established it as a popular genre, was Scott Joplin's 1899 composition, "Maple Leaf Rag."

Among the important factors in the rise of Tin Pan Alley was the rapid growth of vaudeville. Theatres were constructed across the country in great numbers. Names like Strand, Lyceum, Proctor's, Pantages, Keith, and Orpheum sprouted up in towns and villages everywhere. All, including the independent theatres, were supplied talent by booking agencies such as William Morris, Keith-Albee, and Klaw & Erlanger, the majority of which were located in New York City.

Each year, before they set out to troop across the country, vaudeville performers would stop at publishing houses for songs they might use to freshen up their acts. They went to each publisher's Professional Department, where they were taken to one of a series of small rooms, each with an upright piano. At the piano sat an accompanist and, sometimes, a lyricist in a nearby chair. The vaudevillians would listen to new songs, often demonstrated by their composers, and when a singer liked a number, the accompanist would immediately teach it to him or her. On the spot, the song could be tailored to the range and style of the singer, and all possible problems of key or tempo eliminated. For a star, these staff composers and lyricists (with a weekly draw of $25.00 against future royalties) would create special material for exclusive use. The Professional Manager not only supervised these piano rooms and demonstrators but also chose the material for the star performers and directed all plugging activity for the firm.

The record industry began to sell flat discs commercially in 1897. They were an invention of Emile Berliner, who also invented the gramophone on which to play them. Earlier, in 1877, Thomas Edison had invented his phonograph which played cylindrical records, but by 1908 the gramophone and its flat discs became the public's preferred machine and playback device. It wasn't until the 1920's that record sales enjoyed enough popularity to interest Tin Pan Alley. The record companies needed Tin Pan Alley's output, and Tin Pan Alley needed the additional plug capabilities of continual, permanent performances. The publishers also did not mind the two-cents-a-copy royalty given them by the record companies after the Copyright Law of 1909 was enacted. Not until after the Second World War would the recording industry replace the Alley as the mainstay of the music business. With the coming of rock and roll, the transition was complete, and recorded performances became the most important aspect of popular music, rather than sales of the song itself.

Even before talkies, a movie producer often hired a songwriter to compose a theme song with the film's title as the song's title. With the coming of sound, film studios, recognizing their increased need for old and familiar songs as well as new songs for their films, bought established Tin Pan Alley firms and also hired other composers and lyricists to write expressly for their pictures. During the 1930's, most of the successful Tin Pan Alleyites were to be found at one time or another working for the studios.

The most frequently asked question of songwriters is, "Which comes first, the words or the music?" (Lyricist Irving Casear used to say, "What comes first is the contract!") More often than not, the music came first. The Alley composer, once he had thought up a sparkling tune, wrote it down, or, in some cases, played it for a copyist to take down, and then prepared a special sheet, known as a "lead sheet," upon which only the melody appeared. The lead sheet was then given to the lyricist, who usually knew enough about notation to make out the general rhythm and the important accents. The sheet served as his lead or guide, hence the name. Theatre composer Jerome Kern always wrote the music first. Richard Rodgers also wrote the music first when collaborating with Larry Hart. However, when writing with Oscar Hammerstein II, Rodgers wrote his music to Hammerstein's lyrics. Irving Berlin, who wrote both words and music, did it both ways, although writing the words usually came first. In his book GREAT MEN OF AMERICAN POPULAR SONG, David Ewen quotes Berlin: "I usually get a phrase first—words. I keep repeating it over and over, and, the first thing I know, I begin to get a sort of rhythm, and then a tune. I don't say all my songs are written that way. Sometimes I hear a tune first, and then I start trying to fit words to it."

Writing a song for a theatrical production presents special problems for its creators, as most character or plot-specific songs are not potential "hits." The first thing the theatre composer and lyricist do is to plan how many songs they will need and the purpose each will serve in the context of the show. Will a song be used to create a mood, or can this mood be better expressed in dialogue? Would this song be sung by this character at this point in the show? However, creating a potential Tin Pan Alley hit as an independent song required just a kernel of an idea, either verbal or musical.

In the world of Tin Pan Alley, sometimes the title would be the first to come. Sometimes the song would be a true collaborative effort, with two or three people working together at the same time. Sometimes after the heat of fashioning a song, no one remembered who did what. Many a composer contributed lyrics, just as many a lyricist helped with a melodic line. A melodic fragment or a title or a phrase would be enough to start with, and brainstorming could lead to a song's completion.

Conventional wisdom has it that the popular music publishers in New York kept changing their business locations to follow the center of the theatre district in its thirty-year progression uptown. The old-line publishers of the 1870's and 80's first clustered around the Bowery in lower Manhattan, and then Union Square (Fourteenth Street and Broadway). Willis Woodward, who appeared on the scene at the beginning of the 1880's, had his office in the Star Theatre Building, Thirteenth Street and Broadway. In the 90's, West Twenty-eighth Street seemed to attract the upcoming plugging publishers. Between 1903 and 1908, Tin Pan Alley moved uptown again, heading toward West Forty-second Street. By the 1920's, song publishers were entrenched in Upper Longacre Square (West Forty-second to Fifty-sixth Streets), where the Great White Way is still to be found.

Although half of the ten major publishers never set foot on West Twenty-eighth Street (the "Tin Pan Alley" of legend), five of them did, however briefly. At the turn of this century and during its first decade, many minor publishers did have offices there. From 1911 to 1919, most of the majors and minors settled throughout the West Forties, with the Exchange Building, located at 145 West Forty-fifth Street, as the focal point of the small-to-medium-sized publishers. This thirteen-story building seems to have housed nothing but publishers during the second decade of our century. It presaged the coming of the Brill Building.

It wasn't until the Brill Building was built in 1931 at 1619 Broadway (at Forty-ninth Street) that the popular music publishing industry established a permanent location. Named for Morris Brill, who had a clothing store on the ground floor, this building became the last hub of the music business. Among the early tenants were Mills Music, Famous Music, Fred Fisher Music, and Irving Caesar Music. As Hal David, contemporary lyricist and recent President of ASCAP, recalled, "The preponderance of songwriters were in the Brill Building, the energy was in the Brill Building, the publishers were there, and if you had to be some place else, you always wound up back at the Brill Building sometime during the day."

The history of the Alley contains many stories, some true, some half-true, some fables, all of them fascinating. In this chronicle there are some famous stories of who wrote what and how the songs came to be written, along with some stories never before told. A lot of the stories and anecdotes included herein come to us through musical legend and the lore of Tin Pan Alley; many are exaggerated.

Take, for instance, the reported sales figures of most songs during the Alley's "Golden Age." In the hyperbole of the song-hustlers, even the season's worst seller would often be described as "a terrific success." So, what were the genuine million-sellers, the palpable hits?

It has become increasingly evident that in the "Golden Age" the lists of Top Forty hits and of the Hit Parade give a false picture of a song's popularity. Some of the most enduring songs—which became standards—never appeared on these charts and didn't sell a million copies at the time they were first published. There was nothing comparable to the Record Industry Association of America (RIAA) during the years of Tin Pan Alley. The RIAA started issuing Gold Record awards in 1958 to those single discs selling over one million copies and to albums selling five hundred thousand copies. Later, they added the category of Platinum awards for those singles selling over two million and albums over one million. Record companies must now substantiate the accuracy of their figures before an award is given. At Tin Pan Alley's height, there were no trade associations that verified sales figures of the publishers. A look at these charts year by year reveals names of songs, now obscure, which held the number one position for weeks. It is a mistake, therefore, to correlate the best sellers of the day with those songs that became standards, the ones we still hum, those that are a part of our social fabric. This book focuses on the songs—their composers, lyricists, performers and publishers—that have lasted, those songs that have become a most important part of our American heritage.

This book is a reminder that the creators of our musical life are not to be forgotten. Irving Berlin, our greatest songwriter (both lyrics and music) and an important music publisher, took up oil painting in his later years. In his chapter on Berlin in THEY'RE PLAYING OUR SONG, author Max Wilk recounts famed orchestrator Robert Russell Bennett's story about Berlin's young granddaughter who had to write a school paper. She wrote "An Afternoon with My Grandfather." When the teacher asked her, "Who is your grandfather?" she drew herself up to her full height and said, "Irving Berlin is my grandfather."

"Irving Berlin!" said the teacher. "What does *he* do?"

"He paints!" came the granddaughter's reply.

THE BIRTH OF TIN PAN ALLEY

(1886–1899)

THE MAJOR PUBLISHERS:
AN OVERVIEW

According to legend, the naming of Tin Pan Alley came at the turn of the century, when Monroe Rosenfeld, a prolific composer-lyricist, wrote a series of articles for the New York *Herald* on the new and energetic popular music publishing business. For research, he visited the office of Harry Von Tilzer, then located at 42 West Twenty-eighth Street, between Broadway and Sixth Avenue. As more of the fledgling publishers were located on this street of reconstructed brownstone flats than on any other—the "office" usually consisting of a broken-down, out-of-tune piano, a second-hand desk and chair, file cabinets and wooden racks holding the stock of sheet music—he heard a din of competing pianists as he left Von Tilzer's office, and he recorded that this street, with all of the demonstrators working at the same time, sounded like a bunch of tin pans clanging. The street where all of this activity was taking place he characterized as "the Alley."

The entertainment industry in New York City in the 1880's was centered around Union Square on Fourteenth Street. Tony Pastor (1837–1908) had the leading music hall of the day (1875–1906) on East Fourteenth Street near Third Avenue, where the most famous singers entertained. The singers always included old favorites in their acts, as well as new songs which were sung exclusively by them, many created specifically for them. Fourteenth Street between Broadway and Third Avenue was the mecca of musical show business. The premier popular song publisher of the 80's was Willis Woodward, who had his office in the Star Theatre Building, Thirteenth Street at Broadway. Woodward issued such hits as "White Wings," "The Song That Reached My Heart," and "Always Take Mother's Advice." He became the king of the tearjerkers. T. B. Harms & Co. published most of the musical stage songs of the day, while William A. Pond & Company published the Harrigan

1

and Hart songs and the authorized versions of Gilbert and Sullivan music.

Early in the 1890's, a new, young breed of popular music publishers came into being. These publishers were, essentially, salesmen who didn't sit in their offices waiting for performers to come to them, but went out to the entertainment palaces and badgered not only the singers but also the orchestra leaders, dancers, acrobats and comedians to use their numbers. They hustled themselves, as well as their hired singers and whistlers, into the finest theatres and the lowest dives. As the decade progressed, the vaudeville houses began to move uptown, along with the leading restaurants. It is no wonder then that the new popular music publishers moved and expanded their businesses, as did theatrical agents and the show business trade journals.

While Tin Pan Alley had its beginnings in the middle of the 1880's, it was not until 1892 that an Alley publisher had a multi-million-copy hit: "After the Ball," a tear-jerker by Charles K. Harris that sold five million copies in the decade after its first publication. As noted in the Introduction, sales figures of most of the Alley's songs are hard to obtain and impossible to believe. Publishers, as well as songwriters, tended to exaggerate their figures by hundreds of thousands, even by millions, and business records, for the most part, have by now been lost or destroyed. However, "After the Ball" is regarded as the Alley's first hit, and one of its biggest.

Most of the Alley's largest publishers were established during the 1890's, a decade that had, not coincidentally, more songs published and sold than any previous decade. Many of these songs were not very good, and are not remembered today. But such highly acclaimed standards as "The Sidewalks of New York," "The Band Played On," and "Daisy Bell (The Bicycle Built for Two)" did make their debuts during the 1890's.

In the nineties, the cost of publishing and advertising a song was approximately $1,300. That figure, broken down, looked like this: To lithograph a singer's photograph on the cover cost a publisher $50. To print ten thousand copies of the song cost $250. To advertise the song for a year in a trade journal cost $500, and the publisher offered to the singer who introduced the song another $500, sometimes as a flat fee, or as a cash advance against future royalties, depending on the clout and popularity of the performer.

Although the output of Tin Pan Alley appears vast to us now, with seemingly hundreds of publishers publishing thousands of composers and lyricists who cranked out millions of songs, the Alley was, in reality, a very small network of men (and a few women) who helped each other get started, either inadvertently or deliberately.

THE PIONEER PUBLISHERS

Edward B. Marks (1865–1945) was a young notions salesman who liked to write lyrics. He went to Frank Harding, whose father had started a music publishing business in 1860 on the Bowery (Number 229), which Frank had taken over at the same location in 1879. Harding put Marks in touch with William Loraine, a part-time hack composer and full-time lush. Harding published the result of their collaboration ("December and May") in 1893. Marks offered to take samples of Harding's song catalog on the road with him. Harding accepted, as he had no branch office and wanted his music available in places other than New York City. After Marks got his royalty statement for his one song, he decided it would be more profitable to publish his songs himself. He teamed with another salesman who could write melodies, Joseph W. Stern. They opened a small office in 1894 and issued their first collaboration, "The Little Lost Child," that same year. With the help of music hall singers Della Fox and Lottie Gilson, the song became a hit and established the firm of Joseph W. Stern & Company as a major voice in Tin Pan Alley. Marks also created the illustrated song slide, which was used in music theatres to help the audience visualize the lyrics through a series of action and sentimental photographs and illustrations. The slide songs were introduced into nickelodeons—so that audiences could sing the songs between pictures—and vaudeville. The illustrated song slide quickly became a valuable tool in the plugging of popular songs.

Leopold Feist (1869–1930) was a sales manager for a corset company. He liked to write songs, and he managed to convince Ed Marks to publish a couple of them. When sales did not live up to expectations, he decided to give up songwriting, but he liked the business so much that he joined with Joe Frankenthaler to publish other, more successful, songwriters. Among the first songs Feist and Frankenthaler issued were two in 1897 by the prolific Harry Von Tilzer. A year later, Feist issued Abe Holzmann's "Smokey Mokes," their first big hit that firmly established their business. Holzmann not only composed, but became the firm's first arranger. As Feist was an expert salesman, he managed to arrange many performances by approaching orchestra leaders himself and by personally selling copies at various stores. His biggest coup was getting John Philip Sousa to include "Smokey Mokes" in his concerts.

Another old-line publisher, Willis Woodward (d. 1908), who specialized in tear-jerkers, published Isidore Witmark's first song. When Witmark's royalty statement came, he was so disgusted at his meager earnings that he and his brothers went into business for themselves. As the Witmarks prospered, they encouraged the audiences of minstrel, vaudeville, and burlesque shows to learn their songs by distributing handbills upon which the lyrics were printed, and by hiring young boys to sit in the audience and sing along with the star from the balcony, urging the rest of the audience to join them on the repeat of the chorus. The Witmarks were also the first to publish professional copies and distribute them free of charge to performers. They also furnished free orchestrations, which the singers could take with them for engagements.

Charles K. Harris (1867–1930) had his first number, "When the Sun Has Set," published by the Witmarks. When he got his royalty statement six months later, and a postal order for eighty-four cents, he wrote Isidore Witmark that it was the smallest return he had ever received for any song, and that he was going to frame the note with the caption: "The smallest royalty statement on record." When Witmark got his letter, he wrote to Harris: "Would say I am also framing your song and hanging it in a conspicuous place in my office, where all in the profession can see it. Underneath, I am writing this: 'The only song we ever published that did not sell.' " It was this incident that made Harris start publishing his own songs. The first successful one under his imprint was "After the Ball."

Charles K. Harris believed in songs with plots, whether they were sung in musical comedy shows or in sketches in vaudeville. The song itself had to tell a story. Harris practiced what he preached throughout his songwriting career and wrote only sentimental ballads with strong storylines. He also believed that the song title is the most important element, since the lyric is merely an expansion of the title.

Patrick Howley (1870–1918), manager of Willis Woodward & Company, decided that there could be more to publishing than the sentimental ballads his firm bought. In 1893, he joined with Frederick Benjamin Haviland (1868–1932), New York sales manager for the Boston-based Oliver Ditson Company, which at that time was a classical and parlor-music publisher and sheet music wholesaler. As they wanted to test the waters before quitting their jobs, Howley and Haviland started the firm of George T. Worth, a name they made up to protect their identities.

However, their respective employers caught on to their enterprise and forced them to quit their jobs. Thus, Howley, Haviland & Company, one of the most successful of the Tin Pan Alley publishers, was born. This firm had great success with two of the Alley's most popular song styles: the sentimental ballad or tear-jerker, and the "coon song," a generic term at this time for black music, usually presented in comic form, with or without dialect. They exploited these styles vigorously throughout the 1890's, becoming one of the most influential and envied firms of this time. Much of their success with coon songs could be attributed to Bert Cobb (1869–1936) and Edgar Keller (1867–1932), who designed their covers. As their artwork was, in large part, responsible for the sales that these songs enjoyed, the Witmarks soon started using Cobb and Keller too.

One of the first employees of Howley, Haviland & Company was Max Dreyfus (1874–1964), who not only arranged the songs of the firm's top composers, including Paul Dresser (see below), but who also had great skill as an "inside" plugger, teaching performers the firm's songs on the premises. When he went to the Witmarks in 1895 to interest them in his own songs, they did not want his songs but did want him. Witmark's (a larger firm than Howley, Haviland) hired him to arrange and plug its numbers. Dreyfus later joined the old-line firm of T. B. Harms & Company in 1898 as their chief arranger and occasional composer. He purchased a twenty-five percent interest in the firm in 1901. While brothers Thomas B. and Alex T. Harms had the idea of specializing in theatre music, they had outside interests and were not aggressive businessmen. They did not plug their music very effectively, possibly because Tom was more interested in Wall Street. So, their business dwindled, and the newer houses of Stern and Witmark went after their theatre music writers and customers. Dreyfus finally bought out the Harms brothers in 1904, retaining the name and eventually turning it into the most prestigious popular music publishing firm in Tin Pan Alley. Dreyfus discovered and promoted the most distinguished theatre composers of this century: Jerome Kern, George Gershwin, Vincent Youmans, Richard Rodgers, and Cole Porter, among many others. He, in time, published about ninety percent of all Broadway scores and show tunes.

Major songwriters who became publishers did so in the same way. Paul Dresser (1857–1906), who turned out successful sentimental ballads by the dozens, earned so much money in royalties, especially from "On the Banks of the Wabash, Far Away," that Howley and Haviland offered him a partnership.

When Maurice Shapiro and brother-in-law Louis Bernstein purchased printer William Dunn's Orphean Music Company, which included the publishing rights to Harry Von Tilzer's first big hig, "My Old New Hampshire Home," they offered Von Tilzer a partnership in their new business, soon to become Shapiro, Bernstein & Von Tilzer. Von Tilzer thanked them by immediately turning out a million-seller with "A Bird in a Gilded Cage."

Irving Berlin started his career as a singing plugger for Von Tilzer, then joined composer Ted Snyder's company as lyricist. After three years of turning out hits, often co-written with Snyder, and after the enormously successful publication of his own "Alexander's Ragtime Band," Berlin was named a partner in what became Waterson, Berlin & Snyder Company. Eventually, Berlin, as did Dresser and Von Tilzer, branched out as his own publisher.

M. WITMARK & SONS:
ARCHETYPES

Like most new businesses, Tin Pan Alley was a young man's game. But the Witmarks, when they started, made it seem like a kid's game. Isidore (1869–1941), the eldest, was seventeen; Julius (1870–1929), the boy tenor, was sixteen; and baby Jay (1877–1950), the financial head, was all of fourteen when they started publishing music in 1886. "M." Witmark was their father Marcus. His sole function in the firm was to sign legal papers, as his business-minded sons were all underage.

The Witmark brothers decided to enter the music publishing business when Willis Woodward not only neglected to pay Isidore a royalty on his first published number, "A Mother's a Mother after All," but also reneged on his promise to give Julius a percentage of sheet music sales for plugging Jennie Lindsay's "Always Take Mother's Advice," when she was on a bill with the Thatcher, Primrose and West minstrel troupe.

The brothers entered the popular song field with gusto, taking an active lead in plugging their songs instead of waiting, as their competitors Woodward, Harms and Harding did, for singers to come to them. The Witmarks put composers and arrangers—with more than one piano, unusual at the time—on staff to demonstrate their songs. With an eye to a national market, the Witmarks became the first major full-line popular sheet music publisher of the nineties, developing the personal and professional creative and marketing skills that soon became standard throughout the industry.

It was just as true in the 1880's as in the 1980's that political rumors abounded, at first met with denials, and later with an admission of their truth. One day in 1886, Jay Witmark noticed in the newspaper that President Grover Cleveland was going to be married. This news sparked the Witmark brothers' daily business conference. They decided to publish a wedding march to mark the occasion, and Isidore was assigned the task of creating one. After a few hours, he had composed the piece, and the boys rushed to get it printed. During the next few days, it was reported that the announcement had been a hoax and that the President was not going to get married. It was too late to stop the presses, and the boys' publishing career nearly ended before it started. However, a few days after that, the President did announce his forthcoming marriage to Frances Folsom, and the Witmark brothers were ready with their first topical piece, "President Grover Cleveland's Wedding March." It could be said that they had stolen a march over all their competitors—an auspicious beginning to the publishers' business. It was the first attempt of this new breed of music publishers to capitalize on a national event in order to sell sheet music. Although the tune did not become an all-time hit, its creation-on-demand was what publishers in the Alley became famous for, and its publication date marks the traditional beginning of the Golden Age of Tin Pan Alley.

The Witmarks quickly found that topical songs alone were not enough to sustain business. As the 1890's wore on, they branched out to become general publishers of popular music. They handled the show scores of Victor Herbert, Chauncey Olcott, and the precocious George M. Cohan, which led also to the development of their fine Irish song catalog ("Mother Machree," "My Wild Irish Rose," "When Irish Eyes Are Smiling"). As mentioned above, they competed early on with Howley & Haviland in coon songs by hiring Ben Harney ("Mister Johnson, Turn Me Loose") and Sidney Perrin ("Mammy's Little Pumpkin-Colored Coons") to write exclusively for them.

In 1891, Tin Pan Alley became aware of a new development in the copyright laws, which, at first, sharply curtailed its revenues. And, as with President Cleveland's wedding, the Witmarks were the first publishers to leap upon this national event and turn it into profit. Before 1891, copyright laws protected American writers from piracy only within the United States. Similarly, much of what was published in America—royalty free—was the work of Englishmen. Also, tunes from the Continent—embellished with new lyrics by Americans—were published with no fee paid to the composer.

The International Copyright Law of 1891 changed the situation dramatically and, for the first time, afforded copyright protection to foreign compositions sold in America, as well as to American works published abroad. It then became important for American publishers to secure international rights, especially for the English plays and musicals that had been published so freely and easily before. The Witmarks saw the opportunity to convince leading music publishers in London that they needed representation in the United States. They also saw the need to open an office in London to handle their own publications overseas.

Isidore was chosen to go to London to establish representation there. When he arrived, he was faced with a peculiar situation. British music publishers were generally leisurely in their dealings (and advanced in years), and they expected to deal with an American representative of similar attitude and deportment. Isidore, who was then twenty-three years old, resented their attitude. When he could no longer tolerate it, he said at one meeting, "See here! In my country, the type of man you have been expecting to meet in me is retired long ago or relegated to the position of bookkeeper!" He soon won them over and gained contracts with England's second largest publisher, Charles Sheard & Company, as well as one with specialist publisher Reynolds & Company. He also appointed an American actor, Charles Warren, who was living in London permanently, as personal representative of M. Witmark & Sons. Thus, the Witmarks became the first major United States music publisher with an overseas branch.

During 1893, when Julius Witmark was on the road singing his firm's songs with minstrel troupes, he went to Chicago, where the World's Fair was in progress. There he met an old friend, Sol Bloom, who was in charge of some exhibits. Before Julius left, he created a Chicago branch of Witmark's, putting Bloom in charge. It was a restless Bloom, who, several years later, saw a viable business opportunity in acquiring music sections in department stores. He left the Witmarks to pursue it, and later turned publisher himself. After a few successful years as a publisher, he got out of the music publishing business and sold his catalog to the Witmarks. He eventually went into other businesses, finally becoming a Congressman representing New York State.

It was this same year, 1893, that saw the Witmarks move to Twenty-eighth Street from Union Square, becoming the first important firm to move to the still-unnamed "Alley." Their move uptown gave recognition to the shift in the location of the theatrical houses and to the new form of popular entertainment, vaudeville. It also acknowledged that the firm needed larger quarters as its business grew. The Witmarks took over the buildings at 49–51 West Twenty-eighth Street.

As they were settling down in their new building, a new kind of music started to attract the interest of the public. It came at first in high-spirited songs with syncopated accompaniment, and the Witmarks hired Max Hoffman in Chicago to write such "rag accompaniments" for their new coon songs. On the stage, a dance called the cakewalk appeared, with syncopated music written especially for it. Its final form was as an instrumental in two-four time for the piano, and it was called "Rag-Time." It became the sensation of the mid-nineties and vied with the waltz as a favorite time signature.

In 1896, for every "Sweet Rosie O'Grady" that was published, there was a coon song: May Irwin's "Bully Song," Bert A. Williams' "Oh, I Don't Know," Ernest Hogan's "All Coons Look Alike to Me," W. T. Jefferson's "My Coal Black Lady," Ben Harney's "Mister Johnson, Turn Me Loose," Barney Fagan's "My Gal Is a Highborn Lady," and Theodore Metz' "Hot Time in the Old Town."

Two years later, the Witmarks moved again, this time around the corner to 8 West Twenty-ninth Street, a five-story building which they completely occupied. The business had grown to include not only the Professional Department with its staff songwriters and pluggers, but also the Witmark Music Library of special arrangements of medleys, overtures, and popular operatic productions for rental, operatic selections, oratorios, masses, vocal parts for chorus, band scores, and orchestra scores; the Minstrel Department, which furnished not only music but books, gags, scripts, costumes, accessories, make-up, and instruments; and a booming mail-order business outfitting complete minstrel shows for amateur productions. Their mail-order "Black and White Series" not only contained their semi-classical numbers, but also their most famous ballads, standard features and steady sellers through the years. These backlist items carried them through downturns in the economy that produced sluggish frontlist sales, and kept such composers as Ernest Ball and Caro Roma in print. To keep the music world informed of their various activities, the Witmarks began the first of the Alley house-organs, *The Witmark Monthly*.

OTHER PUBLISHERS:

The Rivals of Witmark

Outside the Alley, Will Rossiter (1867–1954) of Chicago became a major publisher when he began operations in 1890. He was the first publisher to hawk his wares in retail stores. Satisfying his urge to perform, he personally demonstrated songs to his customers. This go-getter, styling himself as "The Chicago Publisher," was the first to advertise his songs in trade journals and theatrical papers. He was also the first to issue inexpensive song folios. However, he dropped out of the song publishing business at the end of the decade and didn't resume his publishing career until 1905, when he came back to stay. He helped start the careers of several notable Alleyites by giving advice to Charles K. Harris, and by publishing William Jerome, Fred Fisher, Egbert Van Alstyne, and Percy Wenrich, all of whom, besides being top-notch songwriters, entered the publishing field themselves.

The company of Joseph W. Stern (1870–1934) and his silent partner, Edward B. Marks (1865–1945), became the major competitor of the Witmarks. As general music publishers, Stern and Marks were strong on dance music—waltzes, schottisches, two-steps—and the sensation of the nineties, the syncopated cakewalk. They were quick to hear the difference that the black songwriter made, and hired the most famous and prolific teams—Cole and Johnson (first Bob Cole with comedian Billy Johnson, then Cole with the Johnson Brothers [no relation to Billy], John Rosamond and James Weldon), and Williams (Bert) and Walker (George). The Stern Company was the first New York publisher to latch on to that captivating, toe-tapping piano music from Missouri called ragtime, when they bought the rights to Tom Turpin's 1897 St. Louis publication "Harlem Rag" in 1899. They had their black house arranger, Will Tyers (1876–1924), rewrite it, and it became an enormous hit.

When Leo Feist and Joe Frankenthaler started their concern in August 1897, their first employee was Edgar F. Bitner, who was hired as bookkeeper, porter, errand boy and whatever other general position needed to be filled. By their first decade, Bitner had become general manager of the firm, in charge of the New York office and of all five branches, employing a total of two hundred and fifty people. He eventually became vice-president of the corporation. One of his decisions affected the entire industry. With the cost of paper rising, and in order to keep the cost of sheet music down, he introduced in March 1916 a new music sheet without an insert page. That is, the music was printed complete on the inside of the front and back covers. Not only did this save paper, it also saved on shipping charges. He saved paper again when, in August 1918, he issued a miniature (10¼" × 7") wartime version of the song sheet, also without an insert page.

Charles K. Harris (1867–1930) established an office in New York in 1897, and hired vaudeville artist Meyer Cohen to run his business there, while he concentrated on composing and writing his sentimental ballads-with-a-story in Milwaukee, Wisconsin. Harris never learned to read or write music and depended on Joseph Clauder to arrange and write out his piano and vocal parts for publication. Despite the description of the 1890's as "gay," this was Harris' decade, as the customers devoured his melancholy songs.

Paul Dresser (1857–1906), Harris' rival in creating these melodramas in miniature, was hired by Howley & Haviland to write and plug his own numbers. He became so successful in doing this that he was offered equal partnership in the firm. In 1900, the house became known as Howley, Haviland & Dresser.

Just as Charles K. Harris was essentially a one-type songwriter and publisher (of tear-jerkers), so too, in an opposite vein, was Frederick Allen Mills (1869–1948), who wrote under the name of Kerry Mills. He composed as "Kerry," and published as "F.A.," cakewalks all through the decade, and concentrated almost exclusively on this new, slightly syncopated dance craze. Popularized by the recently-arrived-to-New-York-from-San-Francisco team of Williams and Walker on stage, and by Genaro and Bailey in vaudeville, Kerry Mills turned out a string of instrumental cakewalks which sold in vast quantities. At the end of 1899, advance orders for his "Impecunious Davis" totaled 265,000 copies. It eventually sold nearly 750,000 copies. The cakewalk was almost an industry by itself, as hundreds of other cakewalks were published during the years 1895–1904. (Strangely, the cakewalk enjoyed a short revival in 1915.) The firm of F. A. Mills not only pioneered this dance, but also, through Mills' own compositions, maintained its high quality almost single-handedly. The cakewalk was to be supplanted in the next decade by instrumental ragtime.

MAJOR SONGWRITERS OF THE NINETIES

CHARLES K. HARRIS:
"After the Ball"

Charles Kassell Harris was born in Poughkeepsie, New York, on May 1, 1867. His parents moved soon after to Milwaukee, Wisconsin, where he spent his youth and the first decade of his professional years. For all practical purposes, his dual career as songwriter and publisher existed and was maintained by the extraordinary sales of one song, "After the Ball." Harris' youngest sister, Ada, had a girl friend who lived in Chicago. She invited Ada to visit her and attend a ball given by a social club early in 1892. Charles was asked to chaperone Ada, taking her to Chicago from their home in Milwaukee. The evening of the ball was a momentous one for him for two reasons: he met his future wife there, and he witnessed a scene which he would alter and describe in song. Dancing in those days consisted of the waltz, minuet, quadrille, and schottische. In the group was a charming couple, engaged to be married. Suddenly, Harris heard that the engagement had been broken that very evening. As they were leaving the party, Harris noticed the young man escorting, not his fiancee, but another young lady. The young man felt that by causing his sweetheart a pang of jealousy, she would be willing to forget their quarrel. She, on the other hand, saw only that he was easily consoled. Tears came to her eyes, though she tried to hide them behind a smile and a careless toss of the head. On seeing this little drama, the phrase "Many a heart is aching after the ball" came into Harris' mind and stayed there.

The next day, as he was resting after the journey, he saw the estranged couple of the previous night whose pride had kept them apart. For his song, he created a scene of a little girl climbing on her uncle's knee asking, "Why are you single, why live alone?" The uncle recalls the time when he saw his sweetheart at a ball in the arms of another. She tried to explain, but he wouldn't believe her, thinking her faithless until years later, when he discovered that it was her brother who had been embracing her. When he had finished three verses and a chorus, Harris sent for his arranger, Joseph Clauder, who took the song down on manuscript paper.

Harris' next thought was to get a big star to include it in his repertoire. Playing at the Bijou Theatre in Milwaukee was the touring company of Charles Hoyt's A TRIP TO CHINATOWN. In the cast was the famous

James Aldrich Libbey, who billed himself as "the peerless baritone." Harris knew the company manager and, after hearing Libbey sing on opening night, asked the manager to arrange an appointment with the singer. The following morning Libbey walked into Harris' office and was given the manuscript. Libbey liked the title of the song and proceeded to sing it straight through. He asked for an orchestration and said he would put it into the show the following Wednesday. From the first time he sang it, audience response was overwhelming. He agreed to sing it for as long as the tour lasted. As the company moved from city to city, orders for the song started pouring into the Harris office. His first order was from the Oliver Ditson Company of Boston for seventy-five thousand copies. Another order for one hundred thousand copies came soon thereafter, and within a few months, Harris had sold two million copies, making "After the Ball" the first of the Alley's multi-million-selling hits. It would eventually sell over five million copies. The second edition featured a photograph of the "peerless baritone," who sang it the rest of his professional life.

In addition to Libbey's plugging, John Philip Sousa included it in his daily program at the Chicago World's Fair in 1893, exposing it to crowds from all over the United States. Such a gigantic plug produced continuing sales.

With the money earned on "After the Ball," Harris continued to publish his own songs until he finally established a New York office, where he soon became a full-fledged publisher by taking on other songwriters' numbers. However, the bulk of his success continued to be with the publication of his own songs. He moved to New York permanently in 1903, when he settled at 31 West Thirty-first Street. Another of his own weepers was the Spanish-American War favorite, "Break the News to Mother." He also wrote and published the song that started Al Jolson's career, "For Old Time's Sake," and the great sob-story telephone song, "Hello Central, Give Me Heaven." "Nobody Knows, Nobody Cares" and "Mid the Green Fields of Virginia" are the only other Harris songs which had sales of hit proportions. He continued to publish until his death on December 22, 1930, in New York City.

PAUL DRESSER:
"On the Banks of the Wabash . . ."

Paul Dresser was born Dreiser in Terre Haute, Indiana, on April 21, 1857. He was the older brother of the novelist Theodore Dreiser. His father, a deeply religious man, wanted Paul to become a priest. As Paul's interest was in music, he ran away from home at the age of sixteen and joined a medicine show, changing his last name at this time. Dresser joined several minstrel troupes and wrote songs relentlessly. It was in 1885, when he was with the Billy Rice Minstrels, that he wrote his first hit, "The Letter That Never Came." He followed it two years later with "The Convict and the Bird," published by Willis Woodward, and with his 1891 hit "The Pardon Came Too Late." By this time, Dresser had a solid reputation as the foremost writer of sentimental ballads. When Howley and Haviland started their firm, they hired Dresser to write for them. He continued to write his ballads and to plug them in touring shows. He was in great demand as an actor and singer. It was in 1897 that he created his immortal "On the Banks of the Wabash, Far Away." His brother later took the credit for writing some of the lyrics, but according to the arranger, Max Hoffman, this simply isn't true. Hoffman wrote of witnessing the creation of this famous song, quoted in Isidore Witmark's autobiography, *From Ragtime to Swingtime:*

"I went to his room at the Auditorium Hotel in Chicago where, instead of a piano, there was a small folding camp organ, which Paul always carried with him. It was summer; all the windows were open and Paul was mulling over a melody that was practically in finished form. But he did not have the words. So he had me play the full chorus over and over again for at least two or three hours, while he was writing down words, changing a line here and a phrase there until at last the lyric suited him. He had a sort of dummy refrain, which he was studying; but by the time he finished what he was writing down to my playing, it was an altogether different lyric.

"When Paul came to the line, 'Through the sycamores the candle lights are gleaming,' I was tremendously impressed. It struck me at once as one of the most poetic inspirations I had ever heard.

"I have always felt that Paul got the idea from glancing out of the window now and again as he wrote, and seeing the lights glimmering out on Lake Michigan. We spent many hours together that evening, and when Paul finished, he asked me to make a piano part for publication at the earliest moment. I happened to have some music paper with me, and I wrote one right out, on the spot. This I mailed to Pat Howley, one of Dresser's partners, sending it to the New York Office at Thirty-second Street and Broadway. At Paul's request I also enclosed my bill.

"This piano part contained the lyric as Paul (and no one else) wrote it that night in my presence. The song was published precisely as I arranged it."

In August 1900, the publishing firm became Howley, Haviland & Dresser. He kept pouring out his ballads. On December 7, 1903, Haviland left the firm and by June 1904, Howley, Dresser & Company was bankrupt. Although he wrote what was to be his greatest hit, "My Gal Sal," late in 1905, Dresser didn't have the money to plug it properly, although he did manage to publish it. It was not until his protege, Louise Dresser, who adopted his last name, sang it and Joseph W. Stern & Company took over its publication that it became a hit. Dresser died unexpectedly at his sister's home on January 30, 1906.

JAMES THORNTON:
"When You Were Sweet Sixteen"

James Thornton was born in Liverpool, England, on December 5, 1861. His family came to the United States when he was eight years old, settling in Boston. As a young man, Thornton went to New York City, where he started his career as a singing waiter. He quickly became a drinking companion of John L. Sullivan, the first heavyweight champion of the world. For several years, he was a singing partner of Charles B. Lawlor, the composer of "The Sidewalks of New York," and toured the vaudeville circuits. Thornton's first song hit came in 1892, when his wife Bonnie, with a chance remark, pleaded with him to come home right after his performance, instead of staying out late drinking in saloons. When he refused to promise this, she asked him if she were still his sweetheart. He airily replied, "My sweetheart's the man in the moon." The next morning he remembered the phrase and used it as the title of his song. In 1894, he came up with another sentimental ballad, "She May Have Seen Better Days." But it was in 1898 that he published his most famous song, again inspired by his wife. Asked by her if he did not love her any longer, Thornton replied: "I love you like I did when you were sweet sixteen." Thornton sold "When You Were Sweet Sixteen" outright to two different publishers for fifteen dollars each. When the Witmarks turned it into a giant hit, Joseph W. Stern & Company sued them, as Stern could prove that it had also purchased the song for fifteen dollars. They settled out of court when Witmark paid the Stern company five thousand dollars. The song is still a favorite with barbershop quartets. Thornton's last hit came in 1900, when he wrote "The Bridge of Sighs," inspired by the structure that connects the criminal court building with the Tombs Prison in New York City. He continued as an artist in vaudeville and made his last appearance in Jerome Kern's musical, SWEET ADELINE in 1929. He died broke in New York City on July 27, 1938.

MONROE H. ROSENFELD:

"Take Back Your Gold"

Monroe H. Rosenfeld, the man who named Tin Pan Alley, was born in Richmond, Virginia, on April 22, 1862. As a young man, he was a journalist in Cincinnati, where he came to the attention of old-line publisher Frank Harding. Harding encouraged him to go to New York. Rosie, as he was known, was a most versatile man. He played piano at Herman's Wine Room, wrote articles for newspapers, became a press agent, short story writer, arranger, composer, and lyricist, and he even sold song ideas to other lyricists. He was so prolific that he not only used pseudonyms, but sometimes put novice writers' names on his own works to help them get started. He discovered the talented Emma Carus and had friendships with Helene Mora and Imogene Comer, who helped plug his songs-with-morals.

Although many Alleyites were fond of their drink (see James Thornton, above), Rosenfeld was abstemious. His devastating vice was playing the horses. He was a chronic loser, and most of his earnings went to the track and stayed there. He was often desperate to raise money for his addiction to betting and sold many of his songs outright for a few dollars. He was also known to sell the same song to several publishers, as well as to steal other people's tunes and pass them off as his own. He was a most persuasive salesman, and when he needed cash for the races and didn't have the time to actually write a song, he would sell a publisher an idea for a ballad and receive an advance. He would then go to one of his impoverished writer friends to produce the song for a small consideration, as he acted as a contractor. The next day he would pick up the completed manuscript, take it to the office, convince the publisher that it was going to be a smash hit, and collect another advance on it. On the rare days when this ploy didn't work, he forged checks. Once, when the police were about to arrest him, he jumped out of a second-story window and permanently injured one of his legs. Thereafter, he had a decided limp and wore bell-bottom trousers in an effort to hide the deformity that resulted from his jump.

He started composing while in Cincinnati, and in 1882 he had John Church publish "She's Sweet As She Can Be." His other tear-jerkers included "Good-by, My Boy, Good-by," "With All Her Faults I Love Her Still," and his big ballad hit of 1897, "Take Back Your Gold." One of his few comic songs was titled, "Her Golden Hair Was Hanging down Her Back." Bert Williams created another success when he sang Rosenfeld's coon song, also of 1897, "I Don't Care If Yo' Nebber Comes Back." Probably his last published song was his 1916 "On a Dreamy Summer's Night." Late in his career, he was named founding editor-in-chief of *The Tuneful Yankee*, published by Walter Jacobs, Inc., a magazine for the Trade and would-be songwriters.

Always a supporter of the Alley, and one of its most enduring members, Rosenfeld died in New York City on December 12, 1918.

GUSSIE L. DAVIS:
"In the Baggage Coach Ahead"

Gussie Lord Davis was born in Dayton, Ohio, on December 3, 1863. He moved to Cincinnati in his middle teens and wanted to attend the Nelson Musical College. Because he was black, his application was rejected, so he made a deal with the administration to trade his janitorial services for private lessons. His first song, "We Sat Beneath the Maple on the Hill," was published by Helling & Company, a local printer, in 1880. Whenever the song appeared in a shop window, Davis would point to the song and say, "That's me. I done it."

Before he came to New York and became a full-time songwriter, Davis worked as a Pullman porter. On one train trip he came upon a little girl crying bitterly. When he asked about her trouble, the child informed him that her mother was in the baggage coach ahead, in a coffin. Several years later he remembered that incident, wrote "In the Baggage Coach Ahead," and sold it outright to Howley, Haviland & Company. The publisher turned it into one of its hits of 1896, in part by the plugging of the "Queen of Song," Imogene Comer. The year before, Davis had entered a contest sponsored by the New York *World* to find the ten best songwriters in the United States. He came in second with his tear-jerker, "Send Back the Picture and the Ring." His versatility was shown in that turning-point year of 1896, when he gave T. B. Harms & Company his coon song take-off on Little Egypt's dance at the World's Fair, "When I Do the Hoochy-Coochy in de Sky."

Gussie Davis died at the age of thirty-five on October 18, 1899, at his home in Whitestone, New York.

DANCE OF THE NINETIES

The Cakewalk

This new dance sensation, along with the jaunty music written for it, first appeared in music halls and in the theatres in the middle of the nineties. Its popularity was based on the tuneful, lightly syncopated music written for high-strutting, prancing dance steps. It was composer-publisher Kerry Mills who started the rage for this dance music with his first publication, "Rastus on Parade," in 1895. The song had the further distinction of establishing what soon became a cakewalk harmonic cliche by beginning in a minor key and moving to the relative major, a construction that cakewalk writers later followed with a subdominant trio section. It was another of Mills' cakewalks, however, "At a Georgia Campmeeting" (1897), that became the standard against which all other cakewalks were measured. Although a highly singable and danceable number, it had been rejected by all major publishers of the day, a costly mistake for them, as it firmly set up the house of F. A. Mills for the next twenty years. His 1899 hit, "Whistling Rufus," successfully competed with F. T. McGrath's "A Breeze from Blackville," Bernard Franklin's "Blackville Society," Arthur Pryor's "A Coon Band Contest," Jean Schwartz' "Dusky Dudes," George Rosey's "A Rag-Time Skedaddle," and Abe Holzmann's "Smokey Mokes"—all winners in the glorious "year of the cakewalk." The following year, J. Bodewalt Lampe published his own "Creole Belles" in his hometown of Buffalo, New York. It wasn't until Whitney-Warner purchased it the following year that it became a million-seller. While Kerry Mills went on to compose several lovely Tin Pan Alley songs, some of which ("Meet Me in St. Louis, Louis" and "Red Wing") became standards, he occasionally harked back to his cakewalking roots, as when, in 1909, he produced "Kerry Mills Ragtime Dance" and again in the single revival year of 1915 with "Kerry Mills' Cake Walk."

In their Tin Pan Alley form, cakewalks were 2/4 instrumentals, with occasional vocal trios, founded on a simple march framework and using simple syncopation in a single rhythm pattern. Compositionally, they were unpianistic pieces, involving single-note, easily remembered melody lines that one could sketch out on a piano with a single finger without disturbing their harmony. Though cakewalks were often arranged for piano (as were marches), their sheet music covers typically displayed other instruments, usually trombones and banjos, and they were customarily performed by marching or circus bands, as well as by string bands consisting of violin, banjo and string bass. The earliest cakewalk hits were popularized by the premier concert band of John Philip Sousa, who was responsible for the cakewalk's European popularity. Sousa himself detested the cakewalk but clearly perceived its commercial possibilities. He had his solo trombonist, Arthur Pryor, make the band arrangements and conduct the Sousa band when making cakewalk recordings.

Through Kerry Mills, the cakewalk became the first major dance form of Tin Pan Alley, breaking the dominance of the waltz and adding a syncopated kick.

MUSICAL THEATRE IN THE NINETIES

The Weber and Fields Music Hall

The forerunner of the Weber and Fields shows was the burlesque of Harrigan and Hart, who had their own theatres—first the Theatre Comique and later the Park Theatre—in the 1870's and 1880's, and the services of their own composer, Dave Braham. Their songs were Irish and so were their audiences. New York then had the largest Irish population in the world. By the time Weber and Fields got their own theatre in 1896, coon songs were coming into their own, and John Stromberg, genial composer for Weber and Fields, wrote them and other comic songs and ballads. Weber, Fields and Stromberg published their own material until they sold their catalog to the Witmarks in 1900. (Italian songs came into vogue after 1905, and Yiddish songs about four years later. The ethnic song cycle came to an apex of sorts in 1920 with the publication of "The Argentines, the Portuguese and the Greeks.")

When Joe Weber (1867–1942) and Lew Fields (1867–1941) opened their Music Hall on September 5, 1896, the "Dutch" comedians assembled the finest stars of the popular musical theatre of their time. The 665-seat house was located on the corner of Twenty-ninth Street and Broadway and had been formerly known as the Imperial Music Hall.

Never a success before, under Weber and Fields' management, the place sold out. The first half of their show consisted of variety acts, with such talent as singer Lottie Gilson. It was the second half, though, the burlesque, that made their hall famous. They held matinees on Tuesdays instead of the usual Wednesdays so that their troupe could see the latest dramas at Wednesday matinees to burlesque them in the future. This scheduling also gave the casts who were burlesqued a chance to see how Weber and Fields did it. Some of their famous shows were QUO VASS ISS, FIDDLE-DEE-DEE, HURLY-BURLY, WHIRL-I-GIG, POUSSE CAFE, and TWIRLY-WHIRLY. They were the only burlesque troupe to tour the country year after year. Pete Dailey was their leading comedian, who specialized in extemporizing his lines, throwing the other stars and players into confusion but also keeping them on their toes. Sam Bernard was the German comedian in the company, and David Warfield started his career there as a Jewish comedian. Marie Dressler, William Collier, Collier's wife Louise Allen, Henry Dixey, Lillian Russell, Fay Templeton, Louis Mann, Frankie Bailey, Bessie Clayton, Vesta Tilley, Cissie Loftus, DeWolf Hopper, Carter DeHaven, and the McCoy Sisters were other high-priced stars who appeared at the Hall until it closed in 1904, when Weber and Fields went their separate ways.

WILLIAMS AND WALKER:
"When It's All Goin' Out and Nothin' Comin' In"

Egbert Austin Williams was born on November 12, 1874, in Antigua, British West Indies. His parents brought him to Riverside, California, where he attended high school. He made his way to San Francisco, where he started his career by singing to his own banjo accompaniment. It was there he met George Walker (b. 1873), who came from Lawrence, Kansas, in a touring medicine show. They formed a vaudeville act and were appearing in Chicago when they were asked to perform for the Show Managers of America. Producer Tom Canary, of Canary and Lederer, caught their act and rushed backstage to sign them up to join his new show, THE GOLD BUG (September 21, 1896), with a score by Victor Herbert. They didn't have parts in the show, but they performed their act in the middle of the show and became a hit. It was a short-lived triumph, however, as the show closed at the end of one week. It did bring them to Broadway, though, and to the attention of other managers. They were quickly booked to play Koster and Bial's vaudeville house on Twenty-third Street near Sixth Avenue, where they were kept on for an unusual extended run. It was during this show that Williams and Walker performed and popularized their highly distinctive version of the cakewalk.

For the next thirteen years, they were to popularize many songs, some written by themselves, some by others. Their photographs—a selling tool—appeared on a sheet music cover ("Enjoy Yourselves") as early as 1897. That same year McIntyre and Heath, a famous minstrel duo, sang the Williams and Walker tune, "I Don't Like No Cheap Man," and made it a hit. Their own 1899 hit was "The Medicine Man." In 1901, the team made "Good Morning, Carrie" their biggest song hit written by others, Chris Smith, his vaudeville partner Elmer Bowman, and lyricist R. C. McPherson, who would be better known under his pseudonym, "Cecil Mack." Their 1902 hit, "When It's All Goin' Out and Nothin' Comin' In" featured them on the sheet music cover. In 1905, Williams sang the number that was to be associated with him for the rest of his career, "Nobody." Alex Rogers (1876–1930) wrote the very funny lyrics, and the music was composed by Williams himself. He once wrote of his melodies that "perhaps it would be more correct to say that I assembled them. For the tunes to popular songs are mostly made up of standard parts, like a motor car. As a machinist assembles a motor car then, I assembled the tunes to 'Nobody,' 'Believe Me,' and one or two others." Alex Rogers became a valued member of the Williams and Walker Company, not only for his lyric contributions, but also for his singing and acting in the troupe. He wrote most of Bert Williams' best material and helped Jesse Shipp with the libretti of their three major Broadway musicals. Later he served in the same capacities for composer Luckey Roberts.

Signing with producers Hurtig and Seamon, the Williams and Walker Company created their first vaudeville musical, THE POLICY PLAYERS, which opened at Koster and Bial's on April 3, 1900. It toured the vaudeville houses, and its success encouraged them to continue with their repertory company. The team's next production was SONS OF HAM, which toured for two years, starting in 1900, and finally opened at the Grand Opera House in New York City on March 3, 1902. It was the first Williams and Walker show from which songs were published using a standard show cover, this one featuring drawings of them.

George Walker was the first to marry. In 1899, he wed Aida Overton, a young soubrette with the company. A year later, Bert Williams married dancer Lottie Thompson, also of the company.

Their landmark production of IN DAHOMEY opened on February 18,

1903, at the New York Theatre. This was the first full-length book musical written and performed by blacks at a major Broadway theatre. The Williams and Walker Company contained many of the most creative black talents in show business. The cast included Alex Rogers, Jesse Shipp, J. Leubrie Hill, Hattie McIntosh, George Catlin, and Abbie Mitchell, as well as the stars' two wives. A wonderful song for George Walker was "Me an' da Minstrel Ban'," while Bert Williams scored with Alex Rogers' "I'm a Jonah Man." They enjoyed a seven-month stay with the show in London, where the team appeared before King Edward VII. They returned to tour the show for the 1904–05 season and added "I May Be Crazy But I Ain't No Fool" for Bert Williams. The song's title became a highly popular catch-phrase.

ABYSSINIA was their next production, opening at the Majestic Theatre on February 20, 1906. Their new producer, Melville Raymond, provided elaborate scenery, a large cast and live camels on stage. No songs in the score became popular.

F. Ray Comstock produced the team's last show in which they appeared together on February 3, 1908, again at the Majestic Theatre, called BANDANA LAND. It contained songs by Tom Lemonier, Cecil Mack and Chris Smith, Will Marion Cook and Alex Rogers, J. Leubrie Hill, and Joe Jordan. "Bon Bon Buddy, the Chocolate Drop" became George Walker's theme song, and "You're in the Right Church But the Wrong Pew" became a hit for Bert Williams. This show introduced Williams' famous pantomime "The Poker Game," which became his trademark (it can be seen in a silent film short, "Natural Born Gambler," made in 1916). George Walker became ill during the Chicago run of the tour and retired from the stage. He died in Islip, New York, on January 6, 1911.

Comstock produced the last of the Williams and Walker Company's Broadway shows, MR. LODE OF KOAL, on November 1, 1909, again at the Majestic Theatre, at Fifty-eighth Street and Columbus Avenue. Although George Walker was missing, the critics agreed that Bert Williams carried the show by himself. The big number was Williams' "Believe Me." It was shortly after the show closed that Bert Williams accepted an offer to appear in Florenz Ziegfeld's FOLLIES OF 1910.

For the FOLLIES, Williams composed, with lyrics by Chris Smith and Jim Burris, a riotous song in the "Nobody" vein, called "Constantly," and it became another hit for him. For the ZIEGFELD FOLLIES OF 1911, he created with lyricist Grant Clarke another hit in "Dat's Harmony." It was also in this FOLLIES that he caused a minor sensation singing

Irving Berlin's "Woodman, Woodman, Spare That Tree." For the ZIEG-
FELD FOLLIES OF 1912, Williams came up with "My Landlady" and
"You're on the Right Road But You're Going the Wrong Way." For the
ZIEGFELD FOLLIES OF 1914, he again performed his famous single-handed
poker game and introduced it by singing "The Darktown Poker Club."
For his final ZIEGFELD FOLLIES OF 1919, the one generally acknowledged
as the best of them all, he sang "You Cannot Make Your Shimmy Shake
on Tea," a protest against the coming of Prohibition. His last Broadway
show was the revue, BROADWAY BREVITIES OF 1920, which made popular
"The Moon Shines on the Moonshine." It is fitting that his last song in
this show was written by Chris Smith, who went all the way back to the
beginning of Williams' careeer in New York, "I Want To Know Where
Tosti Went (When He Said Goodbye)." Bert Williams died at his home
in New York City on March 4, 1922.

With all his enormous success, Bert Williams keenly felt prejudice
when he appeared on stage in his own country. In his travels abroad, he
met and performed for royalty and was accepted by them as a talented
artist. At home he was always subjected to race prejudice. He wrote an
article for *American Magazine* (December 1917), in which he stated, "I
have never been able to discover that there was anything disgraceful in
being a colored man. But I have often found it inconvenient—in
America." And, although he ended the article by writing, "I'm having
a grand time," W. C. Fields, who worked with Williams in several of the
FOLLIES, once observed, "He was the funniest man I ever saw and the
saddest man I ever knew."

VICTOR HERBERT:
"Kiss Me Again"

Victor Herbert was born in Dublin, Ireland, on February 1, 1859. He
was educated in Germany and studied cello at the Stuttgart Conservatory. He married Theresa Forster, principal soprano of the Stuttgart
Opera, and they came to New York in the summer of 1886 for her
engagement at the Metropolitan Opera House. A few years later, Herbert
became the leader of the 22nd Army Regimental Band. It was during
this tenure that he began to write music for the theatre. His first success
was THE WIZARD OF THE NILE (November 4, 1895). The most popular
song in the operetta was "Starlight, Star Bright." It was from this show
that the phrase "Am I a wiz?" entered the language and became a fad
question of the day.

Herbert not only led a dual life, writing for the musical stage and composing classical compositions, but also helped establish the careers and made stars of three sopranos. The first was Alice Neilsen, who was introduced to the public in his 1897 production THE SERENADE. As a follow-up to that success, he created THE FORTUNE TELLER (September 26, 1898) for her. In it she played two roles and had a hit song in each part, "Always Do As People Say You Should" and "Romany Life." The biggest hit of the show and one of the greatest songs of all time was sung to her, "Gypsy Love Song" (also known as "Slumber On, My Little Gypsy Sweetheart"). From this show forward, Victor Herbert was published by M. Witmark and Sons.

After three years of devoting his time exclusively to conducting the famed Pittsburgh Symphony Orchestra, Herbert returned to Broadway with BABES IN TOYLAND (October 13, 1903), an extravaganza which included three of his most endearing numbers, "Toyland," "March of the Toys," and "I Can't Do the Sum."

The second of Herbert's soprano discoveries wasn't so much a discovery as the remaking of a career. Fritzi Scheff was singing with the Metropolitan Opera Company when Herbert wanted her for a role in an operetta he had composed. It was a failure, but he made up for it when he wrote MLLE. MODISTE (December 25, 1905) for her and gave her the immortal "Kiss Me Again." When she first heard it, she did not want to sing it, as she felt it was too low for her voice. His lyricist and producer agreed with her, but Herbert was adamant. Her success with this song kept it forever associated with her. One of Herbert's best comic numbers also appeared in this show, "I Want What I Want When I Want It."

The following year, Herbert wrote THE RED MILL (September 24, 1906) for the comedians Dave Montgomery and Fred Stone. Among the fine songs in this score are "In Old New York," "The Isle of Our Dreams," the haunting "Moonbeams," and the rousing "Every Day Is Ladies' Day with Me." The show ran 274 performances, more than any other Herbert show, and has been frequently revived. While the book is dated, the music never fails to captivate its audiences.

Oscar Hammerstein—grandfather of the lyricist who worked with Richard Rodgers—started his career in the 1880's by building and managing vaudeville theatres and opera houses. He eventually built ten of them in New York City alone, starting with the Harlem Opera House. His first Manhattan Opera House was later taken over by vaudeville producers who renamed it after themselves, Koster and Bial's. In 1906, Hammerstein decided to build a second Manhattan Opera House on

Thirty-fourth Street between Eighth and Ninth Avenues and create an opera troupe to compete with the staid Metropolitan. He provided premier performances of THE TALES OF HOFFMAN, PELLEAS ET MELISANDE, THAIS, Strauss's ELEKTRA, and he introduced American audiences to such outstanding performers as Nellie Melba, Mary Garden, Luisa Tetrazzini, and John McCormack. In 1910, Oscar Hammerstein sold his Manhattan Opera Company to the Metropolitan Opera for one million dollars. One condition of the sale was that he was to refrain from producing operas for ten years. So he turned to the Broadway stage. His first Broadway show was Herbert's NAUGHTY MARIETTA (November 7, 1910), which starred the third opera singer Herbert used, Emma Trentini. Possibly because he was working with so many people from opera, including members of the chorus, the orchestra and its conductor, Herbert's score was his most ambitious yet. "Ah, Sweet Mystery of Life" has remained a classic, as has "Italian Street Song," "I'm Falling in Love with Someone," "Tramp, Tramp, Tramp," and " 'Neath the Southern Moon." A remarkable score.

Herbert wrote his last great show for the young actress, Christie MacDonald. It was SWEETHEARTS (September 8, 1913), and it contained such a uniformly fine score that one music critic noted, "The abundant melodic flow is invariably marked by distinction, individuality, and a quality of superlative charm." Among the riches are the title song, "Pretty As a Picture," "The Angelus," "Wooden Shoes," and "Game of Love."

Victor Herbert's last work was a tune composed for the Tiller Girls in the ZIEGFELD FOLLIES. He completed it at noon on May 24, 1924, and sent it to his arranger for scoring. He then went to lunch, overate, felt so poorly that he went to his doctor's office, and there suffered a fatal heart attack.

VAUDEVILLE IN THE NINETIES

When Benjamin F. Keith (1846–1914) opened his first vaudeville palace in 1893, he became known as the "father of vaudeville." He, like Tony Pastor before him, opened his theatre to women and children. He was so successful that he created what was then known as a "chain" of theatres on the East Coast. The jewel among his theatres was the Palace Theatre in New York City. Here, as in lower-case palaces around the country, the star singer introduced new songs, and with her personality (most of the leading vaudeville singers in the nineties were women), imbued the song with unique personal qualities to "put it over." As Tony Pastor once wrote, "The ultimate success of these songs depends very largely on the person who sings them." If the chemistry were right between the singer and the song, the audience bought the sheet music.

MAGGIE CLINE:
"Throw Him Down, McCloskey"

Maggie Cline (1857–1934) began her career in 1879 as the first single-woman comedy Irish singer. Her biggest hit was her 1890 "Throw Him Down, McCloskey." She had met the composer, John W. Kelley, vaudeville's Rolling Mill Man, and asked him if he had any loose songs on him. He told her he had one that no one wanted and that she could have it for two dollars. She bought it from him on the spot, and for twenty-three years she used it in her business. Her performance was spectacular and was a great audience rouser. At the words, "Throw him down, McCloskey!" everybody backstage took whatever they could grab and threw it on the floor with as much force as they could muster. Those who could not find pieces of furniture or iron weights grabbed steam whistles, thunder sheets or any other noisy devices. As she would get encore after encore, she and her backstage crew would become exhausted by the time they finished the performance.

LOTTIE GILSON:
"The Sidewalks of New York"

Lottie Gilson, nicknamed "the Little Magnet" because of her unusual drawing power at the box office, introduced and plugged more songs to hit classification than any other vaudeville star in the nineties. She was the first to have a singer planted in the audience to sing the second chorus along with her. Then, she got the rest of the audience to join in. She made the Joe Stern-Ed Marks 1896 "Mother Was a Lady" an even bigger hit than she did their first song, "The Little Lost Child." Two years earlier in 1894, she made famous Charles Lawlor and James Blake's "The Sidewalks of New York" ("East side, West side"). And, if that weren't enough, she took the John Bratton-Walter Ford song, "The Sunshine of Paradise Alley" (1895) and made such a success of it that she was identified with it thereafter. This was unusual in that Julius Witmark had introduced it for his firm and should have had an edge on the competition. To show her versatility, the same year that she turned the tear-jerker "Mother Was a Lady" into a smashing hit she did the same for the Stanley Carter-Harry Braisted comic song, "You're Not the Only Pebble on the Beach." Throughout the nineties, she was the favorite at Tony Pastor's and the other leading vaudeville houses in New York. In the early nineties when she was on tour, she met and encouraged Harry Von Tilzer to come to New York to try his luck placing his songs. Lottie Gilson remained a favorite for over twenty years.

MAY IRWIN:
"The Bully Song"

May Irwin (1862–1938) started in vaudeville with her sister Flora in 1875 and worked her way up to playing Tony Pastor's. She began to write her own songs in 1893 with "Mamie! Come Kiss Your Honey Boy." Her biggest success came in 1896, when she introduced Charles Trevathan's "The Bully Song." This song established her as the foremost coon-shouter of the day. She was such a favorite that Weber and Fields booked her for their Music Hall, where she developed into a fine comedienne. She then took Ben Harney's "Mister Johnson, Turn Me Loose" into the show COURTED INTO COURT (December 29, 1896), and also introduced her collaboration with George M. Cohan "Hot Tamale Alley," which scored a hit. In 1899, she introduced the fledgling Gus Edwards and Will D. Cobb's coon song, "I Couldn't Stand to See My Baby Lose." She became the first actress to appear on film when she re-enacted the scandalous "kiss scene" from THE WIDOW JONES in 1896! She was beloved by the industry and would appear in benefits long after she retired. She was one of the few performers who invested her money in real estate, so she spent her retirement in great comfort.

OTHER SONG HITS OF THE NINETIES

"The Bowery" (1892) came from Charles Hoyt's record-breaking show A TRIP TO CHINATOWN. The music was composed by Percy Gaunt (1852–1896), with lyrics by Hoyt (1859–1900). The show opened in November 1891, after having been on the road for nearly a year. It played for 657 performances, a record run that wasn't broken for nearly thirty years. That show spawned road companies that toured for five years. During that time, songs came and went, but of the five original songs, "The Bowery" endured and eventually sold over a million copies of sheet music. Two other songs from the show, "Push Dem Clouds Away" and "Reuben and Cynthia," helped convince publisher T. B. Harms that publishing songs from musicals was a profitable venture.

"Daisy Bell" (1892) was written by Englishman Harry Dacre (1860–1922). It was composed, so the story goes, when Dacre came through U.S. customs for the first time. He had brought along his bicycle and was unhappily surprised to find that he had to pay duty on it. A friend who came to pick him up, songwriter Billy Jerome, laughingly told him he was lucky the bicycle was not built for two, or the duty would have been twice as much. The song has always been known as "A Bicycle Built for Two."

"The Sidewalks of New York" (1894) is also better known by the beginning of its chorus ("East side, West side, all around the town"). It was composed by Charles B. Lawlor (1852–1925) and written by James W. Blake (1862–1935). Supposedly, Lawlor, humming the melody, walked into the hat shop where Blake was working, and asked him to write some lyrics about New York. Blake agreed then and there, writing the words down as he waited on customers. When the song was finished, Lawlor took it to Pat Howley, who bought it outright. It was a great hit for Howley, Haviland & Company. Lawlor played and sang it wherever he was appearing, and Lottie Gilson plugged it nightly at the London Theatre on the Bowery and turned it into a hit.

"The Band Played On" was another song perhaps better known by the start of its chorus ("Casey would waltz with a strawberry blonde"). Both words and music were written by John F. Palmer, whose sister called his attention to a hurdy-gurdy melody which was playing outside their house. Palmer took it to publisher Charles B. Ward (1865–1917), who purchased it and gave himself credit as the composer. It was first published in the New York Sunday World on June 30, 1895, and when the sheet music came out, it was dedicated to that newspaper, which, by publishing it first, gave it a wonderful send-off.

"She Is More to Be Pitied Than Censured" ("The Beautiful Sensational Pathetic Song") was written by publisher William B. Gray in 1898. He published it with this note on the cover: "The theme of this song is indeed a delicate one to handle, and is offered in sympathy, and not defense, for the unfortunate erring creatures, the life of one of whom suggested its construction." It became the epitome of the tear-jerker. Today it has come down to us as a parody of itself. The Gay Nineties? Think again.

THE ALLEY GROWS
(1900–1910)
Major Publishers of the Ragtime Era

The most dramatic change in popular music (before the rock era) came at the turn of this century, when the syncopated piano compositions called ragtime caught the public's fancy. For the first time in secular American music there appeared a musical form that could not be sung or danced to—in fact, could only by played and listened to. The work that created the demand for this genre and sparked it as a Tin Pan Alley product was Scott Joplin's "Maple Leaf Rag." Publisher John Stark launched Joplin's career.

JOHN STARK & SON:
The Evangelist for Ragtime

John Stark (1841–1927), a music store owner in Sedalia, Missouri, liked Joplin's original composition enough to publish it in September 1899. The first edition quickly sold out. When Stark wanted to order another edition from the printing firm in St. Louis, he was told he would have to wait his turn, as they were busy with larger orders. This information so infuriated Stark that he went to St. Louis and bought the printing company. He then moved his business, family, and Joplin himself there, where he became a full-time publisher, mostly of rags. His enthusiasm for ragtime was so great that he devoted the rest of his life to plugging it. Certainly, his catalog became the most important, containing many of the significant contributions to the genre. In August 1905, he moved his editorial office from St. Louis to New York City, where he remained at 127 East Twenty-third Street until he moved back to St. Louis permanently in 1910. He continued to publish rags until 1922. His number of published rags was second only to that of the Jerome H. Remick firm.

29

JEROME H. REMICK & COMPANY:
Million-Selling Rags

Jerome H. Remick (1869–1931), a Detroit businessman, bought the old-line firm of Whitney Warner Publishing Company, with offices at 10 Witherell Street, in 1902. It did not take him long to determine that most of the publishing action was in New York City. At the end of 1902, he purchased Charles N. Daniels' Indian intermezzo, "Hiawatha," for the then-unheard-of sum of $10,000 and installed Daniels in Detroit as General Manager. The following year, he bought out Louis Bernstein's half of Shapiro, Bernstein & Company, to become a partner with Maurice Shapiro in the new firm of Shapiro, Remick & Company, proprietors of the Whitney Warner Company, located at 45 West Twenty-eighth Street.

At the end of 1904, Jerome Remick bought out Maurice Shapiro with the stipulation that Shapiro not engage in music publishing in the United States for two years. At the beginning of 1905, he established the firm of Jerome H. Remick & Company. Remick had retained Fred E. Belcher (1869–1919) of the Whitney Warner staff in Detroit to look after his office in New York during the partnership with Shapiro. Upon establishing his own company, Remick kept Belcher in charge of the New York office, where his duties included overseeing the more than fifty retail stores Remick owned around the country. Moses Edwin Gumble (1876–1947), composer and plugger supreme, who had worked in 1902 as branch manager in Chicago for Shapiro, was now brought back to New York and put in charge of Remick's Professional Department, becoming the number two man in the New York office after Belcher.

Remick kept his editorial headquarters in Detroit. Under the direction of composer Charles N. Daniels (usually writing under the pseudonym of Neil Moret), the firm prospered. It not only published well over one hundred rags, but established an enormous catalog of every kind of popular song, with a number of hits. So large was his output that Remick was forced to buy his own printing plant in 1907. His volume of published songs remained the largest of any Tin Pan Alley firm until the end of the First World War. Like other major firms such as Feist, Witmark, Stern, and Shapiro, the Remick Company had a branch office in the theatre-filled city of Chicago, managed for years by Harry Werthan. When Daniels left Detroit in 1912 to move to the West Coast, the Remick editorial office moved to 131 West Forty-first Street in New York City under the guidance of premier plugger, Mose Gumble. Fred

Belcher became Vice-President and Secretary of the Remick Company, supervising the gigantic empire from its new office on Forty-first Street. The firm took a twenty-year lease.

The first million-selling rag produced by Remick was Charles L. Johnson's "Dill Pickles Rag," which had first been published in 1906 by Carl Hoffman in Kansas City. Charles Daniels, who had originally worked for Hoffman, bought the copyright in 1907, launched an extensive plugging campaign, and made it a huge success. The company's next million-selling rag was George Botsford's "Black and White Rag" in 1908. And so they continued until the end of the war.

Eighteen hundred rags were published during this decade, most of them originating from ragtime's regional, small-town roots. For all the spectacular success and enormous influence that ragtime had on the popular music business generally and Tin Pan Alley specifically, the form developed and took root far from New York City. While major publishers Stern, Snyder, Rossiter, Forster, Kremer, Vandersloot, Witmark, Mentel Bros., and Jenkins all issued more rags than the rest of the other publishers, and had their share of ragtime hits, the total output of these nine firms did not equal the combined number of ragtime tunes published by Stark and Remick!

SHAPIRO, BERNSTEIN & COMPANY:

On the Move

Maurice Shapiro (1873–1911) started his outstanding career at the Adelphi Publishing Company at 229 West Twentieth Street on January 1, 1897. By the end of that year, the company's name was changed to Consolidated Music Publishers and the firm moved to 10 Union Square. The next year, he changed the name to Universal Music Department Company and moved the business to 48 West Twenty-ninth Street, but not for long, as the following year it expanded and moved around the corner to the Alley at 49 and 51 West Twenty-eighth Street, as William C. Dunn & Company. When Harry Von Tilzer entered the firm at the end of 1899, the name became Shapiro, Bernstein & Von Tilzer, with a corresponding move two doors away to 45 West Twenty-eighth Street. In the meantime, Shapiro bought the catalogs of Orphean Music Company, Myll Bros., and Horwitz & Bowers. At the beginning of 1902, Harry Von Tilzer left to form his own company. Remick bought Louis Bernstein's share of the business on January 2, 1904, and became Shapiro's partner in Shapiro, Remick & Company. This firm lasted exactly one year, when Remick bought the entire company and its catalog from Shapiro. Returning from his enforced retirement at the end of 1906, Shapiro began again from scratch. He purchased the catalog of Cooper, Kendis & Paley and established a new office in the Maxine Elliot Theatre at 1416 Broadway on the corner of Thirty-ninth Street. He named his new company Shapiro Music Publisher and assembled a brand-new staff. Composer Edgar Selden became his General Manager and served extremely well. Upon Shapiro's untimely death in 1911, his brother-in-law, Louis Bernstein (who had in the meantime become a successful dealer in New York real estate) took over the business, keeping Selden on as General Manager. In 1913 Bernstein changed the name of the firm again to Shapiro, Bernstein & Company. Louis Bernstein (1879–1962) thus re-entered the music publishing business and, matching Shapiro's drive and business acumen, maintained the firm as one of the leading publishers of Tin Pan Alley for the rest of his life.

GOTHAM-ATTUCKS MUSIC COMPANY:
Black Alleymen

Black songwriters, while relatively few in number, were very much on the scene in Tin Pan Alley from the beginning. As mentioned in the previous chapter, such major firms as Joseph W. Stern & Company, Howley, Haviland & Company, and M. Witmark & Sons published talented black composers and lyricists. The tear-jerkers of Gussie Davis sold in the millions, as did the coon songs of the prolific Chris Smith, Ernest Hogan, Irving Jones, Willis Accooe, Shepard Edmonds, and the show music of Tom Lemonier, Cole & Johnson Brothers, Alex Rogers, James Vaughn, James Tim Brymn, Bert Williams, and Cecil Mack.

The first black-owned-and-operated Tin Pan Alley firm was the Attucks Music Publishing Company, started in 1903 by Shepard N. Edmonds (1876–1957). He sold it to Richard C. McPherson (1883–1944) and Will Marion Cook (1869–1944), two years later. They, in the meantime, had started the Gotham Music Company, but with this merger in mid-1905, the new firm became known as the Gotham-Attucks Music Company. They quickly signed Williams and Walker to an exclusive contract and published songs from their shows ABYSSINIA and BANDANA LAND. As a lyricist, McPherson wrote such hits as "He's a Cousin of Mine," "Good Morning, Carrie," "That's Why They Call

Me Shine," and "You're in the Right Church But the Wrong Pew." The firm lasted until 1911, when McPherson decided that running a publishing company was not worth the effort. He continued to write lyrics throughout the twenties and thirties. Probably his most famous lyric was written to James P. Johnson's music for the song which defined the roaring twenties: "The Charleston."

TED SNYDER COMPANY:
A Singing Waiter Makes a Difference

Ted Snyder (1881–1965) came to New York in 1904 after having worked as a staff pianist and plugger for publishing firms in Chicago. He landed a job with the F. A. Mills Company on its professional staff and had some numbers published by Mills. He obtained financial backing from Boston jobber George Krey to start a firm with lyricist Ed Rose (1875–1935). In July 1908, with the backing of Henry Waterson of the Crown Music Company, Snyder created the Ted Snyder Company and became sole owner of the catalog of Rose & Snyder. In September, he published his own phenomenally successful rag, "Wild Cherries." A few months after starting his own firm, singer Amy Butler, a friend of Waterson's, took Snyder down to Jimmy Kelly's saloon, where she had heard a waiter singing original risque parodies of popular songs. She believed his talents as a lyricist would be useful to the firm. Snyder was not overly impressed, but, with Butler's persuasion, he hired the waiter to write lyrics for a weekly draw of twenty-five dollars against future royalties. It is fitting that when Ted Snyder and his new lyricist, Irving Berlin, wrote "Kiss Me, My Honey, Kiss Me," Amy Butler's picture appeared on the cover of the sheet music.

The new team clicked and wrote "Next to Your Mother, Who Do You Love?," "Sweet Italian Love" (which featured a rare photo of Irving Berlin on the cover), "My Wife's Gone to the Country (Hurrah! Hurrah!)" (with lyrics co-written by George Whiting, whose wife divorced him because of this song), and rag songs "That Beautiful Rag," "That Mysterious Rag," and "Wild Cherries Rag." This last was a song version of Snyder's hit instrumental. It, too, became extremely popular. After Irving Berlin's gigantic hit "Alexander's Ragtime Band," he was made a partner in the firm, so in 1912 the name was changed to Waterson, Berlin & Snyder. Berlin left the firm in 1919 to start his own company.

Ted Snyder's biggest hit was published in 1921. In an interview, he told how he wrote it: "I had the melody of the chorus of the 'Sheik' written and I couldn't get any kind of verse that suited me. I have always considered the verse very important, and insist on having a good verse which will show off the chorus of my songs. I played this chorus around the office, but nobody paid any attention to it. In my effort to get a suitable verse, I finally went into the Oriental and at last completed the song under the title of 'My Rose of Araby.'

"Mr. Waterson had just read the book of THE SHEIK and he said that a book that could sell over two million copies was worth writing a song about, and he wanted to call my song 'The Sheik.' However, I couldn't connect the Sheik of the story with my 'Rose of Araby,' as we had written it. Mr. Waterson showed the way and a few days after the song was written, the moving picture was announced. So it was an all-round fortunate combination of circumstances which helped to make the song a hit."

The following year, the same team of Snyder, Harry B. Smith and Francis Wheeler wrote another hit for the company in "Dancing Fool," which was recorded by the most famous dance bands of the day. In 1923 Snyder, Bert Kalmar and Harry Ruby teamed up to write one of the great standards of all time, "Who's Sorry Now." He wrote of it, "Well, everybody knows that song crazes go in cycles. All the publisher can do is try to feel what the public may want next. When I saw all those 'cry' songs and none of them making the headway I thought they should, it made me feel they had not hit on the right idea of that type of song. So I tried my hand and was lucky enough to get the right song. It was a number deliberately written to fit conditions which I felt were in the air. I thought the public wanted that kind of song."

Snyder left his company in the summer of 1927 to go to California. The firm went bankrupt in 1929, and Jack Mills bought its catalog for $5,000 in 1931.

As the new publishers who actively plugged their songs flourished, they needed more physical space. Their plugging methods became more sophisticated, and there was a need to create departments which fulfilled these different kinds of promotion. As it was no longer considered fashionable or productive to see desired performers after their shows, the publishers began to invite performers to their offices to demonstrate the various new songs personally. They needed a fancy suite of demonstration rooms, even a small auditorium, where the performers could try out the tunes under conditions similar to those they faced when they performed in theatres.

The publishers also needed space for their Band and Orchestra Departments, which were responsible for arranging the tunes from lead sheets to orchestral parts. Each Band and Orchestra Department became an industry in itself, arranging different musical combinations and issuing the parts in enticing forms. Orchestral parts didn't have colorful covers as on the piano-vocal sheets; rather, they were sold much the way book clubs sell books today—by establishing a "club" so that performing organizations could "subscribe" to the publisher's works for a year at a time. Not only would the bands and orchestras perform the songs (which constituted plugs), but they were given all of the firm's numbers during the year, fully orchestrated.

The Remick, Feist, Stern, Witmark, and Shapiro organizations either took over entire floors of buildings, or leased entire buildings for their vast and steadily growing departments. Their businesses had outgrown the one-room offices of the previous decade's publishers and now required large spaces for fast-growing operations.

For instance, in January 1903, when Feist moved into its own brownstone at 134 West Thirty-seventh Street, the basement housed the acquired catalog of Century Music, which contained twelve hundred songs. The main floor consisted of the general offices, managed by Edgar Bitner, and the reception room. The second floor housed the Illustrators Department, the Professional Parlor, and Band and Orchestra Department, under Abe Holzmann, who also managed the piano rooms. The third floor included the ladies' reception rooms, Stock Circular Department, more piano rooms, and the Teachers' Department, under the supervision of Robert A. Keiser. The fourth floor housed the Advertising Department, Addressing Department, stock room, Folio Department, and the private office of Leo Feist.

When Remick leased its building at 219–221 West Forty-sixth Street in October, 1912, its set-up was slightly different: the basement held the stock room and Shipping Department; the ground floor had the Band and Orchestra Department (run by Abe Holzmann), the Sales Department (in which F. J. Burt was in charge), the Publicity Department (headed by Sam Speck), and a two-hundred seat auditorium used as a demonstration and rehearsal hall. The second floor was given over to the Professional Department, under Mose Gumble's direction. His assistant Tom Penfold took charge of the fifteen piano rooms. Also on the second floor was the Slide Department, as well as a room devoted to the storage of stationery and advertising campaigns. The third floor contained the executive offices of Fred E. Belcher, Jerome Keit, Belcher's private secretary, and Jerome H. Remick, when he was in town. The Arranging Department, with a dozen arrangers headed by J. Bodewalt Lampe, was also located on this floor.

During these years of quick growth, department stores became an important outlet for the sales of sheet music. The two largest department stores in New York City, Siegel, Cooper & Company ("Meet me at the fountain") at Eighteenth Street and Sixth Avenue and R. H. Macy & Company at Thirty-fourth Street and Broadway, started a famous feud by cutting prices on their items. Macy's began selling sheet music at six cents apiece and daring other stores to undersell them. Five major music publishers got together to stop this price cutting. In August 1907, Leo Feist, M. Witmark & Sons, F. B. Haviland, F. A. Mills, and Charles K. Harris formed the American Music Stores, Inc., to establish their own music counters in the principal department stores of America, and to act as jobbers to the department store business in general. They also wanted to stop the Joseph W. Stern Company from monopolizing the major department store music counters with its contracts to feature Stern music. The American Music Stores managed to secure contracts to supply over fifty stores with their combined publications.

The price-cutting war between Macy and Siegel-Cooper was the publishers' main worry. It was Isidore Witmark's idea to shock the two stores into pricing sheet music at fifty cents. The music cartel did this by announcing a one-day sale—on October 12, 1907—of their most popular songs for one cent apiece at Rothenberg & Company on West Fourteenth Street. This sale was to include Witmark's current hit, "Love Me and the World Is Mine," which was being wholesaled at the department stores for twenty-three cents a copy. In addition to having the sale, the publishers employed people to go to Macy's and to Siegel-Cooper's, demanding that these stores sell their sheets at the same price as Rothenberg's, brandishing before the clerks the "We will not be undersold" ad which appeared in all the dailies the previous day. Rothenberg's put on extra staff and the rehearsed crowd went to Macy's and Siegel-Cooper's. Reports from Macy's said that their floor managers were having trouble with the clerks who, becoming more and more irritated, were calling the floor manager to approve every sale.

One of Isidore Witmark's friends went to the household department and bought some tin pots and pans. He then went to the music department, where he ordered a list of song sheets, which the salesgirl wrapped up. He was prepared to pay a penny apiece for them. When told that the price was six cents a copy, he created a fuss and showed her the Rothenberg ad. After a long harangue, he started to walk away, dropping pieces of tinware along the way, making quite a racket. It took most of the floorwalkers to get him out, but everyone knew he was there.

As the day came to an end, a representative of Macy's called the office of the American Music Stores. When informed that the united publishers would fight the department stores if it took twenty such sales, Macy's capitulated and the price-cutting of sheet music came to an abrupt end.

The format of the popular song, whether tear-jerker or coon song, was the same throughout this decade: there was a verse (which nobody knew) and a chorus (which everybody knew). While the verse might be any length, the chorus was usually thirty-two measures long. During the ragtime age, the tear-jerker gave way to the pleasant love song ("On a Sunday Afternoon," "In the Good Old Summertime," "Meet Me in St. Louis, Louis," "Wait Till the Sun Shines, Nellie," "By the Light of the Silvery Moon," "Let Me Call You Sweetheart"). The more peppy songs used the word "rag" or "ragtime" in their titles and have come to be known as "rag songs." As a musical fact, however, they are constructed exactly as any other popular song: with a verse (which nobody knows) and a chorus (which everybody knows). Such titles during this time were "That _____ Rag" (fill in the blank with "African," "Beautiful," "College," "Devil," "Epidemic," "Fussy," "Gossiping," "Hypnotizing," "Indian," "Kleptomaniac," "London," "Moving Picture," "Nightmare," "Operatic," "Puzzlin'," "Raggedy," "Shakespearian," "Teasin'," "Universal," "Whistling," "X-Ray," "Yodeling," etc., etc.), "Ragging the Baby to Sleep," "The Ragtime Boarding House," "Rag, Rag, Rag," not forgetting the most famous rag song of all, "Alexander's Ragtime Band."

MAJOR SONGWRITERS OF THE RAGTIME ERA

HARRY VON TILZER:
"What You Goin' to Do When the Rent Comes Round?"

While ragtime was rapidly changing the beat of the Alley, and before Irving Berlin started writing his own songs, Harry Von Tilzer, who was to give Berlin his very first job on the Alley—as a plugger, decided to go into business for himself. Amicably leaving Maurice Shapiro in 1902 to form Harry Von Tilzer Music Publishing Company, he remained on Twenty-eighth Street for the first five years of his firm's business life. So prolific was he as a composer, and so successful, that his firm started with million-selling hits as varied as the tear-jerker "A Bird in a Gilded Cage," the waltz song "On a Sunday Afternoon," the coon song "What You Gonna Do When the Rent Comes 'Round?," the friendship songs "Down Where the Wurzburger Flows," "Under the Anheuser Bush," "Wait Till the Sun Shines, Nellie," the kid song "All Aboard for Blanket Bay," the syncopated dance sensation "The Cubanola Glide," and the love song "I Want a Girl Just Like the Girl That Married Dear Old Dad." Von Tilzer was not only prolific, but versatile as well. Unlike Charles K. Harris and Paul Dresser, who stayed with sentimental ballads throughout their careers, Von Tilzer wrote in all genres of popular song with equally stunning success. That he was a master plugger goes without saying, as he was reported to have composed and published more than one hundred songs which sold more than half-a-million copies each, as well as a large number of multi-million-copy selling songs.

In an unsigned article published in *Metropolitan Magazine* in 1902, he wrote about his job as a plugger and of a stunt he created for a song which he had just published:

> "I'm a song promoter. I'm the man who makes the popular songs popular. I earn big money and I've grown into a necessity to the music publishing house that employs me.
>
> The company works one big town at a time. It sends on, by freight, a stack of the music of the song to be made popular. It is not put on sale until I give the word.
>
> I get to a town after the music has been placed in the hands of the leading music houses. I arrange with two or three theatres to aid me in introducing the song.
>
> Maybe I go to the swellest theatre in town Monday night and sit in a lower box, in my evening clothes, like an ordinary patron. During the daytime I will have fixed the orchestra and had the music

run over. Between the first and second act, perhaps, I stand up in my box and begin singing.

The audience is startled. Ushers run through the aisles. A policeman comes in and walks toward the box. About the time the policeman is where he can be seen by all the audience, I step out on to the stage in front of the curtain and begin the chorus, with the orchestra playing and the audience, that is now onto the game, clapping so hard it almost blisters its hands.

I have, maybe, a good whistler in the gallery, whom I have taught during the day. He helps me when I begin teaching the gallery to whistle the chorus. He leads the gods and before I have done they and the whole house have caught the air.

I usually get the orchestra to play the chorus as the audience is going out. Everybody goes home humming or whistling it. But long before the home-going, probably, I have walked singing down the aisle of another theatre between the second and third act, having been led out by an usher and having then come back and stood in front of the orchestra and taught that theatre's audience to sing and whistle the song.

The best thing I ever did to popularize a song was done right here in little old New York, in a roof garden theatre. My wife knew a girl who was making a hit at the garden, so we had to go and see the girl in her act. I put the thing off for a night or two and planned a little surprise.

I met the girl, who did a singing part, and fixed the thing up with her. The orchestra and the manager, an old friend of mine, readily fell into line. I was engaged in promoting the popularity for 'Please Let Me Sleep,' about this time, and I saw a chance to do some noble work.

My wife wanted to sit away up in front so her friend would see her, but I insisted on taking chairs in the rear of the garden, near the elevator landing. The crowd was large. The night was hot and the bill was good.

'I don't know what makes me so drowsy,' I said to my wife as her friend came on. 'I guess they must have put knock-out drops in that last glass of lemonade.'

I leaned back in my chair with one elbow on the table. As the girl sang I began to snore. I snored so loud that it disturbed those listening to the singing. They looked around in disgust. My wife gave me a kick under the table.

'Wake up, Harry,' she said. 'You are attracting attention.' I snored harder than ever. A waiter came over and shook me by the arm. My wife became alarmed and stood up.

Most of the folks in our part of the garden thought I was drunk. One man started toward the manager's office to complain, just as a policeman was brought my way by a second waiter.

The entire audience turned our way. Some persons stood on chairs and others moved out into the aisles. Just as the policeman and the

waiter raised me out of my chair, I stretched and yawned like a man dead for slumber and began singing:
'Please go 'way an' let me sleep. Ah would rather sleep than eat.'
Out of one corner of my eye I noticed a great light spread over my wife's face. I kept singing as I was being carried and led to the elevator. I sang going down and I sang coming up.
As the elevator reached the landing, the girl on the stage struck into the chorus along with the orchestra, and the audience tumbled.
I never saw an audience go so nearly crazy over anything in my life. Men laughed until the tears came and women became hysterical. My wife was the happiest woman in all the town. She admitted for the first time that I was a sure enough actor, which I had made up my mind she should do if I had to scare her half to death to bring about the conviction."

Harry Von Tilzer was born Harry Gumm in Detroit, Michigan, on July 8, 1872. He was one of five sons, all of whom became part of the music publishing business, two of them as successful songwriters. During his early childhood his parents moved to Indianapolis, where he grew up. When he was fourteen, he ran away from home to join Cole Brothers Circus. He next worked for a traveling repertory company, acting, accompanying singers at the piano, and writing songs for the productions. It was at this time that he changed his name, taking his mother's maiden name of Tilzer and adding the Von as a sign of distinction.

When he was performing with a burlesque show in Chicago, he met the popular vaudeville star Lottie Gilson, who took an interest in him. She urged him to devote himself seriously to songwriting and to go to New York to advance his career. He came to New York in 1892 with $1.65 in his pocket. He rented a furnished room and got a job as a pianist and singer in a saloon at fifteen dollars a week. He kept writing songs, some of which Tony Pastor sang in his Music Hall. Several other entertainers bought some of these early works outright for two dollars each.

Six years later, Von Tilzer was still living in a furnished room, sharing one on East Fifteenth Street with his lyricist, Andrew B. Sterling. At one point, they were three weeks behind on their rent. When a final bill was slipped under their door, they used the paper to write a chorus and then a verse of what turned out to be their first successful publication, "My Old New Hampshire Home." Lyricist Bartley Costello heard about their song and advised them to take it to printer-publisher William C. Dunn, who ran the Orphean Music Company. Dunn liked it and bought it for fifteen dollars.

It was shortly thereafter that Dunn sold out to Maurice Shapiro, and Shapiro's edition of the song sold over a million copies. Shapiro then looked up Von Tilzer and asked him to join his firm as a partner and gave him $4,000 in royalties. His first number for the new firm in 1899 was an "oo-oo" song, "I'd Leave Ma Happy Home for You," which featured the vaudeville act of Mr. and Mrs. Joe Keaton on the cover, with their four-year-old son, Buster, who would later make his mark in silent films as a comedian. Von Tilzer's own first million-seller was published in 1900, when he worked out a tune from a lyric written by Arthur J. Lamb. Before he wrote the melody, he insisted that Lamb change the lyric so that the heroine of the story was married to the rich old man, not merely living in sin with him. Later that evening, Von Tilzer went to a party which ended at a house of ill repute. He sat down at the piano in the parlor to compose music to the words. When he finished, he noticed that some of the girls were crying, and their reaction convinced him of the song's possibilities. Von Tilzer later spoke of "A Bird in a Gilded Cage" as "the key that opened the door of wealth and fame" for him. It sold more than two million copies and became a memorable song, typical of the tear-jerker in the public mind. The two teamed up again in 1902 to create a sequel called "The Mansion of Aching Hearts." This song quickly became another million-seller, plugged by a newly-hired boy singer, Izzy Baline, who in a few short years would become the most famous Alley songwriter, Irving Berlin. But, acting as inspiration, Harry Von Tilzer showed the young Berlin how to be a successful publisher and composer. The productive year of 1902, when Von Tilzer started his own publishing company, saw a series of hit songs from his pen. With the always reliable Andrew B. Sterling (1874–1955), he turned out an enormously popular song, the waltz favorite, "On a Sunday Afternoon." When on the beach sunning himself, he thought of the line "they work hard on Monday, but one day that's fun day" and went back to Sterling to have him write the rest of the lyric. With Sterling as his lyricist, Von Tilzer also turned out a series of coon songs which were very popular and whose melodies continue to please. Their previous 1901 collaboration "Down Where the Cotton Blossoms Grow" was featured in vaudeville by Helene Mora. (Did his songwriting brother Albert remember this song when he wrote in 1916, "Down Where the Swanee River Flows" for Al Jolson?) In 1903, the team turned out "Good-bye, Eliza Jane," followed the next year by "Alexander (Don't You Love Your Baby No More)," a title Irving Berlin was to remember seven years later for his all-time hit.

Von Tilzer got his inspiration for his 1905 coon song hit that even topped "Alexander" when he overheard a black couple talking on the platform of a railway station and the wife called her husband "Rufus Rastus Johnson Brown." The rhythmic name was an inspiration to Sterling, who fashioned a complete lyric with the title "What You Goin' to Do When the Rent Comes Round?"

The Harry Von Tilzer Music Publishing Company dominated the industry during this decade mainly by publishing and plugging creatively its owner's wide-ranging songs.

Von Tilzer's 1911 hit with Will Dillon was called "All Alone." This, too, stuck in Irving Berlin's mind when he composed a song with the same name for his 1924 MUSIC BOX REVUE. Another Von Tilzer title, the 1909 "I Love, I Love, I Love My Wife, But Oh, You Kid" was sung by Harry Armstrong and Billy Clark that same year. Also that year, the first parody was published, "I Love My Pipe But Oh, You Pippin!" which spawned other similar song titles. Herbert Ingraham, not to be left out of the pack, entitled his 1910 song "I Love My Husband, But Oh, You Henry!" That same year saw "I Love My Steady, But I'm Crazy for My Once-in-a-While," but it wasn't until 1917 that George W. Meyer came up with "I Love My Billy Sunday, But Oh You Saturday Night."

Von Tilzer's last hit came in 1925, when, with Dolph Singer, he wrote and published "Just Around the Corner." Ted Lewis and his band helped to make it famous. Although he still maintained his office and issued songs, he went, more or less, into retirement and died in New York City on January 10, 1946.

GUS EDWARDS:

"School Days"

Gus Edwards was born in Hohensaliza, Germany, on August 18, 1879. He came to America when he was eight years old and settled in the Williamsburg section of Brooklyn. He soon discovered Union Square and its theatrical center and began to hang around the vaudeville houses. In 1893, Lottie Gilson discovered his sweet singing voice and hired him to act as a stooge for her. His debut occurred in the balcony of Hurtig and Seamon's theatre, where he would sing along with Gilson when she repeated the chorus of such songs as "The Little Lost Child." Gilson was the first to use this particular routine, and Edwards was the first teenage boy to be used in that manner to plug a song. He became such a favorite that he was in demand to sing with Maggie Cline, Helene Mora, and Imogene Comer. One day a vaudeville booking agent discovered him and created an act called the Newsboy Quintet, in which he and four other boys dressed in ragged clothes with newspapers under their arms sang the current hits of the day. Paul Dresser gave pointers to Edwards and allowed him to use a piano at the offices of Howley, Haviland & Company. It was Howley who, in 1898, published Edwards' first tune, a coon song called "All I Wants Is My Black Baby Back." It was featured not only by the Newsboy Quintet, but by Bob Alden, The Rag Time Man. After Edwards met Will D. Cobb, they joined forces to produce "I Couldn't Stand to See My Baby Lose," introduced by the famous coon-shouter, May Irwin. In 1905, Edwards collaborated with Vincent Bryan for the Indian spoof "Tammany." The song was a take-off of the Democratic Party, written for an affair sponsored by the National Democratic Club of New York and well received by this special audience. When Jefferson DeAngelis sang it in vaudeville, it became a hit. The same year, the same team struck it rich for the Witmarks with that great automobile song "In My Merry Oldsmobile." The impetus to write the song came from the newspaper stories about two Oldsmobiles being driven from Detroit to Portland, Oregon, in forty-four days, the first trip by car across country. It is not only the most successful automobile song, but the most memorable. However, try as he might, Edwards could never get the Oldsmobile company to give him one of their cars.

Because of these two hits published by Witmark, Edwards decided to open his own publishing company. He did so near the end of 1905, and it lasted until 1908, when he sold it to the Witmarks. His first numbers were both hits, "Sunbonnet Sue" (which sold over a million copies) and "I Just Can't Make My Eyes Behave" (which Anna Held introduced in the show A PARISIAN MODEL and used as her theme song ever after). Both of these hits had lyrics by Will D. Cobb (1876–1930), who had collaborated with Edwards in 1900 on "I Just Can't Keep from Taking Hold of Things." They did it again with their biggest seller, the 1907 three-million-copy success, "School Days," which they wrote for Edwards' vaudeville act called "School Boys and Girls." Edwards wrote the act, directed and starred in it, and introduced over the years many young performers who would be famous in show business. He played the part of a schoolmaster and some of his "students" who sang, danced, and performed his comedy routines have become legendary: Eddie Cantor, George Jessel, Walter Winchell, Earl Carroll, Lilyan Tashman, Lila Lee, Georgie Price, Groucho Marx, Ray Bolger, Herman Timberg, Charles

King, Mae Murray, Louise Groody, Bert Wheeler, Jack Pearl, Eleanor Powell, Sally Rand, Eddie Buzzell, Mitzi Mayfair, Ona Munson, Ann Dvorak, Larry Adler, and the Duncan Sisters. Georgie Price introduced the Gus Edwards-Edward Madden favorite "By the Light of the Silvery Moon" in 1909. That same year, the song entered the ZIEGFELD FOLLIES, when Lillian Lorraine sang it and boosted its sale to well over two million copies.

During these ragtime years, Edwards created the fine "Merry-Go-Round Rag" and published it at the end of 1908, one of the last tunes issued by the Gus Edwards Music Publishing Company.

Edwards spent most of his years in vaudeville with his school act and later worked in Hollywood, where he died on November 7, 1945.

JOE HOWARD:
"I Wonder Who's Kissing Her Now"

Joseph E. Howard was born in New York City on February 12, 1867. He ran away from home when he was eight years old and made his way to St. Louis, where he eked out a living selling newspapers and singing in saloons. He soon entered vaudeville and next found a job with a traveling stock company. When he was seventeen, he met Ida Emerson and formed a song-and-dance act with her. She was to be the second of his nine wives. They traveled throughout the midwest, coming to Chicago as the stars of their own vaudeville show. They finally came to New York, where they appeared successfully at Tony Pastor's Music Hall. In 1899, T. B. Harms published their marvelous syncopated "ragtime" telephone song "Hello, Ma Baby," which sold over a million copies within a few months and has remained a standard since. In 1904, Howard wrote a follow-up called "Goodbye, My Lady Love," which was featured by Ida. The melody is a variation of his earlier hit and Myddleton's "Down South." Howard continued to perform it in vaudeville, where it was a big hit. He wrote the music for and starred in musical productions in Chicago from 1905–1915, and had his show songs published by Charles K. Harris. His biggest hit and the song most closely identified with him was "I Wonder Who's Kissing Her Now," with lyrics by Will M. Hough and Frank R. Adams, from their 1909 production THE PRINCE OF TO-NIGHT. It wasn't until the motion picture was made of Howard's life using that song title as the title of the film, that Harold Orlob sued to establish that he wrote the melody. Orlob was working for Howard in Chicago, hired to supply music for the shows, with Howard claiming copyright and ownership of the material. When Orlob won his suit, he didn't want money, only the recognition that he was sole composer of that song. Orlob is a classic example of one spending a lifetime in show business but being essentially a one-song composer. He never had another hit. Howard continued to perform in clubs, radio and even television until his retirement, and did benefit shows thereafter. He died while taking a curtain call at the Opera House in Chicago after a show on May 19, 1961.

SCOTT JOPLIN:
"Maple Leaf Rag"

Scott Joplin was born in Bowie County, Texas, on November 24, 1868. He was one of six children of a musical family and was given piano lessons as a child. He made his way as an itinerant pianist throughout the Mississippi Valley, appearing in 1885 at the Silver Dollar Saloon in St. Louis. After performing at the Chicago World's Fair of 1893, he came to the small town of Sedalia, Missouri, where he joined the Queen City Concert Band as second cornetist. Joplin played piano in the Williams Brothers' saloon, whose social club on the second floor was named The Maple Leaf Club. During this time, he enrolled in the George R. Smith College in Sedalia and studied theory, harmony and composition. In 1897 he composed his greatest and most influential piece, "Maple Leaf Rag." It wasn't until 1899, however, that John Stark & Son, of Sedalia, published it. It became the first rag to be nationally popular, eventually selling a million copies of sheet music, and establishing ragtime as a genre of popular music. His "Maple Leaf Rag" was the most imitated rag of all time and set the musical structure of rags from that time forward. It is no wonder, then, that Stark proclaimed in his advertising that Joplin was "King of Ragtime writers." Joplin's use of several sixteen-measure musical themes of complex syncopation with an even, steady duple rhythm was a most revolutionary musical idea at the turn of this century. Popular music would never be the same again. The essential gaiety of the beat fit the national mood; the toe-tapping qualities of this new music filled the air with excitement. This syncopated piano music followed the non-pianistic cakewalk's popularity soon after the slightly syncopated coon song made its debut. The piano rag was more sophisticated musically and technically harder to play than any popular music had been up to this time. Still, the infectious lilt of these syncopated melodies charmed and delighted listeners and sheet music sales soared. Joplin moved from Sedalia to St. Louis, following his publisher John Stark there in 1900.

Joplin's next works were in a different vein, though combining the traditions of Afro-American folk tunes with nineteenth-century European romanticism. His imaginative use of black midwestern folk materials led Alfred Ernst of the St. Louis Choral Symphony Society to call Joplin, in a 1901 article in the St. Louis *Post-Dispatch*, "an extraordinary genius as a composer of ragtime music." That same year saw the publication of "Peacherine Rag" and "The Easy Winners." His "Elite Syncopations" and "The Entertainer" of 1902 proved equally exciting, this last rag being revived in 1974 as background and theme music for the award-winning motion picture THE STING. A recording of the rag that year topped the charts as the number one record for several weeks, seventy-two years after its initial publication!

For the 1904 St. Louis World's Fair, Joplin composed "The Cascades," which became well-known. Following his publisher to New York in June, 1907, Joplin set up his office at 128 West Twenty-ninth Street to compose and arrange ragtime. He made his first New York sale to Joseph W. Stern & Company, which published his "Search Light Rag" and "Gladiolus Rag" that year. His masterpiece in the exceptional year of 1908 was "Fig Leaf Rag," and it was fitting that his mentor, John Stark, issued it. His "Maple Leaf" variation, "Sugar Cane," was also published by the new firm of Seminary Music Company of New York in 1908, as was his brilliant "Pine Apple Rag," later that year. This last tune was such a successful seller that two years later words were added to make a charming "rag song." Joplin was the first to create a syncopated tango instrumental, and his "Solace" of 1909 remains hauntingly beautiful. No ragtime composer has had more influence than Joplin. His thirty-eight rags constitute a major achievement in the history of popular music. He died in New York City on April 1, 1917.

CHARLES L. JOHNSON:
"Dill Pickles Rag"

Charles Leslie Johnson was born in Kansas City, Kansas, on December 3, 1876. He started taking piano lessons at the age of six, and ten years later studied theory and harmony. He had a fine ear and taught himself to play the violin, banjo, guitar, and mandolin. In the twin cities he organized several string orchestras and played in theatres, hotels, restaurants, and dance halls. During the day, he demonstrated songs and pianos for the J. W. Jenkins Sons' Music Company, which published "Scandalous Thompson," his first rag, in 1899. Shortly after, he entered into partnership in the Central Music Publishing Company, which issued his Indian song, "Iola." Interestingly, both this song and Charles N. Daniels' earlier "Hiawatha" were named for towns in Kansas, not Indians. The lyrics to both songs were added after they had become successful as instrumental numbers. "Iola" didn't become a big hit until Charles N. Daniels bought it for Jerome H. Remick & Company and exploited it nationally. Coincidentally, Charles Johnson was working for Daniels' old firm, Carl Hoffman Music Company, at the time of the song's purchase in 1906.

At that time, Johnson was working over a new rag when Hoffman's bookkeeper came in and asked him what the name of it was. The bookkeeper was carrying a carton of dill pickles to accompany his dinner. Johnson noticed them and said, "I'll call it 'Dill Pickles Rag.' " After Daniels bought "Dill Pickles Rag" for Remick in 1907 (it had been published by Hoffman the year before) and turned it into a million-selling hit, Johnson started his own publishing company, which lasted until Harold Rossiter of Chicago purchased the firm in August, 1910, with the stipulation that Johnson not re-enter the publishing business again for one year (shades of Remick and Shapiro!). Charles Johnson was one of the most prolific of the Alley composers, and, like Harry Von Tilzer, wrote all of the types of songs and instrumentals then popular. He was published not only by his own firm, but also by Remick, Vandersloot, Sam Fox, F.J.A. Forster, and Will Rossiter, Harold's older brother. He was so prolific that he had to resort to pseudonyms, especially when he published his own songs, so it would appear that he had more than one composer on his staff. Among his pseudonyms was "Raymond Birch," who was credited with ragtime hits "Powder Rag" and "Blue Goose Rag." Among Johnson's thirty-two rags, "Porcupine Rag" of 1909 and "Crazy Bone Rag" of 1913 became million-selling successes. "Cum-Bac" of 1911 was among his most clever. His 1916 "Teasing the Cat" enjoyed a huge popularity, thanks to the Van Eps Trio's recording on Victor. Johnson's high sense of fun was reflected in his popular and excellently constructed rags. His lyrical talent was evident in his biggest money-making song, the 1919 "Sweet and Low." Unlike other successful Tin Pan Alley composers, he elected to stay in his hometown. His very full career as composer, publisher and arranger came to an end with his death in Kansas City, Missouri, on December 28, 1950.

JEAN SCHWARTZ:
"Chinatown, My Chinatown"

Jean Schwartz was born in Budapest, Hungary, on November 4, 1878. His family came to the United States to live in New York City when he was thirteen. He studied the piano and got a job as a demonstrator in the music department of Siegel-Cooper's, which boasted New York's first department store sheet music counter. He then joined Shapiro, Bernstein & Von Tilzer as staff pianist and plugger. His first published composition was the cakewalk hit "Dusky Dudes" in 1899. He formed a songwriting team with William Jerome (1865–1932) in 1901 and enjoyed a respectable string of hits during the next decade. Schwartz and Jerome started with a coon song made popular by Harry Bulger called "When Mr. Shakespeare Comes to Town," and followed it with "Rip Van Winkle Was a Lucky Man," which Jerome's wife, Maude Nugent, made famous. Schwartz and Jerome's hit with the overwhelmingly popular "Bedelia (The Irish Coon Song Serenade)" was due almost entirely to Mose Gumble's plugging the number for Maurice Shapiro. It sold over three million copies. Blanche Ring sang it in THE JERSEY LILY, and she was constantly identified with the song. Schwartz got back into the syncopated game in 1908 with a huge success in "The Whitewash Man." It was a superior rag and helped reaffirm ragtime's popularity during this decade. He scored twice more with instrumentals in 1910 titled "Black Beauty Rag" and "The Pop Corn Man." This same year saw Remick's publication of Schwartz and Jerome's all-time favorite, "Chinatown, My Chinatown," again plugged to multi-million status by Mose Gumble, now head of Remick's Professional Department.

Jean Schwartz had many of his songs interpolated into Broadway shows, that is, used in shows written by other composers, but it wasn't until 1904 that he wrote his first complete Broadway score PIFF, PAFF, POUF, which starred Eddie Foy. Schwartz and Jerome also owned their own publishing house for a few years before the First World War, when they went their separate ways. Schwartz wrote for Broadway shows throughout the twenties. His biggest successes came during World War One with Al Jolson introducing "Hello Central! Give Me No Man's Land" and "Rock-a-Bye Your Baby with a Dixie Melody" in SINBAD in 1918, with the lyrics for both songs by veterans Joe Young (1889–1939) and Sam M. Lewis (1885–1959). In 1930, Schwartz wrote his last hit, "Au Revoir, Pleasant Dreams," which Ben Bernie used as his radio theme.

Jean Schwartz died in Los Angeles on November 30, 1956.

EGBERT VAN ALSTYNE:

"In the Shade of the Old Apple Tree"

Egbert Anson Van Alstyne was born in Chicago on March 5, 1882. He was a musical prodigy who played the organ for Sunday School when he was seven years old and was given a scholarship to the Chicago Musical College, the Juilliard of its day. It was run by Florenz Ziegfeld, Sr., whose son would later create the famous series revue, the FOLLIES. The Chicago Musical College was the premier school in the midwest for students of classical music. During the first decade of this century, it was unusual for composers of popular music to have any formal training in classical music, and Van Alstyne was exceptional in this regard. (Two other Tin Pan Alleyites, Percy Wenrich and Zez Confrey, would later study there.)

Van Alstyne went into vaudeville with lyricist Harry H. Williams (1879–1922) and turned out a string of hits, starting in 1903 with the fine Indian song "Navajo," introduced by Marie Cahill in her show NANCY BROWN. Van Alstyne and Williams scored again the following year with a great coon song, "Back, Back, Back to Baltimore." In 1905 the team had their greatest hit with "In the Shade of the Old Apple Tree," which sold several million copies of sheet music. The next year the team produced "Won't You Come Over to My House," and followed that up in 1907 with another Indian song, "San Antonio," and the comic "I'm Afraid to Come Home in the Dark," the latter sung to great acclaim by May Irwin. The following year, joined by lyricist Benjamin Hapgood Burt, Van Alstyne composed a sequel, "I Used to Be Afraid to Go Home in the Dark, Now I'm Afraid to Go at All." In 1910 the team scored with the query "What's the Matter with Father?" and in 1911, with a "rag song" harking back to their first hit, "Oh, That Navajo Rag." They produced quite a list of hits.

Van Alstyne was involved with piano rags as early as 1900, when he wrote "Rag Time Chimes," published in his hometown by Will Rossiter. It featured for the first time the "chimes" effect that would later become a cliche. He had a hit for Remick in 1909 with "Honey Rag," whose second strain is a beauty. And in 1912 he wrote "Jamaica Jinger (A Hot Rag)," which again demonstrated his creativity in syncopation.

Van Alstyne was given joint credit with Tony Jackson and lyricist Gus Kahn for the Jackson tune, "Pretty Baby," which, because of its interpolation into the PASSING SHOW OF 1916, became a million seller. His last hit was the 1931 "Beautiful Love." He died in Chicago on July 9, 1951.

THEODORE MORSE:
"Down in Jungle Town"

Theodore F. Morse was born in Washington, D.C., on April 13, 1873. He came to New York City at the age of fourteen and worked for the Oliver Ditson Company as a junior clerk. He joined Howley, Haviland & Company as a staff composer and plugger, left to become manager of F. A. Mills, and then left Mills to open his own firm, Morse Music Company. He sold his catalog two years later to Howley, Haviland & Dresser to become manager of the Professional Department at American Music Company, which published his two-step "Happy Hooligan," based on the comic strip by Frederick Opper, then syndicated by the Hearst newspapers. In December, 1903, Morse and F. B. Haviland left American Music to form F. B. Haviland Publishing Company. It was incorporated in April 1904, with Haviland, Morse, and Richard Nugent as partners. For the new firm, Morse and Edward Madden (1878–1952) began their decade-long collaboration with "Blue Bell," which achieved a notable sale. Another succcess that year from the team was the coon song "I've Got a Feelin' for You (Way Down in My Heart)." As an interpolation in the 1907 show PLAYING THE PONIES, they contributed "I'd Rather Be a Lobster Than a Wise Guy." The following year saw the team's greatest hit, "Down in Jungle Town." The next year, Morse left the Haviland firm to start Theodore Morse Music Company, with Al Cook as his General Manager. Morse's marriage to lyricist Theodora (Dolly) Terriss also gave the composer a new professional collaborator. Their big hits came one after another, beginning in 1911 with the sensational rag song "Another Rag." In 1912, they followed it with "When Uncle Joe Plays a Rag on His Old Banjo," which was featured in vaudeville by The Three Pickert Sisters. The sisters also sang the married team's 1913 "Bobbin' Up and Down" to hit status. Morse teamed with lyricist Howard Johnson in 1915 for the Feist hit "M-O-T-H-E-R." Again for Feist, in 1917, Morse concocted his most famous song, from the music of Arthur Sullivan, when he and Dolly wrote "Hail! Hail! The Gang's All Here." Theodore Morse died in New York City on May 25, 1924.

ALBERT VON TILZER:
"Put Your Arms Around Me, Honey"

Albert Von Tilzer, surnamed Gumm like his older brother Harry, was born in Indianapolis, Indiana, on March 29, 1878. After Harry was made a partner in Shapiro, Bernstein & Von Tilzer, Albert was hired to work in the firm's Chicago office. By 1904, Albert had come to New York, and in that year he founded his own publishing house with his brother Jack. It was called the York Music Company, located at 40 West Twenty-eighth Street. For it, he and Cecil Mack wrote the York firm's first big hit, "Teasin'." When Albert joined vaudevillian Jack Norworth in 1907, they created the hit "Honey Boy" in honor of the old minstrel George Evans. Norworth plugged it in vaudeville, as well as their two 1908 hits: "Smarty," and the song that became the anthem of baseball, "Take Me Out to the Ball-Game." It has been said that Albert had never seen a ball game when the song was written and wasn't to see one until twenty years later! In 1910, he teamed up with vaudevillian Junie McCree to produce the all-time favorite "Put Your Arms Around Me, Honey." He gave up York Music at the beginning of 1913 and joined the new firm of yet another brother: Will Von Tilzer's Broadway Music Corporation, which opened in April at 145 West Forty-fifth Street. With Stanley Murphy and Charles McCarron, Albert wrote "Oh, How She Could Yacki Hacki Wicki Wacki Woo," with which Eddie Cantor made his debut in the ZIEGFELD FOLLIES OF 1917. Charlotte Greenwood helped to popularize "Oh, By Jingo!" in 1919. The next year Albert's smash hit was "I'll Be with You in Apple Blossom Time," which he followed in 1921 with his "Dapper Dan," which Eddie Cantor sang in blackface in THE MIDNIGHT ROUNDERS. His (and Will's) Broadway Music Corporation went out of business in 1922. Albert then went into vaudeville as a headliner on the Orpheum circuit. In 1930, he went to Hollywood to work in film music. He died in Los Angeles on October 1, 1956.

CHARLES N. DANIELS:
"You Tell Me Your Dream . . ."

Charles Neil Daniels was born in Leavenworth, Kansas, on April 12, 1878, and grew up in Kansas City, Kansas. In high school, he studied music theory, piano, and music calligraphy. Upon graduation, he joined the Carl Hoffman Music Company as a song demonstrator during the day, and he accompanied singers for the Kronberg Concert Company at night. In 1898, the Hoffman firm offered a prize of twenty-five dollars for the best two-step by a local composer. Daniels, after much prodding by friends, competed for the prize, winning it with his song "Margery." At that time John Philip Sousa was playing at the Coats Opera House there. Sousa heard of the contest, offered to perform the work, and, much to everyone's amazement, made it an instant success. This collaboration led to a lasting friendship with Sousa which came in handy for Daniels throughout his career. While "Margery" sold 275,000 copies, the Hoffman firm owned the copyright, so Daniels had to be content with his prize money and some favorable publicity. But the tune's success led to his promotion to manager for Hoffman. In December 1898, Daniels, acting for the firm, purchased Scott Joplin's "Original Rags," thus beginning his involvement with ragtime. In time, he became the most significant ragtime entrepreneur after John Stark. He purchased Charles L. Johnson's "Dill Pickles" for Remick's and made it into a million-selling sensation, thereby contributing greatly to the boom years of ragtime. He encouraged the composing of rags by his firm's staff, accepted unsolicited manuscripts, and purchased small-town publishers' rags. He nurtured ragtime until it was a flourishing and significant part of the popular sheet music industry. Curiously, for all his promotion of rags, he composed only a few of them, notably "Classic Rag" in 1909, under his famous pseudonym "Neil Moret," and the rag "Cotton Time" in 1910.

The same year that he purchased Joplin's "Original Rags," Daniels composed his own song, "You Tell Me Your Dream, I'll Tell You Mine," which became a big hit. He also founded the publishing firm of Daniels, Russel and Boone. The next year he left Kansas City for St. Louis, where he managed the sheet music department of the Barr Dry Goods Company. In 1901, his firm published his new Indian song "Hiawatha," which became another success after he prevailed upon Sousa to perform and record it. The following year, when Remick purchased Whitney Warner of Detroit, he paid Daniels $10,000 for his firm so that Remick's could have "Hiawatha." It was the highest sum yet paid for a song. With it went an offer to head up the Whitney Warner company as manager, so Daniels moved to Detroit in 1902. The following year, James O'Dea added words to "Hiawatha," and sales zoomed again when it became a song. Thus started the trend of Indian songs, which were extremely popular during the first decade of the new century. When he moved to San Francisco in 1912, Daniels formed another company, this time in partnership with Weston Wilson. Most notably, they published in 1918 Daniels' title song commissioned by Mack Sennett for his silent film starring Mabel Normand, MICKEY. This was the first motion picture title song. It is remarkable that promoting a silent movie by associating it with a song took as long as it did. The first silent film, "The Sneeze," an extremely short subject starring Fred Ott, was made in 1893. But once producers caught on to this marketing gimmick, they didn't stop, and we still find that most of the songs written for films today are title songs. From 1924 to 1931, Daniels was president of Villa Moret, Inc. in San Francisco. Sensing that movies, with their new "soundtracks," and commercial radio were cutting into sheet music sales, Daniels decided to withdraw from active management in the music business.

During the years he owned his own firms, he composed many hit songs selling well into the millions: "Moonlight and Roses," "Mello Cello," "Song of the Wanderer," "Chloe," "She's Funny That Way," "In Monterey," and "Sweet and Lovely."

Charles N. Daniels died in Los Angeles on January 21, 1943.

DANCES OF THE RAGTIME ERA

The most popular of the ballroom dances during this period was the two-step. Like the cakewalk, it was lightly syncopated and, therefore, easily danced to. At first the tunes were in 6/8 time, but when publishers added the designation "characteristic march and two-step," the public understood it to mean a syncopated number, usually in 2/4 time. As an alternative to piano ragtime, it was easier for the amateur pianist to learn and yet it hinted at the exhilaration that ragtime could provide. Two-steps were published through this decade and into the next, but were succeeded by the "animal dances" and the one-step just before the First World War.

Some of the most successful two-steps include Charles L. Johnson's "All the Money" (1908), S. R. Henry's "The Colored Major" (1900) and "Peter Piper" (1905), Albert Von Tilzer's "Cotton" (1907), Harry Von Tilzer's "The Cubanola Glide" (1909), Duane Crabb's "Fluffy Ruffles" (1907), Malvin M. Franklin's "The Lobster Glide" (1909), William H. Tyers' "Panama" (1911), and Henry Frantzen's "Kentucky Kut Up" (1907).

During this decade the ever-popular waltz was holding its own, as evidenced by the great popularity of such songs as Harry Von Tilzer's "Down Where the Wurzburger Flows," "Under the Anheuser Bush," "On a Sunday Afternoon," George Evans' "In the Good Old Summertime," Egbert Van Alstyne's "In the Shade of the Old Apple Tree," Kerry Mills' "Meet Me in St. Louis, Louis," Gus Edwards' "In My Merry Oldsmobile" and "School Days," and Leo Friedman's "Meet Me Tonight in Dreamland."

This decade in dance was the calm before the storm. The waltz maintained its lead as the universal favorite. The two-step gave the younger generation some kick in their lives, while the older generation clicked its tongues in disapproval. No one could foresee what popular dance would be like in the coming decade.

MUSICAL THEATRE IN THE RAGTIME ERA

GEORGE M. COHAN:
"Forty-Five Minutes from Broadway"

George Michael Cohan was born in Providence, Rhode Island, on July 3, 1878. He could be described, without exaggeration, as having been "born in a trunk," since his parents were touring vaudevillians, and he joined their act as a human prop while still a baby. His first speaking role came at the age of nine. His education consisted mainly of lessons learned on the vaudeville circuit. By eleven he was contributing sketches to his parents' act and acting as their business manager. After his marriage in 1894 to Ethel Levey, who joined the act as a singer-actress, Cohan began to write for the musical theatre and to expand his vaudeville sketches for the legitimate stage.

His first song was published by the Witmarks, who had Walter Ford rewrite the lyrics, turning "Why Did Nellie Leave Home?" from a comic vaudeville number into a tear-jerker. Cohan met May Irwin and, in 1896, collaborated with her on the coon song "Hot Tamale Alley," which she sang in the leading vaudeville houses. Two years later, with his own words and music, Cohan came out with "I Guess I'll Have to Telegraph My Baby," his first real hit song.

A precocious youngster with definite ideas, he set about changing musical comedy in America by giving it an American feeling, his feeling—full of brashness, brightness and patriotic fervor.

Before Cohan, musical comedy consisted of vaudeville stars doing their turns in exotic costumes in front of colorful scenery with scripts that had little or no plot. The more exotic, the more popular, it seemed. Viennese operettas were imported to American stages where the stories unfolded in such foreign locales as "Ruritania." Then came Cohan to write about American characters in American places. He made it acceptable for things American to be written about, and even glorified, on the stage and in song.

In time, Cohan became famous not only as a song-and-dance man, but as a playwright, director, composer, lyricist, publisher, dramatic actor, and producer, the first compleat man of the American theatre. His theatrical talents encompassed the entire scope of the business, and it is hard for us to realize now how one man could dominate an entire musical production doing everything himself—not just once, but time and again for over fifteen years!

His list of Broadway productions, starting with THE GOVERNOR'S SON (February 25, 1901), included twenty-two musicals and thirteen straight plays. His most impressive years as producer-performer-playwright occurred 1904–1920, when he partnered with Broadway producer Sam Harris (1872–1941). Late in his life, Cohan scored a personal triumph as a dramatic actor in Eugene O'Neill's AH, WILDERNESS and again in Kaufman and Hart's I'D RATHER BE RIGHT.

Cohan's first two Broadway shows were merely expansions of his family's vaudeville sketches. It is not surprising that they failed with spectacle-dazed Broadway audiences. However, audiences around the country liked them, and they made money in their out-of-town runs. His first two shows were THE GOVERNOR'S SON and RUNNING FOR OFFICE (April 27, 1903). The first had an interesting song, "I Love Everyone in the Wide, Wide World," and the twelve songs in the score were published by F. A. Mills. The second show also had twelve songs, a good one being "Sweet Popularity," published by the short-lived Cohan, Nobel & Cohan firm.

The eight best Cohan musicals are the ones in which he starred. They also featured his most famous songs during the first decade of this century. LITTLE JOHNNY JONES (November 7, 1904) had a score which contained three genuine hits: "The Yankee Doodle Boy," "Give My Regards to Broadway," and "Life's a Funny Proposition after All." The next important show, FORTY-FIVE MINUTES FROM BROADWAY (January 1, 1906), was the first to star someone other than himself. Three of the six published songs were hits, the title song, "Mary's a Grand Old Name," and "So Long Mary," and one song, a comic number titled "Stand Up and Fight Like Hell," shocked even the sophisticated Broadway audience, as words like "hell" and "damn" were forbidden on stage in the nineteenth century. Cohan's audiences were titillated by his use of them in what was thought to be family entertainment. (It may be remembered that it also took television many years before such language was considered acceptable.)

Unable to stand not starring in his own show, he wrote, produced and

starred in GEORGE WASHINGTON, JR. (February 12, 1906), from which
came the patriotic "The Wedding of the Blue and Gray" and everyone's
favorite "You're a Grand Old Flag." But not everyone was happy with
the song when he originally published it. The first title came from a
conversation Cohan had with a Civil War veteran who had been a color-
bearer during Pickett's charge at Gettysburg. The old man alluded
proudly to the charge saying, "She's a grand old rag." After opening
night and the original publication bearing *that* title and phrase in the
lyric, patriotic societies complained that to refer to our country's flag as
a "rag" was an insult. Cohan recalled the initial sheet music and
substituted "flag" for "rag."

His musical for 1907 was a rehash of RUNNING FOR OFFICE. It was
called THE HONEYMOONERS (June 3, 1907) and featured an unusual (for
him) syncopated tune called "Popularity." The show also included the
comic "If I'm Going to Die, I'm Going to Have Some Fun." The next
musical, THE TALK OF NEW YORK (December 3, 1907), starred Victor
Moore, who had made a splash with his debut in FORTY-FIVE MINUTES
FROM BROADWAY. He made his role of "Kid Burns" so famous that
Cohan wrote a play which featured the character. The show included "I
Want the World to Know I Love You," "I Have a Longing for Long Acre
Square," "When We Are M-A double R-I-E-D," and "When a Fellow's
on the Level with a Girl That's on the Square."

His third show of the 1907–08 season was FIFTY MILES FROM BOSTON
(February 3, 1908), and he provided the score with "Harrigan." THE
YANKEE PRINCE (April 20, 1908) contained "Come On Down Town."
With this show, the producers started their own publishing firm, The
Cohan & Harris Publishing Company, with the Jerome H. Remick
Company as their exclusive selling agent. COHAN & HARRIS' MINSTRELS
(August 3, 1908) starred George "Honey Boy" Evans and included
William Jerome and Jean Schwartz' "Meet Me in Rose Time, Rosie."
THE AMERICAN IDEA (October 5, 1908) featured the song "The Ameri-
can Ragtime."

THE MAN WHO OWNS BROADWAY (October 11, 1909) starred Raymond Hitchcock and featured a song with a show business inside joke,
"I'm All O.K. with K. and E." The "K. and E." referred to was the
theatrical producing colossus, Klaw and Erlanger, which controlled most
of the Broadway theatres through the First World War. The last of
Cohan's own book shows, THE LITTLE MILLIONAIRE (September 25,
1911), starred the author-composer and included Cohan's "bungalow
song," "Come with Me to the Bungalow."

For his last three productions before the end of the War, Cohan explored the revue format. The first, HELLO BROADWAY (December 25, 1914), was subtitled, "A Musical Crazy Quilt Patched and Threaded Together with Words and Music by George M. Cohan." It co-starred Cohan and William Collier and featured "Down by the Erie Canal." THE COHAN REVUE OF 1916 (February 9, 1916) included the cute "The Frisco Melody." For his last Broadway effort of the decade, the COHAN REVUE OF 1918 (December 31, 1917) had a score by Cohan and Irving Berlin. When Cohan managed to fast-talk Berlin into working with him for this revue, it became the first and, so far, only instance of two famous individual composer-lyricists working together on a single Broadway production. "Polly Pretty Polly" had music composed by Berlin and words by Cohan. Thus, the two greatest musical comedy songwriters of the decade joined forces to produce a show.

It is ironic that Cohan's biggest song hit, "Over There," did not come from one of his very successful shows, as that was where he had made his reputation. "Over There" was a patriotic number written expressly for and about the First World War. It was first published by (lyricist William) Jerome Publishing Corporation, which Cohan had financially backed. Nora Bayes introduced it and, by her thrilling performances, turned it into such a hit that Leo Feist bought it for his firm for the then-unprecedented amount of $25,000. He had his pluggers turn it into a more than two-million seller. Cohan immediately donated that money to various war charities. President Woodrow Wilson said it was a "genuine inspiration to all American manhood." The song was so inspiring, in fact, that Congress in 1940, upon the urging of President Franklin D. Roosevelt, issued a special Medal of Honor to Cohan for writing it. Upon Cohan's death in New York City on November 5, 1942, President Franklin D. Roosevelt wrote, "A beloved figure is lost to our national life."

COLE & JOHNSON BROTHERS:
"The Maiden with the Dreamy Eyes"

Bob Cole, a black composer and lyricist, was born in Athens, Georgia, on July 1, 1868. His first big break occurred in 1890, when he was hired as a comedian in Sam T. Jack's Creole Show and also served as its stage manager. In the cast was soubrette Stella Wiley, who would soon marry Cole. Next, he got a job as a playwright and stage manager for Worth's Museum All-Star Stock Company, which James Weldon Johnson described in his book BLACK MANHATTAN as "the first place where a group of coloured performers were able to gain anything approaching dramatic training and experience on the strictly professional stage." Cole's next experience was writing songs and performing the songs of others with BLACK PATTI'S TROUBADOURS, a touring concert-vaudeville show produced by whites. After a dispute about salary Cole left to form his own production company and write his own show. He formed a partnership with Billy Johnson (1858–1916), a fellow actor-dancer who wrote the lyrics and costarred with Cole in A TRIP TO COONTOWN. This was a landmark production when it opened in New York City at the very out-of-the-way Third Avenue Theatre on April 4, 1898, in that it was entirely written, performed and produced by blacks. It was in this show that Bob Cole portrayed a tramp called "Willie Wayside" to great acclaim. Some of the songs in the show were the title song (with words by the new partners and music by Bert Williams), "I Hope These Few Lines Will Find You Well," "The Wedding of the Chinee and the Coon," and "In Dahomey," all with music by Bob Cole and lyrics by Billy Johnson. The show toured the country for two years. After the tour came to an end, so did this Cole-Johnson partnership. The next one that Cole would form would last until his death.

John Rosamond Johnson (1873–1954) and James Weldon Johnson (1871–1938), brothers born in Jacksonville, Florida, joined forces with Bob Cole in 1900. Their first number was "If That's Society, Excuse Me." The team wrote two hits during the next two years which were independent of shows, "My Castle on the Nile" (1901) and "Oh! Didn't He Ramble" (1902), the latter written under the pseudonym "Will Handy."

Their first show assignment was for a white production, THE BELLE OF BRIDGEPORT (October 29, 1900), which starred May Irwin, who sang their "Why Don't the Band Play" and "I've Got Troubles of My Own." These two numbers were published by Joseph W. Stern & Company, which would publish most of their work during this decade. (Howley, Haviland & Company had been the publisher of the first Cole and Johnson team.)

THE SLEEPING BEAUTY AND THE BEAST (November 4, 1901) contained a few of their numbers, "Come Out Dinah on the Green" being the best of them. Another show of that year, THE LITTLE DUCHESS (October 14, 1901), starred Anna Held, who interpolated their famous "The Maiden with the Dreamy Eyes." Marie Cahill starred in SALLY IN OUR ALLEY (August 29, 1902) and interpolated Bob Cole's "Under the Bamboo

Tree," which became so identified with her that she took the song with her into her next show, NANCY BROWN (February 16, 1903). She also sang their "The Katydid, the Cricket and the Frog," and the Johnson Brothers' "Congo Love Song." For the University of Pennsylvania's Mask and Wig Club's eighteenth production, the team supplied four numbers, of which "Won't Your Mamma Let You Come Out and Play" (1906) was the most successful.

Bob Cole and the Johnson Brothers wrote two complete scores for Broadway musicals with white casts. The first was HUMPTY DUMPTY (November 14, 1904), an American adaptation of an English show, which included "Mexico" and "Sambo and Dinah." The second show was IN NEWPORT (December 26, 1904), which starred Fay Templeton and Peter Dailey, former stars of the Weber & Fields Music Hall gang, with Templeton singing "Lindy."

The team wrote only two Broadway musicals for all-black casts. Their first was THE SHOO-FLY REGIMENT (August 6, 1907), in which they co-starred. Their two big numbers were "On the Gay Luneta," and "Who Do You Love?" The team's other Broadway show with an all-black cast was THE RED MOON (May 3, 1909). While the latter didn't have any hits, the entire score was praised by *The Dramatic Mirror*, whose critic tended to be tough on black shows. He wrote, "the score is often quite ambitious and always pleasing to hear." Some of the more "pleasing" songs were "As Long As the World Goes Round," "The Big Red Shawl," and "On the Road to Monterey." The show toured for the rest of the season, at the end of which the team announced their retirement from producing and writing Broadway musicals. The start of the 1910 season saw the team re-enter vaudeville with an act consisting of Bob Cole singing and Rosamond Johnson at the piano. They toured throughout the United States.

James Weldon Johnson died in Wiscasset, Maine, on June 26, 1938.

John Rosamond Johnson died in New York City on November 11, 1954.

Bob Cole drowned in a lake in the Catskills, New York, on August 2, 1911.

THE ZIEGFELD FOLLIES

Before the FOLLIES, which premiered on July 8, 1907, the Broadway revue had been merely vaudeville, extravaganza and burlesque, all dressed up with outrageous costumes and lavish sets. With the coming of Florenz Ziegfeld, Jr., (1867–1932) and his FOLLIES, the revue added girls—not just a handful, but forty to fifty of them, all beauties. For all his meticulous attention to detail, the one element Ziegfeld spent no time with was the music for his shows. He imported stars, dressed (and undressed) his showgirls magnificently, spent fortunes on scenery, but, for the most part, hired hacks to write the FOLLIES songs. Here was glorious, first-class entertainment with little attention paid to the music. Consequently, the talents of Tin Pan Alley weren't as vital to the FOLLIES as might be supposed. Except for the two FOLLIES shows written by Irving Berlin, all of the hit songs in the other editions were interpolations, that is, songs added to the shows and not composed by the original writers of those shows. While it wasn't obvious at the time, one can now see that all of the hits from the FOLLIES (other than the Berlin scores) were songs *not* written with the shows in mind. The original scores never seemed to provide any hits.

The first song hit from the FOLLIES OF 1908 (June 15, 1908) was made by headliner Nora Bayes and her husband Jack Norworth singing their own composition "Shine On, Harvest Moon" as an interpolation. In the FOLLIES OF 1910 (June 20, 1910), Bert Williams and Fanny Brice made their FOLLIES debuts. Williams featured his own tune, "You're Gwine to Get Somethin' What You Don't Expect" and the Ford Dabney-Cecil Mack number, "That Minor Strain." Fanny Brice (1891–1951) scored solidly with Joe Jordan's "Lovie Joe." Ford Dabney (1883–1958), a black writer, managed to place "The Pensacola Mooch" as the show's dance sensation. For the ZIEGFELD FOLLIES OF 1911 (June 26, 1911), Irving Berlin contributed the only standout, with Bert Williams interpreting his "Woodman, Woodman, Spare That Tree." The 1912 edition (October 21, 1912) contained an interpolated hit by James Monaco and William Jerome, with Elizabeth Brice singing their "Row, Row, Row."

By all accounts, the ZIEGFELD FOLLIES OF 1919 (June 16, 1919) was the most important one in the series. Irving Berlin wrote its theme song, one that served this show and hundreds of beauty pageants and fashion shows ever since: "A Pretty Girl Is Like a Melody," which John Steel originally sang. Berlin also created such diverse gems as "Mandy," sung by Van and Schenck, "You Cannot Make Your Shimmy Shake on Tea," performed by Bert Williams, and the million-selling hit that Eddie Cantor sang, "You'd Be Surprised." Alleyites Harry Tierney and Joseph McCarthy had an interpolated hit with "My Baby's Arms."

The 1921 FOLLIES (June 21, 1921) gave Fanny Brice two of her biggest

hits, "Second Hand Rose" and the poignant "My Man," both interpolations. The only hit of the 1922 (June 5, 1922) edition was a specialty
number, composed by the comedians who sang it, entitled "Oh! Mister
Gallagher and Mister Shean." The last Ziegfeld FOLLIES to produce a
song hit was the one that opened on August 16, 1927, when Ruth Etting
introduced Irving Berlin's "Shaking the Blues Away." No other revue
series made such an impression on the public and none created as many
song hits, even though they were mostly interpolated into the shows.

VAUDEVILLE IN THE RAGTIME ERA

BLANCHE RING:
"I've Got Rings on My Fingers"

Blanche Ring (1877–1961) first appeared in vaudeville in her home
town of Boston before coming to New York City, where she made her
debut on Broadway in THE DEFENDER (July 3, 1902). She interpolated
George Evans and Ren Shields' song "In the Good Old Summer Time,"
with which she was identified thereafter. She participated in the song's
creation when she and the two songwriters were having dinner at Coney
Island. Evans looked around and said there was "nothing like the good
old summer time," and Shields picked up the phrase and wrote it down.
When handed the lyrics, Evans practically hummed the tune on the
spot.

From that time forward, Ring became a marvelous interpreter of the
popular songs of the day. Toward the end of this decade, she had three
stupendous hits in a row. The outstanding song success of 1908 was the
John Flynn-Will Cobb "Yip-I-Addy-I-Ay," which she added to her
permanent repertoire. In 1909, she was given her theme song by the
English team of Scott, Weston and Barnes, when they wrote "I've Got
Rings on My Fingers." Ring was asked to join the cast of THE MIDNIGHT
SONS (May 22, 1909) and sang this interpolated number. She had been
successful with it in vaudeville and was even more so in this show. The
song was so closely identified with her that in order to satisfy her fans
she had to interpolate it into her next show, THE YANKEE GIRL (February
10, 1910), where it proved to be the hit of that show, too. The same
year she performed another classic in the Fred Fisher-Alfred Bryan
airplane song, "Come, Josephine, in My Flying Machine." She contin-

ued to be a favorite in vaudeville and on the stage until 1938. She also sang on radio.

NORA BAYES:
"Shine On, Harvest Moon"

Nora Bayes (1880–1928) was christened Dora Goldberg. Her big break in vaudeville came in 1902, when she was asked to perform Harry Von Tilzer's "Down Where the Wurzburger Flows" at the Orpheum Theatre in Brooklyn. On opening day, the composer took a seat in the box nearest the stage and, when Bayes forgot the words halfway through the number, he stood up and sang the rest of the song. She picked it up on the second chorus and got a great hand. The management hired Von Tilzer to repeat the stunt for the rest of the week and generated tremendous interest in the song. Bayes was known for years after as "The Wurzburger Girl." That song made her a star.

She and her husband Jack Norworth wrote "Shine On, Harvest Moon" and featured it in Ziegfeld's FOLLIES OF 1908. It was their biggest song success. Later that year, Norworth wrote the lyrics for Albert Von Tilzer's "Take Me Out to the Ball-Game," and Bayes helped make it the standard it has become by singing it in her act for the next two years. From that time forward, she was a top act in vaudeville and headlined every bill she was on.

In the manner of the time, she interpolated several numbers into the score of THE JOLLY BACHELORS when she starred in it on January 6, 1910. She and her husband rewrote an English song by providing a new title and lyrics and sang "Come Along, My Mandy" to success. Her biggest hit in the show, however, was another English song with Americanized lyrics, entitled "Has Anybody Here Seen Kelly?" It brought the house down nightly.

For LITTLE MISS FIX-IT (April 3, 1911), the team interpolated their sequel to "Shine On, Harvest Moon" and called it "Mr. Moon Man, Turn Off Your Light." Their recording of it demonstrates their star quality (Victor 70038).

George M. Cohan's "Over There" was published by the William Jerome Publishing Company and had a photograph of Nora Bayes on the first edition. This 1917 effort was the biggest seller of the more than one thousand songs written about the War, due in great measure to its plugging by Nora Bayes.

Bayes starred in the Broadway musical LADIES FIRST (October 24,

1918) and sang two interpolated numbers written by George Gershwin. The first was "Some Wonderful Sort of Someone" and was published only with the pre-Broadway show title cover, LOOK WHO'S HERE. The second, "The Real American Folk Song Is a Rag," was not published until 1959, but it was the first song written together by the Gershwin brothers, George and Ira. It was a good song, too, filled with the syncopation that George would cleverly use throughout the 1920's. Ira's lyrics suited the melody perfectly and it was he who gave the song to Ella Fitzgerald in 1959, when she asked to make the first recording of it. Her performance featured the expert backing of ragtime pianist Lou Busch on the LP, ELLA FITZGERALD SINGS THE GEORGE AND IRA GERSHWIN SONG BOOK, Volume Two (Verve MGV-4025).

Although she was to continue as a headliner in vaudeville through the mid-twenties, Bayes' last two big song hits came in 1920. Again for Albert Von Tilzer, she sang "I'll Be with You in Apple Blossom Time" to success, and, for the new team of Richard Whiting and Raymond Egan, she made "The Japanese Sandman" a two-million seller.

EVA TANGUAY:
"I Don't Care"

Eva Tanguay (1878–1948) built her reputation in vaudeville on the idea of her most famous song, the 1905 Harry Sutton-Jean Lenox "I Don't Care." She became known as the "I Don't Care Girl" and, by needling managers, directors, fellow performers and even audiences, her attitude proclaimed loudly that she really didn't care what people thought of her. Her love affairs were commonly known, although she hardly ever gave interviews to the press. She gave everything to putting over a song. With a fairly ordinary voice but with tremendous enthusiasm and energy, Tanguay became vaudeville's highest-paid star.

When she was just seventeen, she first appeared on a sheet music cover: "Shinny on Your Own Side," an 1895 tune by Charles Graham, the composer-author of the classic tear-jerker of 1891, "The Picture That Is Turned to the Wall" (which firmly established M. Witmark & Sons as a major publisher). Tanguay got Blanche Merrill (1895–1966) to write special material for her vaudeville act which parodied her own proclivities. One such song was "Egotistical Eva," and it went over with a bang. In 1910, she had Merrill write her a rag song modestly entitled "The Tanguay Rag." It was published with a photo that showed the famous Tanguay legs on its cover. She had her last two hits in 1915: the

Archie Gottler-Edgar Leslie "America, I Love You" and the veteran team of Monroe H. Rosenfeld and Arthur Lange's "What Money Can't Buy."

She was a human dynamo whose performances truly exhausted her. It could be said of her that she burnt herself out.

OTHER SONG HITS OF THE RAGTIME ERA

"Bill Bailey, Won't You Please Come Home?" (1902) was composed by Hughie Cannon (1877–1912). There are many conflicting stories about who the real "Bill Bailey" was, but everyone seems agreed that there was an actual Bill Bailey, who, after being kicked out of his house by his wife, was let back in. This is one of the greatest syncopated rag songs, but because of its caricature cover, it was considered a coon song. It was so popular that it inspired a host of other songs about Bill Bailey including "I Wonder Why Bill Bailey Don't Come Home," "Since Bill Bailey Came Back Home," "Bill Bailey's Left His Happy Home Again," and "Bill Bailey's Application."

"Sweet Adeline" was composed by Harry Armstrong (1879–1951), with words by Richard H. Gerard (1876–1948). The melody was composed by Armstrong in 1896, but it wasn't until Gerard thought of a title, "You're the Flower of My Heart, Sweet Rosalie," that the song started to take shape. However, publisher after publisher rejected it, until the team saw a billboard advertising the farewell tour of opera singer Adelina Patti. The song was originally titled Rosalie, but the name was changed, not to Adelina, but to Adeline, to rhyme with "pine." The Witmarks published it in late 1903, when the Quaker City Quartette wanted a new number from the firm. The Quartette's lead singer, Harry Ernest, was featured on the cover of the first edition.

"Ida! Sweet As Apple Cider" (1903) was written by Eddie Leonard (1875–1941), a minstrel originally with Primrose and West. During his last performance before he was asked to leave the troupe, he defied the manager by singing this song. It received such acclaim that Leonard was rehired immediately, and afterward "Ida" became his theme song. Eddie Cantor also used it as a theme on radio and television in tribute to his wife, who gave him five daughters.

"The Preacher and the Bear" (1904) was written by Joe Arzonia, a pseudonym of Philadelphia music publisher Arthur Longbrake. It was a fine comic number, revived in the late forties by bandleader-singer-comedian Phil Harris.

"Come Take a Trip in My Airship" was written by the same team who wrote "In the Good Old Summer Time," the minstrel-turned-vaudevillian George "Honey Boy" Evans (1870–1915) and Ren Shields (1868–1913). This was the first of the aviation songs, published by Charles K. Harris in 1904. The most famous airplane song of this or any other era was "Come, Josephine, in My Flying Machine" (1910) by Fred Fisher (1875–1942) and Alfred Bryan (1871–1958).

"The Best I Get Is Much Obliged to You" (1907) was one of the funniest coon songs written in this period. Both words and music were created by Benjamin Hapgood Burt (1882–1950), who was originally an acting member of the Weber & Fields Company. Very much in the "Nobody" vein of Bert Williams, the point of the story here is that no one ever said, "Sylvester, you keep the change." The song was introduced by Louise Dresser in the hit musical THE GIRL BEHIND THE COUNTER (February 4, 1907), which contributed greatly to its success.

"My Pony Boy" (1909) was an interpolation by Charlie O'Donnell and Bobby Heath (1889–1952) into the show MISS INNOCENCE (November 30, 1908). It later acquired hit status and remains a favorite children's song.

"Casey Jones" (1909) is the number one favorite of railroad buffs. It was published in Los Angeles, and the writers two vaudevillians, Eddie Newton composer and T. Lawrence Seibert lyricist, about whom nothing is known. The song inspired the townspeople of Jackson, Tennessee, to place a monument on the grave of the real "Casey," John Luther Jones. He had gotten his nickname from his hometown of Cayce, Kansas.

"Heaven Will Protect the Working Girl" was composed by A. Baldwin Sloane (1872–1925) and written by Edgar Smith (1857–1938) for the show TILLIE'S NIGHTMARE (May 5, 1910), starring Marie Dressler. It was a comic song parodying the tear-jerkers of the nineties, many of which Charles K. Harris made famous. Harris must have had a sense of humor, for he published it. Sloane also had a minor hit written with Clarence Brewster, "When You Ain't Got No Money (Well, You Needn't Come 'Round)" (1898), which May Irwin plugged.

"Meet Me Tonight in Dreamland" was the biggest hit of 1909, music by Leo Friedman (1869–1927), who also published it, and lyrics by Beth Slater Whitson (1879–1930), who was utterly unknown. This perennial favorite featured Asher B. Samuels, equally unknown, on the cover of the first edition. Within three months of its publication, Will Rossiter of Chicago bought the song outright, featured Reine Davies (who featured it in her vaudeville act in Chicago) on his cover, and immediately sold over two million copies. It is estimated that the song has sold around five million in all.

"Let Me Call You Sweetheart" (1910), again by Friedman and Slater, was an even bigger hit. As before, Friedman first issued this song himself, with a photo of Mae Curtis on the cover. Because the team didn't share in the royalties of their previous hit with Will Rossiter, Will's brother Harold, who had worked for him, opened his own publishing company, bought the song from Friedman, and gave him a royalty. It eventually sold over six million copies, making it one of the all-time best sellers. It is interesting to note that in 1904 Chris Smith and Arthur J. Lamb wrote "Let Me Call You Sweetheart Once Again," which didn't set any records.

"Down by the Old Mill Stream" (1910) was the other multi-million selling tune of that year, written and published by Tell Taylor (1876–1937).

This second decade saw the Alley flourishing, having introduced the intoxicating new sounds of ragtime to the scene. Because of the tremendous influx of foreigners to our shores during the last half of the nineteenth century, the Alleyites took advantage of this new audience by making fun of them, as they tried to fit into a new way of life. Ethnic songs proliferated, but hardly any survived this era. Of them, some of the coon songs managed to become memorable when the melody was particularly catchy and the lyrics more than usually funny. Vaudeville was still the most potent plug available to the Alley, and the top stars helped to turn songs into best-selling sheet music hits.

THE ALLEY'S INFLUENCE SPREADS
(1911–1918)
Major Publishers of the Teens

In this period, the ragtime rage continued, with that genre's popularity reaching its height. More piano rags and rag songs were published in this decade's first two years than ever before. The million-seller was commonplace, and a new sound—the blues—was heard for the first time, bringing with it two new major publishers. Like the rag, the blues would have countless imitations and variations and become a vogue word which identified all kinds of songs, especially fox trots.

PACE & HANDY MUSIC COMPANY:
"The St. Louis Blues"

The second black music publishing company was formed in Memphis, Tennessee, by William Christopher Handy (1873–1958) and Harry Herbert Pace (1884–1943). Harry Pace supplied the money and business contacts, while Handy ran the business and composed much of its music. They had written their first song together in 1907, "In the Cotton Fields of Dixie," published by George Jaberg of Cincinnati. The first number they published themselves was the Handy composition "Jogo Blues" in 1913. The idea to start a publishing company actually came the year before when Handy formed Handy Music Company to issue his "Memphis Blues." Shortly after he published it, he sold his copyright to songwriter-publisher Theron Bennett for fifty dollars, after he was assured that the tune was too difficult for the average player. Bennett arranged a year later for words to be added by George A. Norton and transferred the publishing of it to the Joe Morris Music Company. Pace & Handy had a banner year in 1914 with the publication of Handy's "The St. Louis Blues," which became the most famous blues ever written and the

67

most recorded tune by different artists. For his trio, Handy reused the trio section of his "Jogo Blues." The song was slow in getting established because the blues concept was too new for wide public acceptance. It wasn't until Handy's company moved to New York that the tune finally took off. Later in 1914, Handy published his "Yellow Dog Rag," changed in 1919 to "Yellow Dog Blues" when Joseph C. Smith's orchestra recorded it for the Victor Talking Machine Company, featuring the laughing trombone of Harry Raderman.

Sales of the "Rag" version, while not spectacular, were encouraging enough for Pace and Handy to continue the business venture. Being a local publisher in the South, with a small catalog, the firm didn't have national exposure but depended on the Chicago jobbers for its distribution. Their only advertising was done through ads and publicity stories in the black press, notably the Chicago Defender. In 1915, Pace & Handy issued Handy's "Joe Turner Blues" and a take-off on Franz Schubert called "Shoeboot's Serenade." The following year saw the publication of Handy's "Ole Miss Blues" and William King Phillips' "The Florida Blues." The cumulative effect of sales enabled the firm to move to Chicago in 1917, where increased exposure of its blues catalog increased its sheet music sales. The first tunes published in the new office were Charles Hillman's "Preparedness Blues" and Douglas Williams' "The Hooking Cow Blues," to which Handy added some "jazz and blues." That year Handy wrote and published his "Beale Street," the first edition of which was issued appropriately enough in Memphis. It proved to be a huge success.

Other publishers had noted the sales generated by Pace & Handy's catalog and tried to emulate them. Will Rossiter, early in 1915, published Ferdinand Morton's "The 'Jelly Roll' Blues" as an instrumental number. Sheet music sales were sluggish, but the song later became a favorite of jazz bands and pianists.

In September 1917, Handy was asked to bring his band to New York to record for Columbia Records. Early in 1918 Handy decided to settle his publishing partnership in New York and make it a specialty house in Tin Pan Alley. Pace and Handy found offices in the Gaiety Building, at 1547 Broadway. Their New York business began with Eddie Green's (1901–1950) "A Good Man is Hard to Find," which Sophie Tucker immediately turned into a smash hit. The firm quickly followed, in mid-1918, with Clarence A. Stout's "O Death, Where Is Thy Sting," to cash in on Bert Williams' hit recording of it. Handy himself contributed to the war effort that year with "The Kaiser's Got the Blues."

Pace & Handy made a good deal of its money from the mechanical royalties paid on its songs that were recorded. One of the biggest hits was spurred by the Original Dixieland Jazz Band's (ODJB) recording for Victor of "The St. Louis Blues." The money generated from record sales enabled the firm to move in August 1920, to 232 West Forty-sixth Street and again in July 1921, to still more spacious quarters at 165 West Forty-seventh Street. Harry Pace had sold his interest in the firm to Handy in April 1921, when Pace opened the first black-owned-and-operated record company, Black Swan Records. Handy renamed the firm Handy Brothers Music Company. The business is still being run today by his son, Wyer.

WILLIAMS & PIRON MUSIC PUBLISHING COMPANY:
"Royal Garden Blues"

The third black publishing firm, and the second of this decade, was started by Clarence Wiliams (1893–1965) and violinist-orchestra leader Armand John Piron (1888–1943) in New Orleans, Louisiana, in 1915. Called Williams and Piron Music Publishers, it was formed to issue Williams' first song, "You Missed a Good Woman When You Picked All over Me." The firm's partners published their own first collaboration the following year, "Brown Skin, Who You For." It was recorded by Prince's Orchestra for Columbia Records and made money for them. The sale of his 1917 hit, "You're Some Pretty Doll," to Shapiro, Bernstein the following year enabled Williams to move to Chicago, where he opened two music stores and re-established the publishing company later in the year. In 1919 the firm published "Royal Garden Blues" and "I Ain't Gonna Give Nobody None o' This Jelly Roll," both with music by Clarence Williams and words by Spencer Williams (1889–1965), who was no relation to Clarence. When Clarence sold the rights to these to Shapiro, Bernstein, he was able to move to New York City late in 1921, when he secured offices in the Gaiety Building and changed the name of the firm to Clarence Williams Music Publishing Company, having bought out Piron, who did not want to leave New Orleans. Piron subsequently started his own publishing firm there.

Williams started active publishing in New York in 1922 with five hits in his first year: "I Wish I Could Shimmy like My Sister Kate," "Got to Cool My Doggies Now," "That Da-Da Strain," "My Pillow and Me," and " 'Tain't Nobody's Biz-Ness If I Do." In 1923, his biggest hits were "Sugar Blues," which has had many revivals (notably by Clyde McCoy in the mid-thirties), and "Oh, Daddy Blues," made famous by Bessie Smith.

Williams Music Publishing had a great year in 1924, when it issued "Cake Walking Babies from Home," "Mama's Gone, Goodbye," and "Everybody Loves My Baby." The next big year for hits was 1926, when Williams issued James P. Johnson's outstanding "Carolina Shout," Fats Waller's "Squeeze Me" and "How Could I Be Blue," as well as the Jack Palmer-Spencer Williams standard, "I've Found a New Baby." The firm published the King Oliver classic "West End Blues" in 1928, "Baby, Won't You Please Come Home" in 1930, and the famous New Orleans parade-stopper, "High Society," in 1933.

MAJOR SONGWRITERS OF THE 'TEENS

IRVING BERLIN:
"I Love a Piano"

The one man who most personifies Tin Pan Alley in all its glory, as a composer, lyricist, plugger, performer and publisher, is Irving Berlin. He was born Israel Baline in Temun, Russia, on May 11, 1888, and came with his family to the United States when he was four years old.

The young Izzy Baline found a job plugging the songs of Harry Von Tilzer, singing them along with the star from the balcony at Tony Pastor's on Fourteenth Street. When he was eighteen, he became a singing waiter at Pelham's Cafe in Chinatown. He served tables and cleaned up the cafe when it closed for the night, but his main function was to entertain the customers with popular songs of the day. Around the corner from Pelham's was Callahan's, whose proprietor boasted that one of his waiters, George Ronklyn, had just written the lyrics for the newly-published "My Mariuccia Take a Steamboat." Pelham owner Mike Salter, convinced that his waiter could write a better song, went back and encouraged his pianist, Mike Nicholson, to compose a tune for which Izzy would write the lyrics. In frank imitation of their rivals at Callahan's, they called their effort, "Marie, from Sunny Italy." It was published on May 8, 1907, by Joseph W. Stern & Company. On that day Izzy Baline became I. Berlin, which was how he was credited on the cover and on the title page. Not wishing to tempt fate, "I." became "Irving" and the name Berlin stuck. His total royalty on this, his first published song, was thirty-seven cents!

It is well-known that the man who wrote more hit songs than anyone else in all three song categories—pop songs, show tunes, and movie songs—cannot read a note of music, cannot write music, can hardly play the piano, and plays in only one key—F sharp. He got his start in the Alley when he wrote a lyric about the Italian marathon runner, Dorando, who was disqualified after a race in the 1908 Olympics. Berlin went to the young firm of Ted Snyder Company, where Henry Waterson said he would buy the lyric for twenty-five dollars if Berlin would write a melody. Berlin then dictated one to an arranger on the spot. This episode was apparently forgotten when, several weeks later, singer Amy Butler took Ted Snyder to Jimmy Kelly's on Union Square to see and hear Berlin (still a singing waiter) perform some of his parodies of then-current songs. He was hired as staff lyricist for a twenty-five-dollar-a-week draw against future royalties and immediately turned out a song, with music by Ted Snyder, called "She Was a Dear Little Girl," which was interpolated into the show THE BOYS AND BETTY (November 2, 1908) by Marie Cahill (1870–1933). While the song didn't set the world—or the show—on fire, its historic value is obvious. With lyricist Edgar Leslie (1885–1976) making his debut, Berlin wrote the music in 1909 to "Sadie Salome, Go Home," which Fanny Brice used to audition for her first ZIEGFELD FOLLIES (the 1910 edition). That same year Berlin wrote two rag songs of modest success, "That Mesmerizing Mendelssohn Tune," which was plugged by vaudevillian-turned-songwriter Con Conrad, and "Yiddle on Your Fiddle Play Some Rag Time." Also in 1909, Berlin wrote lyrics for Ted Snyder's hugely successful piano rag "Wild Cherries." As Scott Joplin deserved the title "King of Ragtime Writers," Berlin would soon earn the title "King of Ragtime Songs." During the next few years, he would write "That Beautiful Rag," "That Opera Rag," "Stop That Rag," "Dat Draggy Rag," "Dance of the Grizzly Bear," "Everybody's Doin' It Now," "Dying Rag," "Ragtime Violin," "That Mysterious Rag," "Whistling Rag," "Ragtime Jockey Man," "Ragtime Soldier Man," "That Society Bear," "They've Got Me Doin' It Now," "That International Rag," "Ragtime Opera Medley," "When the Band Played an American Rag," "Everything in America Is Ragtime," "Ragtime Razor Brigade," and "That Revolutionary Rag."

His "Alexander's Ragtime Band" (1911) became the most popular and most profitable "ragtime" song ever written, although, of course, it isn't ragtime at all. It is a song *about* ragtime, not a song *in* ragtime. Its march-like feeling is taken from a bugle call and a phase from Stephen Foster's "Swanee River."

At the beginning of 1911, Berlin became a member of the Friars Club and was asked to perform in its annual FROLIC. As this was a special occasion for him, he wanted to write a special song. The year before, he had written the lyrics to a melody by Ted Snyder entitled "Alexander and His Clarionet." Since it had not been a hit, he took these lyrics and rewrote them to fit his new idea and new melody. Old-time coon shouter Emma Carus put it into her vaudeville act in Chicago, where it brought the house down. When Berlin sang it as his contribution to the FROLIC, he received high praise from his audience and from the newspaper critics covering the event. The song was copyrighted on March 18, 1911, and was first published with Emma Carus' photograph on the cover. She is identified underneath her picture, and is wearing a hat on the first edition of this landmark song. The song became so popular that sixty-five performers—a record number—eventually had their photos individually printed on the sheet music cover, as "successfully sung by." On September 9, the Victor Military Band made its famous recorded version for the Victor Talking Machine Company. Snyder then issued the music later that month as a two-step instrumental.

Along with his rag songs, he wrote an exuberant song about the South, "When the Midnight Choo-Choo Leaves for Alabam' " (1912), which became a favorite in vaudeville. It was shortly after this song was published that Berlin was made a partner and the firm's name was changed to Waterson, Berlin & Snyder, Inc.

Berlin had married Dorothy Goetz, sister of songwriter E. Ray Goetz (1886–1954), after a whirlwind courtship of only a few weeks, on February 3, 1912. They honeymooned in Cuba, where she contracted typhoid fever. When she died five months after their wedding, Berlin was inconsolable. His brother-in-law suggested that he assuage his grief by writing a ballad. Later in the year he wrote his first heart-rending ballad, "When I Lost You," which sold two million copies. He would write many other hit ballads, fortunately without such tragedy to inspire them. However, he had a rocky time of it when it came to courting the woman who became his second wife, Ellin Mackay, on January 4, 1926. For her, he wrote "All Alone," "What'll I Do?," "Remember," and, shortly before their wedding, "Always."

There is a story about the writing of "Always," one of Berlin's most popular songs, that Berlin and his then-current pianist were sitting at a table one evening in a Florida restaurant with the pianist's girl friend. As the talk at the table revolved around the Alley and how much hit songs made, the girl gathered up enough nerve to ask, "Mr. Berlin, would you write a song about me sometime?" Berlin, being in an expansive mood, said, "Why sometime, why not right now?" He asked her name again, and she replied, "Mona." With that, Berlin leaned back in his chair and hummed a simple love song, adding words to it. The pianist then copied the tune and words on a napkin, and when he got back to New York, transcribed it onto music paper and put it in the file. A few years later, Berlin had a huge hit in "Remember" and his firm wanted to follow it up with another waltz. Someone went through his file and found the song called "Mona." They played it and said it was a natural. But no one in the office knew who Mona was. When Berlin came in, he said he didn't know, and further, didn't remember even writing the song! Asked to change the lyric, he decided that since Mona is two syllables, why not make the opening, "I'll be loving you, always? That will take care of everybody."

Late in 1914, Berlin created his first complete score for a musical. He had stated in an interview that he wanted to write a ragtime opera. What he meant was that he wanted to include syncopated songs in a musical comedy show, providing toe-tapping music for the latest fad utilizing popular music—ballroom dancing. Dancing schools were opening all over the country to teach the new "animal dances," tango, and others popularized by Irene and Vernon Castle. They had, seemingly overnight, captivated the public with their dancing. It was the work of Broadway producer Charles Dillingham to assemble all the ingredients, putting Irving Berlin together with the Castles to provide Broadway with WATCH YOUR STEP (December 8, 1914). Berlin then created his own publishing entity, Irving Berlin, Inc., to publish his Broadway show songs starting with those in WATCH YOUR STEP. (For all of his other songs, he remained with Waterson, Berlin & Snyder.) He was very proud of his first score and issued all of the numbers in advance of the opening on Broadway. It was unusual for so many songs to be published from one show. Most publishers would test the waters with three or four songs for the out-of-town tryouts, then, after the Broadway opening, would issue a few more of the songs which received audience and newspaper reviewers' approval. With twenty numbers from the show published, only two stood out. "The Syncopated Walk" was highlighted in the overture, as the first act's major production number, the finale to the first act, as an entr-acte, and as the grand finale. It is curious, with the show being hyped as "A Syncopated Musical," that there is very little syncopation in the melody. The verse is practically in even time. The real gem of the show, a song revived in 1950 to standard status, was called "Simple

Melody." It has since become known as "Play a Simple Melody," and it was the first of three numbers Berlin wrote to contain double tunes— two different melodies and lyrics for the same chorus, each sung separately and then combined (requiring two people to sing). One of the melodies to "Simple Melody" is very raggy and certainly justifies the subtitle of the show. Berlin was to write two more of these tricky "double songs": "You're Just in Love" from CALL ME MADAM (1950) and "Empty Pockets Filled with Love" from his last Broadway musical, MR. PRESIDENT (1962).

A new Berlin show followed exactly a year later, with Gaby Deslys and Harry Fox starring in STOP! LOOK! LISTEN! (December 25, 1915). It contained fifteen published numbers, three of them noteworthy. With "Everything in America Is Ragtime," Berlin maintained his rag song crown. "The Girl on the Magazine Cover" made a wonderful production number, one that was re-created in the film EASTER PARADE (1948). The song which became a standard and Berlin's avowed favorite was "I Love a Piano."

The big noise (almost literally) to come from the Alley in 1917 was the new music called jazz. Jazz was both a new style of playing popular songs as well as a term for describing instrumental syncopated melodies for a small (five- to seven-piece) band. The jazz style featured ensemble playing and individual improvisations by the members of the band. It required a tremendous amount of energy to play, to listen to, and, especially, to dance to. Jazz differed from dance band music because, in addition to reading arrangements from printed scores, the jazz band members would syncopate the melody and ad-lib solos in a much faster rhythm and, when playing ensemble, sounded "hotter" than the smooth-flowing sounds of the dance orchestra. What the jazz band was playing and how they played it were the unusual energetic characteristics of jazz music. Because it was featured by bands and was played in nightclubs for dancing, jazz supplanted piano ragtime in popularity. The syncopation involved in jazz was, of necessity, less than it was for piano ragtime, and in time it became more melodious for dancing. New dance steps were created for this fast and wild-sounding music, and the fox trot and, particularly, the one-step became the most suitable ways to dance to it. The new style gave a shot in the leg to all those under thirty and became, thanks to the pioneer recordings of the Original Dixieland Jazz Band (ODJB), a cause celebre among ministers and most older folk. Just under thirty at this time, Berlin sided with youth and wrote an early song about this new music, "Mr. Jazz Himself."

When America entered the First World War, Irving Berlin was drafted. He was assigned to Camp Upton at Fort Yaphank on eastern Long Island and had to get up at five in the morning every day. As he had been accustomed to working until two or three in the morning, he had previously arisen around noon. Something had to be done, so his creativity came to the rescue. He discovered many actors, musicians, and other show business characters also stationed in the camp. He went to his commanding officer and pointed out that if they could use their talents in putting together a show for other soldiers, it would help in recruitment and give a boost to the morale of everyone. The officer gave his permission and, while working on the show, Berlin could get up when he wanted to. This incident gave rise to his most famous war song, "Oh! How I Hate to Get Up in the Morning." He even sang it himself in the show, which was called YIP, YIP, YAPHANK (August 19, 1918). There were ten songs published from this show, including a sort of farewell to ragtime, "Ragtime Razor Brigade," and a hello to jazz, "Send a Lot of Jazz Bands Over There." His soon-to-be-famous "Mandy" was originally written for this show, but in the following year was rewritten, when it was placed in the ZIEGFELD FOLLIES OF 1919 (June 16, 1919).

At the beginning of 1919, Berlin, a civilian once again, dissolved his partnership and severed his connection with the Waterson, Berlin & Snyder Company. On June 1, he and new partner Max Winslow, who also became his Professional Manager, opened Irving Berlin, Inc., taking the third floor of 1587 Broadway (at Forty-eighth Street), with Saul Bornstein as General Manager. The firm's first published song was "The New Moon," written as a theme song for the Norma Talmadge silent film of the same name. Berlin had written it as a favor to his childhood friend, movie producer Joseph M. Schenck, Talmadge's husband. Berlin next wrote "Eyes of Youth" for the "photo-play" of the same name starring Clara Kimball Young. His first million-selling success for his firm was "Nobody Knows and Nobody Seems to Care," which his firm plugged for over seventy weeks!

When Sam Harris broke up his producing partnership with George M. Cohan, Berlin teamed with him to build a new theatre on Broadway. They named it The Music Box, and it opened on September 22, 1921, to general approbation for its architecture and furnishings. The first MUSIC BOX REVUE (with a complete Berlin score) also opened that night to critical acclaim. The hit of the opulent show was "Say It with Music." "The Schoolhouse Blues" was his first nod to this new form of music, blues. (He was late in coming to it.) His next year's REVUE

(October 23, 1922) had three future standards, "Crinoline Days," "Lady of the Evening," and "Pack Up Your Sins and Go to the Devil." The third annual REVUE (September 22, 1923) contained "Learn to Do the Strut," and "An Orange Grove in California." After the opening, Berlin added the classic "What'll I Do?"

THE COCOANUTS (December 8, 1925), starring the Marx Brothers and Margaret Dumont, should have yielded at least one hit, but didn't. When the film was made in 1930, Berlin wrote a new song for it that became popular: "When My Dreams Come True."

Upon star Belle Baker's insistence that he supply her with a song for the Rodgers and Hart show BETSY (December 28, 1926), Berlin wrote "Blue Skies" for her. While revues featured interpolated numbers, it was rare that a book show in the twenties would include one. This was especially true of the Rodgers and Hart shows, which by contract prohibited anyone from interpolating songs into their scores. Berlin would not have contributed his number for any reason except the request of the show's star. Much to Rodgers' and Hart's annoyance, Berlin's song was the only hit to come from that show. It was also the only time they allowed a song to be interpolated into one of their shows (and in this case, very much against their will).

An often overlooked aspect of sheet music publishing is the simplified piano arrangement made for the amateur pianist to accompany the singer. The arrangement must be not only easy to play but also must highlight the melody. The finest of the piano arrangers was Helmy Kresa, who, since 1926, has worked for the Irving Berlin corporation, and does so to this day. When he first came to New York, he was given a job as arranger with the Berlin organization by Berlin's professional manager, Ben Bloom. It was only a temporary job, supposed to last one week while another arranger was on vacation. However, Kresa's work came to Berlin's personal attention (his first job was arranging Harry Woods' "When the Red, Red Robin Comes Bob, Bob, Bobbin' Along"). After Berlin dictated "Blue Skies" to Kresa, Berlin permanently extended Kresa's stay and he became Berlin's personal arranger from that time forward. At this writing, Kresa has been employed by Irving Berlin, Inc., for sixty-two years.

Helmy Kresa is recognized as the premier piano arranger and orchestrator, not only by Berlin but by a list of songwriters who have insisted that Kresa arrange their numbers on a free-lance basis. Among them are: Fred Ahlert, Harry Akst, Rube Bloom, Sam Coslow, Peter DeRose, Cliff Friend, Ferde Grofe, Zez Confrey, Irving Caesar, Sammy Cahn, Hoagy

Carmichael, J. Fred Coots, Walter Donaldson, Jimmy Durante, Duke Ellington, Sammy Fain, Johnny Green, Lou Handman, Gerald Marks, Johnny Mercer, Joseph Meyer, Leigh Harline, Arthur Johnston, Isham Jones, Roger Wolfe Kahn, Vee Lawnhurst, Jerry Livingston, Carmen Lombardo, Jimmy McHugh, Harry Revel, Jean Schwartz, Larry Shay, Mabel Wayne, Pete Wendling, Fred Rose, Harry Ruby, Carl Sigman, Frank Signorelli, Sam H. Stept, Rudy Vallee, Jimmy Van Heusen, Albert Von Tilzer, Harry Warren, Clarence Williams, as well as theatre composers Leonard Bernstein, Harold Arlen, Vernon Duke, George Gershwin, Cole Porter, Burton Lane, Frank Loesser, and Arthur Schwartz.

Kresa always worked out his arrangements in the key of C. Upon completion of his arrangement, he would then determine the actual key in which the song should be published based upon the range of the chorus (most girl singers with bands had vocal ranges of an octave and two notes). While he worked quickly (most piano parts were completed in from one hour to an hour and a half), he caught the essential harmonies and voiced them in the most pleasing manner, making them fun to perform.

His favorite orchestration is the one he did for "God Bless America." Over the years, he has made arrangements for every conceivable combination of instruments and vocal groups. Since "Russian Lullaby" (1927), Kresa has worked on every Berlin song for publication.

While he wouldn't become committed to the movies until 1935, Berlin was asked by Joe Schenck to write more movie theme songs, and he did. In 1928, Berlin wrote three: for COQUETTE, starring Mary Pickford, "Marie," theme song of THE AWAKENING, which starred Vilma Banky (a song Tommy Dorsey was to record with spectacular success nine years later), and "Where Is the Song of Songs for Me" for LADY OF THE PAVEMENTS, or as it was first titled, MASQUERADE, starring Lupe Velez. For King Vidor's "Talking-Singing Picture" HALLELUJAH (1929), Berlin wrote "Swanee Shuffle" and "Waiting at the End of the Road." For his friend Al Jolson's picture MAMMY (1929), Berlin wrote three songs. The best and most characteristic of the Jolson personality was "Let Me Sing and I'm Happy." He also wrote three songs for Harry Richman's film PUTTIN' ON THE RITZ (1929), but only the title song became a hit. For the Douglas Fairbanks-Bebe Daniels film REACHING FOR THE MOON (1930), Berlin obliged once more with a title song.

His first original film score was for TOP HAT (1935), starring Fred Astaire and Ginger Rogers. Because he was allowed to attend all of the story conferences, his songs grew from the plot. The film song which makes the strongest impression when it is first sung in a movie is the one which is firmly rooted to a situation which is a logical outcome of the plot. The song stands a good chance to continue its popularity away from the film, while the generic song, which would seem to have the edge, really doesn't. This is probably why the five songs from TOP HAT have remained standards and the film is generally regarded as the best of the Astaire-Rogers series. The song "Top Hat, White Tie and Tails" is the one immediately identified with Fred Astaire. It matched his persona just as "Let Me Sing and I'm Happy" had matched Jolson's. The others in the score are "Cheek to Cheek," "Isn't This a Lovely Day," "No Strings," and "The Piccolino."

FOLLOW THE FLEET (1936) followed TOP HAT and boasted an original Berlin score of seven songs. While it featured the same stars and production team, the songs didn't seem to be integral parts of the film, so only two have led lives apart from the film: "I'm Putting All My Eggs in One Basket," and "Let's Face the Music and Dance."

ON THE AVENUE (1937) had a score of six published numbers for this Dick Powell-Alice Faye-Madeleine Carroll starrer, with two outstanding hits, "I've Got My Love to Keep Me Warm," and "Slumming on Park Avenue."

ALEXANDER'S RAGTIME BAND (1938) was the title of Berlin's first monumental hit, but this movie proved the song's power again by its place as the biggest-grossing musical film of the thirties. For once, Twentieth Century-Fox's hype was right on the mark when it proclaimed the "Greatest of All Motion Pictures." Starring Tyrone Power, Alice Faye, Don Ameche, Ethel Merman, and Jack Haley, the film consisted mainly of Irving Berlin hits of bygone years. It also holds the record for having more songs published from a single film—32—than any other movie musical.

CAREFREE (1938) starred Fred Astaire and Ginger Rogers, and, of the four new Berlin songs published from it, only "Change Partners" became moderately successful. His next assignment, SECOND FIDDLE (1939) had an even less distinguished score.

Berlin outdid himself with his next film score, HOLIDAY INN (1942), a tuneful film starring Bing Crosby, Fred Astaire, Marjorie Reynolds, and Virginia Dale. He wrote ten new songs and interpolated "Easter Parade" from his 1933 Broadway revue AS THOUSANDS CHEER, since the plot dealt with celebrating different holidays. His blockbuster was "White Christmas," and it won Berlin his only Academy Award for Best Song. Bing Crosby's recording of it (Decca 18429) has sold over twenty-five million copies, and for total record sales the song is the all-time biggest. It further holds the distinction of having been heard more often on YOUR HIT PARADE than any other song in that program's history. It was on thirty-three times, ten times in the number one position. It has sold more than five million copies of sheet music, over a million copies of vocal and band arrangements, and has been recorded in over thirty languages for a total record sale in excess of one hundred and forty million discs. In short, as *Variety* has pointed out, it is the most valuable copyright in the world.

THIS IS THE ARMY (1943) was the movie made from Berlin's Broadway show of the previous year. Berlin had set up a special company, This Is The Army, Inc., to deal with its profits, which he turned over to the Army Relief Fund. Both the Broadway and the film versions were based on his YIP, YIP, YAPHANK of the First World War. This all-soldier revue contained all new material for the Second World War, except for the inclusion of his great "Oh! How I Hate to Get Up in the Morning," which again (on stage and film) featured the composer singing it in his thin voice. When Berlin was recording the song for the soundtrack, a crew member remarked to a colleague, "If the guy who wrote this song could hear the way *this* guy is singing it, he'd turn over in his grave!" The movie cast included two actors who would later become interested in politics, George Murphy and Ronald Reagan. Kate Smith sang "God Bless America," which she had previously introduced on radio on Armistice Day, November 10, 1938. Her Columbia record became a multi-million seller and was used at various events throughout the country, at ball games, political rallies, movie theatres, and presidential birthday balls. In time, it became the best-known patriotic song in the United States. It has been considered our unofficial national anthem and ranks only slightly behind "The Star-Spangled Banner" in performances of a patriotic nature. Berlin assigned all earnings from this song to be shared equally by the Boy Scouts and Girl Scouts of America.

THIS IS THE ARMY also included such hits as "This Is the Army, Mr. Jones," "I'm Getting Tired So I Can Sleep," "With My Head in the Clouds," "How About a Cheer for the Navy," and "I Left My Heart at the Stage Door Canteen."

BLUE SKIES (1946) re-teamed Bing Crosby and Fred Astaire. Its seventeen songs mixed the old with the new. Naturally, the title song was a stand-out, along with the 1921 favorite, "All by Myself," "A Pretty Girl Is Like a Melody," "I'll See You in C-U-B-A," "Always," and the new hit written for the film, "You Keep Coming Back Like a Song."

EASTER PARADE (1948) couldn't help but become a film musical classic because of its stars Fred Astaire and Judy Garland. Set in 1910, it became the perfect vehicle for such golden oldies as "When the Midnight Choo-Choo Leaves for Alabam'," "Snooky Ookums," "I Want to Go Back to Michigan," "Everybody's Doing It," and the title song. His new songs were equally good, as the public put its seal of approval on "It Only Happens When I Dance with You," "We're a Couple of Swells," and "Stepping Out with My Baby."

WHITE CHRISTMAS (1954) deserved and got a delightful cast, with Bing Crosby, Danny Kaye, Rosemary Clooney and Vera-Ellen starring in this charming exercise, another mixture of old Berlin songs and new ones. The new ones included "Sisters" and "Count Your Blessings Instead of Sheep." The latter, as recorded by Eddie Fisher, appeared on the HIT PARADE for sixteen weeks.

THERE'S NO BUSINESS LIKE SHOW BUSINESS (1954) was the last of the Berlin mix-and-match movies. This extravaganza starred Ethel Merman, Donald O'Connor, Marilyn Monroe, Dan Dailey, and Mitzi Gaynor. It contained thirteen numbers, only two of them new. Marilyn Monroe secured her reputation as a sexpot with "Heat Wave," an old song, and "After You Get What You Want You Don't Want It," a new one. The title song has become the unofficial anthem of the entertainment industry, which this film celebrates.

It is fitting that Berlin's last movie assignment was to write a theme for SAYONARA (1957), starring Marlon Brando, thus finishing his movie career as it had begun, writing theme songs.

After writing his late-twenties film themes and with the Depression in full force, Berlin reactivated his career on Broadway. He made his comeback in the revue FACE THE MUSIC (February 17, 1932), which sported the ballad "Soft Lights and Sweet Music," a marvelous comic song "I Say It's Spinach (And I Say the Hell with It)," and, what became a theme song of the Depression, "Let's Have Another Cup of Coffee."

That same year he came out with two of his most haunting ballads, "How Deep Is the Ocean?" and Rudy Vallee's smash hit, "Say It Isn't So."

AS THOUSANDS CHEER (September 30, 1933) was sort of a mid-way high point in his theatrical career. The show was the last one to star Marilyn Miller, the famous FOLLIES star and Ziegfeld favorite. It also featured Clifton Webb, Helen Broderick, and singer-dancer Ethel Waters in her first white show. The score's eight numbers were strangely contrasted, from the tragic "Supper Time" to the joyous "Easter Parade," which was rewritten from his 1917 number "Smile and Show Your Dimple." He had liked the melody of this early number. "Not for All the Rice in China" and "Heat Wave" were the other hits in this show.

LOUISIANA PURCHASE (May 28, 1940) starred William Gaxton, Vera Zorina, Victor Moore, and Irene Bordoni. The score provided no hits, but the optimistic "It's a Lovely Day Tomorrow" was one of Berlin's happiest numbers and was used as a closing theme for THE GARRY MOORE SHOW on television in the 1950's.

ANNIE GET YOUR GUN (May 16, 1946) was Berlin's greatest score, and with 1,147 performances, it was his longest running show. It is a masterful blending of script and music. The Annie Oakley story was originally conceived to have a Jerome Kern score, but Kern's death gave Berlin the opportunity to create one of the most nearly perfect scores in Broadway history. Two of the songs, "Doin' What Comes Natur'lly" and "They Say It's Wonderful," made the HIT PARADE, and "The Girl That I Marry," "I've Got the Sun in the Morning," "I'm an Indian Too," "Anything You Can Do," "You Can't Get a Man with a Gun," and "There's No Business Like Show Business" have become standards. Ethel Merman got her part-of-a-lifetime and was so thoroughly identified with "Annie" that when the show was revived twenty years later, she again played the role.

MISS LIBERTY (July 15, 1949) was only a modest success and, thus, a disappointment after the incredible run of ANNIE. However, the show boasted two memorable songs: "Give Me Your Tired, Your Poor," based on the poem by Emma Lazarus, and "Let's Take an Old-Fashioned Walk," which was in Berlin's happiest waltz vein.

CALL ME MADAM (October 12, 1950) starred Ethel Merman in another role which suited her down to the ground. She portrayed a fabulous party-giver (based on the real-life hostess Perle Mesta) in Washington, D.C., and gave spark to "The Hostess with the Mostes' on the Ball." "You're Just in Love" has been mentioned as one of the "double songs" Berlin had a patent on. "They Like Ike" was so unusually successful that, when the show was done on television in 1968, it was retitled "We Still Like Ike." The most remembered song, however, was "It's a Lovely Day Today."

MR. PRESIDENT (October 20, 1962) also gave Berlin a political subject. His last Broadway musical contained many fresh numbers, including "The Washington Twist," reminiscent of the novelty-dance number in

CALL ME MADAM, the "Washington Square Dance." "Don't Be Afraid of Romance" and his last "double song," "Empty Pockets Filled with Love," provided the ballads for the show.

When ANNIE GET YOUR GUN was revived at the New York State Theatre in 1966, Berlin wrote his final published song for it. It was called "An Old Fashioned Wedding," and it stopped the show nightly.

There is simply no parallel to Irving Berlin's career in Tin Pan Alley. For over seventy years, he has been America's most widely-performed songwriter, in spite of the ever-changing styles of popular music. He has created more standards than anyone else. Of his professional skill, Virgil Thomson once wrote, "I don't know of five American 'art composers' who can be compared as songwriters, for either technical skills or artistic responsibility, with Irving Berlin." And Jerome Kern once said, "Irving Berlin has no place in American music. He is American music."

LEWIS F. MUIR:
"Waiting for the Robert E. Lee"

Lewis Frank Muir was born Louis Meuer in New York City on May 30, 1883. He went to St. Louis for the World's Fair in 1904 and impressed a number of people there with his fantastic piano playing. He had long, tapering fingers and a reach of nearly two octaves. He was known to play only in the key of F sharp. He came back to New York and published his first song with Shapiro Music Publisher, a rag song with lyrics by E. Ray Goetz called "Play That Fandango Rag." It was placed in the FOLLIES OF 1909 and sung in that show by Lillian Lorraine. The following year, Muir went to publisher J. Fred Helf, to whom he submitted another rag song under consideration for the next FOLLIES. It was called "Play That Barber Shop Chord," with words by William Tracey, and Bert Williams performed it in the show. He did such a good job of it that Ballard Macdonald became angry, for he had had the original idea and written the dummy lyric but had abandoned the song. Macdonald sued Helf for leaving his name off the sheet music and was awarded damages of $37,500, which forced Helf into bankruptcy. But before Helf closed shop, he published Muir's piano solo, "Chilly Billy Bee Rag." It stirred enough interest for the publisher to have Ed Moran write words to it. Helf issued the song as "When My Marie Sings Chilly-Billy-Bee." The last song Muir wrote for Helf was "Oh, You Bear Cat Rag," co-composed by Fred Watson, with lyrics by William Tracey (1893–1957).

From Helf, it was but a jump to the house of F. A. Mills, who had published his own brilliant cakewalks, and who encouraged the composing of syncopated music in general. Muir got together with Edgar Leslie in 1911 to write a couple of rag songs, "The Matrimony Rag" and the snappy "When Ragtime Rosie Ragged the Rosary." Both songs attracted attention. The second was fast becoming a hit, vaudevillians thinking it a cute rag song, when a jealous columnist for the trade paper New York *Clipper*, L. Wolfe Gilbert (1886–1970), ingenuously mentioned in his column at the start of 1912 that it was a "crime" to take the rosary and make it the subject of a ragtime song. He also attacked Mills for publishing it and daring to perpetrate such a sacrilege. A few days later, Gilbert ran into Muir, who was hopping mad. Who was Gilbert to criticize his song, anyway? What had Gilbert written? When Gilbert mentioned the few he had published, Muir shot back that he hadn't heard of them and that if Gilbert thought himself a writer, why didn't he prove it by writing a song with him? That evening, the two of them got together at Muir's house and created a summertime love song called "Do You Feel It in the Air?" and a chorus for a Dixie song. The next morning they took their songs to Fred Mills. He listened politely to their ballad and announced that it stank. Gilbert then sang for Mills the Dixie song they titled "Waiting for the Robert E. Lee." Mills said he didn't believe in Dixie songs anymore, that they were passé, but offered Gilbert a batch of professional copies of his songs to let Gilbert see the kind of music his firm published. Gilbert left the office steaming and, after he had walked a few blocks, realized that he hadn't taken the professional copies. He knew that his wife would like to play them, so, back he went. As he entered he door, Mills asked him to step inside and sing his Dixie song again, as he couldn't get the tune out of his mind. Al Jolson introduced it a few weeks later in his show at the Winter Garden Theatre. Soon after, Sophie Tucker plugged it on her tour and newcomer Ruth Roye performed it at the Palace after the opening of that important theatre. The Dixie song sold over two million copies and established the team of Muir and Gilbert. For two years they turned out hit after hit, but none of them sold as many copies or lasted as long as their first collaboration, which is still performed by singers and bands when they want to evoke Mississippi River steamboat days.

Before the song became a hit, Muir wrote another good rag song with Edgar Leslie called "Dancing Dan, the Ragtime Battling Man." With publisher-composer Maurice Abrahams, husband of singer Belle Baker, Muir wrote "Ragtime Cowboy Joe," with lyrics by newcomer Grant

Clarke (1891–1931). It was a smashing success. (With Abrahams, Clarke went on to write the famous automobile song, "He'd Have to Get Under.")

In the meantime, Muir and Gilbert turned out a string of hits in 1912, starting with the great rag songs "Ragging the Baby to Sleep," "Take Me to That Swanee Shore," "Here Comes My Daddy Now," and a song which Al Jolson made famous, "Hitchy Koo." The following year the team quickly followed up with "Little Rag Baby Doll" and the coon song "Mammy Jinny's Jubilee." That same year saw Muir's second and last piano rag published: "Heavy on the Catsup."

The last year of their collaboration, 1914, saw "Buy a Bale of Cotton for Me," "Campmeeting Band," and "Mootching Along."

Lewis F. Muir died of tuberculosis in New York City at the age of 32 on December 3, 1915.

CHRIS SMITH:
"Ballin' the Jack"

Chris Smith was born in Charleston, South Carolina, on October 12, 1879. He started in show business with a black medicine show. He began what was to be a lifelong partnership with childhood friend Elmer Bowman (1879–1916), when they came to New York City with their vaudeville act. There Smith met the best black talents of the day and wrote for them. He also met Cecil Mack, who became his main lyricist. Starting in 1901 with his first big hit, "Good Morning, Carrie," he contributed to the Williams and Walker Company's repertoire. While writing for the Black Patti Company, he and principal comedian Jolly John Larkins wrote a hit comic song in 1904 called "Shame on You." To place a song in MARRYING MARY (August 27, 1906), Smith allowed the show's composer, Silvio Hein, credit on the song. Marie Cahill, the star of the show, made "He's a Cousin of Mine" famous and boosted her career as well. Also in that year, Smith and Mack wrote "All In Down and Out." The songwriting team scored heavily in 1908 with "Down Among the Sugar Cane" and "You're in the Right Church But the Wrong Pew," which Bert Williams made into a hit when he introduced it in BANDANA LAND. In 1909, Smith left Mack and Gotham-Attucks and went to Remick's, with Jim Burris as his lyricist. The new team gave Remick's the ballad "There's a Big Cry-Baby in the Moon" and a marvelous novelty comedy song called "Transmagnificanbamdamuality (or C-A-T Spells Cat)." That same year they went to Joseph W. Stern's with their comic song "Come After Breakfast, Bring 'Long Your Lunch and Leave 'Fore Supper Time," which became a great success in vaudeville. Smith helped Bert Williams write his first ZIEGFELD FOLLIES opener "Constantly" in 1910, as well as "If He Comes In, I'm Going Out."

Smith created the first of his syncopated instrumentals in 1911 with "Honky Tonky Monkey Rag." The following year he went to Haviland with four numbers: "Beans, Beans, Beans," "That Puzzlin' Rag," and the Fanny Brice rag song "That Snakey Rag" (all written with his original partner Elmer Bowman), and the ballad "After All That I've Been to You," with lyrics by Jack Drislane. In 1913, he wrote by himself "Fifteen Cents" and the lyric to Luckey Roberts' fabulous "Junk Man Rag," which was featured by Maurice and Florence Walton, dance rivals of the Castles.

It was while he was at Stern's turning Roberts' rag into a rag song that Smith and Jim Burris created the most famous fox-trot song of the decade, "Ballin' the Jack." Burris' lyrics don't exactly explain the dance step, but nobody cared then and nobody cares now. Chris Smith had composed one of the catchiest syncopated melodies ever, and it immediately caught on with dancers and singers in vaudeville. It was so popular that it was interpolated into THE GIRL FROM UTAH (August 24, 1914), for the star Donald Brian's specialty dance. The song version became so popular that in a reversal from the usual—making an instrumental into a song—bandleader/composer James Reese Europe helped Smith turn the song into an instrumental! The whole world, it seemed, was dance crazy and Chris Smith gave it one reason to be with the era's favorite tune.

In 1915, Smith tried again with the fox-trot "Keep It Up," which was merely a variation of "Ballin' the Jack." This song, too, had a life of its own. The following year Smith had two hits in a row for the Broadway Music Corporation: "Down in Honky Tonk Town," with words by Charles McCarron (1891–1919), and "Never Let the Same Bee Sting You Twice," with words by Cecil Mack. He also published his first blues that year with San Francisco publisher Sherman, Clay & Company, appropriately called "San Francisco Blues."

Throughout the twenties he contributed numbers, including two especially syncopated gems, "I've Got My Habits On" (1921), which he wrote to Jimmy Durante's music, and his own "If You Sheik on Your Mamma, Your Mamma's Gonna Sheba on You" (1924).

Chris Smith died in New York City on October 4, 1949.

PERCY WENRICH:
"When You Wore a Tulip . . ."

Percy Wenrich was born in Joplin, Missouri, on January 23, 1880. He attended the Chicago Musical College and worked for McKinley Music Company, where he wrote melodies to verses would-be lyricists sent in, and also composed songs, rags, intermezzi, waltzes, and whatever else was needed. His initial success came in composing rags. His first major effort was "Peaches and Cream" (1905) for Remick. His biggest rag hit was "The Smiler" (1907), which was published by the Chicago firm of Arnett-Delonais Company. It became so big that Fred Forster bought the copyright and plugged it nationally. His finest rag, "Persian Lamb Rag," was issued the following year by Walter Jacobs of Boston.

Wenrich came to New York City with his wife, vaudevillian Dolly Connolly, in 1908, and became a staff writer for Jerome H. Remick & Company. With lyricist Alfred Byran, he wrote a hit Indian song called "Rainbow." The next year, he immediately turned out a two-million seller "Put On Your Old Gray Bonnet," with lyrics by Stanley Murphy (1875–1919). In 1910, he turned out two rags, "Southern Symphony" and "Egyptian Rag," as well as another million seller, "Silver Bell," with lyrics by Edward Madden. This team then wrote a magnificent rag song for Dolly Connolly, "Red Rose Rag" (1911), which George Burns has been singing ever since, and the harmony quartet's dream, "Moonlight Bay" (1912). Wenrich's ragtime output included the 1911 "Ragtime Chimes" and "Sunflower Rag." "Ragtime Chimes" proved so successful that Edward Madden added lyrics a year later.

In 1912, Wenrich and Homer Howard formed the Wenrich-Howard Company to publish songs. They issued the instrumentals "Kentucky Days" and "Whipped Cream Rag" (both in 1913), and the great rag song "Snow Deer" (also in 1913), with lyrics by Jack Mahoney (1882–1945). Wenrich gave up his publishing company to devote his time to his composing and to performing with his wife in vaudeville. He joined Leo Feist permanently and, with Mahoney, scored heavily in 1914, when they wrote the all-time classic "When You Wore a Tulip and I Wore a Big Red Rose." Dolly Connolly toured vaudeville houses for several years, accompanied by her husband and featuring mostly his songs. She was a great plugger, who also recorded for Columbia Records, which greatly increased sales of the song sheets.

Wenrich had another big hit for Connolly when he and Joe McCarthy wrote "Sweet Cider Time When You Were Mine" (1916).

When America entered the First World War, Wenrich and lyricist Howard Johnson (1887–1941) asked the musical question, "Where Do We Go from Here?"

Wenrich's last great hit was the marvelous syncopated fox-trot song "All Muddled Up" (1922), which Zez Confrey and his Orchestra recorded for Victor with great artistic and commercial success. Percy Wenrich died in New York City on March 17, 1952.

SHELTON BROOKS:
"The Darktown Strutters' Ball"

Shelton Brooks was born in Amesburg, Canada, on May 4, 1886. He grew up in Detroit and started out as a pianist playing ragtime. He then created a comic vaudeville act by doing an imitation of Bert Williams. When Williams saw Brooks' performance, he said, "If I'm as funny as he is, I got nothin' to worry about."

There is a story about Brooks walking around for days with a tune in his head, but unable to find the proper lyrics to fit it. One afternoon he overheard a couple quarreling. "Better not walk out on me, man!" said the angry woman, "for some of these days you're gonna miss me, honey." The song words then fell into place. He spent thirty-five dollars to get the song printed by the William Foster Music Company in Chicago, then showed it to Sophie Tucker, whose maid, a friend of his, introduced them. Tucker liked it so much that she put it into her act the next day. "Some of These Days" (1910) was well received, and the star got Will Rossiter to take over the copyright and give it a big promotion. It was such a hit for Tucker that she used it as her theme song and took the title for her autobiography. The sheet music sold well over two million copies. Brooks' next song, "All Night Long" (1912), was also a Rossiter publication and had a middling sale. It wasn't until 1916, when he wrote the fine fox trot "Walkin' the Dog," that Brooks got his next hit.

In 1917, just as ragtime was starting to be edged off the top of the lists by blues and jazz, Brooks came up with his syncopated smash "The Darktown Strutters' Ball." It was introduced in vaudeville by the team of Benny Fields, Jack Salisbury, and (soon-to-be-songwriter) Benny Davis. It was one of the two selections given to the Original Dixieland Jazz Band to record at their first session for Columbia on January 30, 1917. The disc became such an incredible hit, that Leo Feist bought the publishing rights from Rossiter and plugged the song sheet to over three-million sales. It is still the favorite of dixieland jazz bands. Two years later, Brooks composed "Jean," which became a more modest hit when recorded by the Chicago songwriter-bandleader Isham Jones and his Orchestra for Brunswick Records. Brooks continued to act in vaudeville, films, and on radio, and appeared for two years in Ken Murray's BLACK-OUTS.

Shelton Brooks died in Los Angeles on September 6, 1975.

GEORGE L. COBB:

"Are You from Dixie?"

George Leo Cobb was born in Mexico, New York, on August 31, 1886. Trained in music at Syracuse University, Cobb won a composition contest in Buffalo, where he lived after college. He started out writing rags, then came to the Alley and wrote a few hit songs. He went to work for Boston publisher Walter Jacobs and wrote more rags and everything else, as needed. When Jacobs started publishing the magazine *The Tuneful Yankee* at the start of 1917 [the name was changed the following year to *Melody*], Cobb wrote a monthly column answering the questions of would-be songwriters. He also reviewed current pop songs, and the magazine printed several songs in each issue, often one from the pen of George Cobb. His first rag, "Rubber Plant Rag," was published by Jacobs in 1909 and became fairly well-known. His fine "Canned Corn Rag" was issued by the Bell Music Company of Buffalo in 1910. His "Bunny Hug Rag" of 1913 created a stir, since it was aimed at the new "animal dance" craze. The same year, he and fellow Buffaloan, lyricist Jack Yellen, wrote the syncopated hit "All Aboard for Dixie Land." They got Elizabeth Murray to sing it as an interpolation in Rudolf Friml's operetta HIGH JINKS (December 10, 1913). Murray turned it into a fine hit. Two years later, she would introduce another of their songs, "Listen to That Dixie Band" and score with it also. She could do no wrong for the boys, so later that year they gave her "Alabama Jubilee," which sold nearly a million copies and was revived in the early fifties. The team from North Buffalo, where the winters are below freezing, were so enamored of the South that their last 1915 hit was "Are You from Dixie?"

Then, Cobb came up with a rag for dancer Maizie King called "The Midnight Trot." It was published by Will Rossiter in 1916, and its harmonic changes in the trio are far more adventurous than those written by others that year. He gave Rossiter his 1918 adaptation of Rachmaninoff's "Prelude in C Sharp Minor," and the publisher called it "Russian Rag." It sold over a million copies and was all vaudeville virtuosos' favorite for years. Joe "Fingers" Carr made the definitive recording of it in the early fifties (Capitol 1311). The song was in such demand that in 1923 Rossiter asked him to write another rag using more of the same Prelude. Cobb called it "The New Russian Rag." Amateur pianists have been cursing him for these tricky masterpieces ever since. But pianists with technique love him for it, and so do audiences when they hear Cobb's syncopated gems played well.

George Cobb died in Brookline, Massachusetts, on December 25, 1942.

GEORGE W. MEYER:
"For Me and My Gal"

George W. Meyer was born in Boston, Massachusetts, on January 1, 1884. He came as a songwriter-plugger into the Alley, when Fred Mills published his first song "Lonesome" in 1909 and it became a hit. He wrote the snappy "Brass Band Ephraham Jones" in 1911 with lyricist Joe Goodwin (1889–1943).

Meyer became a publisher for two years, starting in 1912, with the publication of "Variety Rag" by Harry Tierney. He followed it up the same year by issuing "That Entertaining Rag" by Arthur Wellesley and Abe Olman's fabulous "Red Onion Rag." The next year he published Harry Jentes and Pete Wendling's "Soup and Fish Rag," and, in 1914, he issued the vaudeville team Lyons and Yosco's "Mardi Gras Rag."

Al Jolson introduced one of Meyer's great comic hits "Where Did Robinson Crusoe Go with Friday on Saturday Night" (1916), with lyrics by the team of Sam M. Lewis and Joe Young. The next year Meyer's collaborators were Edgar Leslie and E. Ray Goetz, with a two-million selling hit, "For Me and My Gal." (The title is inscribed on the tombstone of Meyer's wife.) "Everything Is Peaches Down in Georgia" (1918) was a collaboration with Milton Ager on the music and Grant Clarke, the lyricist. Al Jolson turned this one into a hit, too.

Reactivating his collaboration with Lewis and Young, Meyer created his greatest triumph, "Tuck Me to Sleep in My Old 'Tucky Home" (1921), which Eddie Cantor helped to make into a multi-million selling hit. In 1923 Meyer collaborated with lyricist Gus Kahn on one of his most beautiful melodies, "Sittin' in a Corner." The following year Meyer wrote the score of his only Broadway show, a black revue first called PLANTATION FOLLIES, then DIXIE TO BROADWAY (October 29, 1924). It contained two of his finest numbers, "I'm a Little Blackbird Looking for a Bluebird" and "Mandy, Make Up Your Mind," a tune jazz bands still enjoy. "Someone Is Losin' Susan" (1926) was given a bouncy treatment by Pete Wendling (Cameo 1021). In 1929, Meyer wrote with Al Bryan "My Song of the Nile" for Richard Barthelmess' film DRAG.

Gus Van made a hit of his 1932 "I'm Sure of Everything But You," which Pete Wendling helped compose to Charles O'Flynn's lyrics. And Meyer and Wendling had another hit two years later, with lyrics by Sam Lewis, in "I Believe in Miracles." Meyer's last hit was "There Are Such Things," co-composed with Abel Baer, with lyrics by Stanley Adams, in 1942.

George W. Meyer died in New York City on August 28, 1959.

ABE OLMAN:

"Oh, Johnny! Oh!"

Abe Olman was born in Cincinnati, Ohio, on December 20, 1888. After working for Chicago publishers, he came to New York City to become manager of the short-lived George W. Meyer Music Company in 1912. This firm was backed by Gus Edwards who, for contractual reasons, couldn't operate it under his own name. In 1914, Olman formed his own company in Chicago, The LaSalle Music Publishing Company, to publish his latest song "Down among the Sheltering Palms," with lyrics by James Brockman. Olman plugged it so well locally that Leo Feist, who had a branch office in Chicago, heard about the song's success and purchased it. Feist then gave it to Al Jolson to sing in one of his stage productions, and that boost turned the song into a three-million copy seller.

Olman's next big hit was published in 1917 by Forster, with lyrics by Ted Snyder's first partner Ed Rose (1875–1935), "Oh, Johnny! Oh!" It was introduced by Nora Bayes and it sold well over a million copies. It was revived by the Andrews Sisters in 1939 and sold over a million again. Olman's last major success was his 1920 hit, originally entitled "O-HI-O," with lyrics by Jack Yellen. It initially sold over three million copies because Eddie Cantor introduced it, and it was then taken up by Lou Holtz, Ted Lewis, Al Jolson, and Van and Schenck in vaudeville and on stage. Unlike today's recording artists, who won't, as a rule, record another's hit, all of these top 1920's performers sang the song, and their fans bought the sheet music in great numbers. As the pop music scene of today seems to require only one version of a song, the impact of several stars making a hit with the same song is not something we are familiar with, and it is our loss, as each artist has something unique to bring to the song. "O-HI-O" was revived by the Andrews Sisters in 1947, under the title "Down by the Ohio," when it sold another million copies.

Olman's lifelong success in the Alley came as a publisher, not only with his own firm, but also as General Manager of The Big Three from 1935. He retired to act as consultant to his nephew Howard Richmond of The Richmond Organization. One of their projects was the formation of The National Academy of Popular Music and its Songwriters Hall of Fame. The Academy came into being in 1969, with Johnny Mercer as its first president. Olman himself gave special attention to the archives of the Academy, which now includes over 50,000 pieces of sheet music, 800 piano rolls, and 3,000 record albums, numerous playbills, and photographs. Further contributions continue to swell this amount, and the purpose of the collection is to make available to those interested in popular music original artifacts for study and enjoyment. This organization is dedicated to the preservation of popular music and it appears to be the only one of its kind in the world. The archives are currently housed at Long Island University's C. W. Post Campus in Brookville, New York.

Abe Olman died in Rancho Mirage, California, on January 4, 1984.

DANCES OF THE TEENS

The Castles

Vernon (1887–1918) and Irene (1893–1969) Castle created and maintained the national craze for ballroom dancing when they returned to the United States from Paris in 1912. They appeared on Broadway in THE LADY OF THE SLIPPER (October 28, 1912) and THE SUNSHINE GIRL (February 3, 1913), which starred Julia Sanderson and featured Julia and Vernon doing the tango, as the song-sheet cover of "The Argentine" illustrates. From the same show, the cover of Dan Caslar's one-and-two-step, "Tres Chic," pictures Irene and Vernon in a pose from their routine. In the same year, Arthur N. Green composed three numbers which featured the Castles on the covers: "Tango Argentine," "Innovation Tango," and "Maxixe Brasilienne." His "Royal Arab" one step and fox trot of 1915 also features the popular Castles on the cover. They starred in Irving Berlin's first complete musical show, WATCH YOUR STEP (1914). The publishing house of Stern, which had been an early booster of ragtime, black songwriters and new fads, showed its intuition by signing the Castles to pose for the covers of a series of dance tunes written by James Reese Europe (1881–1919) and Ford T. Dabney (1883–1958). Dabney had accompanied the Castles with Europe's Society Orchestra. The series of dance-songs consisted of "The Castle Combination" (waltz-trot), "Castle Innovation Waltz," "Castle Lame Duck Waltz," "Castles' Half and Half," "Castle Innovation Tango," "Castle Maxixe," "Castle Perfect Trot," "Castle Valse Classique," "The Castle Walk," "Castles in Europe," and "Castle House Rag."

Vernon was an incredibly skilled and talented dancer who was also a fine comedian and drummer. His picture at the drums is featured on the cover of Carey Morgan's "Trilby Rag" (1915). Irene was slim, tall and graceful, the first to wear her hair bobbed, and unlike Vernon's previous dancing partners, who were too short, she was the right height for her husband. In fact, she was the first tall, slim stage personality in an era whose female stars, notably Sophie Tucker and Emma Carus, were considerably more substantial.

They were featured nightly at Castles-in-the-Air, their own dance pavilion in New York City. During the summers they appeared at Castles-by-the-Sea in Long Beach, Long Island.

They were at the height of their popularity in 1917, when Vernon enlisted in a British flying unit in France to do aerial photography at the front. He was soon transferred to the United States as a flying instructor at the Fort Worth Flying School. He was killed there in a plane crash in 1918, and Irene immediately retired from show business.

Before she did, and while Vernon was away, she appeared as a solo dancer in the revue MISS 1917 (November 5, 1917). She also made a silent movie called PATRIA (1917) for International Studios, and she composed the music for a song of the same name for its theme. She appears on the cover wrapped in an American flag. It was a striking red, white, and blue cover, and it undoubtedly helped stimulate sales.

The Castles' major rivals in vaudeville were Maurice and Florence Walton, who were featured on several song sheet covers, the best being the instrumental composed for them by Paul Biese and F. Henri Klickmann, appropriately entitled "The Maurice Walk" (1913). The following year, silent film star Mae Murray, who also danced in vaudeville, was featured on the cover of "The Murray Walk," also composed by Biese and Klickmann.

Of all the various "animal dances" (grizzly bear, bunny hug, turkey trot), the easiest to do and the most lasting was the fox trot. All these dances featured the music of the Alley's top composers. "The Grizzly Bear Rag" was composed by George Botsford in 1910; "The Turkey Trot" (1912) was composed by J. Bodewalt Lampe under his pseudonym of Ribe Danmark; and "The Bunny Hug" (1912) was composed by Harry Von Tilzer. Some of the Alley's other efforts at composing for these dances were: "Rabbit's Foot" by George L. Cobb, "The Weeping Willow" by Percy Wenrich, "Some Chocolate Drops" by Fred Irvin and Will Vodery, "Doctor Brown" by Fred Irvin, "Sugar Lump" by Fred Bryan, "Supper Club" by Harry Carroll, "Pozzo" by Vincent Rose, "The Kangaroo Hop" by Melville Morris, and "Cruel Papa" by Will Marion Cook. The extraordinarily popular songs "Ballin' the Jack" by Chris Smith and "Walkin' the Dog" by Shelton Brooks were turned into instrumental versions for fox trotting.

THE ORIGINAL DIXIELAND JAZZ BAND (ODJB):
The Phenomenon

Jazz was in the air! As early as 1911, bands were playing in cabarets and for dancing in New Orleans. These were originally called "ragtime bands," as opposed to marching bands, because they tried to imitate piano rags on their various instruments.

A group comprising several members of Jack Laine's Reliance Band went to Chicago in March 1916 to play at Schiller's Cafe. With some personnel changes, this band joined Johnny Fogarty's Dancing Review at McVicker's, a famous vaudeville house, in August. Fogarty had been known to Chicago audiences for his classy society dancing act. His interest in the fox trot was evident from his group's photograph on the sheet music of the fox trot arrangement of Shelton Brooks' "Walkin' the Dog." Johnny Fogarty signed the so-called "Jass" (as it was then called) Band to appear with his act, and *Billboard* reported them to be a sensation. In early November 1916, the band members were chosen to come to New York to make the first jazz recordings at the end of January 1917.

The Original Dixieland Jass Band (ODJB) consisted of New Orleans natives: Nick LaRocca (1889–1961), cornet; Eddie Edwards (1891–1963), trombone; Larry Shields (1893–1953), clarinet; Henry Ragas (1891–1919), piano; and Tony Sbarbaro (1897–1969), drums. The impact that "jass," as it was first spelled—the band would later change the spelling to "jazz" when they discovered that kids as a prank would obliterate the first letter of the word "jass" on their posters—had had in Chicago was immediately felt in the Alley. Chicago-based Henry I. Marshall (1883–1958) and Gus Kahn wrote the first tune about the group called "That Funny Jas Band from Dixieland," which was the first song to use the word for the new musical form in the title. It was published in November 1916 by Jerome H. Remick. Another pair of Chicagoans, Eddie Gray and Jerry Joyce, followed quickly with "When I Hear That 'Jaz' Band Play," issued in late 1916 by Frank K. Root & Company of Chicago. Bert Williams, an early admirer of the band, is featured on the cover of this number. So, the band's popularity did not go unnoticed, especially with the show business crowd. Al Jolson raved about them upon his return to New York from a tour in Chicago, and he sent agent Max Hart to Chicago to hear them. Hart immediately signed them to open at the new Reisenweber's Restaurant, which was going to open its new Paradise Ballroom in mid-January. After the band's first week there, they were asked to open the new 400 Club Room at the end of the month. With Reisenweber's skillful promotion highlighting the jazz band's music for dancing, patrons flocked to the 400 Club Room.

Columbia Records stole a march (nay, a one-step) on its rival, the Victor Talking Machine Company, when it signed the ODJB, as it was now known, to a contract. They were to make two sides on January 30, 1917. When the band arrived at the studio, they were handed two brand-new songs to learn and record that afternoon—Shelton Brooks' "Darktown Strutters' Ball" and James F. Hanley's (1892–1942) and Ballard Macdonald's (1882–1935) "(Back Home Again in) Indiana." Since the others couldn't read music, Henry Ragas and Larry Shields had to play these songs over and over until all of the members knew them and could work out their improvisations. The Columbia engineer was not sympathetic to the band, and neither was the artist and repertoire director. They decided after the session to shelve the two recordings. It was only after ODJB had a hit disc for Victor that Columbia released its recordings in September.

With all of Reisenweber's ballyhoo, Victor executives decided they should be the first to record this new type of band, unaware that the band had already recorded for Columbia. They scheduled a recording session for the band on February 26, 1917.

Taking infinitely more pains than did the Columbia engineer, Charles Souey made hundreds of test recordings to obtain the best placement of the five instruments, and Eddie King, head of Victor's Artists and

Repertoire (A&R) Department, allowed them to record their own compositions. As a result, the Victor acoustic recordings stand up today. We can still enjoy the ODJB's work, as the sound is clear and their enthusiasm and vitality remain contagious. Their first number was "Livery Stable Blues" (published under the ODJB banner as "Barnyard Blues"), followed by the "Dixieland Jass Band One-Step" (later known as "The Original Dixieland One-Step"). When released on Victor 18255 on April 1, these tunes became the first jazz record ever! The Victor Bulletin of March 17 announced their new discovery this way: "Spell it Jass, Jas, Jaz or Jazz—nothing can spell a Jass band . . . Anyway, a Jass band is the newest thing in the cabarets, adding greatly to the hilarity thereof."

The Victor record received nationwide distribution and created a monster, causing as much concern among guardians of the public morality as ragtime had twenty years earlier, foreshadowing the rumpus rock and roll would cause almost forty years later. Everyone, from the clergy to concerned parents to doctors, inveighed against this free expression of the times. The ODJB's collective improvisations on their own compositions created an ensemble sound refreshing to the young, and the tunes, not quite as syncopated as the piano rags, were far more jaunty than the latest pop songs rendered by the brass recording bands or the dance orchestras led by violinists. The initial ODJB recordings for Victor ended with their July 17, 1918 session, with a total of twelve issued sides.

Leo Feist quickly understood the nature of this new jazz sound and signed the ODJB to publish exclusively with his firm. Feist first published several of these original compositions: "Tiger Rag," "Ostrich Walk," "Sensation," "At the Jazz Band Ball," "Barnyard Blues," "Skeleton Jangle," and "Look at 'Em Doing It." During the next year, as their Victor Records kept coming out, Feist issued "Bluin' the Blues," "Clarinet Marmalade," "Fidgety Feet," "Mournin' Blues," and "Lazy Daddy." However, he was surprised to discover, given the music's popularity, that sales were sluggish.

One would expect, as Feist did, that the uptempo, urgently syncopated sounds that were to alter the form and performance of popular music forever, would be popular with Alley publishers and their customers.

Feist labeled the ODJB originals as either "Fox Trots" or "One-Steps." This latter designation was new and used primarily to describe the band's faster numbers. Other good one-steps included "Honky-Tonky" by Chris Smith, "Fluffy Ruffles" by George Hamilton Green, "Step With Pep" by

Mel B. Kaufman, and "Limber Jack" by Don Richardson. The younger members of the piano-playing public couldn't get enough of this good stuff. However, as the piano part in the sheet music arrangements could not convey, much less duplicate, the excitement and the spontaneity of the recorded or live jazz band performances, the Alley publishers reluctantly abandoned the publication of jazz tunes because of poor sales. This decision by the publishers foreshadows what eventually killed the Alley in the 1950's. When the sound of recorded rock and roll songs could not be duplicated from sheet music because so much of the sound depended on the recorded performance, rather than on the content of the music, Tin Pan Alley could not compete with the record companies for dominance of the popular music scene.

MUSICAL THEATRE IN THE 'TEENS

JEROME D. KERN:
"They Didn't Believe Me"

In this era, musical theatre in the United States came a long way from the burlesques of Weber and Fields, the Victor Herbert shows set in some far-off European country, the brashness of the George M. Cohan musicals, and the resplendent revues of the extravagant Ziegfeld. What was wanted now was a musical show which had a strong story line as its base, with songs either adding to the plot or to the characters' personalities to move the show along (but keeping plenty of dancing girls in pretty costumes to gladden the hearts of the audience).

Enter Jerome David Kern, born in New York City on January 27, 1885. He, with librettist Guy Bolton (1884–1979) and lyricist P. G. Wodehouse (1881–1975), would permanently change the face of our musical theatre during this important time in the Alley's history. The new team created a new type of musical comedy on a scale smaller than the overblown imported operettas that dominated the Broadway scene. The Princess Theatre, located on Thirty-ninth Street between Sixth Avenue and Broadway, which was used to house these productions, had only two hundred and ninety-nine seats. The shows produced there dealt exclusively with contemporary American subjects and settings and were intimate productions. Frank Sadler orchestrated most of these scores in a light and lighthearted manner, using an orchestra of eleven instru-

Isidore Witmark, head of the firm that bears his family's name.

The first piece of popular sheet music, "Grover Cleveland's Wedding March," published by Witmark in 1886, marking the traditional beginning of Tin Pan Alley.

The Witmarks rented this building at 8 West 29th Street, the first building entirely occupied by one publisher.

The first building owned by a Tin Pan Alley publisher, located at 144–146 West 37th Street.

The New York Music Publishers Association of 1906. Seated at right, T. B. Harms; above him, F. B. Haviland; second from left, standing, E. T. Paull.

Max Dreyfuss, seated, with brother Louis, owners of Chappell and Harms, the largest publisher of show music in the world.

T. B. Harms was a major publisher of show tunes at the turn of the century. Photo shows Harms' Broadway location in 1891.

Tin Pan Alley on the move uptown. Here, Harms' location at Broadway and 42nd Street in 1910.

Joseph W. Stern and Edward Marks, co-founders of Joseph W. Stern &
Company, publishers of Williams and Walker and Jerome and Schwartz at
the turn of the century.

Leo Feist in 1907, a leading
Tin Pan Alley publisher.

The Big Four of Leo Feist in 1902. From left, Abe Holzmann (plugger and composer), Edgar F. Bitner (general manager), Robert Keiser (major composer) and Leo Feist (owner and former corset salesman).

Maurice Shapiro in 1909, not only a music publisher, but a music distributor as well. He owned 50 music counters in department stores nationwide.

Louis Bernstein in the 1920's when Shapiro, Bernstein was the biggest publisher in Tin Pan Alley.

Shapiro Music publisher in 1910 on Broadway at the corner of 39th Street.

Chicago publisher Will Rossiter in the 1890's, a pioneer of popular sheet music publishing and one of the few successful publishers not located in Tin Pan Alley.

F. B. Haviland, 1906, a major New York music publisher.

Mose Gumble, premier Tin Pan Alley plugger for Shapiro, Bernstein, and later Remick. He popularized "Bedelia" (1902).

Jerome Remick in his office, 1910.

Half-price sale of sheet music at Woolworth's at the turn of the century.

Hillman's, a store devoted to the selling of popular sheet music. Note the demonstrator at the piano at right.

An "unprecedented" sale of sheet music—a penny a sheet—in 1907.

The Brill Building at 1619 Broadway, the traditional and final home of the Tin Pan Alley publishers.

Charles K. Harris, composer of "After the Ball," Tin Pan Alley's first million-copy seller, published in 1892.

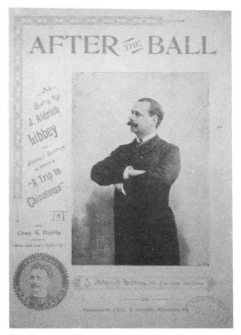

The cover of "After the Ball."

Harry Von Tilzer, "Wait 'Til the Sun Shines, Nellie."

Monroe H. Rosenfeld, composer and the man who gave Tin Pan Alley its name.

Kerry Mills, leading
composer and publisher of
cakewalks, the first
syncopated American
social dance.

Irving Berlin

Berlin, with Victor Herbert, left, and John Philip Sousa.

Berlin, with Al Jolson in the 1920's.

Berlin, with Bing Crosby in the 1930's.

Berlin, with Frank Sinatra at opening
of Sinatra's firm, Barton Music, in
the Brill Building, 1943.

Helmy Kresa, Berlin's arranger for over 60 years.

Scott Joplin, billed by his publisher as
the "King of Ragtime Writers."

Cover of the first edition of
"Maple Leaf Rag."

Charles L. Johnson, composer of pop rags ("Dill Pickles Rag").

Zez Confrey, composer of novelty rags ("Kitten on the Keys").

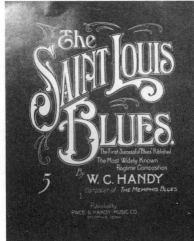

W. C. Handy, king of the blues composers ("The Saint Louis Blues").

Sheet music cover for "The Saint Louis Blues," the most recorded song ever.

The offices of Pace & Handy Music Company, circa 1923.

Walter Donaldson, composer of "Yes Sir, That's My Baby."

From left, Walter Donaldson, Harry Warren and Jerome Kern.

Harry Warren, composer
of "Lullaby of Broadway."

ments, far fewer than the standard Broadway pit orchestra of the time. Above all, the songs were integrated with the plot and could even advance the action because the size of the theater and orchestra allowed the lyrics to be clearly heard. Bolton's stories were always amusing and artfully clever. Wodehouse was the first important literate lyricist of the American musical stage. If Irving Berlin set the standard for pop tunes during the Alley's Golden Age, then Jerome Kern did the same for show tunes, theatre and film songs of his time.

Jerry, as he was called, saw his first musical show when he was ten years old. It was Victor Herbert's THE WIZARD OF THE NILE (November 4, 1895). Legend has it that when he came home, Jerry sat down at the piano and played the score from memory. This show, surely, gave him the incentive to compose for the theatre. After high school, he studied at the New York College of Music, and, to earn extra money and learn the business, he worked after school at Joseph W. Stern's jobbing plant as a bookkeeper, since the main publishing house didn't have a vacancy at the time. However, in September 1902, Stern's subsidiary, the Lyceum Publishing Company, issued Kern's first number, a reverie entitled "At the Casino." Like many other famous Alley composers' first works, this one didn't create much of a stir in the Alley. So, Kern went to Europe for a year's further study. Upon his return in 1904, he attracted the attention of T. B. Harms' publishing head Max Dreyfus, who was at that time producing scores of imported British and European operettas. One result of Kern's new association with that firm was that he was asked to interpolate his own numbers when these shows were to be produced on Broadway, to "Americanize" them. His first such interpolation was "Wine, Wine!" in AN ENGLISH DAISY (January 18, 1904). In MR. WIX OF WICKHAM (September 19, 1904), Kern had four numbers, "Angling by the Babbling Brook" being the most memorable. It wasn't until a year later that he had his first real hit in "How'd You Like to Spoon with Me?", when Georgia Caine sang it in THE EARL AND THE GIRL (November 4, 1905). It was so successful, that it was also used the following year in THE RICH MR. HOGGENHEIMER (October 22, 1906).

During a short stay in London, Kern was asked by American producer Charles Frohman to freshen up Frohman's latest production there, THE BEAUTY OF BATH (1906). The starring actor-manager Seymour Hicks added Pelham Grenville Wodehouse to the show as a resident lyricist and verse writer for the princely sum of £2 a week. For this production, Hicks particularly wanted a show-stopping comic song with several additional choruses for encores. Wodehouse's first meeting with Kern took place at the Aldwych Theatre, where Kern, in his shirtsleeves, was playing poker with several of the actors. "When I finally managed to free him from the card table and was able to talk to him," Wodehouse recalled, "I became impressed. Here, I thought, was a young man supremely confident of himself—the kind of person who inspires people to seek him out when a job must be done." Between them, the composer and the lyricist came up with a song called "Mr. Chamberlain" about the Prime Minister and his then-topical protective tariff policy. When the show opened at the Aldwych on March 19, 1906, the number proved to be everything that Hicks had hoped for, not only stopping the show but also taking London by storm. Had there been a top-forty chart in London in those days, this song would have been at the top. The pleasant Kern-Wodehouse association wasn't to resume for another ten years, when it would produce revolutionary results.

For the next six years, Kern was to interpolate songs in thirty-five musicals in both New York and London, with no major hits.

His first chance to do a complete score for Broadway came when he was called to work on The Red Petticoat (November 13, 1912). The best thing about this flop show was a rag song Kern slipped in called "The Ragtime Restaurant." His second complete score was OH, I SAY! (October 30, 1913), from which the nicely syncopated number "Katy-did" foretold his happiest efforts in LEAVE IT TO JANE. It wasn't until the following year that he enjoyed his second big hit, "You're Here and I'm Here," originally in THE LAUGHING HUSBAND (February 2, 1914) and then put into the post-Broadway tour of THE MARRIAGE MARKET (New York opening: September 22, 1913), where Donald Brian sang it to further popularity. Irene and Vernon Castle added it to the touring version of THE SUNSHINE GIRL (New York opening: February 3, 1913) and turned it into a fox trot showcase. Leo Feist purchased it from Harms and fully exploited it, placing it in six different Broadway shows. Most show songs appeared only once, in the show for which originally written. Feist's professional manager worked overtime to get this number featured in those six productions. The nearest a pop song came to this record was in 1925, when Shapiro, Bernstein's man interpolated "If You Knew Susie," into five Broadway musicals.

THE GIRL FROM UTAH (August 24, 1914) sported seven interpolated numbers by Kern. One of them, "They Didn't Believe Me," became the first of his songs to sell two million copies of sheet music. It has remained a classic. Four more shows found music interpolated by Kern before managers F. Ray Comstock and Elisabeth (Bessie) Marbury took over the

Princess Theatre and turned the productions there into small, two-set shows with small casts and orchestras. When Kern was approached to help create such a show, he informed Marbury that he and Guy Bolton had just completed exactly such a show. Comstock and Marbury produced NOBODY HOME (April 20, 1915), and it was at the opening night that Kern ran into his friend "Plum" Wodehouse in the lobby. Wodehouse was there to see the show as a reviewer for *Vanity Fair*, a magazine "Devoted to Society and the Arts." At a party at his home later in the evening, Kern invited his former partner to join him again in creating shows. Wodehouse accepted, and it was there that he was introduced to Guy Bolton. A classic three-way friendship and collaboration was set to begin.

In addition to writing occasional lyrics for shows, Wodehouse was fast becoming a world-famous humorist, writing the funniest short stories and novels appearing in the *Saturday Evening Post*, *Collier's*, and *Cosmopolitan*. The second Princess show, written by Kern and Bolton, was named VERY GOOD EDDIE (December 23, 1915) and contained the hit song "Babes in the Wood."

HAVE A HEART (January 11, 1917) was billed as "The Up-to-the-Minute Musical Comedy" and was the first to be written by what a New York *Times* drama critic called "the trio of musical fame, Bolton and Wodehouse and Kern." Bolton and Wodehouse fashioned a funny story around which melodious songs were written, most notably "And I Am All Alone" and "You Said Something." The funniest number was sung by comedian Billy B. Van, whose interpretation of "Napoleon" secured Wodehouse's reputation as a humorous lyricist. His renown as the first great theatre lyricist was confirmed later when lyricist Howard Dietz wrote in a letter to Wodehouse, quoted in this author's biography of the lyricist, "Over the years I have held [Wodehouse] as the model of light verse in the song form." And Richard Rodgers wrote in a letter to this author, "Before Larry Hart, only P. G. Wodehouse had made any assault on the intelligence of the song-listening public." In partial answer to what made the trio's Princess shows so influential throughout the twenties, Kern wrote: "It is my opinion that the musical numbers should carry the action of the play, and should be representative of the personalities of the characters who sing them."

The trio didn't have time to rest, as Comstock and Marbury wanted a replacement for EDDIE at the Princess. They complied with OH, BOY! which opened on February 20, 1917, and ran for a record 475 performances. In addition to "Ain't It a Grand and Glorious Feeling?," "Nesting

Time in Flatbush," and "You Never Knew about Me," it also had Kern's favorite of all his songs, "Till the Clouds Roll By," the title M-G-M used for his screen biography.

The team next adapted George Ade's play THE COLLEGE WIDOW and turned it into LEAVE IT TO JANE (August 28, 1917). The score is Kern's happiest, filled with charming and gay melodies, matched superbly by master lyricist Wodehouse. In addition to the title song, "The Crickets Are Calling," "Just You Watch My Step," "The Sun Shines Brighter," "Wait Till Tomorrow," and "The Siren's Song" highlighted the show. The big comic numbers were "Sir Galahad" and "Cleopatterer."

THE RIVIERA GIRL (September 24, 1917) featured one Kern interpolation with Wodehouse lyrics, inspired by the place on Long Island where Wodehouse was then living, "The Bungalow in Quogue" (rhymes with Patchogue).

And finally, on November 5, 1917, an incredible revue called MISS 1917 was produced by Charles Dillingham and Florenz Ziegfeld, with half the numbers written by Kern and Wodehouse, the other half written by Victor Herbert and Wodehouse. The one song to last was Kern's "The Land Where the Good Songs Go."

The last Princess show written by the trio was OH LADY! LADY!! (February 1, 1918). This show ran 219 performances and, prior to its Broadway opening, contained "Bill," one of the all-time classic theatre songs, later to become part of SHOW BOAT. "Before I Met You," "When the Ships Come Home," and "You Found Me and I Found You" were part of this important score. It was of this show that Dorothy Parker wrote: "Well, Bolton and Wodehouse and Kern have done it again. Every time these three gather together, the Princess Theatre is sold out for months in advance . . . I like the way they go about musical comedy. I like the way the action slides casually into the songs. I like the deft rhyming of the song that is always sung in the last act by two comedians and a comedienne."

Composers George Gershwin, Vincent Youmans and Richard Rodgers and lyricists Ira Gershwin and Lorenz Hart were captivated by what they saw and heard at the Princess. They admitted by word and deed that the shows written by this "trio of musical fame" inspired them, and they tried to imitate the Princess shows in form and spirit. Kern's work had a profound effect on theatre music for years to come.

THE NIGHT BOAT (February 2, 1920) contained "Left All Alone Again Blues" and the sprightly "Whose Baby Are You?"—both written with new lyricist Anne Caldwell (1867–1936). In time, she would become the most successful woman writer in Broadway musical history.

Kern's SALLY (December 21, 1920) contained a blockbuster book by Guy Bolton, with such outstanding songs as "The Church 'Round the Corner," lyrics by P. G. Wodehouse and Clifford Grey, and "Look for the Silver Lining" and "Whip-Poor-Will," both with lyrics by B. G. DeSylva. An interpolated Wodehouse lyric was another historical funny, "You Can't Keep a Good Girl Down (Joan of Arc)." With songs like these, the show ran a fantastic 570 performances.

GOOD MORNING DEARIE (November 1, 1921) provided Kern with "Ka-lu-a," his biggest hit since "Look for the Silver Lining." The lyrics were by Anne Caldwell, but what was memorable about the song was its insistent bass line. The bass line was so memorable, in fact, that Fred Fisher successfully sued Kern for using it, claiming Kern had lifted it from "Dardanella" (1919), which Fisher had written and published. Although it was not uncommon to sue over stolen tunes, here was a unique instance in which a bass line was considered a melody.

SITTING PRETTY (April 8, 1924) united the trio one more time. The score was a good one and featured "Bongo on the Congo." That song made a deep impression on Ira Gershwin, who wrote during a later period of self-doubt: "I was still not completely satisfied with my contribution. I was bothered by there being no lyric I considered comic . . . Up to then I'd often wondered if I could do a comedy trio like the ones P. G. Wodehouse came up with—'Bongo on the Congo' from SITTING PRETTY, for instance." Also in that score was "When It's Apple Blossom Time in Sing-Sing," which parodied the 1912 hit "When It's Apple Blossom Time in Normandie." Wodehouse may have recalled his and Kern's earlier parody from OH, BOY!, "(When It's) Nesting Time in Flatbush." (But the boys in the Alley have had fun along these lines, too. How about "When It's Cherry Blossom Time in Tokio," which Peter DeRose wrote for Norma Talmadge, or Irving Berlin's "When It's Night Time Down in Dixieland," or Richard Whiting's "When It's Daylight Saving Time in Oshkosh"?)

SUNNY (September 22, 1925) was written with Otto Harbach (1873–1963) and Oscar Hammerstein II. The score contained over twenty songs, but only "Who?" had a life apart from the show. It sold over a million copies of sheet music and, when revived in a 1937 recording by Tommy Dorsey and his Orchestra, sold over a million records. The reason for the success of Hammerstein's lyric was his choice of the word "who" to sustain the opening note for five beats. It was a word that had enough interest to be repeated five times during the chorus.

SHOW BOAT (December 27, 1927) was the show Oscar Hammerstein wrote based on Edna Ferber's novel that created the modern form of the musical play, as distinct from operetta and the musical comedies of the time. It was the first musical to deal with adult themes in an intelligent fashion as it followed the lives of two couples from the 1880's through the 1920's. The musical score was Kern's greatest endeavor, and Hammerstein's lyrics fitted the music perfectly, one of the highlights of his career. The songs include the classics "Ol' Man River," "Can't Help Lovin' Dat Man," "Make Believe," "Why Do I Love You," "You Are Love," and "Bill." This last song had been written by P. G. Wodehouse for Vivienne Segal to sing in OH, LADY! LADY!! (February 1, 1918) but was dropped during the out-of-town tryouts when it was found to be unsuitable for her voice. As it was a situation song, it had to be featured in a show where it would be pertinent to the plot. Nine years later it found a permanent home in SHOW BOAT and, in Helen Morgan, a singer who immortalized it. The show was a complete success, the third longest-running Broadway show of the twenties, completing 572 performances, and then touring for an entire year. Its London production (1928) ran for 350 performances, with Paul Robeson singing "Ol' Man River." SHOW BOAT has been revived by major companies many times over the years, most notably on Broadway in 1946, for a run of 418 performances. (It was for this revival that Kern wrote his last song, "Nobody Else But Me.") A 1971 revival in London's West End ran for 910 performances! It has had three film versions made of it (in 1929, 1936, and 1951). The show has become one of the few popular entertainments for all time.

SWEET ADELINE (September 3, 1929) contained only one hit, "Why Was I Born?" The show was a nostalgic look at the Gay Nineties. The Wall Street crash put a premature end to the production, as most of the theater audience consisted of the upper middle class which lost much of its disposable income.

THE CAT AND THE FIDDLE (October 15, 1931), called "A Musical Love Story," included the lovely ballad "The Night Was Made for Love" and the coquettish "She Didn't Say Yes," both with lyrics by Otto Harbach.

MUSIC IN THE AIR (November 8, 1932), with lyrics by Oscar Hammerstein, was another of Kern's musical plays with a European setting. The two hits from this show were "I've Told Ev'ry Little Star" and "The Song Is You."

ROBERTA (November 18, 1933) was a reversion to the more ordinary musical comedy show. The lyrics were by Otto Harbach and the story was about a fashion designer. There were the classics "Yesterdays," "The Touch of Your Hand," and the ever-popular "Smoke Gets in Your Eyes." But when Kern first wrote this last song, with its dramatic, yet lyrical, sweep of melodic line, nobody (especially the actress Tamara, for whom it was written) cared much for it, for Kern had written it in a quick march tempo. When he saw the cast's reaction during rehearsal, he recast it, putting it in a more romantic mood to suit the glamorous Tamara, who stopped the show with it nightly. (Incidentally, ROBERTA was Bob Hope's first Broadway musical.)

Kern's film work until 1935 consisted of his adapting SHOW BOAT, SALLY, SUNNY, THE CAT AND THE FIDDLE, SWEET ADELINE, MUSIC IN THE AIR, and ROBERTA for the screen. With ROBERTA (1935), the screen version was superior to the show, using most of the original Broadway score (rare in Kern's other previously filmed shows). It included two new songs which became hits from the film: "Lovely to Look At" and "I Won't Dance," featuring one of Fred Astaire's phenomenal tap routines.

Kern devoted the last part of his career to composing ten original scores for films.

I DREAM TOO MUCH (1935) was his first original film score, but, sadly, it wasn't an auspicious beginning. The only song which attained a modicum of popularity was the lilting "Jockey on the Carousel."

SWING TIME (1936), on the other hand, with lyrics by Dorothy Fields (1905–1974), daughter of Lew Fields (of Weber and Fields), contained an absolutely superb original score. In fact, it was to be regarded as the best score Kern would write for Hollywood. The film starred Fred Astaire and Ginger Rogers and followed their greatest movie, TOP HAT, with Irving Berlin's richest Hollywood score. Kern's music was especially well integrated with the plot and made the movie a stand-out. This new Kern-Fields collaboration included "A Fine Romance," "Never Gonna Dance," and Kern's first Academy Award winner, "The Way You Look Tonight."

With three original film scores in a row producing very little that was memorable, (HIGH, WIDE AND HANDSOME—1937, WHEN YOU'RE IN LOVE—1937, and THE JOY OF LIVING—1938), Kern decided to do another Broadway show with Oscar Hammerstein. They called it VERY WARM FOR MAY (May 17, 1939). It was to be his last show for Broadway, and it wasn't successful. However, one of his best songs and one of the all-time classic melodies, "All the Things You Are," came from this show (which was later made into a film called BROADWAY RHYTHM in 1942). This great song is the most frequent answer given by fellow composers to the two questions, "What song do you wish you had written?" and "Which song do you most admire?"

LADY BE GOOD (1941) was a Hollywood version of the Gershwin brothers' 1924 Broadway show. Into it was interpolated a Kern song he composed out of affection for his friend Oscar Hammerstein, who had written a set of lyrics soon after the Nazis captured Paris in June 1940. They had no thought of using "The Last Time I Saw Paris" in any show or film (Kate Smith had introduced it on the radio), but it fit in this film, with Ann Sothern's poignant rendition. For it, Kern won his second and last Oscar after some controversy, since the song hadn't been written expressly for the film. Kern also felt he should not have won, going so far as to say that Harold Arlen's "Blues in the Night" should have and that the Academy should change its rules so that only songs composed expressly for films could be eligible. The Academy did this, but only after Kern had accepted his award.

COVER GIRL (1944) starred Rita Hayworth and Gene Kelly and paired Kern with lyricist Ira Gershwin for the only time in their careers. The film's best song and another classic, "Long Ago and Far Away," started out with the title "Midnight Music." Gershwin was a slow worker, and his procrastination infuriated Kern. So when Kern became impatient for a lyric for this tune, instead of venting his spleen, he merely sent Gershwin a dummy lyric beginning, "Watching little Alice pee . . ." This, wrote Kern biographer Gerald Bordman, made Gershwin ashamed of his slothfulness, and he immediately wrote the classic that was to become his largest royalty-producer, including all of the songs written with his brother George.

CAN'T HELP SINGING (1944) created the new team of Kern and E. Y. Harburg, who was usually Harold Arlen's collaborator. It gave Deanna Durbin the best song she would ever sing in a film, "More and More," which made the HIT PARADE for fifteen weeks, the last of the Kern songs to become a hit in his lifetime.

CENTENNIAL SUMMER (1946) was the last film for which Kern wrote an original score. Two hits emerged: "In Love in Vain," with lyrics by Leo Robin, and "All Through the Day," written with Oscar Hammerstein. Although both made the HIT PARADE (thirteen and twenty weeks, respectively), they did so after Kern's death.

Jerome D. Kern died of a cerebral hemorrhage in New York City on November 11, 1945. He was hailed as the foremost composer in America. TILL THE CLOUDS ROLL BY, M-G-M's tribute to him, was a spectacular "biography," including fourteen stars and featuring nearly one hundred of his songs, most as background music only. This lavish musical was written by long-time librettist Guy Bolton, who invented an interesting "life" for his old collaborator, one more in the series of Hollywood biographies which bore no relation to their subjects' actual lives.

VAUDEVILLE IN THE TEENS

AL JOLSON:
"Swanee"

Al Jolson (1886–1950) was born Asa Yoelson in Russia. He started his career as a singer in minstrel shows, winding up with the great Lew Dockstader's troupe. He entered vaudeville at the turn of this century and first appears on a sheet music cover for Charles K. Harris' "For Old Times Sake" (1900), as part of the team of Joelson and Moore. His first performance on Broadway was at the Schuberts' newly-opened Winter Garden Theatre on Broadway between Fiftieth and Fifty-first Streets. It was in the revue LA BELLE PAREE (March 20, 1911) that he sang Jerome Kern's "Paris Is a Paradise for Coons." With his next show, the same year, VERA VIOLETTA (November 20), he would headline at the Winter Garden, a tradition that lasted for the next fifteen years. He was such a great entertainer that any song he sang became a hit, so pluggers beat a path to his door. His door was wide open and he was the first performer to insist upon being "cut in" on the writing credit of a song. He became the king of the cut-inners, got co-authorship credit on many copyrights and a share of royalties on many of the biggest hits of his era. It is known that he never wrote anything in his life, yet he shared "authorship" of some of the greatest songs in the Alley!

He secured an historic role for himself in the entertainment industry when he starred in the first talking (more correctly, "singing") film THE JAZZ SINGER (1927). "Mother, I Still Have You" was written especially for the Warner Bros. picture by Louis Silver, Grant Clarke and, oh yes, Al Jolson. His performing trademarks were his blackface and his white gloves. The blackface makeup came early in his career as a vaudevillian, when he acted on the advice of a veteran headliner, who told him to wear it to hide his nervousness.

There is no question that, with his incredible energy and exuberance, he captivated audiences as no other entertainer ever has. He made more hits for Alley writers than any other performer of his time.

In his Broadway shows, movies, records, nightclub performances and touring for the Armed Services, Jolson was the most celebrated singer of the first half of this century. Some of the multi-million selling hits he made were: "Swanee," "April Showers," "Rock-a-bye Your Baby with a Dixie Melody," "My Mammy," "Sonny Boy," "California, Here I Come," "Toot, Toot, Tootsie!" "I'm Sitting on Top of the World," "There's a Rainbow 'Round My Shoulder," "Me and My Shadow," "Back in Your Own Backyard," "The Anniversary Song," and "Is It True What they Say about Dixie?" He was the only subject ever to perform in his own screen biography, not once but twice, when he recorded all of the songs for Larry Parks on the soundtracks of THE JOLSON STORY (1946) and JOLSON SINGS AGAIN (1949).

EMMA CARUS:
"Alexander's Ragtime Band"

Emma Carus (1879–1927) was a vaudeville headliner of the top rank. Drama critic Amy Leslie once wrote, "Emma Carus is about the only one of the big-time singers who has a cultivated and genuine voice. It is a sweet contralto voice with excellent mezzo register and she uses it well."

Carus was discovered by Monroe H. Rosenfeld, and her first song success was his "Take Back Your Gold" (1897).

Carus opened her vaudeville act in the early days by saying, "I'm not pretty, but I'm good to my folks." She belted out her songs and was billed as a coon shouter. She was so effective as a plugger that long after she introduced "Alexander's Ragtime Band" (1911) her name remained on the sheet in its 65 editions, and above the title, at that! In 1914, Jack Glogau (1886–1953) wrote the snappy fox trot "The Carus Breeze" in her honor.

SOPHIE TUCKER:
"Some of These Days"

Sophie Tucker (1884–1966) was billed late in her career as "The Last of the Red Hot Mamas." Earlier, however, she was called "The Mary Garden of Ragtime." She, like Emma Carus, was a large woman with a strong voice and a wide vibrato. Her energy was enormous, and she went to great lengths to put over a song. She started out in vaudeville in blackface, but the first time her trunk with her makeup kit didn't arrive at the theatre for her show, she sang wearing plain stage makeup. Her first hit was the rag song "Dat Lovin' Rag" (1908) by Bernie Adler and Victor Smalley, which convinced her to build her career on that kind of song. She introduced Harry Von Tilzer's "The Cubanola Glide" (1909), and the following year, on the advice of her maid, she introduced black writer Shelton Brooks' "Some of These Days," which was so often requested that she made it her theme song. She also greatly boosted Brooks' "Darktown Strutters' Ball" (1917) after The Original Dixieland Jazz Band made its introductory recording. Throughout the twenties Tucker made hits: "Aggravatin' Papa," "You've Got to See Mama Ev'ry Night," "Papa, Better Watch Your Step," "Old King Tut," "Red Hot Mama," "Mama Goes Where Papa Goes," "Nobody Knows What a Red-Head Mama Can Do," "I Ain't Got Nobody," "After You've Gone," "There'll Be Some Changes Made," "He's a Good Man to Have Around," "Real Estate Papa You Ain't Gonna Sub-Divide Me," and "I'm The Last of the Red Hot Mamas." The last she sang in her first film, HONKY TONK (1929).

Her autobiography SOME OF THESE DAYS (1945) showed her to be a loyal, hardworking performer who loved her business and was always on the lookout for new songs to plug. She was a favorite for decades and continued in clubs, and even on television, until her death, always working as a headliner.

BILLY MURRAY:
"Take Your Girlie to the Movies"

Billy Murray (1877–1954) started his recording career as a tenor singing for the Edison Record Company at the beginning of this century and made his last recording during the Second World War! He was the first singer to make his reputation on recordings rather than by live performance. By the 'teens, he was a star and had recorded most of the hits of this era. His recordings were big plugs for the songs that he chose and were a great boost for the Alley.

SILENT FILM MUSIC IN THE TEENS

This was the decade during which the movie industry first made its mark in the Alley. Even though the screen couldn't talk, music played an important part in the viewing environment as accompaniment to the action on the screen, usually provided by the local pianist in the theater.

Charles N. Daniels, using his pseudonym "Neil Moret," and lyricist Harry Williams wrote the first commissioned title song for a motion picture. The song was "Mickey" (1918) and it was published by Daniels & Wilson of San Francisco to coincide with the release of the film of the same name. It starred Mabel Normand, whose photograph adorns the sheet music cover. The song was acquired later that year by Waterson, Berlin & Snyder Company, which published it in two different small-sized editions. The Mack Sennett star and song got plenty of exposure. This started a vogue for movie title songs, which is still going strong at this writing.

The most famous stars of the silent screen, Charlie Chaplin, Mary Pickford, and Pearl White (star of the PERILS OF PAULINE serials), appeared on sheet music covers as early as 1914 for the two women and 1915 for Chaplin. "March of the Movies" by M. A. Althouse (1915) features a drawing of an audience in a nickelodeon enjoying a film on the screen, watching Chaplin in his tramp costume, with a pianist accompanying in the pit. "Those Keystone Comedy Cops," by Charles McCarron (1915), has a typical photograph of the fabulous Sennett Keystone Kops on its cover, with Ford Sterling at the telephone and Fatty Arbuckle trying to overhear the conversation. Over the next two decades, the movies would provide some of the biggest plugs songs could receive, and major studios would purchase some of the Alley's largest firms to take care of their musical needs.

OTHER SONG HITS OF THE TEENS

"Oceana Roll" (1911) was composed by Lucien Denni (1886–1947) and written by Roger Lewis (1885–1948). It was a great rag song, revived in the early fifties by Teresa Brewer, whose recording of it sold another million copies (London 1083).

"Oh, You Beautiful Doll" (1911) was composed by Nat D. Ayer (1887–1952), with lyrics by Seymour Brown (1885–1947). Earlier that year, the team wrote the comic "If You Talk in Your Sleep, Don't Mention My Name." Ayer left the Alley to take his snappy syncopation to England, where he remained until the end of his life, composing mostly for the theatre.

"Be My Little Baby Bumble Bee" (1912) was composed by Henry I. Marshall and Stanley Murphy, the same team who, two years later, wrote another million-seller, "I Want to Linger."

"Melancholy" was composed by Ernie Burnett (1884–1959), with words by George A. Norton (1880–1923), in 1912. Ragtime composer Theron C. Bennett, who also published W. C. Handy's "Memphis Blues" in the same year, played and sang "Melancholy" first, at Bennett's nightclub, The Dutch Mill, in Denver, Colorado. In late 1914, the title was changed to "My Melancholy Baby." That same year Burnett published his famous piano piece "Steamboat Rag."

"You Made Me Love You (I Didn't Want to Do It)" (1913) was composed by James V. Monaco (1885–1945), with words by Joseph McCarthy (1885–1943), for a new publishing house, Broadway Music Corporation. Al Jolson originally established this standard, which has had periodic revivals.

"Sailing down the Chesapeake Bay" (1913) was the work of famous ragtime composer George Botsford (1874–1949) and lyricist Jean C. Havez (1874–1925). It is among the favorite rag songs of the era, continuing in favor among dixieland jazz bands today.

"The Trail of the Lonesome Pine" (1913) was the work of Harry Carroll (1892–1962) and Ballard Macdonald. The title was taken from a popular novel of the day by John Fox, Jr., the husband of singer Fritzi Scheff. The novel referred to the Cumberland Mountains of Kentucky, but Ballard Macdonald, who obviously hadn't read the book, wrote a lyric about "the Blue Ridge Mountains of Virginia." This was the song which Laurel and Hardy sang in their 1937 film WAY OUT WEST.

"By the Beautiful Sea" (1914) was the second of three million-selling successes in this decade by Harry Carroll, this one with lyrics by Harold R. Atteridge (1886–1938). It is one of the few great and lasting songs about summertime.

"I Ain't Got Nobody" (1914) is a great ballad that both Sophie Tucker and Bert Williams helped to make famous. It was first copyrighted as an unpublished composition in 1914 by Charles Warfield and David Young. A 1916 edition published by Frank K. Root & Company, Chicago, gave credit to the same songwriters. In 1915, the song was again copyrighted as an unpublished composition, credited to Dave Peyton and Spencer Williams, adding the word "Much" to the end of the title. In February 1916, Craig and Company (whose manager was Roger Graham) published the song as being by Spencer Williams, music, and Roger Graham (1885–1938), lyrics. Later in that year, Frank K. Root & Company bought the Craig edition, giving the firm two editions of the same song with two different sets of writers. (So, who really wrote it? I vote for the unsophisticated team of Warfield and Young.)

"The 'Jelly Roll' Blues" (1915) was composed by Ferdinand "Jelly Roll" Morton (1890–1941), one of the greatest jazzmen of all time. This was his first published tune and was issued by Will Rossiter, the Chicago publisher. A great blues number, it has remained a jazz standard.

"Poor Butterfly" (1916) was the hit of the New York Hippodrome's production THE BIG SHOW. It was the only hit of the prolific hack composer Raymond Hubbell (1879–1954) and lyric-writing producer John L. Golden (1874–1955). The song was performed so often that it prompted Arthur Green and William Jerome in 1917 to write "If I Catch the Guy Who Wrote Poor Butterfly."

"Smiles" (1917) was published by its composer, piano roll artist and executive Lee S. Roberts (1884–1949). The lyrics were written by J. Will Callahan (1874–1946). It was lying on the jobber's shelf in New York when Jack Robbins noticed it and brought it to the attention of master plugger and professional manager of Remick's, Mose Gumble. He purchased the copyright for Remick's and plugged it to make it a better than two-million selling success. It has remained a classic.

"After You've Gone" (1918) was composed by John Turner Layton (1894–1978) and Henry Creamer (1879–1930). It was plugged by Sophie Tucker into a standard and became an important number in Broadway Music's catalog. The melody of the chorus starts like "Peg o' My Heart."

"I'm Always Chasing Rainbows" (1918) was the third of Harry Carroll's hits during this decade, even though he took his chorus from Chopin's "Fantasie Impromptu" in C# minor. The original lyrics were by Joseph McCarthy. It was first featured by dancer Harry Fox in the show OH, LOOK!, but its fame increased when the show went on the road with the Dolly Sisters. It again became a hit when it was revived in the movie, THE DOLLY SISTERS (1945).

"Ja-Da" (1918) was written and composed by Bob Carleton (1896–1956). Its catchy melody combined with its nonsense lyric make it a number which is sporadically revived.

"K-K-K-Katy" (1918) was written and composed by Geoffrey O'Hara (1882–1967), and it remains a favorite. During both world wars, it was sung as "K-K-K-K.P." In 1919, an answer was given in the song "Thtop Your Thtuttering, Jimmy."

"Somebody Stole My Gal" (1918) was written and composed by Leo Wood (1882–1929). It had a strange history, first published by Meyer Cohen Music Company and introduced by Florence Milett. The song flopped. It was purchased by Denton & Haskins in 1922 and re-issued, this time recorded by the Original Memphis Five, when it took off and became a hit. It was recorded again by Bix Beiderbecke and his Gang in 1927, when it again sold over a million copies. It has become a standard and a jazz band favorite.

"Beautiful Ohio" (1918) was composed by Robert A. King (1862–1932), using his pseudonym "Mary Earl," with lyrics by Ballard Macdonald. It was by far the biggest-selling song of 1918, topping five million copies, and the largest-selling song published by Shapiro, Bernstein & Company. It has a chromatic theme which is similar to the middle section of Rimsky-Korsakoff's "Song of India." However, the beauty of the song has kept it in the permanent repertoire.

While the Alley published and promoted more songs during the twenties than in any other single decade, it was during the 'teens that the foundation was laid for that feverish activity. The 'teens was the time when Irving Berlin, the greatest songwriter of Tin Pan Alley, came to prominence. It was the decade of the real beginning of Jerome Kern's ascendancy as the greatest influence on the American musical theater. Irene and Vernon Castle established a variety of ballroom dances, giving the public another reason to buy popular music. It was a time when vaudeville reigned supreme and the silent film came into its own as a form of popular entertainment, as stars were created. Songs named for films helped to promote and get audiences to identify with those films and provided yet another outlet for pop music sales. And it was during this volatile period that jazz became popular and added further excitement to the popular music business.

THE ALLEY REIGNS SUPREME

(1919–1929)

Major Publishers of the Twenties

Our involvement in the First World War (1917–1918) changed the American way of life. So did Prohibition (1920–1931). So did radio (starting regular commercial broadcasting in October 1920), records (some million-sellers by 1920), and talking motion pictures (starting in 1927). The biggest change in the sheet music business came when the National Association of Sheet Music Dealers, in April 1919, recommended, and the publishers accepted, a new standard size of sheet music—9¼″ × 12¼″. The standard postwar price was thirty cents a copy.

The two biggest musical influences of this decade were jazz and blues. Although neither of these styles sold well in sheet music form, their records did, and the two new sounds permanently changed popular music.

As had the word "ragtime," the word "blues" became a fad (1919–1924) and was used in the titles of many compositions, whether true blues or not. Many of these so-called "blues" were syncopated fox trots ("Jazz Me Blues," "Chasing the Blues"). Others were ordinary pop songs ("Wang Wang Blues," "Wabash Blues"). Some were even real blues ("Decatur Street Blues," "Laughin' Cryin' Blues"). For years, writers on jazz and blues who are not musicians have stuck to a formula which dictates that a blues is a twelve-measure song of three four-measure lines, with the first two lines being practically identical and the last being the punch line, wrapping up a story. Since this formula describes fewer than half of the songs published as blues, it isn't a worthwhile guide to the genre. To further confound non-musical writers, the term "blues" refers not only to specific songs and instrumentals, but also to a manner in which pop songs can be sung. A good example is the J. Russel Robinson-Roy Turk song "Aggravatin' Papa" (1922). As performed by the Virginians (on Victor 19021), it is a snappy fox trot, but, as performed by Bessie Smith (on Columbia A-3877), it becomes a blues.

112

In the same vein, "jazz" doesn't refer so much to what is played but to how it is played. The ODJB started out with five instruments (cornet, trombone, clarinet, piano and drums). The Original Memphis Five also used those same instruments, as did the Original Indiana Five. Yet these three bands don't sound very much alike. The major difference between the bands is the way in which those instruments were being played. Intonation, or the way in which the brass and reed instruments are blown (and touch for the piano, that is, how the keys are struck) make them sound different. Jazz piano stylist Jelly Roll Morton cannot be mistaken for any other pianist, for his touch and his harmonic choices are immediately recognizable; he makes the piano sound like an entire Dixieland Band. He is easily distinguishable from Eubie Blake, James P. Johnson and Willie "The Lion" Smith, all of whom had original and distinctive styles. As Blake once said, "It's not that I play better than anybody else, but it's the tricks I know."

Discs provide the best way to familiarize oneself with jazzmen and jazz bands of the twenties. Jazz in sheet music form, especially the tunes created for bands, didn't sell well at all and was a discouragement to publishers. Indeed, the great jazz bands—King Oliver's Creole Jazz Band ("Sugar Foot Stomp"), Louis Armstrong's Hot Five ("Heebie Jeebies"), Jimmy Wade's Moulin Rouge Syncopators ("Mobile Blues"), The Original Memphis Five ("Shufflin' Mose"), and The Wolverines featuring Bix Beiderbecke ("Driftwood")—appeared only once or twice each on sheet music covers. Jazzmen such as Jack Teagarden, Muggsy Spanier, Red Nichols, Eubie Blake and Fletcher Henderson appeared on only a few more. The New Orleans Rhythm Kings were not pictured on their famous tune "Tin Roof Blues," but appear only on an edition of Jelly Roll Morton's "Wolverine Blues." Morton himself appeared only on the cover of Folio No. 1 of his famous "Blues & Stomps for Piano." His outstanding band, The Red Hot Peppers, never appeared on a sheet music cover.

These were the most important, creative and best-selling recording jazz bands and soloists of their time, but that popularity did not translate into sheet music sales. In fact, many of the published jazz tunes, which became classics on records, sold so poorly and had such limited press runs that they are almost never found today. The reverse, of course, was true of the pop singers who recorded, whose pictures on covers triggered widespread sales of sheet music.

JACK MILLS, INC.:
Novelty Rags

The emergence of Jack Mills (1891–1979) in July 1919, at 152 West Forty-fifth Street, as a powerful firm was due to his days as a song plugger in the Alley. Most recently, he had been the professional manager of McCarthy & Fisher Company. That experience spurred him to start his own firm. One of his ideas, which established the genre of piano novelty ragtime, was his purchase of Zez Confrey's novelty ragtime masterpiece, "Kitten on the Keys," in July 1921. This, along with the nearly one hundred pieces in this idiom that he eventually issued, gave him the pre-eminence as a publisher of novelty rags he enjoyed throughout this decade. He also published many great blues and jazz numbers like "Down Hearted Blues," "I Just Want a Daddy I Can Call My Own," "Graveyard Dream Blues," "Farewell Blues," and "The Great White Way Blues."

In August 1928, the firm name changed to Mills Music, Inc. The following year, in celebration of its tenth anniversary, Mills bought the catalogs of Gus Edwards Music, Stark & Cowan, Harold Dixon, McCarthy & Fisher, and Fred Fisher Music. In November 1931, Mills obtained the catalog of Waterson, Berlin & Snyder Company (minus the Berlin songs, which were already owned and published by Berlin himself). From 1923 to 1932, the firm was located in the Mills Building at 148–150 West Forty-sixth Street, where it became the most productive publishing house of the twenties.

TRIANGLE MUSIC PUBLISHING COMPANY:
All That Jazz

When Joseph M. Davis (1896–1978) established the Triangle company in 1919, he created a firm to rival the black publishers (he himself was white), issuing mostly blues and popular songs written by blacks. Some of his hits were "I Wanna Jazz Some More," "Papa Will Be Gone," "Whicker Bill Blues," "My Lovin' Mamie," "Daddy, Your Mama Is Lonesome for You," and "Dreaming Blues." During the thirties, Davis dropped the Triangle imprint and replaced it with Joe Davis, Inc.

PERRY BRADFORD:
"You Can't Keep a Good Man Down"

The fourth black publisher to make a mark in Tin Pan Alley (after Gotham-Attucks, Pace & Handy, and Clarence Williams) was Perry

Bradford (1893–1970), a vaudevillian, composer, artists' manager and record producer. While he was playing the Standard Theatre in Philadelphia with his partner Jeanette Taylor in 1916, he published his "Lonesome Blues." Apparently, this edition was a well-kept secret, for he sold the piece to a New York publisher two years later. Moving to New York himself, Bradford became involved with record companies, managing to talk Fred Hager (formerly of the publishing firm of Helf & Hager, 1905–1909), then of Okeh Records, into letting black singer Mamie Smith record two of Bradford's blues compositions. Because of Bradford's tenacity, Mamie Smith, in 1920, became the first black singer to record with a black jazz band (The Jazz Hounds). She was also the first singer to record a blues. Because of her success at selling records, along with the impressive sales of Bessie Smith, Clara Smith, Trixie Smith, Ida Cox, etc., the field of blues singing was dominated by women until the late thirties.

Bradford started his Tin Pan Alley concern by opening the Perry Bradford Music Company in the Gaiety Building at 1547 Broadway, and by publishing his first million-selling hit, "Crazy Blues." Bradford also owned Blues Music Company and Acme Music Publishing Company. His first firm had an important catalog of blues, mostly his own compositions, such as the famous "It's Right Here for You," "That Thing Called Love," which Sophie Tucker helped make popular, "You Can't Keep a Good Man Down," and Lemuel Fowler's "He May Be Your Man, But He Comes to See Me Sometimes." Perry Bradford Music Company lasted until 1928, when it went out of business.

MELROSE BROTHERS MUSIC COMPANY:
"Doctor Jazz"

The Melrose Brothers, Walter and Lester, along with Marty Bloom, owned a music shop before adding to it a brand-new music publishing business in Chicago early in 1923. They issued not only song sheets, but also published orchestrations for dance and jazz bands. Their songs added immeasurably to the jazz and dance band repertoire and helped solidify Chicago's position as the preeminent jazz city during the twenties. Most of the Melrose publications would become standard fare for all dixieland jazz bands. Their first three successes were all-time favorites: "Wolverine Blues" by Jelly Roll Morton (recorded by The Benson Orchestra of Chicago, Albert E. Short and his Tivoli Syncopators, Gene Rodemich and his Orchestra from St. Louis, recording for Brunswick in Chicago, and the New Orleans Rhythm Kings, whose photo is on the cover of the sheet music); "Tin Roof Blues," composed and recorded by the New Orleans Rhythm Kings; and "Sobbin' Blues," written by future bandleader Art Kassell and drummer Vic Berton, initially recorded by the Benson Orchestra and Albert E. Short's Tivoli Syncopators. Melrose also issued "All Night Blues," by Chicago blues pianist Richard M. Jones, which Callie Vassar recorded for Gennett Records.

The following year, 1924, Melrose issued such classics as Charlie Davis' "Copenhagen," which had been recorded instrumentally by jazz and dance bands but got its first recording as a song in the early fifties, when Teresa Brewer sang it; "Someday Sweetheart," which Sophie Tucker belted to fame; "Tia Juana," composed and recorded by St. Louis bandleader Gene Rodemich and his trombonist Larry Conley, although the classic recording was by Jelly Roll Morton; and "Mobile Blues," by Fred Rose and Al Short.

The Melrose Brothers came back strongly in 1925 with Charlie Davis' "Jimtown Blues," a favorite of Jimmy Wade's Moulin Rouge Syncopators; "Whoop 'Em Up Blues," introduced by the Benson Orchestra; and the now standard "Spanish Shawl," pianist Elmer Schoebel's clever tune which Boston-based Edwin J. McEnelly's orchestra recorded with a superb piano solo by newcomer Frankie Carle. "Sugar Babe" was Boyd Senter's fine tune which he plugged nightly with his Senterpedes.

"Sugar Foot Stomp" (1926), the King Oliver classic, which he recorded with his Creole Jazz Band, featuring Louis Armstrong, was better known to jazz fans as "Dippermouth Blues." "Hangin' Around" (1926), was a collaboration between pianist Jack Gardner and bandleader Fred Hamm of Chicago.

Two jazz classics were first published in 1927: King Oliver's "Doctor Jazz," which Jelly Roll Morton's Red Hot Peppers catapulted to fame, and "Willie the Weeper," recorded initially by three big Chicago jazz bands: King Oliver's, Louis Armstrong's, and Doc Cook's. The famous gospel composer Thomas A. Dorsey's solid blues "It's Tight Like That" was issued by the company in 1928.

The Melrose Brothers folios of Jelly Roll Morton compositions and Louis Armstrong's "50 Hot Choruses" were landmarks in jazz publishing. The numbers that the Melrose Brothers issued, as well as the bands and soloists they helped to record, gave Chicago pride of place in the jazz world during the twenties.

EDWARD B. MARKS MUSIC CORPORATION:
Hanging On

The biggest name change in publishing came in December 1920, when Joseph W. Stern retired and the firm was retitled the Edward B. Marks Music Corporation, retaining its old address at 102–104 Thirty-eighth Street, until February 1922, when Marks purchased the building at 223–225 West Forty-sixth Street, adjacent to the Jerome H. Remick Building.

ROBBINS MUSIC CORP.:
A New Face

A new company was formed on January 1, 1922, when Maurice Richmond, a major jobber and a minor publisher (who had bought the F. A. Mills catalog in 1915), created a firm with his nephew and general manager, John J. Robbins (whose nickname was Jack) (1894–1959), to form Richmond-Robbins at 1658 Broadway. When Robbins became a partner with Harry Engel two years later (Robbins-Engel), the new firm stayed at the same address. From 1927–1935 (when Robbins sold out to M-G-M studios), the firm was known as Robbins Music Corporation, at 799 Seventh Avenue.

AGER, YELLEN & BORNSTEIN:
Writer-Publishers

Songwriters Milton Ager and Jack Yellen, with professional manager Ben Bornstein (who had been with Harry Von Tilzer for twenty years), formed their company in August 1922, and stayed together until they were bought out by Warner Brothers in 1936. Thereafter, the firm was known as Advanced Music.

DeSYLVA, BROWN & HENDERSON, INC.:
The Hot Team

Proving songwriters could make a go of it, the fabulously successful twenties team of DeSylva, Brown and Henderson formed their own publishing company at the end of 1926, with Robert Crawford as President and General Manager. He had been with Irving Berlin, Inc. as Sales Manager since that company's inception. The founding team maintained the company until 1934 at 745 Seventh Avenue. The current owner of the catalog is Chappell.

SANTLY-JOY, INC.:
A Plugger Makes His Move

Joe Santly (1886–1962), long a plugger and composer in the Alley, decided to open his own firm in 1929, with brothers Lester (1894–1983) and Henry (1890–1934), as Santly Brothers. Shortly after moving into the Brill Building in 1935, they became partners with George Joy, and changed the name of the firm to Santly Bros.-Joy. In 1938, it became known as Santly-Joy-Select until 1943, when it was permanently changed to Santly-Joy, Inc.

Hollywood Buys Into the Alley

With the coming of talking pictures, Hollywood changed Tin Pan Alley by buying up most of the larger publishers. Warner Brothers made the first move to acquire song catalogs when it bought out Witmark and Harms (from Max Dreyfus) in 1929 and Jerome H. Remick Company from Jerome Keit later that year. M-G-M bought Leo Feist, Inc. in 1934 and Robbins Music Corp. in the following year. Adding Miller Music, Inc., M-G-M then formed the combine known as Robbins-Feist-Miller, The Big Three. Paramount Pictures created Famous Music Corporation in 1928, and soon bought out Spier & Coslow to add to the Famous catalog.

These new firms created new ways to plug songs, using the various media new to this decade to advantage. Radio became the most important way to plug a song, and bandleaders and singers were constantly badgered by pluggers. Harry Von Tilzer, still at it in the twenties, sang his own songs over the radio and even made a talking picture plugging his then-latest number, demonstrating at the piano how he wrote "Just Around the Corner May Be Sunshine for You." The Roaring Twenties saw more popular songs published than has any other decade before or since.

MAJOR SONGWRITERS OF THE TWENTIES

WALTER DONALDSON:
"Yes Sir, That's My Baby"

Walter Donaldson was born in Brooklyn, New York, on February 15, 1891. He loved writing songs so much that he was fired from his first job in the Alley for doing so during business hours, when he was supposed to be plugging the firm's tunes for performers. His first published song was "Just Try to Picture Me Back Home in Tennessee," issued in 1915 by Waterson, Berlin & Snyder. As was the case with Albert Von Tilzer, who didn't see his first baseball game until twenty years after he wrote "Take Me Out to the Ball Game," it was many years after Donaldson published the tune that he finally saw the state which was so closely identified with him in song. In fact, states and cities proved to be lucky for him, as his next published song that year was the hit "We'll Have a Jubilee in My Old Kentucky Home." He followed this one with "On the Gin, Gin, Ginny Shore," "Carolina in the Morning," "Kansas City Kitty," and "Lazy Louisiana Moon." His first post-World War One number to become a million-selling success was "How Ya Gonna Keep 'Em Down on the Farm" (1919). During the war, when he was stationed at Camp Upton as an entertainer, he wrote the famous "The Daughter of Rosie O'Grady." It was at this camp where he met his future employer, Irving Berlin, who was also serving his country in khaki.

In Donaldson's first year as a civilian working for Waterson, Berlin & Snyder (1919), he teamed with the lyric duo of Sam M. Lewis and Joe Young for four hits: the aforementioned "How Ya Gonna Keep 'Em Down on the Farm," "Don't Cry Frenchy, Don't Cry," "I'll Be Happy When the Preacher Makes You Mine," and "You're a Million Miles from Nowhere."

At the beginning of the new decade, Donaldson began roaring with a Hawaiian number, "My Little Bimbo Down on the Bamboo Isle," with lyricist Grant Clarke. He then wrote, in 1921, with Lewis and Young providing the words, "My Mammy," which Al Jolson made "his" song, performing it on bended knee with white-gloved hands outstretched. This song became Jolson's trademark, and from that time forward any interpreter of mother songs became known as a "mammy singer."

Donaldson next wrote "Georgia" (1922), with lyrics by Howard Johnson (1887–1941), a lovely melody made famous by Paul Whiteman and his orchestra.

Donaldson's next collaboration was with the celebrated lyricist Gus Kahn (1886–1941), a Chicagoan who refused to live in New York, remaining in the windy city before going to Hollywood. Their first number, "My Buddy" (1922), was a hit. They followed it up with "Carolina in the Morning" the same year. The next year, they scored with "Beside a Babbling Brook."

In 1925, the team of Donaldson and Kahn had a banner year with four multi-million selling songs: "My Sweetie Turned Me Down," which the Dixie Stars (singer Al Bernard and pianist-composer J. Russel Robinson) made famous on a Columbia Record; "That Certain Party," popularized by Eddie Cantor; and two great Charleston numbers, "I Wonder Where My Baby Is Tonight?" and "Yes Sir, That's My Baby." This last was not only written for Eddie Cantor, it was written at Eddie Cantor's house. One of Cantor's five daughters had a mechanical toy pig which attracted Gus Kahn's attention. As the pig jiggled across the floor, Kahn recited the lines, "Yes sir, that's my baby, no sir, don't mean maybe" to the movements, and another of their hits was born. Gene Austin made a best-selling record for Victor.

The following year Donaldson produced "What Can I Say After I Say I'm Sorry?" with bandleader Abe Lyman. It was sung with great success by two singers, torcher Ruth Etting and jazzbaby Bee Palmer. With Gus Kahn, he produced two more hits in 1926, "There Ain't No Maybe in My Baby's Eyes" and "Let's Talk about My Sweetie."

If 1925 was a big year for Donaldson, 1927 was even bigger. He again had four hits, but their sales figures were much greater. With Gus Kahn, he wrote "He's the Last Word." Donaldson then started writing both words and music and came up with "At Sundown," introduced at the Palace Theatre by Cliff Edwards, "Changes," featured by Paul Whiteman's Orchestra (and given a spectacular piano roll arrangement by Vee Lawnhurst on Welte 75333), and "Sam, the Old Accordion Man," made famous by Ruth Etting. For his only collaboration with George Whiting, Donaldson came up with "My Blue Heaven." Gene Austin recorded it for Victor, selling several million copies, and Eddie Cantor plugged it in vaudeville and in the ZIEGFELD FOLLIES OF 1927. It was the biggest-selling song in the history of Leo Feist, Inc., according to Feist's son Leonard. It sold over five million copies of sheet music.

On June 1, 1928, Donaldson formed a publishing house with Walter Douglas and ace plugger Mose Gumble. Their first issues were the songs from the score of Donaldson's only Broadway show, WHOOPEE! (December 4, 1928). Gus Kahn wrote the lyrics, and Eddie Cantor starred with

Ruth Etting and Tamara Geva. Two songs were hits and became standards: "Making Whoopee" and "Love Me or Leave Me." When the show was made into a movie two years later, Donaldson and Kahn added "My Baby Just Cares for Me," which Eddie Cantor turned into a hit.

By himself, Donaldson wrote "Because My Baby Don't Mean Maybe Now" in the first year of his publishing company. It was recorded into hit status by Paul Whiteman and his Orchestra, Ruth Etting, and George Olsen and his Music. It has been a favorite of jazz bands and singers ever since. In the following year, Donaldson wrote with Edgar Leslie the wonderfully comic "'Tain't No Sin to Dance Around in Your Bones."

Before he went to Hollywood in 1930, Donaldson wrote for newcomer Ethel Merman "Little White Lies" and one of his biggest hits, initially made famous by Rudy Vallee and later by Guy Lombardo and his Orchestra, "You're Driving Me Crazy," which seems to be revived every twenty-five years or so.

Donaldson went to Hollywood, but his output slowed down considerably. He contributed a score to Eddie Cantor's KID MILLIONS (1935), which included "Okay Toots." For HERE COMES THE BAND (also 1935), he and Harold Adamson (1906–) wrote "Tender Is the Night." The following year, again with Adamson, he wrote for Jean Harlow's SUZY "Did I Remember?" In 1936, the team of Donaldson and Adamson wrote "It's Been So Long" and "You," for THE GREAT ZIEGFELD. This last song later became the theme song of Art Linkletter's House Party on television. Donaldson and Kermit Goell (1915–) wrote "Tonight" for the all-star Universal movie FOLLOW THE BOYS (1944). Soon after this, he was forced to retire due to ill health.

Walter Donaldson died in Santa Monica, California, on July 15, 1947.

RICHARD A. WHITING:
"Till We Meet Again"

Richard A. Whiting was born in Peoria, Illinois, on November 12, 1891. He started writing songs while in high school, but didn't try to publish them until a friend persuaded him to travel to Detroit for an interview with Jerome H. Remick. The great publisher was so impressed that he bought three of Whiting's songs and offered him the recently-vacated job of professional manager of the Detroit office. As the salary was only twenty-five dollars a week, Whiting supplemented his income by playing piano for six Hawaiians in a hotel band. He had to wear brown makeup nightly to pretend he, too, was a "native."

His first song was "The Big Red Motor and the Little Blue Limousine," with lyricist Earle C. Jones, who had previously worked with former manager Charles N. Daniels. His second number, a ragtime song, "I Wonder Where My Lovin' Man Has Gone," was written in collaboration with Charles L. Cooke (1891–1958), who had written a marvelous rag, "Blame It on the Blues" (1914), and was, a decade later, known as Doc Cook, leader of the Dreamland Orchestra in Chicago.

The following year Whiting wrote "It's Tulip Time in Holland" and acquired a Steinway grand piano. He had longed for one and approached Remick with the idea of signing over his rights to this song if Remick would get him the piano. Remick, a good businessman, accepted the deal. While Whiting was ecstatic at first, he got the worst of the bargain, as "Tulip Time" had a sale of one and a half million copies, which would have netted him more than $50,000. Steinway nine-foot, Model D concert grands, at this time, cost about $1,600.

In 1916 Whiting teamed with a Detroit bank clerk, Raymond Egan (1890–1952), who hung out at the Remick office during his lunch breaks. He and Whiting were to write many hits. Their first effort was "Mammy's Little Coal Black Rose," which Blossom Seeley helped sell. Shortly after, the team created another hit with "They Made It Twice as Nice as Paradise and They Called It Dixieland." The following year, Al Jolson helped sell "Where the Black-Eyed Susans Grow."

His next hit became his biggest seller of all and one of the First World War's greatest numbers. The lyricist was, again, Ray Egan. When Whiting first submitted the song to Remick, the publisher said he liked the tune but didn't think the title, "Auf Wiedersehen," was saleable when American soldiers were being killed by the Kaiser's army. When asked what it meant in English, Whiting replied, "Till We Meet Again." Remick thought that a good title, and so did over five million Americans who bought the sheet music!

The roaring twenties really did roar for Whiting. His first two songs published in this decade were multi-million sellers, both with lyrics by Ray Egan. "Japanese Sandman" was a catchy tune, repeating two notes in a sing-song way. Nora Bayes delighted audiences with it, Zez Confrey made a superb arrangement of it for QRS piano roll, and Paul Whiteman's orchestra sold over a million copies of their Victor record.

After he wrote the melody for "Bimini Bay," Whiting showed it to two lyricists, Ray Egan and Gus Kahn. This trio proved successful, as Ted Lewis plugged this one, and Van and Schenck plugged "Ain't We Got Fun" to sell well over a million copies each. "Bimini Bay" was introduced by Arthur West in SATIRES OF 1920.

"Sleepy Time Gal" (1925) was co-composed with pianist Ange Lorenzo, who followed it up with his own "Dreamy Dream Girl," which was not a hit. Cliff Edwards made the hit recording of "Sleepy Time Gal," and Canadian pianist Vera Guilaroff made a wonderful novelty solo recording of it.

"Ukulele Lady" (1925) was a natural for Nick Lucas to plug. It had lyrics by Gus Kahn and it made a nifty song for Vaughn DeLeath to sing to success on radio. The following year Al Jolson turned Whiting's "Breezin' Along with the Breeze" into a hit, while Lou Breese made it his orchestra's theme song. "Horses" had lyrics by Byron Gay (1886–1945) and was made famous by Roger Wolfe Kahn's orchestra. "Honey" (1928) was introduced by Rudy Vallee who made it a hit, while Sophie Tucker made "She's Funny That Way" successful. The melody of "She's Funny That Way" was composed by Charles N. Daniels, and the lyrics were written by Whiting. Ruth Etting made the most of the torch song "Guilty," which Whiting, Harry Akst and Gus Kahn wrote for her in 1931.

By then, Whiting was heavily involved with the movies. He started very early in the talkie game, when he signed with Paramount to compose music for their films. They teamed him with a new lyricist, Leo Robin (1900–1984), to write the score for INNOCENTS OF PARIS (1929), starring Maurice Chevalier in his American debut. The big hit was "Louise," which Chevalier was to keep in his repertoire for the rest of his career. In DANCE OF LIFE (1929), Hal Skelly scored with "True Blue Lou," later revived by Frank Sinatra.

Writing the score for MONTE CARLO (1930), Whiting and Robin came up with a Depression-era rouser for Jeanette Macdonald in "Beyond the Blue Horizon." It was a genuine hit with several revivals. For PLAYBOY OF PARIS (1930), the team came up with what became Whiting's own favorite of his songs, "My Ideal." The song's best interpreter is his daughter, Margaret Whiting, whose first recording was of that song and who turned it into a gigantic hit, as well as a standard.

ONE HOUR WITH YOU (1932) was the last film on Whiting and Robin's contract for Paramount. It was an undistinguished film but "(I'd Love to Spend) One Hour with You" became a standard when Eddie Cantor made it his radio theme, and carried it over to his popular television show in the fifties.

That same year, 1932, brought Whiting to Broadway, collaborating with Nacio Herb Brown and B. G. "Buddy" DeSylva on the show TAKE A CHANCE (November 26, 1932), starring Ethel Merman, Jack Haley and Jack Whiting. The hit song was "You're an Old Smoothie," which was kept current by its use on both radio and television by Old Gold Cigarettes as the song which opened their commercials.

When Whiting was asked to write a song for Shirley Temple in her first starring film, BRIGHT EYES (1934), he couldn't get an idea. His daughter Margaret, licking a large lollipop, came to see him and he told her to get away from him with all that sticky stuff. He then realized that the lollipop might be a subject, and wrote one of the most famous children's songs ever, "On the Good Ship Lollipop."

In 1937, Whiting went to Warner Brothers, where he was teamed with lyricist Johnny Mercer for what would be his last three films. The first, READY, WILLING AND ABLE (1937), contained a great production number, "Too Marvelous for Words," which outlasted the film's success to become a standard. HOLLYWOOD HOTEL (1937) was a movie based on the popular radio show of the same name hosted by gossip columnist Louella Parsons. The song which has become a standard was used as the opener, "Hooray for Hollywood," the unofficial theme song of the film industry. It was sung in the film by Johnny "Scat" Davis and Frances Langford, backed by Benny Goodman's Orchestra. It was later used by Jack Benny to close his radio show every Sunday evening.

While working on a Dick Powell feature, COWBOY FROM BROOKLYN (1938), Whiting suffered a heart attack. His last song was "Ride, Tenderfoot, Ride," written with Johnny Mercer.

Richard A. Whiting died in Beverly Hills, California, on February 10, 1938.

FRED FISHER:
"Chicago"

Fred Fisher was born in Cologne, Germany, on September 30, 1875. He came to the United States in 1900 and settled in Chicago, where a black saloon pianist gave him lessons. His first hit, for which he wrote both words and music, was "If the Man in the Moon Were a Coon" (1905), the first song published by Will Rossiter, who had just re-entered the music business after a five-year absence. It eventually sold over three million copies and gave Fisher the start of his career. The next year he wrote "I've Said My Last Farewell," with lyrics by Ed Rose.

In 1910 he wrote, not one, but two million-selling songs. "Any Little Girl That's a Nice Little Girl Is the Right Little Girl for Me" was the first syncopated number to become a hit that year, and "Come, Josephine, in My Flying Machine" was the second and bigger of the songs.

It became the most familiar of all airplane songs and remains a classic, with cheerful lyrics by Alfred Bryan. With Bryan doing lyrics again in 1913, Fisher had another hit with "Peg o' My Heart," which drew inspiration from the play of the same name starring Laurette Taylor. When it was revived by the Harmonicats in 1947, the disc sold over two million copies and continued the song's popularity.

It was around this time that Fisher started to compose songs with foreign cities or countries in the title. Since many of them became hits, it seems his idea was sound. It started in 1913 with "I'm On My Way to Mandalay" and continued with "When It's Moonlight on the Alamo," "I Want to Go to Tokio," "Norway, the Land of the Midnight Sun," "Siam," "Ireland Must Be Heaven for My Mother Came from There," "In the Land o' Yamo Yamo," "Lorraine, My Beautiful Alsace Lorraine," "When It's Night Time in Little Italy," and ending with "Fifty Million Frenchmen Can't Be Wrong."

Dolly Connolly helped make "There's a Broken Heart for Every Light on Broadway" (1915) famous, while Sophie Tucker did the same for "You Can't Get Along with 'Em or Without 'Em" (1916). Eddie Cantor slayed 'em with "They Go Wild, Simply Wild, Over Me" (1917). Fisher's biggest hit came in 1919, when he wrote the lyrics for and published Johnny Black's phenomenal tune "Dardanella." It was first recorded by Ben Selvin's Novelty Orchestra (Victor 18633) as an instrumental, selling more than six and one half million discs, but the song with Fisher's lyrics had a sheet music sale of more than two million. What made it so popular, however, was not an especially clever melody, but the highly original bass line. There had been nothing like it before, and as was discussed earlier, when Jerome Kern wrote "Ka-lu-a" for his show GOOD MORNING DEARIE using the identical recurring bass pattern, Fisher sued and won, the judge ruling that Fisher's one measure of music was "essential and substantial" to his song.

In 1921, Fisher, in collaboration with Willie Raskin (1896–1942), wrote the lovely "I Found a Rose in the Devil's Garden," which Pete Wendling (1888–1974) made into a fine piano roll arrangement (QRS 1411).

Another multi-million seller in sheet music sales occurred because of Max Kortlander's brilliant piano roll arrangement of "Chicago" (1922) for the QRS company (QRS 2021) and Paul Whiteman's scintillating version of the song for Victor records (Victor 18946). As the home of jazz during this decade, Chicago is perfectly evoked as "that toddlin' town."

Fisher found himself with another hit when Bix Beiderbecke recorded "There Ain't No Sweet Man That's Worth the Salt of My Tears" (1927) in Tom Satterfield's arrangement for the Paul Whiteman Orchestra, with the Rhythm Boys as vocalists.

Sophie Tucker got another Fisher favorite in "Happy Days and Lonely Nights" (1928). It became so popular that Ruth Etting interpolated it two years later into SIMPLE SIMON.

With the coming of talking pictures, Fred Fisher went to Hollywood in 1929. When he met producer Irving Thalberg at MGM and was asked if he could write a symphony, he replied, "When you buy me, you're buying Chopin, Liszt and Mozart. You're getting the very best!" His first song hit there was "I Don't Want Your Kisses" from SO THIS IS COLLEGE (1929). His next one was "Blue Is the Night" for Norma Shearer in THEIR OWN DESIRE (1930).

In 1931, he wrote a pop song "I'm All Dressed Up with a Broken Heart," which bandleader Ben Bernie played to success. And at the end of that decade, he wrote "Your Feet's Too Big," which Fats Waller made his own. Waller was so closely identified with it that it was included in a potpourri of his own songs for the hit revue AIN'T MISBEHAVIN' (1978).

Fred Fisher died in New York City on January 14, 1942.

CON CONRAD:
"Ma! (He's Making Eyes at Me)"

Con Conrad was born Conrad K. Dober in New York City on June 18, 1891. His debut in show business was as a pianist at the Vanity Fair Theatre on 125th Street. He soon met Jay Whidden (1886–1968), a boilermaker who wanted to be a violinist. They teamed up to play on the Keith circuit, had their first song published with "Down in Dear Old New Orleans" (1912), and were signed for a London revue. Conrad came back home from the War and wrote the hit "Oh! Frenchy" (1918).

At the beginning of the twenties, he teamed with pianist-composer J. Russel Robinson and turned out three hits in a row. Their first was "Margie" (1920), with words by Benny Davis (1895–1979); their second was "Singing the Blues," with words by Sam Lewis and Joe Young; and their third was "Palesteena," which they wrote by themselves. The Original Dixieland Jazz Band recorded a double-sided best-seller (Victor 18717) which produced *three* hits, as the "Margie" side included a chorus of "Singing the Blues" (as noted on the record label) and "Palesteena" was recorded by itself and put on the other side of the disc. The pianist for this recording, not very coincidentally, was Robinson. The record sold over two million copies. In one form or another, these recorded performances were in print from the time of the record's release in September 1920 to late 1975, when the ODJB LP was finally deleted from the Victor catalog. No other record has been in print continuously for so long a time.

"Ma! (He's Making Eyes at Me)" was Conrad's 1921 entry in the hit parade. With words by Sidney Clare (1892–1972), it gave Eddie Cantor another in the series of songs permanently identified with him. Cantor featured it in his revue THE MIDNIGHT ROUNDERS. And Eubie Blake made an outstanding piano recording that year (Emerson 10450). Another song that year, for which Conrad wrote both words and music, was "Moonlight." It was a beautiful ballad which received its major boost from Paul Whiteman's recording (Victor 18756).

Starting in 1923, Conrad teamed up with Billy Rose (1899–1966), and they wrote three songs which are still played by jazz bands. The first was "Barney Google," based on Billy De Beck's comic strip. Olsen and Johnson first featured it in their vaudeville act by having an actor in a horse costume ridden in the aisles by another actor dressed like Barney Google while the team sang the song. It caught on, with Eddie Cantor plugging it and with Georgie Price's recording. The writers capitalized on the song with a follow-up, "Come On, Spark Plug!" The covers of both songs had drawings by De Beck to help sell them. The last of their 1923 hits became a jazz standard, "You've Got to See Mamma Ev'ry Night (Or You Can't See Mamma at All)," initially made famous by "the last of the red-hot mamas," Sophie Tucker.

"Lonesome and Sorry" (1926), with Benny Davis again as lyricist, was featured by Davis in vaudeville. It was also featured by the young comedian Milton Berle. Jean Goldkette and his Orchestra recorded it for Victor.

Conrad went to California to write for the movies. His first assignment was for William Fox in 1929 to write the score for the FOX MOVIETONE FOLLIES. "Walking with Susie" was the best of the lot. In 1931, Conrad discovered Russ Columbo and became his manager, writing for him "Prisoner of Love" and "You Call It Madness But I Call It Love," to do vocal battle with his rival, Bing Crosby.

Conrad teamed with Herb Magidson (1906–1986) to write for films from 1934. That year, they won the first Oscar given for Best Song with "The Continental," from RKO's THE GAY DIVORCEE, starring Fred Astaire and Ginger Rogers.

Con Conrad died in Van Nuys, California, on September 28, 1938.

J. RUSSEL ROBINSON:
"Margie"

J. Russel Robinson was born in Indianapolis, Indiana, on July 8, 1892. He and his brother John were known as the "Famous Robinson Brothers" as they toured theatres, with Russel at the piano and John playing drums. Russel had his first composition, "Sapho Rag," published in 1909 by John Stark. "That Eccentric Rag" was published in his hometown in 1912 by a local music store, but when published by Jack Mills in 1923 as "Eccentric" (and with a recording by the New Orleans Rhythm Kings (Gennett 5009)), it became a favorite of jazz bands and remains a standard in their repertoire. From 1917 to 1925, he worked for the Imperial Player Rolls company and later for QRS, where he was introduced in their catalog as "the White Boy with the colored fingers." During the day he worked as a demonstrator for the Leo Feist Company in its Chicago branch. In 1919, Feist published a tune Robinson had written with Theodore Morse called "Lullaby Blues in the Evening," which was melodically the parent of "Margie."

Robinson came to New York and joined Pace & Handy as an arranger and as Handy's personal manager. He met minstrel singer Al Bernard (1888–1949) and they formed a vaudeville team, the Dixie Stars. They recorded for Columbia, Brunswick, Cameo and Okeh. They were the white version of Sissle and Blake, as Bernard sang while Robinson played piano (and occasionally joined in singing). They composed and made famous "Blue-Eyed Sally," "Let Me Be the First to Kiss You Good Morning," "Never Gettin' No Place Blues," and "Let My Home Be Your Home," among others.

Robinson briefly joined the ODJB for their tour to London in 1919, then rejoined them on their return to this country to make six extremely successful sides with the band, including the aforementioned "Margie" and "Palesteena."

Robinson teamed with Roy Turk (1892–1934) to write the successful "Aggravatin' Papa (Don't You Two-Time Me)" (1922) and "Beale Street Mama" (1923). Also in 1923 came "St. Louis Gal," which was featured by the St. Louis orchestra leader, Gene Rodemich. In 1926, Robinson wrote the classic "Mary Lou," which was introduced by Abe Lyman and his Orchestra and recorded by Pete Wendling on Cameo with a vocal by Frances Sper. Under the pseudonym "Joe Hoover," Robinson wrote another jazz favorite, "Rhythm King," which was first recorded by Bix Beiderbecke and His Gang. He moved to California to freelance and, in 1936, wrote "Swing, Mister Charlie."

J. Russel Robinson died in Palmdale, California, on September 30, 1963.

JIMMY DURANTE:
"Inka Dinka Doo"

Jimmy Durante was born in New York City on February 10, 1893. He began his career as a pianist at Coney Island in Brooklyn, where he was known as "Ragtime Jimmy." He also organized a five-piece jazz band there. While he is best known as a comedian, first with the team of Clayton, Jackson and Durante, in the mid-twenties, and later as a single in radio, movies and television, he composed his own specialty numbers ("Inka Dinka Doo," "I'm Jimmy the Well-Dressed Man," and "Umbriago"). He also turned out a batch of songs in the early twenties which created quite a stir.

His big year was 1921, first with the smash hit "I've Got My Habits On," which he composed to the lyrics of Chris Smith and Bob Schafer (1897–1943). Bennie Krueger, the original alto saxophonist with the ODJB, had his own dance orchestra and created a big plug with his recording (Brunswick 2181). This reception of a Durante tune led Joe Davis to sign Durante to a contract as a staff composer with his Triangle Music firm. With the same team, Durante wrote "Daddy, Your Mama Is Lonesome for You." Then, with Schafer and Dave Ringle (1893–1965), he wrote "Sweetness." With Sam Coslow, he wrote the harmonically interesting "I Didn't Start in to Love You," a tricky piece, which, when well played, is a mighty fine blues number. "I'm on My Way to New Orleans" and "One of Your Smiles" were written with Bartley Costello (1871–1941).

"I Ain't Never Had Nobody Crazy over Me" (1923), a fine, jazzy blues number, was co-written with two drummers, Johnny Stein and Jack Roth. "Papa String Bean" (1923) had lyrics by Al Bernard, the partner of J. Russel Robinson.

Jimmy Durante died in Santa Monica, California, on January 29, 1980.

PETE WENDLING:
"Oh! What a Pal Was Mary"

Pete Wendling was born in New York City on June 6, 1888. He was a self-taught pianist who learned to play from watching and listening to his idol, Mike Bernard, a ragtime champ who performed at Tony Pastor's Music Hall. When he was eighteen, Wendling won a national ragtime piano contest sponsored by *The Police Gazette*. He was proud of the gold medal he won, but even prouder when F. A. Mills took him on as a staff pianist. He joined Rhythmodik in 1914 as a piano roll artist, and later went with QRS (in 1919), where he made a great many rolls until he left in 1925.

He was a staff pianist at Waterson, Berlin & Snyder, where he met Lewis F. Muir and became Muir's vaudeville partner. They would eventually play the London Hippodrome.

Wendling's first rag was a collaboration with Harry Jentes entitled "Soup and Fish Rag" (1913), published by George W. Meyer & Company. With instruction in songwriting from both Muir and Irving Berlin, Wendling sold over one million copies of his first published song, "Yaaka Hula Hickey Dula," with Joe Young and E. Ray Goetz. Of course, it helped that Al Jolson used the song in his show ROBINSON CRUSOE, JR. (1916). Jolson also provided Wendling with his million-selling World War I favorite, "Oh! How I Wish I Could Sleep Until My Daddy Comes Home," with lyrics by Lewis and Young.

Wendling formed a partnership in 1919 with Bert Kalmar and Edgar Leslie. They produced two million-sellers and two nearly as successful. The two close-to-a-million sellers were "All the Quakers Are Shoulder Shakers Down in Quaker Town" and "Take Your Girlie to the Movies." The two million-sellers were "Oh! What a Pal Was Mary" and "Take Me to the Land of Jazz."

In August 1926, Wendling made some rare recordings at Cameo Records, four sides including two of his own brand-new songs, "Usen't You Used to Be My Sweetie?" and "I Meet Her in the Moonlight (But She Keeps Me in the Dark)," this last sung on the recording by Frances Sper. Although he made more than a thousand piano rolls, these four recordings do more to show the kind of pianist he was, for they demonstrate a light, bouncy touch with a lilting swing unlike that of any other pianist. It is a real loss that he didn't record more songs.

Wendling scored again in 1927 with "There's Everything Nice about You," with lyrics by Alfred Bryan. Two other songwriters, Al Bernard and Sammy Stept, made a lovely recording of it (Cameo 1141). "Red Lips, Kiss My Blues Away" (1927), also with lyrics by Alfred Bryan, had a marvelous recording by Mike Markel's orchestra (Okeh 40805) and a superb arrangement on piano roll by Jack Ward (Welte 75273).

Wendling and Jack Meskill wrote "There's Danger in Your Eyes,

Cherie!" (1929) for Harry Richman to sing in his film PUTTIN' ON THE RITZ.

The last major hit Wendling had was "On the Street of Regret" (1942), with John Klenner's lyrics (1899–1955), published by Loeb-Lissauer.

Pete Wendling died in Maspeth, New York, on April 8, 1974.

EUBIE BLAKE:
"I'm Just Wild about Harry"

James Hubert (Eubie) Blake was born in Baltimore, Maryland, on February 7, 1883. His first published compositions were "The Chevy Chase," a rag with an especially fine trio section, and "Fizz Water," both published in 1914 by Joseph W. Stern & Company. He met his lifelong friend and lyricist, Noble Sissle (1889–1975) in 1915, and they soon wrote their first song together, "It's All Your Fault," which Sophie Tucker introduced in her vaudeville act. It didn't do much commercially, but it did pave the way for their own sensational act, which they called the "Dixie Duo." As headliners in vaudeville, they featured their own songs with Blake at the piano. They made many recordings of their works and were the most successful black act of their time. They wrote the first all-black musical to play Broadway since Cole and Johnson's THE RED MOON in 1909. Their SHUFFLE ALONG (May 23, 1921) ran for a record-breaking 484 performances. Among the hits were "Bandana Days," "Gypsy Blues," "Good Night, Angeline," "I'm Craving for That Kind of Love," "I'm Just Simply Full of Jazz," "If You've Never Been Vamped by a Brownskin (You've Never Been Vamped at All)," "In Honeysuckle Time," "Love Will Find a Way," "Low Down Blues," and their biggest hit and most durable song, "I'm Just Wild about Harry." This last was composed by Blake as a waltz, but when his star Lottie Gee complained, he turned it into a snappy fox trot. Sissle's lyrics were virtually the same as the ones he did for their 1916 song, "My Loving Baby."

In 1923, the team made a sound-on-film short for broadcast pioneer Lee De Forest, called "Sissle and Blake's Snappy Songs," which included their "Affectionate Dan" and "All God's Chillun Got Shoes." This short, perhaps the very first film musical ever made, has survived and has been shown on several television documentaries about Eubie Blake.

For ANDRE CHARLOT'S REVUE OF 1924, the team wrote "You Were Meant for Me" (not to be confused with the song of the same title written by Nacio Herb Brown and Arthur Freed in 1929). This was the first song that Noel Coward and Gertrude Lawrence sang together in a show.

THE CHOCOLATE DANDIES (September 1, 1924) was the team's next Broadway show. While it was a slick and lavish production, the only song to emerge was the beautiful "You Ought to Know." (The haunting "Jassamine Lane" and Blake's own favorite of his songs, "Dixie Moon," were also in this score.) The team finally recorded "You Ought to Know" in March 1926 (Edison Bell Winner 4417). "I Wonder Where My Sweetie Can Be" (1925) appeared under the Jack Mills imprint and was recorded by the writers (Edison Bell Winner 4371), with an especially fetching ragtime solo chorus by Blake.

For BLACKBIRDS OF 1930 (October 22, 1930), Blake wrote "You're Lucky to Me," "That Lindy Hop," and his lovely "Memories of You," all with lyricist Andy Razaf. Even though Will Morrissey's HOT RHYTHM (August 21, 1930) was a flop, Blake's "Loving You the Way I Do" was definitely a hit.

An anthology revue of his works titled EUBIE! (September 23, 1978) had a successful run of 439 performances on Broadway. The show's namesake attended several performances and even performed several songs himself on opening night.

Eubie Blake died in Brooklyn, New York, on February 12, 1983, five days after his one-hundredth birthday.

ZEZ CONFREY:
"Kitten on the Keys"

Zez Confrey was born Edward Elzear Confrey in Peru, Illinois, on April 3, 1895. He studied at Florenz Ziegfeld, Sr.'s Chicago Musical College, where he was exposed to the French impressionist composers, who had a profound influence on his own composition. In 1915 he obtained a job demonstrating music for the Chicago branch of the Harry Von Tilzer Music Publishing Company. At the start of World War I, he enlisted in the Navy and was featured in a skit with a touring show, LEAVE IT TO THE SAILORS. Part of the routine paired Confrey and a violinist from Waukegan who eventually became known as Jack Benny. When the show broke up and he left the Navy, Confrey auditioned for the QRS piano roll company, where he was hired as an arranger and pianist. During his stay with QRS, he arranged and played one hundred and twenty-three rolls. His arrangements were consistently tasteful and filled with rollicking inspiration. His success in making rolls and composing hit tunes led him into recording (piano solos for Brunswick, Edison and Emerson, playing with an orchestra for Victor) and appearing in vaudeville. His first novelty rag was the revolutionary "My Pet," closely followed by his "Greenwich Witch," "Poor Buttermilk," "You Tell 'Em Ivories," "Coaxing the Piano," and, in 1921, his landmark "Kitten on the Keys." To insure the proper effect, Confrey said of "Kitten on the Keys' " third section, "Be sure to scramble up the octaves in the part which is supposed to sound like a cat bouncing down the keyboard. In other words, make a fist when simulating the cat running up and down, otherwise it won't sound real." The sheet music sold over one million copies, as did his recording of it (Victor 18900). It was like "Maple Leaf Rag" all over again: another difficult piano rag had defined a genre and had become a hit at the same time. "Kitten" was the most technically advanced rag yet to be published, and it sold quickly and enormously.

In 1922, Zez Confrey had three hits, "Dumbell," "Tricks," and the perennial favorite, "Stumbling," the first pop song to use a 3/4 rhythm inside a 4/4 time signature. Its opening chorus used the five-tone scale, later used by Irving Berlin in "Always," Richard Whiting in "Louise" and in "Breezin' Along with the Breeze," Vincent Rose in "Linger Awhile," and Hoagy Carmichael in "Ole Buttermilk Sky."

The following year, Confrey came out with another smash novelty piano rag, "Dizzy Fingers" and the clever "Nickel in the Slot." He was such an outstanding talent that he was asked to participate in an historic concert at Aeolian Hall. Held on February 12, 1924, the concert was billed as "Paul Whiteman and his Palais Royal Orchestra will offer an Experiment in Modern Music, assisted by Zez Confrey and George Gershwin." Later that year, he contracted to make piano rolls exclusively for Ampico. In 1933, he and Byron Gay wrote the hit "Sittin' on a Log (Pettin' My Dog)." He composed more than ninety pieces which influenced the playing of his contemporaries and created the vogue for novelty rags in the twenties.

Zez Confrey died in Lakewood, New Jersey, on November 22, 1971.

FATS WALLER:

"Ain't Misbehavin' "

Thomas "Fats" Waller was born in New York City on May 21, 1904. As a performer, he was the best known exponent of stride, a black piano style of the twenties, perfected by his teacher James P. Johnson, composer of "Charleston." Waller made piano rolls, as well as over five hundred records, had his own weekly network radio program, performed in Europe and England, and was featured in such films as HOORAY FOR LOVE, KING OF BURLESQUE, and STORMY WEATHER. After winning a Harlem piano contest with James P. Johnson's "Carolina Shout," he became a protege of the composer. Waller wrote scores for the musicals KEEP SHUFFLIN' (February 27, 1928), HOT CHOCOLATES (JUNE 20, 1929), AND EARLY TO BED (June 17, 1943).

He was a prolific songwriter who knocked 'em out for hamburger money. His first big hit was with Clarence Williams, "Squeeze Me," in 1925. His biggest year was 1929, with such standards emerging as "Ain't Misbehavin'," "Sweet Savannah Sue," "What Did I Do to Be So Black and Blue?," "Honeysuckle Rose," "I've Got a Feeling I'm Falling," and "My Fate Is in Your Hands." He continued in 1930 with "Blue Turning Grey over You," and in 1932 with "Keeping Out of Mischief Now." Most of these had lyrics by Andy Razaf (1895–1973). A revue featuring his songs (and songs associated with him) entitled AIN'T MISBEHAVIN' (May 9, 1978) had a run of 1604 performances on Broadway.

Fats Waller died of bronchial pneumonia aboard a train in Kansas City, Kansas, on December 15, 1943.

JELLY ROLL MORTON:
"Wolverine Blues"

Ferdinand "Jelly Roll" Morton was born in New Orleans, Louisiana, on October 20, 1890. He was a unique figure in American popular music. Everything he did was sparked with originality and almost everything had its controversial element. He created a style of arranging which encompassed other jazzmen's styles and yet retained his own conceptions. Morton's individual piano style was distinctive and, once heard, was never forgotten or confused with anyone else's. He had definite ideas about his music and was the most articulate jazzman of his time. There was nothing haphazard or accidental in his performing, arranging or composing, as each musical device was well thought out and deliberately executed. As both composer and performer, he created more diverse moods in his works than anyone else of his time. He also used unexpected rhythmic patterns to sustain audience interest. His use of sixths in the left hand provided uncommon voicings. What made his piano sound so distinctive, besides his touch, was his desire not to sound like a solo pianist, but to sound like an entire jazz band. His extraordinary left hand not only kept a steady rhythm like that of a tuba or string bass, but also incorporated the counterpoint of a trombone. His right hand alternated between the clear-cut melody line, as usually played by a trumpet, and the embellishments and flourishes of a clarinet. In performance, to complete the resemblance to a band, he would usually place a drumstick in his inner left shoe to beat against his bench or chair while playing.

Jelly Roll Morton had a vaudeville comedy act and was the first jazzman to travel extensively around the country, from the time he was fourteen until he settled in Chicago in 1923 at the age of 33. There he became a staff arranger and composer for the newly-formed Melrose Brothers Music Company. Although he had had one piece published earlier ("The 'Jelly Roll' Blues," issued by Will Rossiter in September 1915), his steady publishing, recording and performing careers dated from his arrival in Chicago. Encouraged by the sales of "Wolverine Blues" (1923), Walter Melrose set up recording sessions with Gennett Records of Richmond, Indiana. It was this company which eventually recorded every major dixieland jazz band, with the sole exception of the ODJB, and most of the important individual jazzmen of the twenties.

Between the eleven months of July 1923 and June 1924, Morton recorded nineteen now-classic piano solos, sixteen of them his own compositions, all of these eventually published by Melrose. The solo piano recordings were the start of his legend among his peers. His publications are important, not only as vehicles for himself, but as permanent parts of the jazz repertoire. The majority of his work was published by Melrose between 1923 and 1928.

"King Porter Stomp" was recorded more often by Morton and others than any of his other compositions. It was the first piano solo (Gennett 5289) he recorded at his first solo session on July 17, 1923, and it was among the last piano solos (General 4005) he recorded at his last solo session on December 14, 1939. This song started the swing era, when Fletcher Henderson arranged it for Benny Goodman's band in 1935. It has the distinction of being in the ragtimer's repertoire as well as those of dixieland bands and swing bands. Melrose published it in 1924.

"Milenberg Joys" led the eight Morton tunes published in 1925. Although it is a standard today and has been recorded by both dance and jazz bands through the years, it is the only one not recorded by Morton himself. His famous rags "Kansas City Stomp" and "Grandpa's Spells," as well as his "Chicago Break Down" and "Shreveport Stomp,"

"New Orleans Blues," "London Blues," and "Tom Cat Blues," were all issued during this same year.

Morton published six compositions in 1926. His "Sweetheart o' Mine" was a reworking of the earlier "Frog-I-More Rag," the lead sheet of which was entered for copyright in 1918. "Stratford Hunch" was the last of his original piano solos to be issued. Melrose obtained a contract with the Victor company for Morton to record with a seven-piece band of his choosing. It was to be an ideal band, for Morton was allowed to request his favorite musicians, those usually working in other people's bands. In an unusual arrangement, Morton hand-picked his band for recordings only and called his group the Red Hot Peppers. He did not have a working band at this time. Even though the personnel of the Red Hot Peppers changed during its four years of recording, the group never failed to provide stimulating jazz. The remaining tunes published in the exciting year of 1926 came directly from the recordings of the Red Hot Peppers: "Black Bottom Stomp," "Sidewalk Blues," "Dead Man Blues," and "Cannon Ball Blues."

Two old solos and four new ones account for his 1927 output. "The Pearls," with its clever use of the rudimentary timekeeping of the left hand, and "Mr. Jelly Lord" were finally issued. "Billy Goat Stomp," "Jungle Blues," "Wild Man Blues," and "Hyena Stomp" were other Red Hot Peppers tunes.

In 1928, Melrose published his "Boogaboo" and "Georgia Swing," a reworking of an earlier Melrose tune, Santo Pecora's "She's Crying for Me."

Morton reminisced, played, and sang his life story to Alan Lomax for the Library of Congress during a six-week period in May and June 1938, still the greatest documentary of a jazzman yet recorded.

Jelly Roll Morton died in Los Angeles, California, on July 10, 1941.

ELMER SCHOEBEL:
"Nobody's Sweetheart"

Elmer Schoebel was born in East St. Louis, Illinois, on September 8, 1896. His first jobs were playing piano and organ in movie houses. He went to Chicago in 1919, and, in 1922, he recorded with the Friar's Society Orchestra (which later changed its name to the New Orleans Rhythm Kings). He was an excellent jazz pianist and his work caught the jazz spirit, as exemplified by his first published compositions in 1923, "Blue Grass Blues," "The House of David Blues," "Bugle Call Rag," and

"Railroad Man," all with lyrics by Billy Meyers. Schoebel's "Farewell Blues" (1923) became the New Orleans Rhythm Kings' theme song and one of the standard tunes of the dixieland repertoire. Cornetist Paul Mares and clarinetist Leon Roppolo shared composer credit.

In 1924, Schoebel wrote a great jazz tune called "Prince of Wails," a punning title which referred to the then-popular Prince of Wales (later to become King Edward VIII), who was a jazz fan. His Friar's Society Orchestra made a superb recording of it in 1929 (Brunswick 4652), which featured Schoebel's marvelous piano playing. That year he also wrote, with the ubiquitous Gus Kahn and Ernie Erdman, what would become the standard "Nobody's Sweetheart."

Schoebel joined Isham Jones' orchestra in 1925, and played with them briefly in New York, where he composed "Everybody Stomp." Back in Chicago, he played with Louis Panico's band and also with Art Kassell's. During the day, he arranged and transcribed tunes for the Melrose Brothers Music Company, which published his "Spanish Shawl" (1925).

As did all of the better Chicago composers, he wrote with Gus Kahn. Besides "Nobody's Sweetheart," they wrote "Ten Little Miles from Town" (1928).

Schoebel spent over a decade (beginning in the mid-thirties) in New York City, where he was the chief musical arranger for the Warner Bros.-owned Music Publishers Holding Corporation.

Elmer Schoebel died in St. Petersburg, Florida, on December 15, 1970.

JAMES F. HANLEY:
"(Back Home Again in) Indiana"

James Frederick Hanley was born in Rensalaer, Indiana, on February 17, 1892. He attended Chicago Musical College and had his first hit with the World War I number "The Ragtime Volunteers Are Off to War" (1917), with lyrics by Ballard Macdonald. It was a featured number for Emma Carus. Later that same year, the team created "(Back Home Again in) Indiana," first recorded by the ODJB. Joe Goodwin joined the team to help produce "Breeze, Blow My Baby Back to Me" (1919).

Fanny Brice sang the Hanley-Macdonald "Rose of Washington Square" (1920) in the ZIEGFELD MIDNIGHT FROLIC, and it became a smash hit. Hanley followed it up the next year, with Grant Clarke writing the words to his "Second Hand Rose," which Fanny Brice sang in the ZIEGFELD FOLLIES OF 1921. The Virginians made a hit recording of the

Hanley-Goodwin collaboration "Gee! But I Hate to Go Home Alone" (1922). With B. G. DeSylva, Hanley wrote "Just a Cottage Small" (1925) for John McCormack, who sang it to success. For HONEYMOON LANE (September 20, 1926), Hanley collaborated with Eddie Dowling on the score, the big hit of which was "The Little White House (At the End of Honeymoon Lane)." And with Gene Buck, Hanley produced "No Foolin' " for ZIEGFELD'S AMERICAN REVUE OF 1926(June 24, 1926). Sam Lanin's Troubadours made a nifty version on disc (Banner 1753). His last hit came when he wrote "Zing! Went the Strings of My Heart" for Hal LeRoy and Eunice Healey to dance and sing in THUMBS UP! (December 27, 1934). Judy Garland sang it in LISTEN, DARLING (1938). James F. Hanley died in Douglaston, New York, on February 8, 1942.

MACEO PINKARD:
"Sweet Georgia Brown"

Maceo Pinkard was born in Bluefield, West Virginia, on June 27, 1897. He started with a theatrical agency in Omaha, Nebraska, where he had his first song published. It was called "I'm Goin' Back Home" (1915). From this inauspicious beginning, he came to New York, where he collaborated with William Tracey on his first million-selling hit, "Mammy o' Mine" (1919). His next success was "I'm Always Stuttering" (1922), which was styled after Zez Confrey's "Stumbling." This similarity was not lost on Confrey, who was asked to arrange it for piano roll (QRS 2079). Confrey took full advantage of the resemblance in his arrangement by including "Stumbling" rhythms whenever possible.

It wasn't until the mid-twenties that Pinkard hit his stride. For five years, he knocked out hit after hit, starting with "Sweet Georgia Brown" (1925), with lyrics by Ken Casey (1899–1965). It was introduced by bandleader Ben Bernie who, for plugging purposes, cut himself in on the song as co-composer, although he did no writing. The same year, this time with Roy Turk as his collaborator, Pinkard wrote "Sweet Man," a fox trot which was given a royal treatment on piano roll by Zez Confrey.

The team of Pinkard and Turk hit it big again in 1926 with "Gimme a Little Kiss, Will Ya Huh?," which was introduced by Guy Lombardo and given another big boost by Whispering Jack Smith, who cut himself in on the writing credits. The same year, the team created the snappy fox trot, "I Wonder What's Become of Joe?," introduced by Harry Reser's Seven Little Polar Bears.

Working with Billy Rose, Pinkard turned out "Here Comes the Show Boat" (1927), introduced by Ethel Waters in AFRICANA and later used in the first movie version of SHOW BOAT (1929). It was also used as the radio theme for MAXWELL HOUSE SHOW BOAT, a variety program. The same year, with Sidney Mitchell, he composed "Sugar," popularized by Ann Howe.

In 1928, Pinkard teamed with Archie Gottler (1896–1959) and Charles Tobias (1898–1970) to produce two big hits, "Don't Be Like That," which became a Helen Kane favorite, and "Lila," which Waring's Pennsylvanians recorded on a big-selling disc.

Pinkard alone wrote "I'll Be a Friend with Pleasure" (1930), which Bix Beiderbecke and his Orchestra recorded successfully, the orchestra including such latter-day bandleaders as Benny Goodman, Jimmy Dorsey, and Gene Krupa. For his last two hits in this depression year, Pinkard returned to his first New York partner, William Tracey, to write "Okay, Baby," recorded by McKinney's Cotton Pickers, and "Them There Eyes," which had several revivals, including a recording by Billie Holiday. Throughout his songwriting career, Pinkard seemed to collaborate only with white lyricists. If he weren't the only black composer to do this, he was certainly the first.

Maceo Pinkard died in New York City on July 21, 1962.

FRED ROSE:
"Red Hot Mamma"

Fred Rose was born in Evansville, Indiana, on August 24, 1897. A pianist as well as composer, singer, and eventual publisher, Rose started in Chicago, playing and singing in honky-tonks. He also made records for Brunswick and had his own radio show there. Since Chicago was the real hometown of twenties jazz, Rose's earliest compositions show the city's influence more than the songs of most of the composers of his day. They are highly syncopated.

Rose's first hit was "Sweet Mama, Papa's Getting Mad" (1920), recorded by the ODJB and featured in vaudeville by Sophie Tucker and her Kings of Syncopation. "Don't Bring Me Posies" (1921) was his next hit. He wrote several more songs, but it wasn't until the end of 1923 that he scored again, with the classic "Mobile Blues," which he wrote in collaboration with bandleader Albert E. Short. Jimmy Wade's Moulin

Rouge Syncopaters made the hit recording of it, quickly followed by Muggsy Spanier and his Bucktown Five.

"Red Hot Mamma" (1924) was a favorite of jazz bands, especially after the Original Memphis Five's version. Ray Miller's dance band came out with a recording of it and Sophie Tucker plugged it in vaudeville, where she was readily identified with it. As if to show his versatility, Rose produced the waltz-ballad "Honest and Truly" (1924), which sold over a million copies and started a short-term collaboration with Paul Whiteman and publisher Leo Feist. With Whiteman, in 1925, Rose wrote "Charlestonette" and "Flamin' Mamie," both recorded and plugged heavily by Whiteman. The last hit Rose produced in 1925, for Feist, was "Red Hot Henry Brown," which the Charleston Chasers made famous.

Back in Chicago, Rose wrote " 'Deed I Do" (1926), which Ben Bernie popularized, and "Deep Henderson" (1926), which was plugged and recorded by the unique Coon-Sanders Nighthawks.

In the thirties, Rose settled in Nashville, where he composed a series of country hits, started the most successful publishing company of hillbilly music, Acuff-Rose, and was most influential in creating the sound of country and western music of the forties. As a publisher, he is credited with the discovery of Hank Williams.

Fred Rose died in Nashville, Tennessee, on December 1, 1954.

LOU HANDMAN:

"Blue (and Broken Hearted)"

Lou Handman was born in New York City on September 10, 1894. Like the archtypical composers of the twenties, he started out as a piano accompanist for singers in vaudeville and then worked as a demonstrator for publishing firms.

Handman's first big hit was "Blue (and Broken Hearted)" (1922), with lyrics by Grant Clarke and Edgar Leslie. The Virginians, a "jazz" band within the Paul Whiteman Orchestra, made the hit recording for Victor, while Marion Harris started her association with Handman songs by making it a hit on Brunswick. Zez Confrey made an outstanding arrangement for QRS piano rolls. Later, Mildred Bailey revived it.

"My Sweetie Went Away" (1923) found its best plug in the Cotton Pickers' version (Brunswick's name for the Original Memphis Five), and Joe Raymond and his Orchestra recorded it for Victor. "Lovey Came Back" (1923), with words by the veteran team of Lewis and Young, sounded good to Marion Harris, who had previously scored with "Blue," and Ray Miller and his Orchestra performed it often. The Original Memphis Five (under their real name) liked it, too, and plugged it on Banner.

"I Can't Get the One I Want" (1924) was a favorite with the dance bands, as Paul Whiteman, Vincent Lopez, Paul Specht, Ray Miller, and Lanin's Arcadians all recorded it.

"I'm Gonna Charleston Back to Charleston" (1925) was not only a cute play on words, but a gem of a dance number as well. The California Ramblers, as well as Lou Gold's orchestra, featured it.

"Are You Lonesome Tonight?" (1927) was the musical question Handman asked, and Little Jack Little answered with a hit recording. Elvis Presley revived it with his hit recording in 1960.

Although Handman composed throughout the thirties, only "Puddin' Head Jones" (1933) was successful, featured by the upcoming Ozzie Nelson Orchestra.

Lou Handman died in Flushing, New York, on December 9, 1956.

TED FIORITO:
"Charley My Boy"

Ted Fiorito was born in Newark, New Jersey, on December 20, 1900. He became a demonstrator, playing piano for composer-publisher Al Piantadosi. Next, he formed a band to open the Oriole Terrace in Detroit, with Dan Russo as co-leader. Nick Lucas, later "The Singing Troubadour" in vaudeville, was their vocalist.

As a songwriter, Fiorito's most successful time was during the twenties, although his heyday as a bandleader came in the thirties. The Oriole Terrace Orchestra was in such demand that he took it to Chicago for a record-breaking four-year engagement at the Edgewater Beach Hotel. It was during this stay in Chicago that Fiorito wrote with master lyricist Gus Kahn.

Their first song hit, "Toot, Toot, Tootsie, Goo'bye!" (1922), was written with Ernie Erdman (1879–1946) and Dan Russo (1885–1956). The song was interpolated into BOMBO (October 6, 1921), where it was enthusiastically sung by Al Jolson. Jolson would eventually sing it in four movies spanning his entire career. The Oriole Terrace Orchestra's recording of it would seem to be definitive (Brunswick 2337), as the co-leaders of the group were half of the team who wrote it.

The next Fiorito-Kahn song hit was "No, No, Nora" (1923), thanks to Ruth Etting's plugging it and the Benson Orchestra's making a record of it. Max Kortlander made a wonderful arrangement for piano roll (QRS 2398).

The new team scored again the next year with "Charley My Boy" (1924). As might be expected, Charley Straight made one of his knockout arrangements for QRS, and Bennie Krueger's Orchestra helped to make it a success. Just a few years later, it became popular all over again when Lindbergh made his historic flight.

Their other 1924 number, "I Need Some Pettin' " with Robert A. King (1862–1932) as co-composer, became the jazz lovers' favorite because of the recording made by the Wolverine Orchestra (Gennett 20062) in June. The group consisted of Bix Beiderbecke on cornet; Jimmy Hartwell, clarinet and alto sax; George Johnson, tenor sax; Dick Voynow, piano; Bob Gillette, banjo; Min Leibrook, tuba; and Vic Moore, drums.

"Alone at Last" (1925) was another hit with Gus Kahn, this time because of the Coon-Sanders recording of it (Victor 19728). The band featured the beautiful ballad nightly at the Congress Restaurant. "I Never Knew" (1925) was the team's last hit together, and Roger Wolfe Kahn's recording helped it along.

"King for a Day" and "Laugh Clown Laugh" (both 1928) were written with Sam Lewis and Joe Young, the latter song as the theme for Lon Chaney's film of the same name. Again with Lewis and Young as collaborators, Fiorito had his last hit with "Then You've Never Been Blue" (1929).

His band took up much of Fiorito's energies during the thirties, when, at different times, he had young Betty Grable and June Haver as vocalists before they became movie stars. Fiorito and his orchestra appeared in films with Dick Powell and did many radio shows. He continued to lead an orchestra on the West Coast until the 1960's.

Ted Fiorito died in Scottsdale, Arizona, on July 22, 1971.

ISHAM JONES:

"It Had to Be You"

Isham Jones was born in Coalton, Ohio, on January 31, 1894. He started his musical training early and became proficient on the tenor saxophone. His first published composition, for which he wrote both words and music, "At That Dixie Jubilee," was published by him when he was living in Saginaw, Michigan, in 1915. From there he moved to

Chicago, where he organized a band that played at the Green Mill. In 1920, he opened the Rainbow Gardens and started recording for the new Brunswick Records, which was headquartered in Chicago. The band quickly established a national reputation through its recordings and, in 1922, added Louis Panico as lead trumpeter. Al Eldridge was pianist and shared the arranging chores with Jones. Eldridge wrote a beautiful number, "Think of Me" (1923), which the band recorded (Brunswick 2374) and on which he is featured. The band then moved to the College Inn at the Hotel Sherman for six years, where they became the preeminent dance band in Chicago. In 1924, Roy Bargy (1894–1974), composer-pianist for the Benson Orchestra, joined Jones to become his chief arranger and pianist after Eldridge died. Bargy was featured on their recording of "Charleston" (Brunswick 2970). Jones' band changed its style at the beginning of the thirties. He was the first to change the tempo of "Star Dust" from a snappy fox trot to a dreamy ballad, and his recording of it sent the song on its way to becoming the most recorded of all time. The band reached its peak of popularity during the years 1932–34. Jones finally broke up the band in 1936, with Woody Herman, his clarinetist, hiring most of the players and reforming them into another band and making it a cooperative venture.

Jones' songwriting career was a typical twenties success story, with his thirties efforts not meeting with such success. In 1922, he and James P. Johnson composed "Ivy," with words by Bert Williams' lyricist, Alex Rogers. It was a middling success, recorded by the band. Also in 1922, Jones teamed with the prolific Gus Kahn, who was to be his collaborator for several years. They wrote "Broken Hearted Melody" and "On the Alamo." By 1923, when they wrote the hardy perennial "Swinging Down the Lane," Jones was so famous that Leo Feist put his photograph on the cover of the sheet music.

The number of million-sellers which the team created in 1924 is truly amazing. Jones' wife gave him a baby grand piano for his birthday that year and *within an hour*, so the story goes, he composed "I'll See You in My Dreams," "The One I Love Belongs to Somebody Else," "Spain," and "It Had to Be You." Such a burst of creativity remains unparalleled, as each one is now a part of the standard repertoire. With such major hits, other good songs have been overlooked. One such was his 1924 ballad "Never Again," which his band recorded (Brunswick 2577) and to which Ruth Mack gave a sumptuous arrangement on a piano roll (Vocalstyle 12994). Another was their "Why Couldn't It Be Poor Little Me?" (1924), which Jones recorded with Ray Miller's Orchestra (Brunswick 2788). But jazz fans will always associate this song with the version cornetist Muggsy Spanier (1906–1967) made with The Stomp Six (Autograph 626), which included: Guy Carey, trombone; Volly de Faut, clarinet; Mel Stitzel, piano; Joe Gish, tuba; and Ben Pollack, drums.

Jones created many other songs, but it wasn't until 1931 that he and Charles Newman (1901–1978) wrote "You're Just a Dream Come True," which became the band's new theme song.

Isham Jones died in Hollywood, California, on October 19, 1956.

MILTON AGER:
"Ain't She Sweet?"

Milton Ager was born in Chicago, Illinois, on October 6, 1893. He began his career plugging and demonstrating music at the Chicago branch of Waterson, Berlin & Snyder in 1910. From there he became the vaudeville accompanist to Gene Greene, who was at that time singing "Melancholy Baby." (Earlier, Greene had sung his and Charley Straight's "King of the Bungaloos," a wonderful ragtime song.) When Ager came to New York in 1914, he learned what made a song popular by scoring for the staff writers at Waterson, Berlin & Snyder. He met Pete Wendling there and wrote a few undistinguished fox trots. When he returned from his military service at Fort Greenleaf, Georgia, he got a job with Leo Feist and collaborated with George Meyer and lyricist Grant Clarke on two "experience-based" songs: his first hit was the 1918 "Everything Is Peaches Down in Georgia," followed in 1919 by "Anything Is Nice If It Comes from Dixieland." These were both peppy numbers, not very far removed from the instrumental fox trots he had been turning out several years before.

Ager met his permanent lyricist Jack Yellen (1892–), and the two of them formed Ager, Yellen & Bornstein, with professional manager Ben Bornstein, in 1922. Their first published number was "Lovin' Sam (The Sheik of Alabam')," a song Sophie Tucker turned into a hit. It started Yellen's association with Tucker. He was to write special material for her over the next twenty years.

"Louisville Lou" and "Mamma Goes Where Papa Goes" were 1923 hits by the partners. Sophie Tucker introduced both numbers, and the comedy team of Greenlee and Drayton helped promote the first, while Jane Green with the Virginians recorded the second. Belle Baker also helped it along in vaudeville.

"I Wonder What's Become of Sally" was their big number for 1924. It was introduced by Van and Schenck, who made it a million-seller. The team wrote three more numbers that year. The first was "Big Boy," a super tune which the Wolverines recorded for Gennett, featuring Bix Beiderbecke not only on cornet, but also briefly on piano, quickly returning to cornet for the rest of the number. Sophie Tucker wasn't the only singer who liked the Ager-Yellen songs. Margaret Young did, too, and she recorded many of them on Brunswick. "Hard Hearted Hannah" was introduced on Broadway by Frances Williams in INNOCENT EYES. Paul Whiteman covered it, as did Herb Wiedoeft's Orchestra, on disc. The team's comedy number that year was "Big Bad Bill Is Sweet William Now," which enjoyed great popularity with Margaret Young's record, and with Healy & Cross in vaudeville.

"Could I? I Certainly Could" was one of their two 1926 novelty entries, which Sophie Tucker introduced. Bob Haring's Orchestra recording on Cameo almost matched Sid Sydney's for Victor for cleverness in arrangement. This was a fine, spirited comic song which would be heard over the next year, along with the others. The other novelty was "Hard-To-Get Gertie," given a peppy treatment by Irving Aaronson and his Commanders (Victor 20100).

If 1924 was Isham Jones' big year for hits, 1927 was Ager's and Yellen's big year, with five huge successes. "Ain't That a Grand and Glorious Feeling" was the first that year, followed by a big comic number, "Crazy Words, Crazy Tune (Vo Do De O)," which Irving Aaronson's orchestra made into a hit (revived in the mid-fifties by Jerry Lewis). "Is She My Girl Friend?" was given a huge send-off by the Coon-Sanders Nighthawks (Victor 21148). The Ager-Yellen ballad "Forgive Me" was sung by Lillian Roth, while Nat Shilkret made a beautiful arrangement on Victor records. Their "charleston" number, "Ain't She Sweet?," was their biggest hit. Frank Banta recorded it as a marvelous piano solo (Victor 20610).

"Hungry Women" (1928) was interpolated by Eddie Cantor into WHOOPEE and brought the house down. The team wrote most of the score of RAIN OR SHINE (February 9, 1928), and only the title song made a stir. "My Pet" (1928) was given a boost by Ernie Golden's Orchestra recording (Domino 4146).

The team went to Hollywood, where, in 1929, they wrote the score for Sophie Tucker's first film, HONKY TONK, which gave her "I'm the Last of the Red Hot Mamas." They also wrote the theme song for Dolores Costello's GLAD RAG DOLL. And for the MGM musical CHASING RAINBOWS, they wrote what became the theme song of the New

Deal, the song Democrats have used as their party's theme ever since, "Happy Days Are Here Again." It was revived by Barbra Streisand in 1963.

Milton Ager died in Los Angeles, California, on April 6, 1979.

HARRY AKST:
"Baby Face"

Harry Akst was born in New York City on August 15, 1894. He took classical piano lessons at the age of five but learned ragtime so that he could become a demonstrator for Leo Feist. For a brief time, he accompanied Nora Bayes in her vaudeville appearances. He was drafted during World War One and was sent to Camp Upton, where he met Private Walter Donaldson and Sergeant Irving Berlin. At war's end, Akst joined Berlin in his new publishing company as a staff pianist and as his amanuensis. He and Berlin wrote "Home Again Blues" in 1921 and scored with their effort. Aileen Stanley made the best recording of it. "A Smile Will Go a Long Long Way" (1923) was a collaboration between Akst and lyricist Benny Davis. Henry Santrey's plug began its sale of a million copies, and it later became the theme song of Sam Lanin and his Orchestra.

"Dinah" (1925) was Akst's first collaboration with the old pros Lewis and Young. It was introduced in THE NEW PLANTATION CLUB REVUE by Ethel Waters, who also made the first recording of it. It was a late interpolation by Eddie Cantor into KID BOOTS (December 31, 1923) and has been performed throughout the years in various films. Dinah Shore used it as her theme on radio and television. "Steppin' in Society" (1925) was a syncopated fox trot made popular by Ben Selvin (Vocalion 15038).

"Everything's Gonna Be All Right" (1926) had another Benny Davis lyric and was featured on record by Jane Gray, accompanied by Rube Bloom (Harmony 128), and by the Coon-Sanders Nighthawks on Victor. Akst and Davis' huge success that year was "Baby Face," which Eddie Cantor made famous. The first recording was made by Jan Garber's Orchestra, with lyricist Benny Davis as vocalist (Victor 20105). Al Jolson eventually sang it on the soundtrack of JOLSON SINGS AGAIN. Art Mooney's orchestra also revived it in the late forties.

The last major song by Akst was written with Grant Clarke for Ethel Waters' first film, ON WITH THE SHOW (1929). She brought the house down with her poignant rendition of "Am I Blue?" Her recording, accompanied by the Dorsey brothers and Frank Signorelli, was enormously popular.

Harry Akst later toured with Al Jolson as his accompanist. Akst died in Hollywood, California, on March 31, 1963.

JOSEPH MEYER:

"California, Here I Come"

Joseph Meyer was born in Modesto, California, on March 12, 1894. He entered the Alley in 1922 with an enormous hit, "My Honey's Lovin' Arms," with lyrics by Herman Ruby (1891–1959). It was a favorite of dance bands and jazz combos, with Isham Jones, Ray Miller, The Virginians, and Jazzbo's Carolina Serenaders (really the Original Memphis Five) making solid arrangements on records.

"California, Here I Come" (1924) was an inspiration of B. G. DeSylva. Its message echoed the composer's life, as he had come from California to New York, and wrote the song in New York. It would be some six years before he followed his own advice. When cut in on the writing credit, Al Jolson interpolated it into BIG BOY. The song was a natural for Jolson, and he helped make it a million-seller. He also sang it in the films ROSE OF WASHINGTON SQUARE (1939), THE JOLSON STORY (1946), and JOLSON SINGS AGAIN (1949). It was used as the theme song of the California Ramblers.

"A Cup of Coffee, a Sandwich and You" (1925) was placed in CHARLOT'S REVUE OF 1926 and sung by the stars Gertrude Lawrence and Jack Buchanan. Billy Rose and Al Dubin wrote the lyrics. "Sugar Plum" (1925), with lyrics by B. G. DeSylva, was interpolated into GAY PAREE and made famous by George Olsen and His Music for Victor Records. "If You Knew Susie" (1925) was originally written for Al Jolson, but, for once, he failed to deliver the expected hit, and it was Eddie Cantor who used it for the rest of his career. The song was placed in five different Broadway shows where it was featured by musical comedy stars. Practically every male performer in vaudeville sang it, and the sheet music sold well over a million copies. "Clap Hands! Here Comes Charley!" (1925) became the other famous Charley song, with lyrics by Billy Rose and Ballard Macdonald. Van and Schenck helped to popularize it, and the Goofus Five made a hit recording for Okeh.

"Crazy Rhythm" (1928) had lyrics by Irving Caesar, and Roger Wolfe Kahn (1907–1962) co-composed it and recorded it for Victor after having introduced it in HERE'S HOWE.

Joseph Meyer died in New York City on June 22, 1987.

HARRY RUBY:
"Three Little Words"

Harry Ruby was born Harry Rubinstein in New York City on January 27, 1895. His first love throughout his life was baseball. He probably wished he had written "Take Me Out to the Ball Game," and he actually played in an exhibition game in 1931 with the Washington Senators against the Baltimore Orioles. He once bragged to writer David Ewen, "I also played in a few major league exhibition games, and in four official games in the Coast League with the Hollywood Stars and Los Angeles Angels. All this, you will admit, is more than Mozart, Berlin, Gershwin, and Chopin can say." Max Wilk recounts the story of a lunchtime discussion at the Metro commissary between Joseph L. Mankiewicz and Ruby, wherein Mankiewicz put Ruby to the supreme test. "Let's assume you're driving along a mountain road, high up," he hypothesized. "You see a precipitous cliff with a sheer six-hundred-foot drop. Two men are hanging there, desperate. One of them is Joe DiMaggio, the other is your father. You have time to save only one of them. Which one do you save?"

"Are you kidding?" replied Ruby instantly. "My father never hit over .218 in his life!"

Ruby's musical life began when he got his first job working as a staff pianist for Gus Edwards in his publishing house. While doubling in vaudeville as the pianist of the Messenger Boys Trio, he met dancer Bert Kalmar (1884–1947), who also had a publishing company with Harry Puck (1890–1964), and he persuaded Kalmar to give him a job as staff pianist with his firm. (Puck worked with his sister Eva, and Kalmar and Puck had written the 1913 success "Where Did You Get That Girl?") It wasn't until he worked for Waterson, Berlin & Snyder that Ruby came up with his first hit, "What'll We Do on a Saturday Night When the Town Goes Dry?" (1919), for which he wrote both words and music. His mind was still on Prohibition when, the following year, he teamed with Bert Kalmar to write "Where Do They Go When They Row, Row, Row?" That same year the team came up with "So Long, Oo-Long." "My Sunny Tennessee" (1921) was featured by Eddie Cantor in THE MIDNIGHT ROUNDERS. "I Gave You Up Just Before You Threw Me Down" (1922) was made into a hit by Arthur Fields' Banner recording. In the same year, Kalmar and Ruby wrote for Van and Schenck "The Sheik of Avenue B," a take-off of Ted Snyder's mammoth hit, "The Sheik (of

Araby)." And the team wrote the lyrics to Ted Snyder's 1923 melody "Who's Sorry Now?"

They wrote the score for THE RAMBLERS (September 20, 1926), which starred Clark and McCullough, who made a hit of "All Alone Monday." For the score of THE 5 O'CLOCK GIRL (October 10, 1927), they wrote "Thinking of You." This song later became Kay Kyser's theme song. In GOOD BOY (September 5, 1928), they had "I Wanna Be Loved by You," and Helen Kane with her boop-boop-a-doop made it a hit in that show. For Groucho Marx in ANIMAL CRACKERS (October 23, 1928), they wrote "Hooray for Captain Spaulding," which was not published as a single sheet until 1956, when it became Groucho's theme for his television program.

Kalmar and Ruby went to Hollywood and shored up Amos 'n' Andy's film debut in CHECK AND DOUBLE CHECK (1930) by inserting their multi-million-selling "Three Little Words." It was next popularized on radio by Rudy Vallee.

"Nevertheless" (1931) was made into a hit by both Bing Crosby and Rudy Vallee. It was revived in a recording made in 1950 by the Mills Brothers.

For the film WAKE UP AND DREAM (1945) Ruby wrote the lyrics to Rube Bloom's music for "Give Me the Simple Life."

In 1950, MGM made a film biography of Ruby and Kalmar, THREE LITTLE WORDS, with Red Skelton playing Harry Ruby and Fred Astaire as Bert Kalmar. The score was, of course, an anthology of their hits. One song of Ruby's we'll never get to hear is the gag title he once asked Eddie Cantor to sing: "I'm Sorry I Made You Cry But Your Face Looks Cleaner Now."

Harry Ruby died in Woodland Hills, California, on February 23, 1974.

RAY HENDERSON:
"Five Foot Two, Eyes of Blue"

Ray Henderson was born Raymond Brost in Buffalo, New York, on December 1, 1896. After being trained at the Chicago Conservatory of Music, he came to the Alley to take a job as song plugger with Leo Feist. Shortly after that, he joined the Fred Fisher Company, where he was promoted from staff pianist to arranger. He next went to Shapiro, Bernstein & Company, where Louis Bernstein personally took an interest in him and got him jobs accompanying vaudevillian Elizabeth Brice, comedian Lew Brice, and several dance teams. These jobs gave him additional experience and insight into the specific musical needs of performers in the two-a-day crucible of vaudeville. His first published song was "Humming" (1920) for T. B. Harms, with lyrics by Lou Breau. Henderson had luck with collaborators named Lou (or Lew), as Bernstein soon introduced him to lyricist Lew Brown, who became a collaborator and partner in the most famous songwriting trio of the twenties. His first song with Brown was "Georgette" (1922), which was included in the revue GREENWICH VILLAGE FOLLIES OF 1922, played by Ted Lewis, whose band also made a successful recording of it.

His next with Brown was "Annabelle" (1923), which didn't set the world on fire, but later that year with Mort Dixon and Billy Rose, Henderson composed "That Old Gang of Mine," which did create sparks. This same team wrote "Follow the Swallow," which was placed in the GREENWICH VILLAGE FOLLIES OF 1924 and enjoyed a fine arrangement on George Olsen's recording. They also came up with "I Wonder Who's Dancing with You Tonight," "Lucky Kentucky," and "You're in Love with Every One" (this last without Billy Rose).

The big year for Henderson was 1925, when, with assorted collaborators, he turned out six hits in a row. "Alabamy Bound," with lyrics by B. G. DeSylva and Bud Green, sold over a million copies of sheet music. Al Jolson introduced it, but it was more often associated with Eddie Cantor, who interpolated it into KID BOOTS. " 'Bam, 'Bam, 'Bammy Shore," with lyrics by Mort Dixon, was made into a hit by Roger Wolfe Kahn's recording, and "If I Had a Girl Like You" (with help from Billy Rose) became a success largely because of Bennie Krueger's disc on Brunswick. The Henderson-Dixon-Rose team then wrote "Too Many Parties and Too Many Pals." "Don't Bring Lulu" had Rose and Lew Brown as lyric writers and was helped to hit status by performances of The Avon Comedy Four in vaudeville and on records by Jan Garber's Orchestra.

The two other Henderson hits in that fabulous year of 1925 had lyrics by Sam Lewis and Joe Young. "Five Foot Two, Eyes of Blue" didn't sell a million copies in its own time but has remained a favorite through the years. It caught the flapper era musically as John Held, Jr.'s illustrations did visually. It became a song for women singers, strangely enough, as Jane Gray (Harmony 114) and Esther Walker (Brunswick 3008) recorded it, each with accompaniment by Rube Bloom. "I'm Sitting on Top of the World" embodies the optimistic outlook of the times and was given beautiful arrangements on disc by Isham Jones' Orchestra and Roger

Wolfe Kahn's. The Canadian pianist Vera Guilaroff made an exquisite piano solo (Gennett 5750).

"Bye Bye Blackbird" (1926) had lyrics by Mort Dixon and was the last song for years that Henderson would write with anyone other than his soon-to-be partners, Lew Brown and Buddy De Sylva. This song was heavily plugged by Eddie Cantor, Georgie Price, and the Duncan Sisters. (The De Sylva, Brown and Henderson partnership is discussed in the theatre section of this chapter.)

After the partnership broke up, with Buddy De Sylva remaining in Hollywood as a film producer, Henderson and Brown stayed together for another three years. During that time, they wrote the score for GEORGE WHITE SCANDALS OF 1931. The biggest hit of that show was "Life Is Just a Bowl of Cherries," which was introduced and recorded by Ethel Merman and Rudy Vallee. Other hits from that revue were "This Is the Missus," "My Song," "That's Why Darkies Were Born," and "The Thrill Is Gone." This last became a favorite with Tony Martin years later.

For the Shirley Temple film CURLY TOP (1935), Henderson, with lyricists Ted Koehler and Irving Caesar, wrote her all-time favorite "Animal Crackers in My Soup."

Ray Henderson died in Greenwich, Connecticut, on December 31, 1970.

JIMMY MCHUGH:
"On the Sunny Side of the Street"

Jimmy McHugh was born in Boston, Massachusetts, on July 10, 1895. He became a song plugger for the Boston office of Waterson, Berlin & Snyder, joining the more than twenty others who bicycled around town playing and singing the firm's songs. He came to New York City in 1921 and joined the new Jack Mills organization as a staff pianist. "Stop Your Kiddin' " (1922) was a joint effort with Ferde Grofe and was plugged extensively on disc by the Original Memphis Five. His first hit was written with singer Gene Austin, "When My Sugar Walks Down the Street" (1924). "The Lonesomest Girl in Town" (1925) had lyrics by Al Dubin. "Everything Is Hotsy Totsy Now" (1925) was done with Irving Mills. "I Can't Believe That You're in Love with Me" (1926) was written with Clarence Gaskill.

BLACKBIRDS OF 1928 (May 9, 1928) was the first Broadway show that McHugh and Dorothy Fields (1905–1974) wrote. It Contained "Digga

Digga Do," "Doin' the New Low-Down" for Bill Robinson's great tap dance, "I Must Have That Man," and the frequently revived "I Can't Give You Anything but Love." (It has been said that McHugh bought the last song from Fats Waller and Andy Razaf and that Fields had no knowledge of this. Her name went on the song because she and McHugh were contractual partners for the show.) The song originally appeared in the flop revue HARRY DELMAR'S REVELS (November 28, 1927), but was placed in this all-black revue with great success. (When Andy Razaf was inducted into the Songwriter's Hall of Fame, Don Redman's wife asked which of his songs was his favorite. Razaf, in a wheelchair, motioned her closer and sang softly in her ear, "I can't give you anything but love, baby . . .").

THE INTERNATIONAL REVUE (February 25, 1930) was the next show the McHugh-Fields team wrote, and two hits emerged from the score. "Exactly Like You" and "On the Sunny Side of the Street" were both given to Harry Richman. Over the years, "On the Sunny Side of the Street" has been used in seven films and has been a favorite of such jazz performers as Louis Armstrong, Connee Boswell, Benny Goodman, Peggy Lee, Louis Prima and Fats Waller, all having made recordings of it.

EVERY NIGHT AT EIGHT (1935) was the first film to have a complete score by McHugh and Fields. "I Feel a Song Coming On" and "I'm in the Mood for Love" were the hits.

KING OF BURLESQUE (1935) sported McHugh tunes and Ted Koehler lyrics. Alice Faye sang "I'm Shooting High," while Fats Waller made the most of the cute "I've Got My Fingers Crossed."

STREETS OF PARIS (June 19, 1939) was a Broadway revue for which McHugh and Al Dubin wrote the score. It featured Carmen Miranda, who scored big with "South American Way." When she went to Hollywood the next year, she sang it in her film debut, DOWN ARGEN-TINE WAY.

HERS TO HOLD (1943) contained a Deanna Durbin wartime hit, "Say a Pray'r for the Boys Over There." Also in that year, McHugh and Harold Adamson wrote one of the better World War II songs, "Comin' in on a Wing and a Prayer."

A DATE WITH JUDY (1948) contained one of McHugh's happiest songs, "It's a Most Unusual Day," sung by Jane Powell. Margaret Whiting recorded it (Capitol 57-724) and helped make it a standard.

Jimmy McHugh died in Beverly Hills, California, on May 23, 1969.

HARRY WOODS:
"Side by Side"

Harry Woods was born in North Chelmsford, Massachusetts, on November 4, 1896. He was born with no fingers on his left hand, yet he learned to play the piano and could manage enough of a two-note bass line so that he could occasionally play professionally throughout his songwriting career.

Woods loved fishing and farming in his native New England. He began to dabble in songwriting in 1923, when he collaborated with Abner Silver (1899–1966) on "I'm Goin' South," which Al Jolson sang successfully in BOMBO. Lanin's Arcadians and Bennie Krueger's Orchestra recorded "Long Lost Mamma (Daddy Misses You)" (1923), which enjoyed substantial sales. But songwriting was still a hobby for Woods, who remained away from the Alley and stayed on his farm on Cape Cod. But when Cliff Edwards interpolated Woods' "Paddlin' Madeline Home" (1925) in SUNNY, Woods began to have second thoughts about songwriting.

The clincher that turned Harry Woods into a fulltime songwriter was his 1926 song, "When the Red, Red, Robin Comes Bob, Bob, Bobbin' Along," which sold over a million copies. The same year, he had minor hits with "Poor Papa (He's Got Nothin' at All)," with lyrics by Billy Rose, which was recorded successfully by both Fred Rich and Irving Aaronson. "Me Too" had words by Al Sherman and Charlie Tobias. Tobias introduced it in vaudeville and got Paul Whiteman to make a record of it.

"Side by Side" (1927) was a tremendous hit when Paul Whiteman recorded it, and the Duncan Sisters sang it in vaudeville. Kay Starr revived it in 1953 for another million-selling success.

"Just Like a Butterfly That's Caught in the Rain" (1927) was the work of Woods and lyricist Mort Dixon (1892–1956). It was sung successfully by Blossom Seeley. This new team came up with a perennial that same year when they wrote "I'm Looking Over a Four Leaf Clover." The Jean Goldkette recording featuring Bix Beiderbecke helped make the million sales. In 1947 it again topped the charts with Art Mooney's recording (M G M 10119), featuring the ex-Paul Whiteman banjoist, Mike Pingatore. It is the theme song of the Mummers' Parade held in Philadelphia each year.

"She's a Great, Great Girl" (1928) received a nice arrangement on Roger Wolfe Kahn's Orchestra's recording.

"A Little Kiss Each Morning (A Little Kiss Each Night)" and "Heigh Ho! Everybody, Heigh Ho!" (both 1929) were written for Rudy Vallee and his Connecticut Yankees for their film debut in THE VAGABOND LOVER.

"The Man from the South" (1930) was a collaboration with Rube Bloom (1902–1976), which Ted Weems and his Orchestra made into a hit record.

"When the Moon Comes over the Mountain" (1931) became Kate Smith's radio theme and the title of her first film. "River, Stay 'Way from My Door" (1931) had lyrics by Mort Dixon and was given a splendid piano roll arrangement by Lou Penn (Paramount 5876).

Before Woods went to England in 1932 to write for British-Gaumont films, he and Mort Dixon collaborated on "Pink Elephants," which Guy Lombardo plugged. This was also the year of his only collaboration with Gus Kahn. They wrote "A Little Street Where Old Friends Meet," which was played on radio and in clubs by Vincent Lopez. Later that year, he joined the English songwriting-publishing team of Reg Connelly and Jimmy Campbell to write "Try a Little Tenderness," which Ruth Etting and Eddie Duchin made popular in America, and Ray Noble and his Orchestra made popular in England. Campbell, Connelly and Woods also collaborated on "Just an Echo in the Valley," which Bing Crosby sang in the film GOING HOLLYWOOD (1933).

In 1935, Woods wrote the cute "I'll Never Say 'Never Again' Again."

A favorite story about Harry Woods typifies both the insouciance and the values of the Alleymen of his day. Woods' terrible temper and his love for strong drink were well known to his songwriter friends, as well as to the bartenders and customers of the clubs he played piano in. Woods once got into a yelling match with an equally inebriated customer. When the row escalated to the physical, the bartender called the police. As the police arrived, they found Woods sitting astride the chest of his foe, clutching his throat with his right hand and pounding a dent in the unfortunate patron's forehead with the stump of his left hand. As the combatants were separated, a woman entering the bar recoiled from the bloody sight. "Who is that horrible man?" she asked. Woods' crony, sitting at the bar, replied proudly, "That's Harry Woods. He wrote 'Try a Little Tenderness.' "

Harry Woods died in Glendale, Arizona, on January 14, 1970.

DANCES OF THE TWENTIES

The Shimmy

At the beginning of this decade, the shimmy introduced by Gilda Gray (1898–1959) was the craze in vaudeville and on Broadway. Ethel Waters (1900–1977) started her career as a shimmy dancer before she began singing and acting. Joe Gold and Eugene West summed it up in their song "Everybody Shimmies Now" (1918), which had a photo of Mae West (1893–1980) on the cover. That the dance was still going strong four years later was evidenced by Armand J. Piron's song "I Wish I Could Shimmy Like My Sister Kate" (1922).

The Charleston

The dance that captivated the nation and defined the defiant spirit of the twenties is the Charleston, which first appeared in the Broadway show RUNNIN' WILD (October 29, 1923). Elisabeth Welch introduced the song in this show, composed by James P. Johnson (1891–1955) and written by Cecil Mack. (They also wrote the standard "Old Fashioned Love" for this production.) Not only did the "Charleston" influence other songs with its rhythm, it also inspired a host of numbers that used the word in its title: "Charleston Baby of Mine," "Charleston Ball," "Charleston Cabin," "Charleston Capers," "Charleston Charlie." Zez Confrey wrote "Charleston Chuckles," and Fats Waller wrote "Charleston Hound." Others included "The Charleston Didn't Come from Charleston," "Charleston Rhythm," "Charleston Stampede," "Charleston Your Blues Away," and, finally, in 1926, William Holmes' "Everybody's Charleston Crazy." James P. Johnson and Cecil Mack followed their original hit with "Everybody's Doin' the Charleston Now."

Two other dances, novelties and variations of the Charleston, didn't last very long. However, their songs lasted and have become standards. One was the De Sylva-Brown-Henderson "Black Bottom," which first appeared in GEORGE WHITE'S SCANDALS (June 14, 1926). It was introduced by little Ann Pennington, who had performed in the ZIEGFELD FOLLIES since 1913. The same team wrote "The Varsity Drag" (1927) for their show GOOD NEWS, for a dance which featured the entire chorus line.

The Fox Trot

Fox trots became the staple of the social dance floor, making the jazz bands and dance bands very important. Describing the new recording of "Dumbell" by Zez Confrey and his Orchestra, the writer of the blurb in the Victor Records bulletin of March 1923, commented, "The fox trot today is the greatest social dance of the entire world. It has gone far beyond the waltz, the polka, the tango. Where the oldtime dancer 'knew' a dozen dances, the fox trotter only needs to know one. Everything that can be readily stepped off has been incorporated into it—the light kicks of the polka, the whirls of the waltz, the long curves of the tango, a lot of baby-steps anyone ought to pick up without trouble in two minutes, and a lot more from dances the present generation never heard of . . . Instruments appear when least expected, and do the least expected things; but you are fox trotting all the time, without a falter, and wondering, probably, why it is you are dancing so well."

There were many fine bands playing throughout the country, most of them recording in either New York or Chicago studios. Some record companies went in search of regional talent, Okeh and Victor among the more prominent, carting their not-so-portable equipment from town to town. Much good local music, which would be otherwise lost to us, is to be found on dance records from the twenties. The nationally known bands were recording for Brunswick, Columbia, Okeh and Victor, the latter having the largest talent roster and the largest distribution in the country. Paul Whiteman had the largest and most famous orchestra of the time.

PAUL WHITEMAN:
"Whispering"

Paul Whiteman (1890–1967) was a large man, and it seemed that the size of his original band (nine) increased in proportion to his waistline as his career flourished during the twenties. (His band stopped at thirty-four, but his waistline didn't.) His first group, called the Ambassador Orchestra, made its first recording for Victor on August 9, 1920. Whiteman was leader and violinist; Henry Busse, trumpet; Buster Johnson, trombone; Gus Mueller, clarinet and alto sax; Hale Byers, soprano sax, alto sax and flute; Ferde Grofe, piano and arranger; Mike Pingatore, banjo; Sammy Heiss, tuba; and Harold McDonald, drums. There were three sessions before a record was finally released, the first being "Japanese Sandman" backed with "Whispering" (Victor 18690). It sold well over a million copies, made both songs hits (and standards), and established Whiteman as a major force in popular music.

Ross Gorman (1890–1953) was soon to replace Gus Mueller and become the most influential reed player in dance orchestras. He played every reed instrument (the bass clarinet is a particularly nice touch on "Nobody Lied When They Said That I Cried over You") and was the creator of the three-octave clarinet run at the beginning of the "Rhapsody in Blue." He played the "Rhapsody" at its Aeolian Hall debut and on the two recordings the band made for Victor (the first acoustical on Victor 55225, the second electrical on Victor 35822).

The band's first arranger was Ferde Grofe (1892–1972), who composed the well-known "Grand Canyon Suite" (from which "On the Trail" was the most famous section, thanks to its use by Philip Morris cigarettes as their theme for radio commercials). Grofe created memorable arrangements of pop songs in the "symphonic jazz" style that gave the band its distinctive sound. He orchestrated the first version of Gershwin's "Rhapsody in Blue" for the concert held on February 12, 1924, as well as all of the other selections performed that evening. Grofe was also in charge of making the arrangements for the tunes The Virginians recorded. This was a sub-group of the Whiteman orchestra used by Victor to fill the loss of the ODJB to the company when they disbanded. Victor didn't want another real jazz band like the ODJB but did want a group it could call a jazz band, one which played with less abandon. The only problem for jazz fans was that everything the Virginians recorded was scored, whereas real jazz bands improvised. That Grofe succeeded at all was due to his skill in writing what sounded like improvisations. The Virginians were led by Ross Gorman, who, in the year of the group's creation, co-wrote the hit "Rose of the Rio Grande" (1922) and recorded it (Victor 19001) with Grofe's arrangement.

From the jazz fan's perspective, the most interesting band Whiteman ever had existed from November 1927 through September 1929, when it included Bix Beiderbecke on cornet, the Dorsey brothers—Tommy on trombone and Jimmy on clarinet and alto sax—Frank Trumbauer on C melody sax, and Bill Challis as arranger.

The Whiteman band performed in the pit for such Broadway musicals as GEORGE WHITE'S SCANDALS OF 1922 (August 28, 1922), LUCKY (March 22, 1927), and JUMBO (November 16, 1935), wherein Whiteman rode an elephant while conducting his orchestra! The band made its first film in 1930, KING OF JAZZ, a title bestowed upon Whiteman by his press agent after the historic concert at Aeolian Hall.

The Rhythm Boys (Harry Barris, Al Rinker and Bing Crosby) became the band's first vocal group. Mildred Bailey was its first female vocalist. Some of the sidemen and vocalists during the thirties included Ramona Davies, Johnny Mercer, Jack Teagarden, Bunny Berigan, Miff Mole, Frank Signorelli, Clark Dennis, Joan Edwards, and The Modernaires.

Throughout the thirties, Whiteman appeared on radio, with his own show and as a frequent guest on other programs. He appeared in the films THANKS A MILLION (1935), STRIKE UP THE BAND (1940), ATLANTIC CITY (1944), and RHAPSODY IN BLUE (1945). Whiteman became involved with television early on and hosted a teenage dance show in the early fifties. He was a most important influence in American popular dance music.

JEAN GOLDKETTE:
"Sunday"

Jean Goldkette (1899–1962) formed his big dance band, which started recording for Victor in 1924, when he bought and ran Detroit's Greystone Ballroom. His recording band made a mere twenty sides from October 12, 1926, until September 15, 1927, and is arguably the finest dance band in the United States during this decade. With minor changes through the year (the addition of Billy Murray as vocalist on "I'm Looking over a Four Leaf Clover," Danny Polo's replacing Don Murray on clarinet, or Itzy Riskin's replacing Paul Mertz on piano), the band's personnel consisted of: Bix Beiderbecke, cornet; Fuzzy Farrar and Ray Lodwig, trumpets; Bill Rank and Spiegle Wilcox, trombones; Don Murray, clarinet, alto sax and baritone sax; Doc Ryker, alto sax; Frank Trumbauer, C melody sax; Joe Venuti, violin; Paul Mertz, piano; Howdy Quicksell, banjo; Eddie Lang, guitar; Steve Brown, string bass; Chauncey Morehouse, drums; and Bill Challis as arranger.

COON-SANDERS NIGHTHAWKS
"Here Comes My Ball and Chain"

The Coon-Sanders Original Nighthawk Orchestra was a unique band. Its amazing popularity transcended its own time and is vividly remembered today by a fan club which meets annually, with a festival devoted entirely to it and its tunes. The original band, its arrangements and particular band members, created a sound and spirit unlike any of the hundreds of other bands throughout the twenties.

Carleton A. Coon (1894–1932) and Joe L. Sanders (1896–1965) met in a Kansas City, Missouri, music store. As a result of that chance meeting, they formed a dance band which was jazz-oriented. Coon was the drummer and shared vocal duties with Sanders, the pianist and arranger. The distinctive arrangements made by Sanders featured the spreading of the voicings in the saxophone section, letting each of those instruments be clearly heard, whether in solo or ensemble playing. The Sanders arrangements included modern harmonies and sophisticated modulations, sometimes within a measure of an ancient ragtime break. Their careful blend of old and new sounds made this band distinctive from its heyday forward. Sanders also composed special instrumentals, as well as pop songs, which became audience favorites.

This band was one of the first to appear on radio, with a nightly show over station WDAF in the Muehlebach Hotel in Kansas City. They broadcast from eleven at night till two in the morning, forming the "Knights and Ladies of the Bath" and giving themselves the name Nighthawks. Western Union installed a ticker tape in the ballroom so that the leaders could play requests and acknowledge their fans while on the air. During those pioneering radio days, the band, broadcasting late at night, could be heard halfway around the country. Their announcer, or as they called him, "The Merry Old Chief," was Leo Fitzgerald. Sanders was a grand showman and air personality, full of warmth and good cheer. Coon and Sanders were featured on practically every number, either alone or in a duet, their voices blending perfectly.

In 1924 the Nighthawks went to Chicago, where they played at the Congress Hotel. They started making their more than eighty sides for the Victor Talking Machine Company in April of that year. Their first recording was of their theme song, "Night Hawk Blues" (1924), with words and music by Sanders. The band became so popular that, when the Blackhawk Restaurant opened in 1926, it booked the Coon-Sanders Orchestra. They also began broadcasting nightly over station WGN, solidifying their nationwide popularity. When they went on tours, playing college dances and other one-night stands, they were always sold out.

The Sanders instrumentals included "High Fever" (1926) (Victor 20461), "Brainstorm" (1926) (Victor 20390), "Roodles" (1927) (Victor 20785), and "Blazin' " (1928) (Victor 21680). Sanders' pop songs included "Sluefoot" (1927) (Victor 21305), "What a Girl! What a Night!" (1928) (Victor 21803), "Little Orphan Annie" (1928) (Victor 21895), with lyrics by Gus Kahn, and "Tennessee Lazy" (1929) (Victor 21939), with lyrics by Carleton Coon. During the twelve years it was together (1920–1932), the band's personnel remained amazingly constant. The men's personalities reflected their lively, happy music and they were a contented group. For the last seven years, the personnel didn't change at all. The band consisted of: Bob Pope and Joe Richolson, trumpets; Rex Downing, trombone; Harold Thiell, John Thiell, Floyd Estep, on clarinet, alto sax, and tenor sax respectively; Joe Sanders, piano and vocal; Russ Stout, banjo; Elmer Krebs, tuba; and Carleton Coon, drums and vocal. The band's big request number was "Here Comes My Ball and Chain" (1929), a marvelous comic song written by J. Fred Coots and Lou Davis (Victor 21812). They also scored heavily with "Darktown Strutters' Ball" (Victor 22342), "Some of These Days" (Victor 19600), and "On Revival Day" (Victor 22979).

The Coon-Sanders Orchestra was truly a twenties musical highlight.

ORIGINAL MEMPHIS FIVE:
"Great White Way Blues"

The exciting, vibrant sounds of the Original Memphis Five are still overwhelmingly joyous to hear. The Original Memphis Five was unlike any other small jazz band of the twenties. To begin with, they are hardly ever mentioned in jazz history books, and yet they exerted the greatest influence of all jazz bands on the public. They did not play at the usual dance halls (or unusual ones, for that matter), nor did they make the obligatory tours which so exhaust musicians. They were a studio group, in existence only to make records, not perform live for the public. And make records they did—more than any other group of their time! Just how many they made is still a question, as they recorded for many record companies under a host of pseudonyms. In addition to their "official" name, they recorded as Bailey's Lucky Seven, The Cotton Pickers, Jazzbo's Carolina Serenaders, Ladd's Black Aces, Lanin's Southern Serenaders, McMurray's California Thumpers, New Orleans Blackbirds, and the Tennessee Ten.

Their "official" name is misleading, as they didn't come from Memphis, nor were they always five in number. The founding members, Frank

Signorelli (piano) and Phil Napoleon (trumpet), were the original groupies of the ODJB. They and their friends, Miff Mole (trombone), Jimmy Lytell (clarinet), and Jack Roth (drums), would follow the ODJB from job to job, even sitting in with their idols when one or several didn't show up for the evening. Frank Signorelli (1901–1975) was the luckiest of the admirers, as he actually got to record with the ODJB.

The Original Memphis Five's prolificacy gave them a unique standing in the record business. Their special sound (mainly emanating from Napoleon) and easy tempos made their music ideal for dancing. The distinctive sound of this group is at its purest when the two leaders play a chorus together. Phil Napoleon (1901–) invariably mutes his trumpet for an intimate feeling, allowing Signorelli's sensitive and rhythmical piano backing to provide the basic animation and impetus for the rest of the band. Jimmy Lytell's clarinet is directly inspired by the ODJB's Larry Shields, but with a fuller tone. The Original Memphis Five's drive and the ability to ad-lib made their music ideal for listening and fun to dance to. As a result, the Original Memphis Five made a profound impression on the record-buying public during the 1920's, one which is still not fully appreciated. This is probably the only jazz group to remain fairly anonymous despite a readily identifiable sound. Their collective record sales were phenomenal.

It is not surprising to find Jack Mills publishing the compositions of the Original Memphis Five (or, more properly, those by Napoleon and Signorelli), as the band was plugging all of Mills' hot numbers on records. The best of the published Napoleon-Signorelli tunes seem to come from the year 1923, although their recordings of them started in late 1922. "Memphis Glide" became the group's theme song (Perfect 14132). "Great White Way Blues" (Vocalion 14527) and "Shufflin' Mose" (Perfect 14150) were published by Mills and achieved some success in sheet music. "Snuggle Up a Bit" and "Teasin' Squeezin' Man o' Mine" (both on Pathe 036043) and "Just Hot," written with Jimmy McHugh (Brunswick 2507), were hot record sellers. "Sioux City Sue" (1924) (Pathe 036072), written with Walter Donaldson, is not to be confused with the 1945 pop song of the same name. The first one didn't go anywhere. Also in 1924, Napoleon and Signorelli composed "The Meanest Blues" (Perfect 14323) and "Mama's Boy" (Pathe 036168). In the thirties, Signorelli became a composer of song hits, such as "A Blues Serenade," "I'll Never Be the Same," and "Stairway to the Stars."

While their output was unusually large, the Original Memphis Five's repertoire was not correspondingly large, because they would record the same tune for a dozen different recording companies. But this apparent drawback affords us the rare opportunity of listening to just how creative they were, as each rendition was a separate and individual one, not using the same stock arrangement take after take. The band still communicates its excitement and enthusiasm to its listeners through its original recordings.

KING OLIVER'S CREOLE JAZZ BAND:
"Dippermouth Blues"

Joe "King" Oliver (1885–1938) assembled the first of the great black jazz bands in Chicago. He came from New Orleans, where he had played in Kid Ory's band. He left New Orleans permanently in 1918 and became popular with the Chicago public. He assembled his Creole Jazz Band in mid-1922 for a job at the Lincoln Gardens on Chicago's South Side. He brought Louis Armstrong (1901–1971) from New Orleans, and the band made its first recordings for Gennett Records in various sessions from April 6 to October 5, 1923. The band consisted of: King Oliver and Louis Armstrong, cornets; Honore Dutrey, trombone; Johnny Dodds, clarinet; Lil Hardin, piano; Bill Johnson, banjo; and Warren "Baby" Dodds, drums.

The Creole Band was the most popular band on the South Side at that time, and its two cornets playing spontaneously at the same time created tremendous excitement. The amazing gift that Armstrong had of improvising a second cornet part to King Oliver's lead has never been duplicated. They ad-libbed duets!

As with the ODJB, the Creole Jazz Band's importance to the history of jazz lies in its contribution to jazz composition. The tunes were mostly composed by King Oliver, some with the help of Armstrong, others with Lil Hardin (later the second Mrs. Armstrong). Oliver's compositions included: "Canal Street Blues," "Chimes Blues," "Dippermouth Blues," "Snake Rag," "Alligator Hop," "Zulu's Ball," and later tunes, "Snag It," "West End Blues," and "Doctor Jazz." When Melrose finally published "Dippermouth Blues" in 1926, its name was changed to "Sugar Foot Stomp." It was only one of two times the band's photo appeared on a sheet music cover.

LOUIS ARMSTRONG'S HOT FIVE:

"Muskrat Ramble"

Louis Armstrong was the most creative and inspiring cornetist in jazz history. More trumpeters (and other jazzmen, such as Earl Hines) took inspiration straight from his phrasing and either directly copied him or tried to make his ideas their own.

He began recording with his Hot Five in November 1925, for Okeh Records. The personnel included: Louis Armstrong, cornet; Kid Ory, trombone; Johnny Dodds, clarinet; Lil Armstrong, piano; and Johnny St. Cyr, banjo. Along with the ODJB and King Oliver recordings, the Hot Five and Hot Seven discs provide the basic jazz repertoire. Kid Ory's classic "Muskrat Ramble" was initially recorded by the Hot Five, as was Boyd Atkins' "Heebie Jeebies" (1926). "Heebie Jeebies" is the only song sheet to feature a photo of the Hot Five on a sheet music cover. Armstrong composed such tunes for his band as "My Heart," "Cornet Chop Suey," "Potato Head Blues," "Wild Man Blues," "Struttin' with Some Barbecue," and the later "Someday You'll Be Sorry."

Throughout his working life, Louis Armstrong was a source of inspiration to jazzmen and songwriters. In 1964, his recording of "Hello, Dolly" displaced the Beatles from their accustomed place at the top of the charts. In 1988, Armstrong once again led the list, with his 1967 performance of "What a Wonderful World," which was used on the soundtrack of GOOD MORNING, VIETNAM.

MUSICAL THEATRE IN THE TWENTIES

GEORGE GERSHWIN:

"Fascinating Rhythm"

George Gershwin was born Jacob Gershvin in Brooklyn, New York, on September 26, 1898. After taking classical piano lessons, he was told by his friend Ben Bloom, who was working for Jerome H. Remick, that the company had an opening for a demonstrator and song plugger. In May 1914, Gershwin applied for and obtained that job, which paid fifteen dollars a week. There was a conflict of interest, however, as Gershwin was much more interested in showing off his own compositions than in playing the firm's. When he finally submitted some of his own songs for consideration by Remick's, he was told that he was hired as a demonstrator, not as a composer.

Gershwin got his first break when Sophie Tucker took his manuscript of "When You Want 'Em, You Can't Get 'Em, When You've Got 'Em, You Don't Want 'Em" to Harry Von Tilzer. Von Tilzer liked it, and on May 15, 1916, he became the first publisher to print a Gershwin song. As lyricist Murray Roth had sold his share in the song to Gershwin for fifteen dollars, Gershwin decided to gamble on a royalty. He got only five dollars in advance, but the song sold so few copies that this was the only money he would make on it.

Gershwin's piano playing was a cause of comment around the Remick offices. He was using advanced harmonies and striking rhythms in his playing, not just "pounding it out" like his colleagues. Other pluggers who heard Gershwin when they were working the music stores agreed that he had "something else." In late 1915, Gershwin started making piano rolls for the Standard Music Roll Company, manufacturers of Perfection Rolls. He turned them out with regularity and they appeared, not only under his own name, but also as being played by James Baker, Bert Wynn or Fred Murtha, all "house names" of fictitious Perfection artists. Felix Arndt, composer of "Nola," was instrumental in getting him to make rolls for the Aeolian Company in 1916. Aeolian was a large outfit with several different labels, and Gershwin was to make over one hundred rolls for them.

It is ironic that after Gershwin left Remick's in March 1917, the firm immediately accepted a rag he wrote with Will Donaldson (1891–1954) and published "Rialto Ripples" in June, with Mose Gumble as house plugger. It was in late September that Gershwin became the rehearsal pianist for MISS 1917, an extravaganza with music by Victor Herbert and Gershwin's idol Jerome Kern (with lyrics by P. G. Wodehouse). Gershwin not only met the eminent composers, but got a chance to play some of his songs for the chorus and stars. After the show closed, one of the young stars, Vivienne Segal, took "You-oo Just You," with words by Irving Caesar (1895–), to sing in vaudeville. It, too, was published by Remick's, but this time the sale was handled much differently. Seated behind his desk was the formidable Fred Belcher, general manager of the largest publishing house in the Alley. The young and inexperienced Irving Caesar sang while Gershwin played their song for the great man. Each had been hoping that they might make twenty-five dollars apiece for their effort. After the demonstration, Belcher said, "Well, boys, how about two hundred and fifty dollars?" Caesar and Gershwin looked at each other, speechless. Seeing them hesitate, Belcher then said, "Tell ya what, boys, I'll pay you five hundred dollars instead."

Early in 1918, Gershwin was hired by Max Dreyfus at T. B. Harms to write songs for thirty-five dollars a week, plus a fifty dollar advance and three cents a copy royalty on each song accepted. From this point forward, Harms was Gershwin's publisher. The first occasion Dreyfus had to place a Gershwin song was in Nora Bayes' show LADIES FIRST (October 24, 1918), where she sang "Some Wonderful Sort of Someone." The lyrics were by sometime Kern lyricist Schuyler Greene (1880–1927), and the published song was issued when the show was in tryouts on the road and still titled LOOK WHO'S HERE.

The next interpolation came in February 1919, when GOOD MORNING JUDGE opened with two Gershwin-Caesar songs. "I Was So Young (You Were So Beautiful)" became a hit.

The first complete Broadway score by Gershwin was for LA, LA LUCILLE, which opened on May 26, 1919. It contained seven published songs, none distinguished, but Gershwin had a score to his credit. The show ran a respectable 104 performances and produced "Nobody But You," which was added after the opening. The post-Broadway tour was mounted by the son of the show's producer, Alex Aarons, who, with Vinton Freedley, would produce six Gershwin musicals, five of them hits!

It was later in 1919 that Gershwin was asked to write a couple of numbers for the opening of the Capitol Theatre, a new movie palace on Broadway. This event was to be celebrated by a revue called DEMI-TASSE (October 24, 1919). One Gershwin entry was "Swanee," with lyrics by Irving Caesar. It was used in the show as a production number, with dance master Ned Wayburn choreographing the song for sixty chorus girls with electric lights on their slippers. Despite this impressive setting, the demand for the sheet music sold in the lobby was next to nothing. It wasn't until Irving Caesar took the song to his friend Al Jolson and asked him to sing it that the song became a hit. Jolson put it into his SINBAD, his current show at the Winter Garden, and made a recording of it for Columbia (A-2884). With a full-page headshot of Jolson on the cover, "Swanee" sold over a million copies of sheet music and two million copies of his disc. It became the biggest-selling song Gershwin would have in his life.

George White (1890–1968), the dancer-director turned impresario, created his SCANDALS to rival Ziegfeld's FOLLIES. For the second SCANDALS, the edition of 1920, Gershwin composed six songs that were published. Of them, "Scandal Walk" achieved a mild success and was introduced in the show by dimple-kneed Ann Pennington, herself usually a star of the FOLLIES.

"Waiting for the Sun to Come Out" was George's first collaboration with his brother Ira (1896–1983). Ira wrote it under the combined names of one of his brothers and one of his sisters, "Arthur Francis." It was interpolated into THE SWEETHEART SHOP (August 31, 1920) and later published with a show cover. Previously, Ira had written lyrics to George's music for "The Real American Folk Song (Is a Rag)" (1918) for LADIES FIRST, but it wasn't published until 1959, after Ella Fitzgerald had included it in an album of Gershwin songs, with a special ragtime piano accompaniment by Lou Busch, then better known as Joe "Fingers" Carr.

"The Yankee Doodle Blues" had lyrics by Irving Caesar and B. G. De Sylva and was interpolated into SPICE OF 1922. It didn't sell much sheet music until Al Jolson started plugging it and jazz bands recorded it. The best versions came from The Virginians and Ladd's Black Aces. The Black Aces record on Gennett competed with that of Jazzbo's Carolina Serenaders (a second pseudonym for the same band, the Original Memphis Five) on Cameo. Isham Jones' orchestra also did a nice version for Brunswick.

GEORGE WHITE SCANDALS OF 1922 provided one big Gershwin hit and a monumental flop which led to the strangest commission of all. The hit was "I'll Build a Stairway to Paradise," which Winnie Lightner sang to success backed by an impressive production featuring George White himself with the rest of the dancing cast. The resounding flop really had no business in a revue. It was a one-act opera called BLUE MONDAY, which Gershwin composed to a libretto by De Sylva. It was a twenty-five minute ballet, which, after opening night, White decided was too gloomy, so he shelved it. But it impressed Paul Whiteman, whose orchestra was playing the show. Whiteman filed away the fact that Gershwin was trying to incorporate jazz and blues elements in popular music inside a more "serious" setting, and commissioned him to write his "Rhapsody in Blue" for the Whiteman concert at Aeolian Hall a year and a half later.

For the Charles Dillingham revue, NIFTIES OF 1923, Gershwin saw his and Irving Caesar's "Nashville Nightingale" interpolated. Waring's Pennsylvanians recorded it, as did Phil Ohman and Victor Arden, the two-piano team who would shortly become the mainstays of the orchestras for several Gershwin shows.

It was "Rhapsody in Blue" which firmly established Gershwin's reputation as a composer. One critic called it "the foremost serious effort by an American composer," while another described it as "one of the most significant works in twentieth century music." The two Whiteman recordings, with the composer at the piano, sold incredibly well, the acoustic performance being put on Victor's classical blue label. The "Rhapsody" has since been performed extensively in concert halls both here and abroad, and it has been used as the basis of several ballets. It was sold to Universal Studios for a record price for use in KING OF JAZZ (1930), in which pianist Roy Bargy is featured with the Whiteman orchestra. Although it was originally scored for jazz band and piano, and then written out for two pianos, it has been transcribed for every conceivable combination of instruments and even for unaccompanied chorus.

The last of the SCANDALS for which Gershwin would compose a score was the sixth edition in 1924. It boasted eight published songs, one of which became a smash hit, thanks to Paul Whiteman's recording. As with Gershwin's other SCANDALS hit of two years before, it fell to Winnie Lightner to introduce "Somebody Loves Me." The lyric was by DeSylva and Ballard Macdonald, and the song was sung on Brunswick Records by Marion Harris. It has remained timeless.

The first of Gershwin's complete Broadway scores since LUCILLE was LADY BE GOOD! (December 1, 1924). With seven songs published, four were hits and another was an impressive syncopated dance number. The show starred Fred and Adele Astaire, and had in the orchestra the duo-piano team of Victor Arden and Phil Ohman. This double-piano innovation was repeated by the Gershwins in four of their other shows (TIP-TOES, OH, KAY!, FUNNY FACE and TREASURE GIRL). "Oh, Lady Be Good" became popular as sung by Walter Catlett in the show. Artie Shaw revived it in a swing arrangement in 1939 which gave jazz bands and dancers a perennial favorite. "Fascinating Rhythm" provided the Astaires with a great song-and-dance number and gave Arden and Ohman a chance to make a nice recording of it with Carl Fenton's Orchestra. "Little Jazz Bird" gave Cliff Edwards a solo in the show. "The Half of It, Dearie, Blues" was interestingly structured, but the best of all, "The Man I Love," was dropped from the show during the Philadelphia tryouts, when audiences failed to respond to Adele Astaire's performance. The song was tried in three later shows, only to be dropped from each of them. Finally, the song was so well known through vaudeville and nightclub performances that the brothers stopped trying to put it into a show. It had become a standard despite production flops. TIP-TOES (December 28, 1925) was produced by Alex Aarons and Vinton Freedley, the team that produced the Gershwin brothers' previous show, and the book was written by Guy Bolton and Fred Thompson, the same team who had written LADY BE GOOD. "Looking for a Boy" was introduced in the show by Queenie Smith, who had last starred in the Kern-Wodehouse show SITTING PRETTY (1924). The Knickerbockers and Roger Wolfe Kahn's Orchestra made lovely recordings of it. "Sweet and Low-Down" and "That Certain Feeling" were the two other songs from the show which have remained standards.

It is generally agreed that the score for OH, KAY! (November 8, 1926) is the brothers' best, and the book, by P. G. Wodehouse and Guy Bolton (concerning rum-running), was the funniest written during the twenties. Altogether, Aarons and Freedley gave this material their usual attractive production, which starred Gertrude Lawrence, Oscar Shaw and Victor Moore. It was perfect casting. The title song is one of the Gershwins' gems and so, in their ways, are "Fidgety Feet," "Clap Yo' Hands," and "Do-Do-Do." The last two numbers, by a strange coincidence, were usually to be found back-to-back on the same double-sided disc, paired by the various artists who recorded them. Gershwin himself recorded them as piano solos (Columbia 809-D), while Ohman and Arden recorded the same pair with their orchestra, as did Fred Rich's orchestra, the Missouri Jazz Band, and, curiously, Victor split a recorded pairing, with Roger Wolfe Kahn's orchestra doing "Clap Yo' Hands" on one side and George Olsen and his Music's "Do-Do-Do" on the other side (Victor 20327).

Gertrude Lawrence, who became a star with this show, introduced the most-played number, "Someone to Watch over Me." She recorded the song twice—once accompanied by Tom Waring at the piano (Victor 20331), and, in London for the show's production there a year later, accompanied by His Majesty's Theatre Orchestra, led by Arthur Wood (English Columbia 4618). As late as the mid-nineteen eighties, pop singer Linda Ronstadt backed by Nelson Riddle's Orchestra had a hit recording of the song. George Gershwin also made a piano solo of it and coupled it with "Maybe" (Columbia 812-D). "Maybe" is a lovely ballad, which, in the show, contrasted nicely with "Heaven on Earth," a show-stopper featured by comedian Victor Moore. When OH, KAY! was revived off-Broadway in 1960, an original cast album was made (Fox 4003), with Wodehouse rewriting lyrics for "The Twenties Are Here to Stay," "The Pophams," and "You'll Still Be There."

With a book by George S. Kaufman, the first production of STRIKE UP THE BAND (1927) never made it to Broadway. It included "The Man I Love" and the title song, which was used with the rewritten book in 1930.

The next Aarons-Freedley production with the Gershwins was FUNNY FACE (November 22, 1927), which was called SMARTY during the tryouts. The producers opened a new theatre called the Alvin, the first syllable of each's given name, with this show, which starred Fred and Adele Astaire, Victor Moore, and Allen Kearns. "The Babbitt and the Bromide" was Ira's attempt to write a Wodehousian comic number and it succeeded. "High Hat," "He Loves and She Loves," "How Long Has This Been Going On," "Let's Kiss and Make Up," "My One and Only" (originally published as "What Am I Gonna Do?"), and " 'S Wonderful" were the hit songs from the show. FUNNY FACE was the basis of the Broadway production called MY ONE AND ONLY (May 1, 1983), proving again the durability of the Gershwins' songs.

Florenz Ziegfeld, Jr. produced an elaborate show for his star Marilyn Miller, ROSALIE (January 10, 1928), with music by both Sigmund Romberg and George Gershwin. Romberg used lyricist P. G. Wodehouse. Gershwin used his brother Ira and, for two numbers, Wodehouse. The two collaborations with Wodehouse, "Oh Gee! Oh Joy!" and "Say So!," were the only hits in the show.

SHOW GIRL (July 2, 1929) was a flop which starred Ruby Keeler, Al Jolson's nineteen-year-old wife, and the comic team of Clayton, Jackson and Durante. The only song which attained any status was "Liza," which was intended to be sung by Nick Lucas and danced by Ruby Keeler. On opening night, however, Al Jolson, who was in the audience, leaped onto the stage and sang it to his wife while she came down a huge staircase. He was to sing it again on THE JOLSON STORY'S soundtrack.

When the revised version of STRIKE UP THE BAND (January 14, 1930) came to Broadway, it had a new book by Morrie Ryskind and included the hit "I've Got a Crush on You," which Frank Sinatra would revive in the late forties, the cute "Mademoiselle in New Rochelle," "Soon," and the title song, which would be sung in the 1940 movie of the same name, by Judy Garland and Mickey Rooney.

The last of the great Aarons-Freedley-Gershwin shows was GIRL CRAZY (October 14, 1930), starring Ethel Merman, Ginger Rogers, Allen Kearns, Willie Howard, and William Kent. Ethel Merman became a star when she introduced "Sam and Delilah" and "I Got Rhythm." Gershwin liked this last song so much that he used it as the basis for a concert work, "Variations on I Got Rhythm" (1934). It has been a favorite of jazz pianists, too. Ginger Rogers introduced the two beautiful ballads of the show, "But Not for Me" and "Embraceable You." For this last number, former Gershwin star Fred Astaire helped choreograph, and he taught the routines to Rogers. Two films were made called GIRL CRAZY, though only the second used the show's storyline. For the 1932 version, which starred Bert Wheeler and Robert Woolsey, the Gershwins wrote "You've Got What Gets Me," and for the 1943 Judy Garland-Mickey Rooney film, "Treat Me Rough!" was finally published. The Foursome, a male quartet, introduced "Bidin' My Time" in the 1930 show.

With the help of George S. Kaufman and Morrie Ryskind, the Gershwins embarked on a short series of politically-conscious shows, starting with OF THEE I SING (December 26, 1931). This was an election year, so it was logical to build a musical around the Presidency. The stars were William Gaxton, Lois Moran and Victor Moore. It was the first musical to win a Pulitzer Prize (for drama), and the award went to Kaufman, Ryskind and Ira Gershwin. It seemed that George's musical contribution didn't count with the committee. The score included "The Illegitimate Daughter," "Love Is Sweeping the Country," "Who Cares?" and the title song. The original production had the longest Broadway run of all the Gershwin shows and had the further distinction of having its libretto published by Knopf, the first hardcover presentation ever for a book of a musical. It is curious that it was not until the show was revived in 1952 that "Wintergreen for President" was first published.

Gershwin's last work for the stage was, many feel, his finest. PORGY AND BESS (October 10, 1935) starred Todd Duncan, Anne Brown, John W. Bubbles, and Warren Coleman. The songs, most of which are classics, include "Bess, You Is My Woman (Now)," "My Man's Gone Now," "A Woman Is a Sometime Thing," "I Got Plenty o' Nuttin'," "It Ain't Necessarily So," and, with a lyric by librettist DuBose Heyward, perhaps George's most majestic song, the one with which Abbie Mitchell opened the show, "Summertime." Anne Brown sang "Summertime" in RHAPSODY IN BLUE (1945), the biographical Gershwin film.

Even before the movies could talk, theme songs were written to promote them. Irving Berlin wrote several, and Gershwin wrote one. It was called "The Sunshine Trail" (1923), for the film of the same name, starring Douglas MacLean and produced by Thomas H. Ince. Gershwin's debut in a film for which he wrote the entire score did not come until

1931, the Janet Gaynor-Charles Farrell starrer, DELICIOUS. None of the songs were especially memorable, although "Blah-Blah-Blah" has continued to have a life in cabarets over the years. Ira spoofs the Moon-June-Croon-Spoon type of Alley lyrics typical of the twenties and thirties, possibly thinking specifically about the J. Fred Coots-Lou Davis song "I'm Croonin' a Tune about June" (1929).

When the Gershwin brothers returned to Hollywood in 1936, it was to work for RKO on two pictures, both with Fred Astaire, the star of the Gershwin Broadway shows LADY, BE GOOD! and FUNNY FACE. The first film was with Astaire's dancing-singing partner Ginger Rogers, who had made her Broadway debut in GIRL CRAZY. It was called SHALL WE DANCE (1937), in which the brothers returned to their more light-hearted, pre-thirties, less socially-significant themes with "Slap That Bass," "Walking the Dog" (which was published many years later as "Promenade"), the great comic number "Let's Call the Whole Thing Off," and one of George's most endearing and enduring ballads, "They Can't Take That Away from Me."

A DAMSEL IN DISTRESS (1937) was the next film to have a complete score by the Gershwins, with Fred Astaire once again in the leading role (but for the first time in four years, without Ginger Rogers). Joan Fontaine, a dramatic actress, was given the assignment of the heroine in the book, basically taken from P. G. Wodehouse's 1919 novel of the same name. (He also contributed to its screenplay.) George Burns and Gracie Allen were a delight in this film and surprised audiences with their dancing abilities, sharing equally with Astaire in a tap routine and then doing an extended dance through an amusement park, winding up in front of trick mirrors. Allen sang the comic "Stiff Upper Lip," while Astaire sang "A Foggy Day (In London Town)." The film's hit song was the amusing "Nice Work If You Can Get It."

After DAMSEL, the brothers went to work for Samuel Goldwyn on the score for THE GOLDWYN FOLLIES (1938). Five songs for the film had been completed when George suddenly became incapacitated by headaches. Two ballads became hits, "Love Walked In" and "(Our) Love Is Here to Stay," the last song George ever wrote. It was more or less thrown away in this film, but when it was used in Gene Kelly's AN AMERICAN IN PARIS (1951), it became the standard it should have been all along.

George Gershwin died of a brain tumor in Los Angeles, California, on July 11, 1937.

VINCENT YOUMANS:
"Tea for Two"

Vincent Youmans was born in New York City on September 27, 1898, just one day after George Gershwin, and their careers in the Alley occurred at roughly the same time. Youmans worked with Ira Gershwin as lyricist on the first Broadway show for each of them. As George Gershwin was the first to experiment with blues and jazz ideas in Broadway music, so Youmans took the temper of the times and expressed himself just as individually. There is no mistaking much of Youmans' or Gershwin's music as coming from any time but the 1920's.

As Gershwin began his recording career for Aeolian, so too did Youmans, also in 1916. Felix Arndt, as he had done for Gershwin a few months earlier, hired Youmans to orchestrate songs for piano rolls and taught him many tricks for making richer-sounding arrangements.

Youmans enlisted in the United States Navy during the First World War and was stationed at the Great Lakes Training Station, where he was to prepare musical shows for the sailors and act as rehearsal pianist. The bandmaster there was none other than John Philip Sousa (1854–1932), who liked one tune Youmans had written, programmed it in his concerts frequently, and gave it to other Navy bands to play. Nine years later, with words added, it became "Hallelujah," the runaway hit of HIT THE DECK (1927).

Upon returning to civilian life in 1919, Youmans got a job with Mose Gumble at Remick's, where Gershwin had worked just a few years before. Youmans was given the same duties, that of demonstrating house songs to performers and plugging them in stores. He was soon given a chance to work for Victor Herbert on Herbert's OUI MADAM (1920), which closed out of town. Youmans, in a rare interview later in his life, said, "There are no treatises or instruction books on how to write an opera or musical comedy. Working with a man like Victor Herbert was the luckiest thing that happened to me. No money could have bought the training I received in less than a year."

Youmans published his first song in January 1920, when Remick's issued his "The Country Cousin," with lyrics by Alfred Bryan. It was inspired by a silent movie of the same name, starring Elaine Hammerstein, whose photo appears on the cover. Unfortunately, like most first songs by top composers, this one didn't create a ripple in the Alley's pond.

By the fall of 1920, Youmans was ready to write for the theater, so he took his wares to Max Dreyfus who, as he had done for Gershwin, hired Youmans just to compose. It was at Harms that he met lyricist Irving Caesar and the Gershwin brothers. George took an immediate liking to Youmans. When they learned of the proximity of their birthdays, Youmans called George "Old Man," and George responded by calling Youmans "Junior."

When young Alex Aarons, who had produced the road tour of Gershwin's LA, LA LUCILLE, began his next show, TWO LITTLE GIRLS IN BLUE (May 3, 1921), George urged Aarons to hire Youmans to write the score, and Youmans, in turn, asked Ira to write the lyrics. One of the first songs they worked on turned out to be the hit of the show. Ira recalled that when he wrote "Oh, Me! Oh, My! (Oh, You!)" it was merely a dummy lyric to translate the rhythm into sounds. Later on, he thought he would find a real lyric subject and change it, but Youmans expressed delight with that original inspiration. Ira later said, "That was fine with me because I couldn't think of anything else." Another set of dummy lyrics would provide Youmans with his greatest hit just a few years later. (See below.) One of the reasons "Oh, Me! Oh, My!" became such a smash was Paul Whiteman's Victor recording of Ferde Grofe's orchestration, which caught the public's attention with its snappy syncopation.

WILDFLOWER (February 7, 1923) was Youmans' second Broadway score and his longest running show, with 477 performances. The two hit songs, "Bambalina" and "Wildflower," firmly established Youmans as one of the leading composers of the early twenties.

His next two shows, MARY JANE McKANE (December 25, 1923) and LOLLIPOP (January 21, 1924), were moderately successful but didn't contain any outstanding songs. Youmans had a penchant for revising and reusing songs in future shows. One of his greatest hits "Sometimes I'm Happy," with lyrics by Irving Caesar, was placed first in A NIGHT OUT (1925), which closed during its pre-Broadway tour in Philadelphia, and later put into HIT THE DECK (1927), when it became a classic. The song was originally known as "Come On and Pet Me," with lyrics by Oscar Hammerstein II and William Cary Duncan, from MARY JANE McKANE. Also from that show was the song "My Boy and I," the melody of which later turned up in NO, NO, NANETTE (1925) as the title song, with a lyric by Otto Harbach.

NO, NO, NANETTE (September 16, 1925) had a strange history. It was first performed in a Detroit tryout on April 23, 1924, where it ran into horrendous book problems. Before the show moved to Chicago (where it was a smash hit), the book was overhauled and completely changed, the cast members were replaced, and five new songs were written. The lyricist Irving Caesar remembers working a long day with Youmans on one of the new songs and trying to get a brief nap before they were to attend a party. He had just fallen asleep on the couch when Youmans woke him, wanting to play a new tune he had just worked out. Couldn't it wait until tomorrow? No. Caesar was dragged to the piano to hear it. Youmans wanted a lyric. Couldn't it wait? No, again. He wanted it now. While Youmans played it over, Caesar sleepily jotted down dummy lyrics to fit the rhythm, intending to replace it the next day with a permanent set. When Caesar was finished, Youmans thought the lyrics and title were great and insisted on keeping what Caesar had just written. The song, Youmans' greatest hit, was "Tea for Two." The other NANETTE song which has remained a favorite also has charming lyrics by Caesar, "I Want to Be Happy." And, not to be outdone by his idol Jerome Kern, who had flirted with the blues in an early twenties show, Youmans wrote " 'Where Has My Hubby Gone?' Blues" for this score. By the time NANETTE opened on Broadway, it had had nearly a year's run in Chicago, as well as two road companies and a London production (March 11, 1925), which ran for 665 performances. The Broadway production ran for 321 performances, and when NANETTE was revived on Broadway on May 16, 1973, it ran for 861 performances.

OH, PLEASE! (December 17, 1926) was the next Youmans show. It starred Beatrice Lillie and it bombed. However, it contained one of his catchiest melodies, "I Know That You Know," which jazz pianists still like to perform. The initial recording by Ohman and Arden with their Orchestra started it on its way. (An interesting sidelight is that both of Youmans' future wives came from the chorus of this show.)

HIT THE DECK (April 25, 1927), the first show produced by Youmans himself, had a successful Broadway run of 352 performances. The two major songs were the classic "Hallelujah!," with words by Leo Robin and Clifford Grey, and "Sometimes I'm Happy," with lyrics by Irving Caesar, used without Caesar's permission in this show. However, as it became a hit, Caesar benefitted tremendously.

GREAT DAY! (October 17, 1929), with lyrics by Billy Rose and Edward Eliscu (1902–), contained three all-time standards: "Great Day!," "Without a Song," and the gorgeous ballad, "More Than You Know." The show was a flop, but these songs are evergreens.

SMILES (November 18, 1930) was a Ziegfeldian bomb. Starring Marilyn Miller and Fred and Adele Astaire, this lavish production should have been a success but lasted only 63 performances. However, with lyrics by Harold Adamson and Mack Gordon, Youmans turned out the enduring "Time on My Hands."

THROUGH THE YEARS (January 28, 1932) was another flop for Youmans, with only a twenty-performance run. But, as had been the case with his other unsuccessful shows, two standards emerged: "Drums in My Heart" and "Through the Years," both with lyrics by Edward Heyman.

TAKE A CHANCE (November 26, 1932) was Youmans' last Broadway show, but he didn't write the entire score. His biggest contribution was "Rise 'n' Shine," sung by Ethel Merman.

Youmans' only original movie score was for RKO'S FLYING DOWN TO RIO (1933), in which Fred Astaire and Ginger Rogers had supporting roles and danced together for the first time. Their first dance was to Youmans' "Carioca," a wonderful samba with a maxixe tinge, with lyrics by Gus Kahn and Edward Eliscu. "Orchids in the Moonlight" was another hit from the score, danced to by Astaire and Dolores Del Rio as a tango. Clearly, Youmans was in the vanguard of Latin American music, which swept the country in the forties. "Flying Down to Rio" became a hit thanks to Astaire's forceful performance of it.

Youmans had a comparatively brief career on Broadway and an even briefer one in Hollywood. But he created some of the best-loved songs of all time, and their lasting qualities say much for this gifted composer.

Vincent Youmans died of tuberculosis in Denver, Colorado, on April 5, 1946.

DESYLVA, BROWN AND HENDERSON:

"The Best Things in Life Are Free"

The songwriting team of DeSylva, Brown and Henderson was unique in the Alley. Although Buddy DeSylva and Lew Brown nominally wrote the words and Ray Henderson the music, these three functioned as one creator, sharing the same thought, feeling, purpose and style. Each contributed to both words and music. Before their teaming, each had written hits with others: DeSylva's "Look for the Silver Lining" with Jerome Kern, "Somebody Loves Me" with George Gershwin, and "A Kiss in the Dark" with Victor Herbert; Lew Brown's "I'm the Lonesomest Gal in Town," "Oh, By Jingo" and "Dapper Dan (The Sheik of Alabam')" with Albert Von Tilzer, "I Wanna Go Where You Go," with

Cliff Friend, and "Collegiate" with Moe Jaffe; Henderson's "That Old Gang of Mine," "Five Foot Two, Eyes of Blue," and "I'm Sitting on Top of the World." As a trio they would come up with an unusual number of hits, mostly in the theatre, some in the movies, and, occasionally, as pop tunes.

The trio formed when George White needed a composer for his new SCANDALS in 1925 after George Gershwin, who had composed the music to the last five editions, decided to concentrate on book musicals. White hired Ray Henderson to write the music for his new production and, independently, hired Buddy DeSylva and Lew Brown to write the lyrics. The score the team produced (June 22, 1925) was published by Harms and not distinguished, but they created their first hit soon after they began their own publishing company. "It All Depends on You" (1926) was sung by Al Jolson (in whiteface, for a change) in his show BIG BOY. "South Wind" (1926) was given a jazzy interpretation by The Dixie Jazz Band (Oriole 896).

The next year, for GEORGE WHITE'S SCANDALS OF 1926 (June 14, 1926), the team turned out hit after hit, including "(This Is My) Lucky Day," "The Girl is You and the Boy Is Me," and "The Birth of the Blues," all of which were introduced by Harry Richman in the show, and "Black Bottom," a challenge to the "Charleston," which was sung and danced by Ann Pennington, the McCarthy Sisters, Frances Williams, and Tom Patricola. It was George White himself who created the spectacularly frenetic dance with which Ann Pennington stopped the show nightly and which helped make this edition the best of all his SCANDALS. Ohman and Arden with their Orchestra (Brunswick 3242) and Howard Lanin's Orchestra (Columbia 689-D) gave the audiences something to remember the show by on discs.

The songwriting team went from this revue to a Broadway book musical comedy for their next offering. They chose college life, as Bolton-Wodehouse-Kern had done ten years earlier, to showcase the fads of the day that appealed to their audiences. The show was awash with raccoon coats, porkpie hats, ukuleles, and sorority emblems embroidered on tight-fitting sweaters. It featured George Olsen and his band running down the aisle yelling college cheers before jumping into the pit, where they struck up the overture. Even the ushers wore college jerseys. The show, GOOD NEWS (September 26, 1927), ran for 551 performances and made a star of the high-kicking Zelma O'Neal, who introduced "Good News" and "The Varsity Drag," the team's answer to "Charleston." The bright, fresh show abounded with other hit songs, such as "Lucky in Love," "Just Imagine," and "The Best Things in Life Are Free."

As well as clicking their first time out with a book show's score, the team wrote three solid pop songs in this creative year of 1927, and another one under a pseudonym. The pseudonymous song was "The Church Bells Are Ringing for Mary" (1927), credited to "Elmer Colby." Belle Baker made "(Here I Am) Broken Hearted" famous, while their "Just a Memory" was interpolated into MANHATTAN MARY. Lou Gold's orchestra helped make "Magnolia" a hit that year.

Their GEORGE WHITE SCANDALS OF 1928 can be summed up nicely by a song title from the show, "Not As Good As Last Year." So the team plunged ahead with their next book show, HOLD EVERYTHING (October 10, 1928), a show about boxing, which starred Ona Munson, Betty Compton, Jack Whiting, Bert Lahr, and Victor Moore. Their resounding and memorable song in that show was "You're the Cream in My Coffee." Ted Weems' orchestra recorded it and helped establish its place on the all-time hit parade.

While Al Jolson was making THE SINGING FOOL (1928) for Warner Bros., the team was on the road in Atlantic City, New Jersey, trying out HOLD EVERYTHING. One night they received a phone call from Jolson, asking DeSylva to write a song immediately. It had to be about a child, Jolson's son in the movie, and he wanted it to make the audience cry. As soon as DeSylva hung up, the team went to work, as related by David Ewen in GREAT MEN IN AMERICAN POPULAR SONG, "not on a beautiful ballad, but on the corniest creation they could dream up—just one more practical joke. In no time at all, they called Jolson back, all three singing into the receiver. Jolson loved it. 'It'll be the biggest ballad I've ever sung,' he told the songwriters excitedly. The three could hardly keep from laughing, but they solemnly assured Jolson that they would send him the words and music immediately. When he finally hung up, they started to laugh—and never stopped. What they had written as a joke was the hit of the picture, 'Sonny Boy.' It sold a million and a half copies of sheet music and became a best-seller in Jolson's recording."

"Together" was the team's pop hit of 1928. Cliff Edwards and Franklyn Bauer made the first recordings. Mindy Carson's record in 1944 made it a hit again, and in 1961 Connie Francis made yet another best-selling recording of the song.

The big song in FOLLOW THRU (January 9, 1929), the trio's show about golf, was "Button Up Your Overcoat" which was sung by Zelma

O'Neal and Jack Haley in the show. After a vocal chorus, Eleanor Powell tap-danced to it. Helping to make it big on records were Fred Waring's Pennsylvanians. It was revived in the mid-fifties on disc by the Glenn Brown Trio (Coronet 550).

The team's only original film score was for SUNNY SIDE UP (1929), which featured Janet Gaynor and Charles Farrell singing the hit "If I Had a Talking Picture of You." The title song was sung by Janet Gaynor, as well as "I'm a Dreamer, Aren't We All?"

The team's last Broadway show, FLYING HIGH (March 3, 1930), exploited the aviation craze, reflected in the headlines about Charles Lindbergh, Amelia Earhart and Admiral Byrd. The score boasted one enduring song, "Thank Your Father," which was sung by Grace Brinkley and Oscar Shaw.

Hollywood used the cream of their catalog in a "biography" of the team starring Dan Dailey, Gordon MacRae and Ernest Borgnine. It was called THE BEST THINGS IN LIFE ARE FREE (1956).

RUDOLF FRIML:
"Indian Love Call"

Rudolf Friml was born in Prague, Czechoslovakia, on December 7, 1879. He studied at the Prague Conservatory under Antonin Dvorak and became an accompanist to violinist Jan Kubelik, who toured Europe and the United States. On his visit to America in 1906, Friml decided to stay permanently. It was while he was pursuing a concert career that he was asked to work on an operetta for opera star Emma Trentini, who had just scored a huge success in Victor Herbert's NAUGHTY MARIETTA. Herbert was expected to write her next show, with a book by Otto Harbach, but he and Trentini had a serious falling-out, so he withdrew from the musical. Thus it was that publisher Rudolph Schirmer obtained the commission for Friml.

THE FIREFLY (December 2, 1912) was the musical that resulted, and it was Friml's first success. "Love Is Like a Firefly," "Sympathy," and "Giannina Mia" were the outstanding songs in the score. When it was turned into a film (1937) starring Jeanette MacDonald and Allan Jones, Friml turned his "Chansonette" (of 1923) into "The Donkey Serenade." It is always included in revivals of the stage show.

Friml continued to compose for the Broadway stage steadily thereafter, but it wasn't until 1924 that he wrote his next great success. In the midst of the jazziness and turbulence of the roaring twenties, ROSE

MARIE (September 2, 1924), an old-fashioned European-styled operetta set in the Canadian Rockies, signaled a brief return to more gracious times. The score included five major songs: "Rose Marie," "Song of the Mounties," "The Door of My Dreams," "Totem Tom-Tom," and the million-selling "Indian Love Call," with lyrics by Otto Harbach and Oscar Hammerstein II. This show, too, was turned into a film of great popularity, starring Jeanette MacDonald and Nelson Eddy (1936).

THE VAGABOND KING (1925), with lyrics by Brian Hooker, starred Dennis King. The rich score included the stirring "Song of the Vagabonds," "Huguette Waltz," "Love Me Tonight," "Some Day," and "Only a Rose." The film version (1930) starred Dennis King and Jeanette MacDonald and has sustained the score's popularity through the years.

THE THREE MUSKETEERS (March 13, 1928), with lyrics by P. G. Wodehouse and Clifford Grey (1887–1941), was Friml's last important show. It starred Dennis King and Vivienne Segal, who shared "March of the Musketeers" and "Your Eyes," both with Wodehouse lyrics, and "My Sword and I," "Ma Belle," "All for One and One for All," and "The He for Me," with lyrics by Clifford Grey.

Rudolf Friml died in Los Angeles, California, on November 12, 1972.

SIGMUND ROMBERG:
"Lover, Come Back to Me"

Sigmund Romberg was born in Nagy Kaniza, Hungary, on July 29, 1887. He came to the United States in 1909 and got jobs playing piano in Hungarian restaurants in New York City. He later began conducting a small orchestra in salon music at Bustanoby's, a fashionable restaurant. After he instituted the playing of American trots and glides for social dancing, the place became the favorite rendezvous of the rich and famous. Romberg's first published compositions in the Alley were "Some Smoke" and "Leg of Mutton," both issued by Joseph W. Stern & Company in 1913.

When Louis Hirsch resigned as staff composer of the Shubert producing empire, J. J. Shubert hired Romberg as the replacement and gave him his first assignment: to write the score for the Shubert Brothers' elaborate revue at the Winter Garden, THE WHIRL OF THE WORLD (January 10, 1914). Unlike Friml's debut, Romberg's was inauspicious. While his trots had brought him some attention and the notice of J. J. Shubert, his popular songwriting left a lot to be desired. It took him fifteen other Shubert musicals (in three years) before he struck it rich.

As he kept learning his craft at the expense of his audiences, he became something of hack, churning out uninspired tunes to suit the various stars of the shows.

MAYTIME (August 16, 1917), with lyrics by Rida Johnson Young, had one outstanding song, "Will You Remember (Sweetheart)?" It was spotted as a leitmotif throughout the story. When the movie was made (1937), Jeanette MacDonald and Nelson Eddy sang it to immortality.

LOVE BIRDS (March 15, 1921), with lyrics by Ballard Macdonald, sported a cheerful song called "I Love To Go Swimmin' with Wimmen'," which has gone unnoticed except that for over twenty-five years, Al Stricker has sung it with the St. Louis Ragtimers. Their recording of it is one of their highlights (Paseo 102).

BLOSSOM TIME (September 29, 1921) had lyrics by Dorothy Donnelly (1880–1928) and was based on the life and music of Franz Schubert (1797–1828). This was one of the most popular shows of all time, with various touring companies playing it for over thirty years. Romberg picked his thematic material well, as the score's well-known numbers include "Three Little Maids," "The Serenade," "My Springtime Thou Art," "Tell Me Daisy," and the major hit, "Song of Love," taken from the first movement of Schubert's UNFINISHED SYMPHONY.

THE STUDENT PRINCE (December 2, 1924), again with lyrics by Dorothy Donnelly, proved to be Romberg's finest score. He had found his metier in the Viennese-operetta tradition instead of the Alley's, and in the year of Friml's success with ROSE MARIE, Romberg's PRINCE had a run of 608 performances. The score is filled with standards: "Students' Marching Song," "Serenade," "Just We Two," "Drinking Song," "Golden Days," and the everlasting favorite of them all, "Deep in My Heart, Dear." Rise Stevens and Nelson Eddy made the hit recording (Columbia 4510-M).

THE DESERT SONG (November 30, 1926) took its theme from the headlines of the day. It was great romantic stuff and, with the help of Otto Harbach and Oscar Hammerstein II, Romberg fashioned a superb score, rich in memorable songs. They include "The Riff Song," "It," "The Desert Song," and the hauntingly beautiful "One Alone."

According to Gerald Bordman in his biography of Kern, at a bridge game Jerome Kern tried to give his partner Sigmund Romberg a clue as to how many trumps he was holding by humming Romberg's "One Alone." When the scheme failed and the hand was lost, Kern got him aside and said, "You dumb Dutchman. What was I humming to you?"

Romberg replied, "One of my songs." Kern: "What was the title?" Romberg: "Who knows from lyrics?"

THE NEW MOON (September 19, 1928), with lyrics by Oscar Hammerstein II, was the last of the great operettas that Broadway produced in the flurry which spanned seven years (from BLOSSOM TIME to THE NEW MOON). For this successful show (519 performances), Romberg created five hits: "Softly, As in a Morning Sunrise," "One Kiss," "Stout Hearted Men," "Wanting You," and the perennial "Lover Come Back to Me."

THE NIGHT IS YOUNG (1935) was an MGM film for which Oscar Hammerstein II wrote lyrics to Romberg's music. It contained "When I Grow Too Old to Dream," made famous by Nelson Eddy (Victor 4285). Sigmund Romberg died in New York City on November 9, 1951.

VAUDEVILLE AND RADIO

EDDIE CANTOR:
"If You Knew Susie"

Eddie Cantor (1892–1964) was born Edward Israel Iskowitz. He joined the Gus Edwards troupe in vaudeville, along with his friend George Jessel. He next formed an act with Lila Lee and went on to play the Palace Theatre. He became famous when he sang "That's the Kind of a Baby for Me" in the ZIEGFELD FOLLIES OF 1917. He then played in the FOLLIES OF 1918 and 1919, BROADWAY BREVITIES OF 1920, MIDNIGHT ROUNDERS OF 1921, MAKE IT SNAPPY (1922), ZIEGFELD FOLLIES OF 1923, and starred in KID BOOTS (1924) and WHOOPEE (1928). His last Broadway show was BANJO EYES (1942).

He began his movie career in 1930 and made fourteen films. In 1953, THE EDDIE CANTOR STORY starred Keefe Brasselle in the title role.

Cantor's recording career began in 1917 and continued into the era of the LP. He was an early star of radio in the twenties and had a top-rated program throughout the thirties and forties, with "One Hour with You" as his closing theme. He helped singers Deanna Durbin and Bobby Breen achieve stardom in the thirties, and helped Dinah Shore in the forties. Eddie Fisher was the recipient of his good offices during the early fifties. His COLGATE COMEDY HOUR television show was a consistent favorite.

With these various media activities, Cantor was the biggest plugger on Broadway during the twenties and the most influential in selling songs. Throughout his career, he was known for "You'd Be Surprised," "Margie," "Oh! Gee, Oh! Gosh, Oh! Golly I'm in Love," "No, No, Nora," "Dinah," "If You Knew Susie," "Oh! Boy, What a Girl," "Ida," "Makin' Whoopee!," "Yes Sir! That's My Baby," and "Now's the Time to Fall in Love." He wrote two autobiographies, MY LIFE IS IN YOUR HANDS and TAKE MY LIFE.

RUDY VALLEE:
"My Time Is Your Time"

Rudy Vallee (1901–1986) was born Hubert Pryor Vallee in Island Pond, Vermont. After graduation from Yale, he worked at the Heigh-Ho Club in New York City in 1928, leading the Connecticut Yankees, whose name he took from the Rodgers and Hart show of the previous season. His pianist Cliff Burwell wrote with lyricist Mitchell Parish one great hit, "Sweet Lorraine," which Vallee plugged to success. Vallee was famous in the pre-electric microphone days for using a megaphone while singing in front of his band. He was also an alto saxophonist who changed his first name in honor of the great alto sax virtuoso, Rudy Wiedoeft. Vallee's rise to stardom was swift. His first movie, THE VAGABOND LOVER (1929), featured his song "I'm Just a Vagabond Lover." His NBC radio show made Alice Faye, Frances Langford, and Edgar Bergen into stars and revived the career of comedian Frank Fay. Vallee's theme song was "My Time Is Your Time." In addition to plugging the songs of others, Vallee wrote a few hits himself, notably "Deep Night" (1929) and "Betty Co-Ed" (1930), while he helped make famous "Good Night Sweetheart," "The Whiffenpoof Song," and the "Stein Song." He made a comeback as the star of Broadway's long-running musical, HOW TO SUCCEED IN BUSINESS WITHOUT REALLY TRYING (October 14, 1961), and he played the same role in the film version (1967). His peak as a hitmaker came at the end of the twenties, and his popularity lasted through the thirties.

OTHER SONG HITS OF THE TWENTIES

1919

"Alice Blue Gown" was composed by Harry Tierney (1890–1965), with lyrics by Joseph McCarthy, for IRENE (November 1, 1919), the longest running musical up to that time (a record held for the next twenty-eight years), with 675 performances. This waltz was introduced in the show by star Edith Day.

"I'm Forever Blowing Bubbles" was written by "Jaan Kenbrovin and John William Kellette," pseudonyms for James Kendis (1883–1946), James Brockman (1886–1967) and Nat Vincent (1889–1979). It was introduced in THE PASSING SHOW OF 1918, but was made famous by June Caprice.

"In Soudan" was composed by Nat Osborne (1878–1954), with words by Ballard Macdonald. It was in the "Tin Pan Alley Oriental" style of the day, coming at the height of "Dardanella's" popularity. Zez Confrey, making piano rolls for QRS, was given many such songs, and he could usually come up with a brilliant arrangement, at once fresh and unstereotypical. He worked wonders with this one (QRS 786).

"Oh" was the inspiration of Byron Gay (1886–1945) and bandleader Arnold Johnson (1893–1975). Its catchy melody made it suitable for Ted Lewis' Jazz Band (Columbia A-2844). Pee Wee Hunt and his dixieland band sold over a million copies with a recording of it in 1953 (Capitol 2442).

"Rose Room" was composed by San Francisco bandleader Art Hickman (1886–1930) as his instrumental theme in 1917. He published it and plugged it himself at the St. Francis Hotel, where his band performed in the Rose Room. His recording (Columbia A-2858) did so well that Sherman, Clay & Company took it over and published it as a song, with words by Harry Williams (1879–1922).

"The World Is Waiting for the Sunrise" was written by two Canadians, Ernest Seitz and Eugene Lockhart. The Benson Orchestra's arrangement by Roy Bargy (Victor 18980) caused a sensation. So Did Frank Banta's piano solo in 1928 (Victor 21821). The Firehouse Five Plus Two's revival in 1950 (Good Time Jazz L-12010) made it fresh and new all over again.

1920

"Avalon" was "composed" by Vincent Rose (1880–1944), a California pianist and bandleader, who was a trained classical musician. The main melodic theme of the chorus was stolen from the tenor aria, *E Lucevan le Stelle*, in Puccini's (1858–1924) TOSCA (1900). J. Bodewalt Lampe made the popular arrangement for Jerome H. Remick & Company, who reportedly settled out of court with a $25,000 payment to Puccini.

"Jelly Bean" was the work of Jimmy Dupre, Sam Rosen and Joe Verges, New Orleans songwriters who published the song with their Universal Music Publishing. It was revived in 1949 by "Chuck Thomas" and His Dixieland Band (Capitol 1011), in reality Woody Herman, who also sang it, with piano backing by Lou Busch.

"The Love Nest" was Louis A. Hirsch's only big hit. He started writing for the Shubert organization (preceding Sigmund Romberg), then wrote for several ZIEGFELD FOLLIES productions and many other shows and revues. He never got anywhere (except for getting lots of work) until this one. It was introduced by Janet Velie and Jack McGowan in MARY, with book and lyrics by Otto Harbach and Frank Mandel. It was used for years as the radio and (later) television theme of THE BURNS AND ALLEN SHOW.

"San" was pianist Lindsay McPhail's (1895–1965) only major song. It was subtitled "Oriental fox trot" and it competed successfully with Whiting's "Japanese Sandman." Paul Whiteman had the hit version (Victor 19381), although the Benson Orchestra, The Georgia Melodians, Mike Markel's Orchestra and Ben Selvin didn't do badly with it. It was revived by Abe Lyman's Sharps and Flats in 1928 (Brunswick 3964), and again by Pee Wee Hunt in 1953, to sell more than a million discs (Capitol 2442).

"Whispering" was composed by John Schonberger (1892–1983) and Vincent Rose, with lyrics by Richard Coburn (1886–1952). It was a hit due solely to Paul Whiteman's recording (Victor 18690), which sold over two million copies. It is still being performed, a deserving classic.

1921

"April Showers" was composed by Louis Silver, with words by B. G. DeSylva, and sung with enormous success by Al Jolson, who introduced it in BOMBO (after the show had opened on Broadway) and sang it on the soundtracks for his two biographical films, THE JOLSON STORY (1946) and JOLSON SINGS AGAIN (1949).

"Down Yonder" was the work of L. Wolfe Gilbert, usually a lyricist, but here writing both words and music. He even published it himself. It was interpolated by the Brown Brothers, a saxophone sextet, in TIP TOP after that show's Broadway opening. It was spectacularly revived by pianist Del Wood (Tennessee 775) in 1951. Joe "Fingers" Carr also sold over a million copies with his version (Capitol 1777).

"Strut Miss Lizzie" was written by John Turner Layton and Henry Creamer. It was introduced by Van and Schenck in the ZIEGFELD FOLLIES OF 1921.

"Sweet Lady" was composed by Frank Crumit (1889–1943) and Dave Zoob, with lyrics by Howard Johnson, for Julia Sanderson in TANGERINE. It became a hit with Carl Fenton's Orchestra (Brunswick 2143) and Paul Whiteman's Orchestra (Victor 18803), but Eubie Blake recorded it as a piano solo with a vocal chorus by Irving Kaufman (Emerson 10450) and this version sold tremendously.

"Three O'Clock in the Morning" was written by Julian Robledo and Dorothy Terriss, a pseudonym of Theodora Morse. Its middle strain echoes the famous Westminster Chime of London's Big Ben. It was first heard in GREENWICH VILLAGE FOLLIES OF 1921, and Paul Whiteman's recording sold over two million copies (Victor 18940).

1922

"Angel Child" was composed by Abner Silver (1899–1966), with lyrics by Benny Davis. It was introduced by George Price in SPICE OF 1922. The Benson Orchestra (Victor 18870) had the big recording.

"Bees Knees" was composed by Ted Lewis (1892–1971) and Ray Lopez, with words by Leo Wood (1882–1929). Ted Lewis' Band made the first recording of this great syncopated fox trot (Columbia A-3730), but the Boston Syncopators (another pseudonym of the Original Memphis Five) made an outstanding version (Grey Gull 1138).

"China Boy" was the work of Phil Boutelje (1895–1979) and Dick Winfree. Arnold Johnson's Orchestra made a hit recording (Brunswick 2355), and it was revived in 1952 by Pete Daily and his Dixieland Band (Capitol 2041).

"He May Be Your Man But He Comes to See Me Sometimes" was written by blues pianist Lemuel Fowler, who sold it to two different publishers, Perry Bradford in New York and Ted Browne in Chicago. When the Bradford edition sold extremely well, Browne stepped in and sued him. The best selling instrumental version was by the Original Memphis Five (Pathe 202855).

"Hot Lips" was written by Henry Lange (1895–1985), Henry Busse (1894–1955) and Lou Davis (1881–1961), when the first two were with Paul Whiteman's orchestra. It became a popular feature for trumpeter

Busse, and Whiteman's recording of it (Victor 18920) sold over a million copies. When Busse had his own orchestra in the thirties, he used it as a theme song.

"Runnin' Wild" was composed by Arthur Harrington Gibbs (1895–1956), with lyrics by Joe Grey (1879–1956) and Leo Wood. It was such a hit that a show was named after it in 1923. The Southland Six made a fine recording (Vocalion 14476).

"Way Down Yonder in New Orleans" was written and introduced by J. Turner Layton and Henry Creamer in SPICE OF 1922. It has been revived in practically every decade since, starting with the Frankie Trumbauer recording featuring Bix Beiderbecke in 1927 (Okeh 40843). Astaire and Rogers danced to it on film in 1939, Betty Hutton sang it in a film in 1952, and Freddie Cannon made a hit recording of it in 1960.

"Who'll Take My Place When I'm Gone" was composed by Billy Fazioli (1898–1924), with lyrics by Raymond Klages (1888–1947). Fazioli was the pianist-arranger with Ray Miller's orchestra (Columbia A-3695), but it was Bennie Krueger and his Orchestra which had the finest recording (Brunswick 2303).

1923

"Blue Hoosier Blues" was composed by Abel Baer (1893–1976) and Cliff Friend (1893–1974) and written by Jack Meskill. Vincent Lopez and his Hotel Pennsylvania Orchestra (Okeh 4869) made the hit recording, in a heavily competitive field.

"I Cried for You" was composed by two bandleaders, Abe Lyman (1897–1957) and Gus Arnheim (1897–1955), and written by Arthur Freed (1894–1973). It was assured of success with two bandleaders as composers, each plugging it in nightclubs, radio and recordings, but when the lyricist became an executive producer for MGM, its continued success was certain. Judy Garland sang it in BABES IN ARMS (1939), and it became identified with her from that time on.

"I Love You," by Harry Archer (1888–1960) and Harlan Thompson (1890–1966), was their only hit from LITTLE JESSIE JAMES. It was introduced in the show by John Boles and Margaret Wilson. Paul Whiteman's orchestra (Victor 19151) and Carl Fenton's orchestra (featuring the duo pianists Arden and Ohman) (Brunswick 2487) had the hit recordings.

"Struttin' Jim" was written by Bob Carlten and Cliff Dixon. Its big recording was done by the Original Memphis Five (Perfect 14155).

"Yes! We Have No Bananas" was credited to Frank Silver (1896–1960) and Irving Conn (1898–1961), and supposedly taken from the street cry of a Greek fruit peddler. However, it is known that the entire staff of Shapiro, Bernstein had a hand in it. Sigmund Spaeth, in A HISTORY OF POPULAR MUSIC IN AMERICA, traced the musical pedigree of this tune ". . . the song had a most distinguished background, for its chorus melody was borrowed, consciously or unconsciously, from Handel's 'Hallelujah Chorus,' the finish of 'My Bonnie,' 'I Dreamt That I Dwelt in Marble Halls' (the middle strain), and 'Aunt Dinah's Quilting Party' (by way of Cole Porter's 'An Old-Fashioned Garden'). It makes an amusing trick to sing the original words wherever possible, creating this extraordinary text: 'Hallelujah, Bananas! Oh, bring back my Bonnie to me. I dreamt that I dwelt in marble halls–the kind that you seldom see. I was seeing Nellie home, to an old-fashioned garden; but, Hallelujah, Bananas! Oh, bring back my Bonnie to me!' " The Pennsylvanian Syncopators made a fine recording (Emerson 10623) and Spike Jones and his City Slickers revived it in 1950 (Victor 20-3912).

1924

"Doo Wacka Doo" was written by Clarence Gaskill (1892–1947), Will Donaldson (1891–1954) and George Horther. Paul Whiteman successfully featured it (Victor 19462), and Marion McKay's orchestra created a hit recording (Gennett 5615).

"Doodle-Doo-Doo" was composed by pianist Mel Stitzel (1902–1952), with lyrics by bandleader Art Kassel (1896–1965). Naturally, when Kassel had a band, it was used as his theme song, but Jack Linx and his Orchestra also made an exciting disc (Okeh 40188).

"How Come You Do Me Like You Do?" was written by Gene Austin (1900–1972) and Roy Bergere (1889–1969). It was introduced by Gene Austin in vaudeville and was sung by Rosa Henderson, accompanied by Fletcher Henderson (Vocalion 14795), Marion Harris, accompanied by Phil Ohman (Brunswick 2610), and played by The Original Memphis Five (Perfect 14322). Bill Krenz revived it as a piano solo in 1954 (Coral 9-61248).

"I'm All Broken Up over You" was composed by Joe Murphy and Carl Hoeffle, with lyrics by Joe Burke and Lou Herscher. Ted Weems and his Orchestra did a magnificent arrangement (Victor 19286), featuring Dewey Bergman's novelty piano chorus and Walter Livingston on bass clarinet and alto saxophone.

"It Ain't Gonna Rain No Mo' " was taken by Wendell Hall (1896–1969) from an old Southern folk song and made into a hit by Carl Fenton's Orchestra (Brunswick 2568).

"Me and the Boy Friend" was composed by Jimmy Monaco, with words by Sidney Clare. Margaret Young made a hit recording of it (Brunswick 2736), as did Ray Miller and his Orchestra (Brunswick 2753).

"There'll Be Some Changes Made" was composed by W. Benton Overstreet, with lyrics by Billy Higgins. Marion Harris helped make it a hit, and Benny Goodman revived it in 1939 (Columbia 35210).

"Those Panama Mamas" was composed by publisher Irving Bibo (1889–1962), with words by Howard Johnson. Eddie Cantor helped make it a hit (Columbia 256-D), as did Belle Baker (Victor 19609), and the Cotton Pickers (yet again the Original Memphis Five!) made a splendid version (Brunswick 2879), as did the Varsity Eight (Lincoln 2289).

1925

"Angry" was composed by Dudley Mecum (1896–1978), Henry and Merritt Brunies, and Jules Cassard. They all recorded it as Merritt Brunies and His Friars Inn Orchestra in Chicago in November 1924 (Autograph 610). And George Brunies (Merritt's brother) recorded it with the New Orleans Rhythm Kings in July 1923 (Gennett 5219), in Richmond, Indiana. The Arcadian Serenaders recorded it in St. Louis, Missouri, in October 1925 (Okeh 40517). Ray Miller and his Orchestra recorded it with Muggsy Spanier on cornet and Jules Cassard on string bass in Chicago in January 1929 (Brunswick 4224). Bob Crosby's Bob Cats in New York revived it in November 1939 (Decca 2839) in a best-selling disc.

"Cheatin' on Me" was composed by Lew Pollack (1895–1946) and written by Jack Yellen. Eddie Frazier and his Orchestra made a sensational recording (Sunset 1100), as did Warner's Seven Aces (Columbia 305-D). Sophie Tucker introduced it in vaudeville.

"Show Me the Way to Go Home" was by "Irving King," a pseudonym for the English songwriter-publishers Reg Connelly and Jimmy Campbell. They adapted it from an old Canadian folk song. Perry's Hot Dogs made a superb recording (Banner 1615).

1926

"Charmaine" was originally published in 1926 by Belwin as a theme song for the silent film WHAT PRICE GLORY?, with composer credit going to Erno Rapee (1891–1945) and lyrics by "Louis Leazer." When it was published with a new copyright in 1927 by Sherman, Clay, the lyricist's name appeared as Lew Pollack. When the song was first performed, Pollack thought it lousy and didn't want his name associated with it. When it became a hit a year later, he reconsidered and thought his name should appear in its rightful place.

"Coney Island Washboard" was composed by Wade Hampton Durand (1887–1964) and Jerry Adams, with words by Ned Nestor and Claude Shugart. It became a favorite of jazz bands during the dixieland revival of the forties and has become a standard. The big recording came from Bob Scobey's Frisco Band (Good Time Jazz 49).

"Heart of My Heart" was written by Ben Ryan (1892–1968) and was also known as "The Gang That Sang 'Heart of My Heart'." It was a big hit in the late forties and into the early fifties with recordings by Frankie Laine, Curt Massey, and The Four Aces.

"Hello, Bluebird" was composed by Cliff Friend. It was featured by Harry Reser's Clicquot Club Eskimos (Columbia 795-D). It was revived in a best-selling record in 1952 by Teresa Brewer (Coral 60873).

"High, High, High Up in the Hills" was composed by Maurice Abrahams (1883–1931), with words by Sam Lewis and Joe Young. Abrahams wrote it for his wife, Belle Baker, who introduced it. Nat Shilkret and his Orchestra made a splendid recording (Victor 20436).

"Hugs and Kisses" was composed by Lou Alter (1902–1980), with lyrics by Raymond Klages, for EARL CARROLL'S VANITIES—FIFTH EDITION. Art Landry and his Orchestra had the hit recording (Victor 20285).

"I Never See Maggie Alone" was composed by Englishman Everett Lynton, with lyrics by Harry Tilsley. Irving Aaronson and his Commanders made the hit recording (Victor 20473). It was revived by the Hilltoppers in 1949.

"If I Could Be with You" was composed by James P. Johnson and written by Henry Creamer. Ruth Etting made it popular in vaudeville, and the composer recorded it as a piano solo in 1944 (Decca 24883). McKinney's Cotton Pickers used it as their theme. It has become a favorite of jazz bands and their singers.

"In a Little Spanish Town" was composed by Mabel Wayne (1904–1978), with words by Sam Lewis and Joe Young. Vincent Lopez made the hit recording.

"Moonlight on the Ganges" was composed by Englishman Sherman Myers, with lyrics by Chester Wallace. Paul Whiteman and his Orchestra had the best-selling record (Victor 20139).

"Tonight You Belong to Me" was composed by Lee David (1891–1978), with words by Billy Rose. Gene Austin made a hit of it then, and Patience and Prudence revived it in 1956.

1927

"Bye-Bye Pretty Baby" was composed by pianist Jack Gardner (1903–1957) and bandleader George "Spike" Hamilton (1901–1957). Jan Garber and his Orchestra had a marvelous version (Victor 20833), and composer-singer-pianist Fred Rose accompanied himself for a touching rendition (Brunswick 3616).

"Diane" was written by Erno Rapee and Lew Pollack, as the theme song for the Janet Gaynor-Charles Farrell film SEVENTH HEAVEN. Published by Sherman, Clay, it became an outstanding hit.

"Did You Mean It?" was written by bandleader Abe Lyman and comedians Phil Baker (1896–1963) and Sid Silvers (1907–1976). Baker and Silvers were a duo in vaudeville. This was written for Marion Harris, who sang it in the revue A NIGHT IN SPAIN, also featuring the comedians.

"(I Scream, You Scream, We All Scream for) Ice Cream" was composed by Robert King, with lyrics, most appropriately, by Howard Johnson (1887–1941) (not the ice cream chain owner, however) and Billy Moll (1905–1968). The Six Jumping Jacks made a cute recording (Brunswick 3782), as did Waring's Pennsylvanians (Victor 21099).

"I'm Gonna Meet My Sweetie Now" was composed by Jesse Greer (1896–1970), with lyrics by Benny Davis. Jean Goldkette and his Orchestra made a fabulous recording (Victor 20675), as did vocalist Jane Green (Victor 20509).

"The Kinkajou" was composed by Harry Tierney, with words by Joseph McCarthy, for RIO RITA (1927). The song's title is the name of a bandit in the show. Most recordings featured this song backed by the show's title song. One of the best performances was by the Knickerbockers (Columbia 893-D). The song was copyrighted in 1926, while the show opened on Broadway on February 2, 1927.

"Lucky Lindy," composed by Abel Baer (1893–1976), with lyrics by L. Wolfe Gilbert, was the first song to celebrate Charles Lindbergh's landing in Paris. It was the best of nearly twenty other Lindy songs.

"Me and My Shadow" was composed by Dave Dreyer (1894–1967), with lyrics by Billy Rose. It was heavily plugged by Al Jolson, who sang it on radio, and it was introduced in HARRY DELMAR'S REVELS by Frank

Fay. It later became the theme song of Segar Ellis and his Orchestra. Ted Lewis used it as a feature in his performances.

"(Who's Wonderful, Who's Marvelous?) Miss Annabelle Lee" was composed by Lew Pollack, with words by Sidney Clare. It was introduced by Harry Richman. The Knickerbockers made a lovely dance arrangement (Columbia 1088-D), and Jane Gray, probably accompanied by Rube Bloom, made a nice version of it (Diva 2464-G).

"My Sunday Girl" was composed by Sam H. Stept, with words by Herman Ruby and Bud Cooper. It was given a superb recorded performance, with a fabulous novelty piano break by Frankie Carle, by Edwin J. McEnelly's Orchestra (Victor 20589). On the Clicquot Club Eskimos' recording (Columbia 921-D), Harry Reser's banjo gets a good working over.

"Who's That Pretty Baby?" was written by Bobby Heath (1889–1952) and Alex Marr. Jack Crawford and his Orchestra had a splendid recording (Victor 20847).

1928

"Back in Your Own Back Yard" was composed by Dave Dreyer, with lyrics by Billy Rose. When Al Jolson first introduced it, the title was "It's Nobody's Fault But Mine." Under its new title, it became a hit.

"Oh, Baby" was written by Owen Murphy (1893–1965) for the show RAIN OR SHINE. Jay C. Flippen plugged it.

"Sweet Sue" was composed by Victor Young (1900–1956), with lyrics by Will J. Harris (1900–1967). It was identified with the young actress Sue Carol. Charley Straight and his Orchestra made a fine recording (Brunswick 3900), as did Pauline Alpert, as a piano solo, in 1946 (Sonora 1041).

" 'Tain't So, Honey, 'Tain't So" was written by Willard Robison (1894–1968), and popularized by Paul Whiteman and his Orchestra (Columbia 1444-D).

"That's My Weakness Now" was composed by Sam H. Stept (1897–1964), with lyrics by Bud Green (1897–1981), for Helen Kane. Sam Lanin and his Orchestra made a hit recording (Perfect 14999).

"When Sweet Susie Goes Steppin' By" was written by bandleader Whitey Kaufman, Fred Kelly and publisher Irving Bibo. Nat Shilkret's Orchestra made a fine recording (Victor 21515).

"When You're Smiling," composed by Larry Shay (1897–1988) and Mark Fisher, with lyrics by Joe Goodwin (1889–1943), was made famous by Vincent Lopez and Rudy Vallee. Louis Armstrong made the first recording and it has remained in the standard repertoire ever since.

1929

"Can't We Be Friends?" was composed by Kay Swift (1905–   ) with lyrics by her (then) husband James P. Warburg (1896–1969), writing under the pseudonym "Paul James." It was introduced by Libby Holman in THE LITTLE SHOW.

"Do Something" was another song by the team of Sam Stept and Bud Green. They wrote it for Helen Kane to perform in the film NOTHING BUT THE TRUTH. It has been revived in the eighties by the contemporary vaudevillian Ian Whitcomb, in his act with piano accompanist Dick Zimmerman.

The twenties saw the most prolific outpouring of songs of all the decades in Tin Pan Alley's history. The good times were reflected in the popularity of jazz bands and in the number of dance bands that were being recorded around the country. The entertainment industry was going full-blast, with the sale of player pianos and piano rolls peaking in 1926. Vaudeville attendance was at an all-time high and so were the number of musical comedy productions on Broadway (the 1927–28 season produced fifty-three musicals, according to *Variety*). Everything came to a halt by the end of 1929 when, in *Variety*'s famous headline, "Wall Street Lays An Egg."

By the start of the thirties, radio had become a most important force in the popular music industry, reaching vast numbers of people comprising pop music's audience, and heralding the age of the disc jockey. Talking pictures created another outlet for music publishers, as movie musicals were starting to appear in great numbers. Films became a most important source of income for the songwriters and publishers of Tin Pan Alley, as film producers had to buy songs. Film companies found it more convenient to purchase already-established publishing firms with a catalog of favorite songs for their ever-growing roster of films. The Depression saw the cost of sheet music drop from thirty to twenty-five cents. Ironically, during the early thirties, dance bands were increasing in size from twelve to fifteen players and they came to be known as the big bands. Pluggers went after those performers with radio shows and sought bandleaders with permanent ballroom jobs.

Mitchell Parish, one of
Tin Pan Alley's most prolific
lyricists of hit songs
("Stardust," "Deep Purple").

Harold Arlen, composer of
"Blues in the Night."

Ethel Waters and Eubie Blake in the early 1930's.

Hoagy Carmichael, with
Duke Ellington at the piano,
in the 1940's.

Jimmy Van Heusen, Academy Award-winning Hollywood composer ("Three Coins in A Fountain").

Song sheet cover for the first jazz tune recorded by the Original Dixieland Jazz Band.

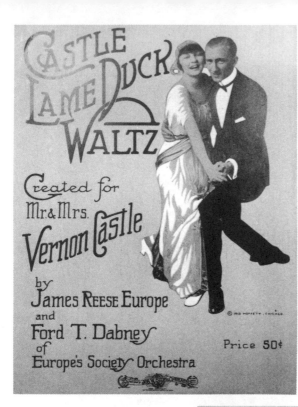

Song sheet cover for a tune popularized by Irene and Vernon Castle, who created ballroom dancing.

Bert Williams, whose performances popularized "I Ain't Got Nobody," and turned the sheet music edition into a hit.

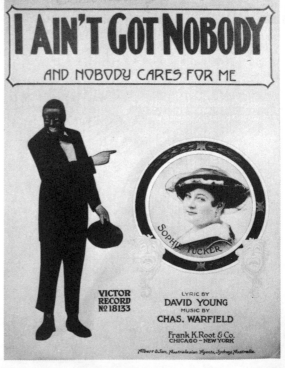

Sheet cover for song written by Bob Cole and J. Rosamond Johnson.

THEATER COMPOSERS

George M. Cohan, pictured on the cover of one of his songs.

George Gershwin, left, with his idol, Jerome Kern.

A rare appearance of a Kern song in a Ziegfeld Follies production.

When The Lights Are Low

ZIEGFELD FOLLIES 1916

PRODUCED AT THE
NEW AMSTERDAM
THEATRE
NEW YORK

LYRICS BY
GENE BUCK
MUSIC BY
JEROME KERN

Vincent Youmans, composer of many standards ("Tea for Two," "More Than You Know").

Cole Porter, Irving Berlin's favorite composer-lyricist.

Richard Rodgers, seated, with Lorenz Hart, in the early 1930's.

Richard Rodgers at the piano with Oscar Hammerstein II, at a rehearsal of "Oklahoma," 1943.

Frederick Loewe, seated, with Alan Jay Lerner.

THE PERFORMERS

Weber and Fields, pictured on an edition of a song they popularized.

Eva Tanguay, the highest paid female vaudeville performer of her era, pictured on the cover of a rag named after her.

Nora Bayes, pictured on her foxtrot.

Sophie Tucker, the Mary Garden of ragtime, featured on one of her many hits.

Bandleader Paul Whiteman, who had the most famous dance band in the 1920's.

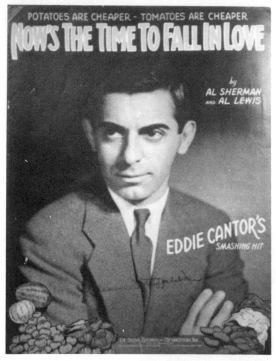

Performers' popularity helped sell songs they sang. Here, Eddie Cantor.

Rudy Vallee.

Bing Crosby.

Benny Goodman.

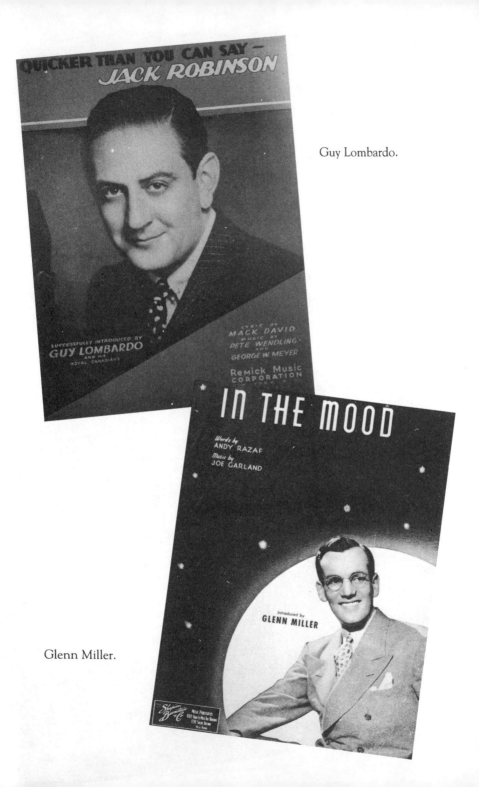

Guy Lombardo.

Glenn Miller.

Xavier Cugat.

Frank Sinatra and
Xavier Cugat.

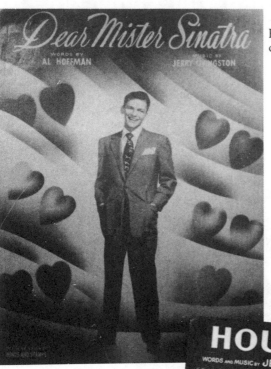

Frank Sinatra, pictured on cover of "Dear Mister Sinatra."

Elvis Presley.

THE ALLEY AND THE MOVIES

(1930–1939)

New Publishers in the Alley

$\mathbf{W}$hile this decade saw consolidation of Tin Pan Alley publishers, with major film companies buying companies for their large catalogs, it also saw a few new names starting up.

Southern Music

Southern Music began in 1930. It specialized in publishing songs that were recorded first, rather than creating songs and then trying to get them recorded. This firm started in the Paramount Building, but became the first tenant in the Brill Building a year later.

Chappell & Company

Chappell & Company, the old-line English firm owned by Louis Dreyfus since 1926, created an American branch headed by his older brother Max Dreyfus. It took offices in the RKO Building in 1934, and quickly became a power in the Alley by specializing in publishing songs from Broadway shows. When Chappell bought T. B. Harms, with Jerome Kern and Oscar Hammerstein as partners, from Warner Brothers, and added Williamson Music (the Rodgers and Hammerstein catalog) to its lists, the firm developed the most complete catalog of show music.

Jerry Vogel Music Company

Jerry Vogel (1897–1980), long-time manager of Plaza Music, a major jobber in New York City, opened his own firm in 1934, when George M. Cohan gave him all of the Cohan copyrights in order to keep them in print. Vogel inherited the F. B. Haviland Publishing Company two years later. His firm's specialty lay in acquiring copyright renewals of proven hits. Mainly a reprint house, Vogel's slogan was "Old Songs Are the Best Songs."

MAJOR SONGWRITERS OF THE THIRTIES

HARRY WARREN:
"Lullaby of Broadway"

Harry Warren was born Salvatore Guaragna in Brooklyn, New York, on December 24, 1893. He started his show business career as a stage hand at the Liberty Theatre, a combination vaudeville and picture house in Brooklyn. He then went to the Vitagraph Studio in Flatbush, where he became a property man. In those fledgling movie days, he did whatever needed to be done, as a movie extra, an assistant director, an off-stage mood music pianist for the various love scenes, cabaret sequences and chases. In short, he was a general utility man. The young Warren's love for the movies never left him.

While working as the house pianist at Healy's Cafe in Sheepshead Bay, he was heard by two songwriters who recommended him for a job as rehearsal pianist and song plugger for Stark and Cowan. It was there that he had his first song published and had his first hit, "Rose of the Rio Grande" (1922). It was co-composed by Whiteman reed virtuoso Ross Gorman, with lyrics by Edgar Leslie. Naturally, Gorman's band, The Virginians, was the first to record it (Victor 19001). "Chuck Thomas" (alias Woody Herman) and his Dixieland Band revived it in 1949.

Warren went to Shapiro, Bernstein & Company in 1925, where, with Bud Green, he wrote "I Love My Baby (My Baby Loves Me)." Waring's Pennsylvanians helped make it a hit (Victor 19905). Two years later, Warren and Green scored again with "Away Down South in Heaven." And with Henry Creamer, Warren wrote "Clementine (From New Orleans)," which Blossom Seeley introduced, and which Jean Goldkette and his Orchestra, featuring Bix Beiderbecke, made into a classic recording (Victor 20994).

"Nagasaki" (1928), with Mort Dixon, which Paul Mares' Friars Society Orchestra recorded (Okeh 41574), and which Bill Robinson featured in the Cotton Club, was the perennial favorite of stride pianist Willie "The Lion" Smith, who played and sang it at almost every engagement he had.

SWEET AND LOW (November 17, 1930) was a revue for which Warren wrote two hits, "Cheerful Little Earful," with lyrics by Ira Gershwin and Billy Rose, and "Would You Like to Take a Walk?" with lyrics by Mort Dixon and Billy Rose.

"Cryin' for the Carolines" (1930), with words by Sam Lewis and Joe Young, was written for the film SPRING IS HERE and sung in the film by Lawrence Gray. It was popularized by Guy Lombardo and his Royal Canadians. Lombardo also turned the Warren and Edgar Leslie song "By the River Sainte Marie" into a hit in 1931. The same year found Warren writing for the revue THE LAUGH PARADE (November 2, 1931), to star Ed Wynn. Warren's big song, written with Mort Dixon and Joe Young, was "You're My Everything," which was introduced by Jeanne Aubert and Lawrence Gray.

Billy Rose was a great title man. He wrote serviceable lyrics, but his forte was creating song titles and selling the resulting songs for more money than anyone else could have gotten for them. In 1926, he created the title "I Found a Million Dollar Baby" and wrote the lyrics to music by Fred Fisher. It didn't go anywhere, but, as Rose still liked the title, he gave it to Warren and Mort Dixon. They fashioned "I Found a Million Dollar Baby in a Five and Ten Cent Store" for the revue BILLY ROSE'S CRAZY QUILT (May 19, 1931), which featured Ted Healy, Fanny Brice (Mrs. Billy Rose at the time), Phil Baker, and Lew Brice. Bing Crosby's recording gave it the necessary boost. It was also used in two movies called MILLION DOLLAR BABY (1935 and 1941).

Warner Brothers offered Warren a chance to compose a complete score for an original movie musical and to team with Al Dubin (1891–1945) as lyricist in 1932. The film they wrote was FORTY SECOND STREET (1933), and it became the prototype of the backstage musical and established Busby Berkeley as the most creative choreographer and director of ensemble production numbers in the history of Hollywood. Harry Warren's music inspired many Berkeley extravaganzas. For this film, Warren and Dubin wrote "Shuffle Off to Buffalo," "Forty-Second Street," and "You're Getting to Be a Habit with Me." All became standards, the last one the most frequently performed.

GOLD DIGGERS OF 1933 was the next Warren-Dubin film which boasted a number of hits. "The Gold Digger's Song (We're in the Money)" became a hopeful anthem during the Depression. "Pettin' in the Park" was an answer to the anti-petting ordinances in some cities. "The Shadow Waltz" also became a hit.

"I Only Have Eyes for You" (1934) came from DAMES and was first sung by Dick Powell. It received a much more felicitous rendering when it was revived in TEA FOR TWO (1950) by Doris Day and Gordon MacRae.

"Lullaby of Broadway" came from DAMES' sequel GOLD DIGGERS OF

1935, and it won the first of Warren's three Oscars for Best Song. It has been a standard ever since. A movie with the song's title was made in 1951 with Doris Day and Gene Nelson. It would seem natural that Hollywood moguls, who were making money hand-over-fist with movie musicals, would trust their songwriters' talents, but such was not the case. Jack Warner did not want "Lullaby of Broadway" in GOLD DIGGERS OF 1935. When Warren played it for Al Jolson, Jolson went back to Warner to demand that he be allowed to use it in his current film, then in production. When Berkeley heard about Jolson's designs on the song, he demanded that Warner put it back into DIGGERS, as originally planned. Warner relented and the song became one of the Alley perennials.

"Lulu's Back in Town" (1935) came from the film BROADWAY GON-DOLIER, sung by Dick Powell and the Mills Brothers. It was made into a hit recording by Fats Waller and his Rhythm (Victor 25063), and was revived in 1964 by Jerry Vale for Columbia Records.

"With Plenty of Money and You" (1936) came from GOLD DIGGERS OF 1937, introduced by Dick Powell. Doris Day revived it in the film MY DREAM IS YOURS (1949).

"September in the Rain" (1937) was sung by James Melton in MELODY FOR TWO, and was revived in 1949 by pianist George Shearing, whose first hit it was.

"You Must Have Been a Beautiful Baby" (1938) was the beginning of a short working relationship with lyricist Johnny Mercer. It was written for the film HARD TO GET and sung by Dick Powell to Olivia de Havilland. Bobby Darin revived it in a 1961 best-selling record.

"Jeepers Creepers" (1938) was another Warren-Mercer collaboration, written for Louis Armstrong in the film GOING PLACES. Armstrong used it throughout the rest of his career.

"Down Argentine Way" (1940), with lyrics by Mack Gordon, was introduced by Don Ameche and Betty Grable in the film of the same name.

"Chattanooga Choo Choo" (1941), again with lyrics by Mack Gordon, was played in the movie SUN VALLEY SERENADE (1941) by Glenn Miller and his Orchestra, featuring the individual band members, and underscoring a spectacular tap routine by the Nicholas Brothers. Glenn Miller's band made a million-selling disc (Bluebird 11230), which has kept it a favorite number with the public.

ORCHESTRA WIVES (1942) again featured Glenn Miller and his Orchestra, taking acting parts as well as performing "At Last," "Serenade in Blue," and "I've Got a Gal in Kalamazoo." Pat Friday sang the songs that actress Lynn Bari lip-synched in the film.

"I Had the Craziest Dream" (1942) was sung by Harry James' vocalist Helen Forrest in the film SPRINGTIME IN THE ROCKIES.

"You'll Never Know" (1943) was written by Warren and Gordon for Alice Faye in HELLO, FRISCO, HELLO. It won Warren his second of three Oscars. It also proved to be his biggest seller in sheet music. Dick Haymes' recording for Decca sold over a million copies.

"I Wish I Knew" and "The More I See You," both with lyrics by Mack Gordon, were written for BILLY ROSE'S DIAMOND HORSESHOE (1945).

"On The Atchison, Topeka and the Sante Fe" (1945) was used in THE HARVEY GIRLS (1946), first as a production number and later sung by Judy Garland. It won Warren his third Oscar (and Mercer his first), and Johnny Mercer and the Pied Pipers had a best-selling disc (Capitol 195).

"That's Amore" (1953), with lyricist Jack Brooks (1912–1971), was written for Dean Martin in the film THE CADDY. Martin also made a best-selling recording (Capitol 2589), which was used in the 1987 film MOONSTRUCK.

"An Affair to Remember" (1957), with words by Harold Adamson and Leo McCarey, was Warren's last big hit and was used as the theme for the film of the same name. It was sung by Vic Damone under the titles and was further popularized by his recording.

Harry Warren died in Los Angeles, California, on September 22, 1981.

JOE BURKE:

"Tip Toe Through the Tulips"

Joe Burke was born in Philadelphia, Pennsylvania, on March 18, 1884. In 1924, he teamed with lyricist Benny Davis and bandleader Mark Fisher (1895–1948) to write the million-selling hit "Oh, How I Miss You Tonight," recorded by the Oriole Orchestra (Brunswick 2874), with a vocal by the leader and co-composer and Oriole banjoist, Mark Fisher.

"Yearning (Just for You)" (1925), with lyrics by Benny Davis, made the best-seller list of that year with recordings by Ben Bernie and his Hotel Roosevelt Orchestra (Vocalion 15002) and Roger Wolfe Kahn and his Hotel Biltmore Orchestra (Victor 19616). "She Was Just a Sailor's Sweetheart" (1925) was both composed and written by Burke, and it was featured by the Six Jumping Jacks (Brunswick 3094). It was revived in the early fifties by the Frank Petty Trio (MGM 11186).

"Just the Same" (1927), with lyrics by Walter Donaldson, was given a splendid treatment by Roger Wolfe Kahn and his Orchestra, featuring Joe Venuti on violin and Eddie Lang on guitar (Victor 20634).

"Carolina Moon" (1928), with lyrics by Benny Davis, was originally plugged and recorded by Gene Austin, but it was Guy Lombardo's Orchestra that had the hit record. Later, it was used by singer Morton Downey as his theme on radio.

GOLD DIGGERS OF BROADWAY (1929) brought Burke together with lyricist Al Dubin for two memorable songs, "Painting the Clouds with Sunshine" and "Tip Toe Through the Tulips with Me," both sung in the film by Nick Lucas. The second song was revived in the late sixties on a best-selling record by Tiny Tim.

"Dancing with Tears in My Eyes" (1930) was written with Al Dubin for the film DANCING SWEETIES, but was not used. Burke was so angry that he left Hollywood and returned to the Alley. He proved the movie moguls wrong when he got Rudy Vallee to introduce the song on his radio program. It became a smash. The team then wrote "For You," which was successfully recorded by Glen Gray and The Casa Loma Orchestra with vocalist Kenny Sargent. Ricky Nelson revived it with his best-selling recording in 1964. DANCING SWEETIES (1930), however, did use one Burke-Dubin song, "The Kiss Waltz," which was sung by Sue Carol. It, too, sold many copies.

When he resettled in the Alley in the mid-thirties, Burke teamed with Edgar Leslie, and they knocked out seven of the biggest hits of this decade. In 1935 alone, they had four huge successes: "On Treasure Island," "A Little Bit Independent," "In a Little Gypsy Tea Room," and "Moon over Miami," the last introduced by Ted Fiorito and his Orchestra. Frankie Masters also helped plug it into a hit.

The new team of Burke and Leslie scored twice more in 1936 with "Midnight Blue," an interpolation into THE NEW ZIEGFELD FOLLIES OF 1936, and "Robins and Roses," which Bing Crosby made famous.

"It Looks Like Rain in Cherry Blossom Lane," one of Burke's loveliest melodies, took him twenty minutes to compose. Leslie's lyrics fit perfectly and Guy Lombardo's recording helped to make it another hit. Poppa John Gordy revived it in the fifties.

Burke's last big hit came in 1948 in "Rambling Rose," with words by Joseph McCarthy, Jr.

Joe Burke died in Upper Darby, Pennsylvania, on June 9, 1950.

FRED E. AHLERT:
"I'll Get By"

Fred E. Ahlert was born in New York City on September 19, 1892. He worked as a staff arranger for Waterson, Berlin & Snyder and had his first number published by them. "Beets and Turnips" (1915), a syncopated fox trot, was composed with Cliff Hess (1894–1959). Vic Meyers and his Orchestra made a fine recording of it in 1924 (Brunswick 2664), as did the Varsity Eight (Cameo 640) for a revival.

"I'd Love to Fall Asleep and Wake Up in My Mammy's Arms" (1920) was Ahlert's first big hit, with lyrics by Sam Lewis and Joe Young. It was helped along by the Benson Orchestra's recording (Victor 18697).

"Maybe She'll Write Me (Maybe She'll Phone Me)" (1924) was a cute novelty co-composed with Ted Snyder, with lyrics by Roy Turk (1892–1934). Paul Whiteman and his Orchestra gave it a nice treatment (Victor 19284).

"There's a Cradle in Caroline" (1927) was written by Sam Lewis and Joe Young. Frankie Trumbauer and his Orchestra with Bix Beiderbecke made a lovely recording of it with a vocal by Seger Ellis (Okeh 40879).

"I'll Get By" (1928), written with Roy Turk, was Ahlert's biggest seller. Ruth Etting sang it to hit status originally, and the Irving Aaronson Orchestra recording gave it a boost. It was revived in the film A GUY NAMED JOE (1943), sung by star Irene Dunne. The King Sisters made a best-selling record the following year, while Dan Dailey sang it in the film YOU WERE MEANT FOR ME (1948). It was used later as a theme song for a film of the same name in 1950.

"Mean to Me" (1929) was another big success for Ahlert and Turk. Again, Ruth Etting had success with it, as did Helen Morgan. When Ruth Etting's life got the Hollywood treatment in LOVE ME OR LEAVE ME (1955), Doris Day, who portrayed Etting, sang it in that film.

"Walkin' My Baby Back Home" (1930) continued the Ahlert-Turk team's streak, and was featured by singer Harry Richman. It was revived in 1952 by Johnny Ray, and was sung by Donald O'Connor in the 1953 film of the same name.

"I Don't Know Why (I Just Do)" (1931), again by the Ahlert-Turk combination, gave Kate Smith one of her early hits. It was revived during the forties and fifties by the Andrews Sisters, Tommy Dorsey's Orchestra, the King Cole Trio, Frank Sinatra, and Bobby Sherwood and his Orchestra.

"Where the Blue of the Night (Meets the Gold of the Day)" (1931) was written by the team, along with Bing Crosby, who sang it to success and made it his theme song. He was so identified with it that he was asked to include it in THE BIG BROADCAST (1932).

"I'll Follow You" and "Love, You Funny Thing!" (1932) were the last two hits written by the team. The first was a Kate Smith favorite, while the second was made famous by Bing Crosby.

"I'm Gonna Sit Right Down and Write Myself a Letter" (1935) was Ahlert's last big hit, and it was written with Joe Young. Fats Waller introduced it and his recording became a best-seller. It was revived in 1956 by Billy Williams on an MGM record that sold over two million copies.

Fred E. Ahlert died in New York City on October 20, 1953.

J. FRED COOTS:
"You Go to My Head"

John Frederick Coots was born in Brooklyn, New York, on May 2, 1897. He started in the Alley as a stock clerk and piano demonstrator in the New York branch of Chicago's McKinley Music. His first big hit, "Doin' the Raccoon" (1928), with lyrics by Ray Klages, was made by the George Olsen band's recording. The same year Coots and Lou Davis wrote "A Precious Little Thing Called Love," which was introduced by Nancy Carroll in THE SHOPWORN ANGEL (1929). It sold over two million copies of sheet music.

"I Still Get a Thrill Thinking of You" (1930), with words by Benny Davis, was popularized by Hal Kemp and his Orchestra. It was revived in 1950 by Dinah Shore.

"Love Letters in the Sand" (1931) was written with Charles and Nick Kenny. It was introduced by Dolly Dawn and became the theme song of George Hall and his Orchestra. Russ Columbo made a hit recording of it. It was revived with a best-selling record by Pat Boone in 1957. Boone also sang it in the film BERNADINE.

"Two Tickets to Georgia" (1933) has lyrics by Joe Young and Charles Tobias. It was introduced by Ted Lewis and popularized by The Pickens Sisters.

"For All We Know" (1934), with lyrics by Sam M. Lewis, is one of the most beautiful ballads ever composed. Introduced by Morton Downey, it was featured by Isham Jones. In a revival, The Voices of Walter Schumann made a magnificent recording for Capitol Records.

"Santa Claus Is Coming to Town" (1934), with lyrics by Haven

Gillespie (1888-1975), is Coots' all-time Christmas standard. It was introduced by Eddie Cantor on his radio program and became an instant hit, selling over four million copies. The hit recordings were made by Bing Crosby with the Andrews Sisters (Decca 23281), the Pied Pipers with Paul Weston's Orchestra (Capitol 15004), Ozzie Nelson and his Orchestra (Columbia 35786), and Tommy Dorsey and his Orchestra (Victor 25145).

"A Beautiful Lady in Blue" (1935) has lyrics by Sam M. Lewis. Jan Garber and his Orchestra had the hit recording.

"You Go to My Head" (1938), with lyrics by Haven Gillespie, became the theme song of Mitchell Ayres and his Orchestra. The first recording was by Larry Clinton and his Orchestra, with a vocal by Bea Wain (Victor 25849). This classic was later recorded by Glen Gray and the Casa Loma Orchestra, Frank Sinatra, Doris Day, and Billy Eckstine.

J. Fred Coots died in New York City on April 8, 1985.

SAMMY FAIN:
"That Old Feeling"

Sammy Fain was born in New York City on June 17, 1902. He got a job as staff pianist at the Jack Mills firm. His first big hit was also his first published song, "Nobody Knows What a Red Head Mamma Can Do" (1924). The lyrics were by Al Dubin and Irving Mills, and the best-selling recordings were by Margaret Young (Brunswick 2806) and Ray Miller and his Orchestra (Brunswick 2778).

"Let a Smile Be Your Umbrella" (1927) has lyrics by Irving Kahal (1903-1942) and Francis Wheeler. Roger Wolfe Kahn and his Orchestra made a splendid recording (Victor 21233). Milton Berle, "The Wayward Youth," plugged it in vaudeville, and it was revived in the film GIVE MY REGARDS TO BROADWAY (1948).

"Wedding Bells Are Breaking Up That Old Gang of Mine" (1929) has lyrics by Kahal and Willie Raskin (1896-1942). Johnny Perkins introduced the song, and it was revived in the fifties by The Four Aces.

"You Brought a New Kind of Love to Me" (1930) was co-composed with Pierre Norman Connor (1895-1952), with lyrics by Irving Kahal. It was introduced by Maurice Chevalier in THE BIG POND. The Chevalier style of singing it became so identifiable that when the Marx Brothers wanted to kid Chevalier, they used this song in MONKEY BUSINESS

(1931). It was revived in 1963, when it was used as the theme for the film A NEW KIND OF LOVE.

"Was That the Human Thing to Do?" (1931) has lyrics by Joe Young and was introduced and made famous by Guy Lombardo and his Royal Canadians.

"By a Waterfall" (1933), with lyrics by Irving Kahal, was introduced by Dick Powell and Ruby Keeler in FOOTLIGHT PARADE. It was given an incredibly elaborate twelve-minute sequence in the film, a very splashy interlude featuring Busby Berkeley's exotic choreography.

"That Old Feeling" (1937) was written with Lew Brown for Virginia Verrill in the film VOGUES OF 1938. Count Basie and his Orchestra (Columbia 36795) helped it to success, and later it was revived by Peggy Lee (Capitol 10012). Jane Froman sang it on the soundtrack of WITH A SONG IN MY HEART (1952).

"I Can Dream, Can't I?" was written with Kahal for Tamara to sing in the show RIGHT THIS WAY (1937). It was revived on a best-selling record by the Andrews Sisters in 1949.

"Are You Having Any Fun?" (1939) was written with Jack Yellen for Ella Logan to sing in GEORGE WHITE'S SCANDALS OF 1939. She also made the hit record (Columbia 35251).

"I'll Be Seeing You" (1938), again with lyrics by Kahal, was placed in the ROYAL PALM REVUE, a Los Angeles showcase which starred Harry Richman, Tony Martin, Abe Lyman, Rudy Vallee, and the DeMarcos. It was next used in the film of the same name (1944), where it scored solidly. Hit recordings were made by Hildegarde (Decca 23291) and by Frank Sinatra with Tommy Dorsey's Orchestra (Victor 26539).

"Dear Hearts and Gentle People" (1949) has lyrics by Bob Hilliard (1918–1971). It was an enormously popular song thanks to Dinah Shore (Columbia 38605) and Bing Crosby (Decca 24798).

"Secret Love" (1953), with lyrics by Paul Francis Webster (1907–1984), was written for Doris Day in the film CALAMITY JANE (1953). It earned the first of the two Oscars given to Fain for Best Song. Doris Day's Columbia record sold over a million copies.

"Love Is a Many-Splendored Thing" (1955), again with lyrics by Webster, written for the film of the same name, won the second Oscar for Fain. The recording by The Four Aces sold over a million copies.

"A Certain Smile" (1958) was written with Webster as a film's title song. Johnny Mathis made the million-selling record for Columbia.

"A Very Precious Love" (1958), with Webster's lyrics, appeared in the film MARJORIE MORNINGSTAR, introduced by Gene Kelly. Doris Day made the hit recording for Columbia.

"April Love" (1957), with lyrics by Webster, came from the movie of the same name. Pat Boone's recording for Dot Records sold over a million copies.

"Tender Is the Night" (1961), with lyrics by Webster, was an important part of the plot of this non-musical film of the same name based on the Scott Fitzgerald novel. The recording by Johnny Mathis was a best-seller.

HARRY BARRIS:
"Wrap Your Troubles in Dreams"

Harry Barris was born in New York City on November 24, 1905. He started as a professional pianist at age fourteen and became one of Paul Whiteman's Rhythm Boys in late 1926, teamed with Al Rinker and Bing Crosby.

"Mississippi Mud" (1927) was his first song hit and one that he wrote while a member of the Rhythm Boys trio. Paul Whiteman and his Orchestra recorded it, with Bix Beiderbecke on cornet and the Rhythm Boys as vocalists (Victor 21274). "From Monday On" (1928) was another great feature for the Rhythm Boys and was recorded on the same disc as "Mississippi Mud."

"It Must Be True" (1930) was written with bandleader Gus Arnheim and Gordon Clifford (1902–1968) for Bing Crosby and the Rhythm Boys. Ted Weems also featured this hit.

"I Surrender, Dear" (1931) also has lyrics by Gordon Clifford and was featured by Bing Crosby. Kate Smith, as well as Guy Lombardo's band, also plugged it successfully.

"Lies" (1931), with lyrics by George Springer, was introduced by Russ Columbo. Guy Lombardo's Orchestra also helped to turn it into a standard. This song has the shortest note-span in all of pop music. Only four full tones are used in verse and chorus!

"Wrap Your Troubles in Dreams" (1931) has lyrics by Ted Koehler and Billy Moll. It was a big hit for Bing Crosby.

"It Was So Beautiful" (1932) was written with film producer Arthur Freed for Connee Boswell. It was sung by Kate Smith in the film THE BIG BROADCAST (1932).

"I'm Satisfied" (1934) has lyrics by Ralph Freed (1907–1973) and was introduced by Horatio Zito.

"Little Dutch Mill" (1934) also has words by Ralph Freed and was a hit for Bing Crosby.

Harry Barris died in Burbank, California, on December 13, 1962.

NACIO HERB BROWN:
"Singin' in the Rain"

Nacio Herb Brown was born in Deming, New Mexico, on February 22, 1896. He started his career as piano accompanist to vaudeville singer Alice Doll and toured with her for a year on the Orpheum circuit. Wanting to be part of the Hollywood scene, he opened up a custom tailor shop, attracting clients such as Charlie Chaplin, Rudolph Valentino, and Wallace Reid. He then went into Beverly Hills real estate and became extremely successful. He started composing songs in his spare time. His first number, with lyrics by King Zany, was "Coral Sea," which Sherman, Clay & Company published in 1920. Paul Whiteman and his Alexandria Hotel Orchestra started plugging it in Los Angeles. When Whiteman recorded it later that year, it became a modest hit. His first real smash, a novelty piano rag called "Doll Dance" (1927), was interpolated into the HOLLYWOOD MUSIC BOX REVUE, featuring Doris Eaton. It was almost as big as Zez Confrey's "Kitten on the Keys" had been six years earlier. Sheet music sales boomed for this marvelous, technically difficult composition written in the seldom-used key of D major, because of the tricky fingering required, the easiest key in which to play it. Frank Banta, using the pseudonym of "Jimmy Andrews," made a spectacular recording of it (Banner 6116).

At the urging of his publisher, Brown followed it up with "Rag Doll" (1928), not quite as overwhelming but selling over half a million copies. San Francisco vaudeville pianist Edna Fischer made the hit recording (Victor 21384).

Brown was asked by MGM Production Chief Irving Thalberg to compose the score for MGM's first all-sound musical, THE BROADWAY MELODY (1929), with lyricist Arthur Freed, who was soon to become an MGM producer of musical films. "You Were Meant for Me," "Broadway Melody," and "Wedding of the Painted Doll" became enduring hits.

"Singin' in the Rain" (1929), by the new team of Brown and Freed, was put into MGM's next musical HOLLYWOOD REVUE (1929). It was introduced by Cliff Edwards. It was later given to Judy Garland in LITTLE

NELLIE KELLY (1940). Finally, it became the title song of the greatest film musical of all time (1952), sung by the film's three stars, Donald O'Connor, Debbie Reynolds and Gene Kelly. Kelly also sang and danced to it in an elaborate sequence. The majority of the score reprised earlier hits by Brown and Freed, and this film remains the movie musical fans' favorite.

THE PAGAN (1929) introduced "Pagan Love Song," sung by star Ramon Novarro. "Should I?" came from LORD BYRON OF BROADWAY (1929). "Paradise" (1931) was the waltz theme of Pola Negri's A WOMAN COMMANDS, and it has been used in several non-musical films through the years.

"Temptation" (1933) was the huge success of GOING HOLLYWOOD, dramatically sung by Bing Crosby, who later made a hit recording. Perry Como revived it with a best-selling disc in 1945. Red Ingle and Jo Stafford sold a million copies of their take-off "Tim-Tayshun" in 1948 (Capitol 412).

"All I Do Is Dream of You" (1934) was the Brown-Freed hit from SADIE MCKEE, introduced by Gene Raymond. It was revived successfully by Debbie Reynolds in SINGIN' IN THE RAIN.

"You Are My Lucky Star" (1935) was featured in THE BROADWAY MELODY OF 1936 (1935) by Eleanor Powell. From the same year's Marx Brothers movie, A NIGHT AT THE OPERA (1935), was "Alone," sung by Kitty Carlisle and Allan Jones.

"Would You?" (1936) was sung by Jeanette MacDonald in SAN FRANCISCO.

"Good Morning" (1939) was introduced by Judy Garland and Mickey Rooney in BABES IN ARMS. It was revived by Debbie Reynolds, Donald O'Connor and Gene Kelly in SINGIN' IN THE RAIN.

"Love Is Where You Find It" (1948) was written with Edward Heyman and Earl Brent for Kathryn Grayson in THE KISSING BANDIT. Her recording of it helped put over this last gem by Brown (MGM 30133).

Nacio Herb Brown died in San Francisco, California, on September 28, 1964.

RALPH RAINGER:

"Thanks for the Memory"

Ralph Rainger was born Ralph Reichenthal in New York City on October 7, 1901. Before starting law school, Rainger had his first rag published, "Piano Puzzle" (1923), which he also recorded (Bell P-193). After graduating from law school, he got a job as rehearsal pianist and (later) pianist in the pit for the Broadway show QUEEN HIGH (1926). He joined with Edgar Fairchild to become a duo-piano team on Broadway and in vaudeville that rivalled Victor Arden and Phil Ohman. Rainger next accompanied the vaudeville team of Clifton Webb and Mary Hay. When Webb went into the revue THE LITTLE SHOW (1929), Rainger went into the orchestra as pianist. During rehearsals a blues song was needed, so Rainger and lyricist Howard Dietz supplied "Moanin' Low." It was Rainger's first song, and like Sammy Fain's, his first big hit. Libby Holman sang it with great success in that show, and she and Webb performed a sensuous dance to it.

Rainger was a very fine pianist and musician, as evidenced by his remarkable novelty rag "Pianogram" (1929), which Robbins Music published. It has very interesting rhythms not often found in music of its time.

Rainger was offered a job with Paramount Pictures at the end of 1930, when he was teamed with Leo Robin (1900–1984). The first film they worked on was THE BIG BROADCAST (1932), wherein Bing Crosby introduced "Please." He first sang it in a rehearsal scene with Eddie Lang accompanying him on the guitar. Later, Crosby sang it with a full orchestra at the end of the film. It was the first of many standards this fine team would produce. Bing Crosby's recording was a best-seller (Brunswick 6394).

"Love in Bloom" (1934) was written for Bing Crosby in SHE LOVES ME NOT. His recording helped make this a half-million sheet music seller. The song's greatest success came from Jack Benny's use of it as his radio and television theme, and as his practice piece when taking violin lessons from Professor LeBlanc.

"June in January" (1934) was introduced by Bing Crosby in HERE IS MY HEART. Its title came first, an unusual occurrence, as Rainger preferred to compose the tune first.

"I Wished on the Moon" (1935) was written with Dorothy Parker for Bing Crosby to sing in THE BIG BROADCAST OF 1936 (1935).

"Blue Hawaii" (1937) was another Bing Crosby feature in WAIKIKI WEDDING (1937). It was also used as the title song for an Elvis Presley film (1961) and in Presley's PARADISE, HAWAIIAN STYLE (1966). Presley's recording in 1962 was a best-seller.

"Thanks for the Memory" (1937) was written for Bob Hope and Shirley Ross in THE BIG BROADCAST OF 1938 (1937). It won the

Academy Award for Best Song. The next movie that Hope made was named for the song (1938). Hope started his radio show later that year and used it as his theme song. He maintained its use on his television shows, and it will be forever identified with him, as "Love In Bloom" is with Jack Benny.

Ralph Rainger died in an air crash in Beverly Hills, California, on October 24, 1942.

HOAGY CARMICHAEL:

"Star Dust"

Hoagland Howard Carmichael was born in Bloomington, Indiana, on November 22, 1899. He learned to play piano by listening to his mother, who accompanied silent movies, and from a local black pianist, Reggie Duval. While attending Indiana University's law school, he became friendly with Bix Beiderbecke and invited Beiderbecke's Wolverines to play at many parties his fraternity gave. As a result of that friendship, his first composition "Riverboat Shuffle" was recorded by the Wolverines (Gennett 5454) in May 1924. Jack Mills published it in 1925, giving co-composer credit to Wolverine pianist Dick Voynow and to publisher Irving Mills. Mitchell Parish added lyrics in 1939.

"Washboard Blues" (1928) was Carmichael's next tune, which he wrote with lyrics by Fred B. Callahan. Paul Whiteman and his Orchestra recorded it in November 1927, with Beiderbecke on cornet and Carmichael as pianist, also performing his first vocal on record (Victor 35877).

It was in 1927 that Carmichael composed the tune to "Star Dust," one evening at the University when he went over to the Book Nook to play the broken-down upright piano there. His school friend Stuart Gorrell named the tune that resulted because "it sounded like dust from stars drifting down through the summer sky." Carmichael first recorded the tune as a "stomp" with Emil Seidel's band, under the name of Hoagy Carmichael and his Pals (Gennett 6311). Carmichael played the piano on this recording of October 31, 1927. Mills Music published it as an instrumental number in January 1929. In May of that year, Mitchell Parish added the lyrics. The song didn't begin to be popular until Isham Jones and his Orchestra recorded it as a dreamy ballad with an arrangement by Jones' pianist-arranger Victor Young (Brunswick 4886), in May 1930. RCA-Victor Records broke music tradition when it issued a single record containing two completely different versions of the song. Benny Goodman, using a Fletcher Henderson arrangement, recorded it with his orchestra on April 23, 1936. Tommy Dorsey, with vocalist Edythe Wright, had recorded the song on April 15 that same year. Both versions were issued back-to-back on Victor 25320. The two biggest swing bandleaders of the day proved their popularity by making this disc a best-seller. Artie Shaw and his Orchestra made their recording in 1940, which sold over two million copies (Victor 27230). The song has since been recorded over a thousand times in the United States alone. Carmichael recorded it several times during his long career, and the best is his 1942 version, accompanied by Artie Bernstein on string bass, and Spike Jones on drums (Decca 18395).

"Rockin' Chair" (1930) was Carmichael's next important song. He recorded it with Louis Armstrong and his Orchestra (Okeh 8756) in December 1929, with vocals by the two of them. Carmichael also sang it with what now looks like an all-star band in May 1930: Bix Beiderbecke and Bubber Miley (from Duke Ellington's band), cornets; Tommy Dorsey, trombone; Benny Goodman, clarinet; Bud Freeman, tenor sax; Joe Venuti, violin; Irving Brodsky, piano and vocal; Eddie Lang, guitar; Harry Goodman, tuba; and Gene Krupa, drums. Hoagy Carmichael joined in on Brodsky's vocal (Victor 38139).

"Georgia on My Mind" (1930) had lyrics by Carmichael's school chum Stuart Gorrell. Carmichael first recorded it with his own hand-picked group in September 1930 (Victor 23013). Fats Waller recorded it. (Victor 27765) in 1941, and Ray Charles revived it in 1959 for a best-selling disc on ABC-Paramount. The Ray Charles recording prompted the Georgia state legislature to make it the state's official song. Charles performed it in the legislative chamber on the day of the voting for a new state song.

"Lazy River" (1931) was written with New Orleanian Sidney Arodin. Carmichael sang it on a record with another all-star band that he brought together (Victor 23034). The Mills Brothers also recorded a best-selling disc (Decca 28458). It was revived in 1961 by Bobby Darin and also by Si Zentner, whose orchestral performance won him a Grammy Award.

"Come Easy, Go Easy, Love" (1931), with lyrics by Sunny Clapp (1899–1962), was recorded by Clapp's band with Carmichael as vocalist. Sidney Arodin, co-writer of "Lazy River," is the clarinetist in the band, with Clapp playing alto saxophone (Victor 22776).

"Lazybones" (1933) has lyrics by Johnny Mercer. If ever there were a natural collaboration between similar musical personalities, this was it.

Carmichael recorded it (Victor 24402), as did Mercer (Varsity 8031). It was also popularized by Mildred Bailey, Ben Bernie and Rudy Vallee.

"Little Old Lady" (1936) has lyrics by Stanley Adams (1907–   ). It was written for the revue THE SHOW IS ON. During rehearsals, the producer wanted to remove it, as he felt it didn't have a proper setting. E. Y. Harburg, working on the show, liked the song so much that he created a special situation for Mitzi Mayfair and Charles Walters, who sang and danced to it.

"The Nearness of You," with lyrics by Ned Washington (1901–1976), was written for Gladys Swarthout in the film ROMANCE IN THE DARK (1938). It wasn't published until 1940, as a song, with no mention of its film connection.

"Heart and Soul" had lyrics by Frank Loesser for a Paramount short, A SONG IS BORN (1938), which featured bandleader Larry Clinton and his Orchestra. The Loesser-Carmichael team also wrote "Two Sleepy People" for Bob Hope and Shirley Ross in the film THANKS FOR THE MEMORY (1938).

"Hong Kong Blues" (1939) was an independent number that didn't take off until the composer himself sang it in the film TO HAVE AND HAVE NOT (1944). From this time on, Carmichael would add film acting to his varied career.

"Doctor, Lawyer, Indian Chief" (1945) had lyrics by Paul Francis Webster for the Betty Hutton film THE STORK CLUB. Her recording made it a hit (Capitol 15230).

"Ole Buttermilk Sky" (1946) was written with Jack Brooks for Carmichael himself to sing in the non-musical film CANYON PASSAGE.

"In The Cool, Cool, Cool of the Evening" (1951), with lyrics by Johnny Mercer, was written for Bing Crosby and Jane Wyman in HERE COMES THE GROOM. It received the Academy Award for Best Song, Mercer's second of four Oscars.

Hoagy Carmichael died in Palm Springs, California on December 27, 1981.

MITCHELL PARISH:
"Sophisticated Lady"

Mitchell Parish was born in Shreveport, Louisiana, on July 10, 1900 and is one of only two lyricists featured in this book. For the most part, he has written his lyrics without benefit of collaboration. Many of his hits resulted when he put words to a melody long after the melody had been composed. In some cases, the tune had been a hit before his lyrics appeared. What makes Parish so distinguished on Tin Pan Alley is that his lyrics fit perfectly with the melody, and in every case, the song became a greater hit, and often a standard, because of the addition of his words.

Parish began his career when publisher Joe Morris hired him to write special material for vaudeville singers—recitations, punch lines, extra verses and alternate lyrics to songs.

Parish's first published song was "Carolina Rolling Stone" (1921), with music composed by the husband and wife team of Eleanor Young and Harry Squires. It was published by Morris and was featured by Willie and Eugene Howard in vaudeville. Bailey's Lucky Seven made a fine recording (Gennett 4868).

His big chance came when he was hired as staff lyricist by Jack Mills for his firm. Mills was the first publisher to give Parish already-famous melodies to turn into songs. "Sweet Lorraine" (1928) was composed by Cliff Burwell and was helped to popularity by Rudy Vallee on radio. It was this song which started jazz pianist Nat "King" Cole's singing career in 1937, when a drunk in a club insisted that he sing it. He agreed reluctantly, as he had never sung in public, having achieved popularity as the pianist in the King Cole Trio. The reception was so great that he henceforth included singing in his act.

"Lazy Rhapsody" (1929) was composed by Harry Sosnik and Howard Jackson. Over the years it has become a standard in nightclubs. It was given special treatment in an album of the same name arranged and performed by Lou Busch (Capitol T-1072).

When "Star Dust" (1929) was first given to Parish, he declined to write lyrics for it, as he didn't like it as a swing tune. But he was prevailed upon to write its lyrics and he did so after he heard Victor Young's ballad arrangement of the melody for the Isham Jones Orchestra.

"Mood Indigo" (1931) was ostensibly written by Irving Mills to music by Duke Ellington and Barney Bigard. It was actually Bigard's melody and Parish's lyric, but Ellington and Mills claimed credit. It is the only

Parish song for which he as lyricist is not named on the sheet music.
"Sentimental Gentleman from Georgia" (1932) was composed by
Frank Perkins (1908–). The Boswell Sisters helped make this a
standard. "The Scat Song" (1932) was composed by Perkins with help
from Cab Calloway, who made this "his" song.

"One Morning in May" (1933) was composed by Hoagy Carmichael,
who also introduced it.

"Sophisticated Lady" (1933) is probably Duke Ellington's most famous
melody. Until Parish put lyrics to it, it was only a piece of special
material for the Ellington band. Since then, it has become an evergreen.

"Hands Across the Table" (1934) was composed by Jean Delettre for
Lucienne Boyer in the revue CONTINENTAL VARIETIES.

"Sidewalks of Cuba" (1934) has a melody of Ben Oakland's (1907–
1979). It was introduced in the twenty-fifth edition of the COTTON
CLUB PARADE. Woody Herman and his Orchestra revived it in 1946.

"Stars Fell on Alabama" (1934) has a marvelous melody by Frank
Perkins. It has been identified with Ozzie Nelson and his Orchestra, and
with Woody Herman in the forties. Jack Teagarden also performed it
memorably.

"Stairway to the Stars" (1935, 1939) was taken from a theme in Matty
Malneck (1904–1981) and Frank Signorelli's "Park Avenue Fantasy,"
first published in 1935. After Parish wrote the lyrics, it became a
smash hit, featured in Glenn Miller, Ozzie Nelson and Paul Whiteman
renditions.

"Organ Grinder Swing" (1936) and "Mr. Ghost Goes to Town" (1936)
both had melodies by swing bandleader Will Hudson (1908–).

"Don't Be That Way" (1938) was arranger Edgar Sampson's melody.
It was recorded by Chick Webb and his Orchestra as an instrumental in
November 1934 (Decca 483). By the time Parish wrote the words, Benny
Goodman's name had been added as co-composer. Goodman also helped
make it a hit (Victor 25792).

"Riverboat Shuffle" was published in 1925 as an instrumental by
Hoagy Carmichael. In 1939, Parish made it famous again by putting
words to it.

"Deep Purple" (1939) was another example of a famous instrumental
becoming even more popular after Parish worked his miracles. Peter De
Rose (1900–1953) wrote this beloved melody in 1934, but after the
Parish lyrics, Larry Clinton's Orchestra with vocalist Bea Wain had a
best-selling recording (Victor 26141). It has been recorded through the

years, and in 1963 Nino Tempo and April Stevens revived it in an Atco recording which received a Grammy Award.

"Moonlight Serenade" (1939) was composed by bandleader Glenn Miller, who made it his theme song. It has been a constant favorite through the years.

"All My Love" (1950) was composed by Paul Durand from Ravel's "Bolero." Patti Page made a best-selling recording.

In 1950, Parish wrote lyrics to "The Syncopated Clock," "Serenata," and "Sleigh Ride," all composed by Leroy Anderson (1908–1975). He later added words to Anderson's "Blue Tango" (1952) and "Forgotten Dreams" (1962).

"Tzena" (1950) was an Israeli pop tune which Julian Grossman adapted, with words by Parish. Gordon Jenkins and the Weavers made the hit recording.

"Ruby" (1953) was composed by Heinz Roemheld for the non-musical film RUBY GENTRY. It was popularized by Les Baxter and his Orchestra.

"Volare" (1958) was composed by Domenico Modugno, who made it popular. Dean Martin had the best-selling recording on Capitol.

"Ciao, Ciao, Bambina" (1959) was the last big hit Parish had, to the music of Domenico Modugno.

STARDUST (February 19, 1987) was a magnificent Broadway revue which brought together the best of Mitchell Parish's songs. It was a richly-deserved tribute to one of the Alley's most creative lyricists.

DANCES OF THE THIRTIES

The Jitterbug

For swinging hepcats, the jitterbug was "real gone." Many rugs were cut by "killer-dillers" and "gates" in this dancing decade. This dance, which captivated bobbysoxers in the Depression years, literally swept people off their feet. It started in Harlem's Savoy Ballroom, the block-long building on Lenox Avenue, between 140th and 141st Streets, and was first known as the Lindy, a dance which started in the late twenties (in honor of flying ace Charles Lindbergh). By the mid-thirties, when swing was taking the country by storm, this fast, exhibition-style dancing was called the jitterbug, and at the Savoy they danced to the music of Chick Webb and his Orchestra. Johnny Hodges composed "Jitterbug's Lullaby" (1938), Harold Arlen wrote "The Jitterbug" for THE WIZARD

OF OZ (1939), Rube Bloom wrote "Jitterbug Jamboree" (1939), and Fats Waller composed "The Jitterbug Waltz" (1942).

BENNY GOODMAN:
"Let's Dance"

Benny Goodman (1909–1986) was known as "The King of Swing." The name wasn't just press agentry. Unlike Paul Whiteman's "King of Jazz" tag, the masterful clarinetist deserved his title. Most of the big bands changed their personnel regularly as sidemen grew to star stature and others made their reputations, but when asked, "Which was your favorite big band?" and "Which did you enjoy playing in the most?" many sidemen over the years give the same answer: "Benny Goodman had the most exciting band of all, and we had a ball playing in it. But, my God, what a taskmaster!" While Goodman was not the most exacting of leaders (Glenn Miller comes to mind), he did expect precision playing which called for regularly-scheduled rehearsals. For men scarcely out of their teens, this kind of discipline was too much like work. But the talented musicians, and the skilled arrangers led by pioneer Fletcher Henderson, made the members remember this orchestra with utmost affection.

Goodman was born and grew up in Chicago, where he took clarinet lessons at Hull House. He started his professional career at age thirteen. He came to New York City with the Ben Pollack band and began to record extensively as a sideman. His beautiful, full tone was easily identifiable and his forceful sound soared through many recordings, even though his name was not often to be found on these early record labels. He also did pit band work for Broadway musicals, and was even busier doing freelance work in radio bands.

In the summer of 1932, he organized his first band, which accompanied singer Russ Columbo. He next formed a band in the summer of 1934 to play at Billy Rose's Music Hall. This second band also made some fine recordings. He and the band started to get some recognition when, from December 1934 to May 1935, they appeared on the weekly three-hour NBC radio program LET'S DANCE. They shared the program with Xavier Cugat's Latin music and Kel Murray's sweet dance music.

After six months on the program, the Goodman band toured the country with disastrous results until they hit the Palomar Ballroom in Los Angeles, where their hot swing was a huge success. They went on to play at Chicago's Congress Hotel for eight months, during which time they were heard nightly on radio. The band's first hit recording featured Fletcher Henderson arrangements of the two kinds of tunes the band would perform throughout this decade, the medium bounce hot instrumental, and the slow, dreamy ballad. The disc that put them on the map was Jelly Roll Morton's "King Porter Stomp" and Vincent Youmans' "Sometimes I'm Happy" (Victor 25090).

The band's theme, "Let's Dance," a 1935 song by Gregory Stone, Fanny May Baldridge and Joe Bonime, wasn't recorded until 1939 (Columbia 35301). Their closing theme was "Good-Bye" (1935) by bandleader Gordon Jenkins (Victor 25215).

Besides breaking up the fourteen-piece band into sections and having them compete with one another (e.g., the brass section accompanying his clarinet solo, or alternating between the brass and reed sections) and turning a section into the soloist, Fletcher Henderson, the band's premier architect-arranger, used the riff as the underlying motif throughout the pieces. The "riff" was any phrase of two measures which was repeated in the background. It became the basis for many jazz-inspired songs, such as "Sing, Sing, Sing," "One O'Clock Jump," and "String of Pearls." Other arrangers who contributed over the years to the Goodman band's distinctive sound were Edgar Sampson, Jimmy Mundy and Horace Henderson.

As Paul Whiteman wanted to make (what he considered) jazz respectable for the educated and middle and upper classes in the 1920's, so did Benny Goodman want to do the same for what he was calling jazz in the 1930's. On January 16, 1938, Goodman and his band rented Carnegie Hall to present the first jazz concert ever held in that bastion of classical music. It was a complete success, as the recordings made during the concert have indicated. They were finally issued in 1950 as a set of two long-playing records that has become an all-time best seller (Columbia OSL-160, CARNEGIE HALL JAZZ CONCERT). The musicians for that concert included: Harry James, Ziggy Elman and Gordon Griffin, trumpets; Red Ballard and Vernon Brown, trombones; Benny Goodman, clarinet; Hymie Schertzer and George Koenig, alto saxes; Arthur Rollini and Babe Russin, tenor saxes; Jess Stacy, piano; Allen Reuss, guitar; Harry Goodman, string bass; Gene Krupa, drums; and Martha Tilton, vocalist.

The band's specialty hot numbers included "Stompin' at the Savoy" (Victor 25247), "House Hop" (Victor 25350), "Riffin' at the Ritz" (Victor 25445), "Rosetta" (Victor 25510), "Sing, Sing, Sing" (Victor 36205), "Don't Be That Way" (Victor 25792), "Lullaby in Rhythm"

(Victor 25827), "And the Angels Sing" (Victor 26170), "Jumpin' at the Woodside" (Columbia 35210), "Stealin' Apples"/"Opus Local 802" (Columbia 35362), "Benny Rides Again" (Columbia 55001), "Solo Flight" (Columbia 36684), "Air Mail Special" (Columbia 36254), "Clarinet a la King" (Okeh 6544), "Jersey Bounce"/"String of Pearls" (Okeh 6592), and "Six Flats Unfurnished" (Columbia 36652).

Besides his big band, Goodman also featured, at various times, his Trio, Quartet, Quintet, Sextet and Septet. They all contributed to his success.

Goodman and the band appeared in several films, with prominent roles in HOLLYWOOD HOTEL (1938), THE POWERS GIRL (1943), THE GANG'S ALL HERE (1943), and SWEET AND LOWDOWN (1944). They made a soundtrack for the Disney film MAKE MINE MUSIC (1946). Goodman's life was given the Hollywood treatment, with Steve Allen in the title role, in THE BENNY GOODMAN STORY (1956).

TOMMY DORSEY:
"I'm Gettin' Sentimental over You"

Tommy Dorsey (1905–1956) was the greatest trombonist of all time at playing popular ballads. He and his older brother Jimmy (another top bandleader, and master of the clarinet and alto saxophone) grew up in Shenandoah, Pennsylvania, playing in their father's parade and concert band. They both came to New York City in 1925, and, as freelancers, quickly became established as recording studio sidemen and as hot soloists. They organized the Dorsey Brothers' Orchestra in 1928, mostly for recording purposes, and started their dance band in 1934. They broke up in September 1935. Jimmy stayed with their band, and Tommy took over the nucleus of the Joe Haymes band.

Tommy recorded extensively for RCA-Victor for the next fifteen years. His theme song was "I'm Gettin' Sentimental over You," composed by George Bassman (1914–) and written by Ned Washington (1901–1976) (Victor 25236). He had his own radio shows, as well as feature spots on other programs, but he finally hit it big when he recorded, on January 29, 1937, his arrangement of "Song of India," backed by Irving Berlin's "Marie," with the band singing riffs behind Jack Leonard's straight vocal (Victor 25523). The "Marie" arrangement was originally created for Doc Wheeler's Sunset Royal Serenaders, but Tommy traded Wheeler eight Dorsey arrangements for that one. It was a profitable trade, since over the next few years, the Tommy Dorsey Orchestra would record other hits in that style: "Who?" (Victor 25693), "Yearning" (Victor 25815), "Blue Moon" (Victor 26185), and "East of the Sun" (Bluebird 10726). This last number had a lead vocal by Frank Sinatra. Tommy Dorsey's band would change personnel considerably over the years, but the band which gave him his first double-sided hit consisted of: Bunny Berigan, Steve Lipkins, Joe Bauer and Bob Cusumano, trumpets; Tommy Dorsey, Les Jenkins and Artie Foster, trombones; Joe Dixon, clarinet and alto sax; Fred Stulce and Clyde Rounds, alto saxes; Bud Freeman, tenor sax; Dick Jones, piano; Carmen Mastren, guitar; Gene Traxler, string bass; Dave Tough, drums; Jack Leonard, vocals.

Some of Tommy Dorsey's biggest hit recordings included: "Once in a While" (Victor 25686), "Music, Maestro, Please" (Victor 25866), "I'll Be Seeing You" (Victor 26539) (which had on the other side Frank Sinatra's first hit with the band, "Polka Dots and Moonbeams"), "I'll Never Smile Again" (Victor 26628), and "This Love of Mine" (Victor 27508).

Tommy formed a "band within the band," his Clambake Seven, a modern dixieland combo which made some hit recordings.

The Tommy Dorsey band appeared in the following movies: Las Vegas Nights (1941), Ship Ahoy (1942), Dubarry Was a Lady (1943), Girl Crazy (1943), Presenting Lily Mars (1943), Broadway Rhythm (1944), Thrill of a Romance (1945), and, in 1947, both Dorseys starred in their biographical movie The Fabulous Dorseys.

ARTIE SHAW:
"Begin the Beguine"

Artie Shaw (1910–) was the most feisty bandleader of the swing era. He was a virtuoso of the clarinet, with a gorgeous tone, especially telling on show tunes and ballads. His solos were very well thought out, and his arrangements were startlingly effective. He joined Irving Aaronson in California in 1929, and came with him on tour to New York City, where he remained.

Shaw became an elite freelancer in the recording studios and, especially, in radio bands. After leading various combos, he formed a swing band in the spring of 1937 called "Artie Shaw and his New Music." It didn't do particularly well until Jerry Gray arranged Cole Porter's flop song "Begin the Beguine" (Bluebird 7746) for a July 1938 recording, which firmly established the band and made the song a classic. Shaw's own radio show, many recordings and prestigious dance hall engagements kept his band on top. At the time of the "Beguine" recording, the personnel consisted of: Chuck Peterson, John Best and Claude Bowen, trumpets; George Arus, Ted Vesley and Harry Rogers, trombones; Artie Shaw, clarinet; Les Robinson and Hank Freeman, alto saxes; Tony Pastor and Ronnie Perry, tenor saxes; Les Burness, piano; Al Avola, guitar; Sid Weiss, string bass; and Cliff Leeman, drums.

Among his hits were: "What Is This Thing Called Love?" (Bluebird 10001), "It Had to Be You" (Bluebird 10091), "Donkey Serenade" (Bluebird 10125), "Rose Room" (Bluebird 10148), "Out of Nowhere" (Bluebird 10320), "Oh, Lady Be Good" (Bluebird 10430), and "All the Things You Are" (Bluebird 10492). With a thirty-two piece band that included a thirteen piece string section, Shaw recorded, on March 3, 1940, "Frenesi," the biggest selling recording of the Second World War years (Victor 26542). In the fall of 1940, Shaw created his band-within-the-band, the Gramercy Five, with Johnny Guarnieri playing harpsichord! The group scored a hit with "Moonglow" (Victor 27405).

Shaw is almost as well-known for his wives as for his music. Among his eight were novelist Kathleen Winsor, actresses Lana Turner, Ava Gardner, Doris Dowling and Evelyn Keyes.

The Shaw band appeared in two movies, DANCING CO-ED (1939) and SECOND CHORUS (1941). His bands had the highest musical standards and contained some of the country's finest musicians.

GUY LOMBARDO:
"Boo Hoo"

Guy Lombardo (1902–1977) played "The Sweetest Music This Side of Heaven." Because of his brother Carmen's lead alto saxophone, with its wide vibrato, his brother Lebert's lead trumpet sound, and their eminently danceable tempos, Guy Lombardo and his Royal Canadians were the most successful dance band of all time.

Carmen (1903–1971) was the key member to the band's success. He wrote many of their arrangements, took vocal solos, led the vocal trio, and composed several hits, including: "Coquette" (1928), co-written with Johnny Green (Green's first published song), lyrics by Gus Kahn (Columbia 1345-D); "Sweethearts on Parade" (1928), lyrics by Charles Newman (Columbia 1628-D); "Boo Hoo" (1937), co-composed with John Jacob Loeb (1910–1970), with lyrics by Edward Heyman (Victor 25522); "Seems Like Old Times" (1946), again with Loeb, used by

Arthur Godfrey as his radio and television theme (Decca 18738); "Powder Your Face with Sunshine" (1948), lyrics by Stanley Rochinski; and "Get Out Those Old Records" (1950), written with John Jacob Loeb.

The band's personnel was a most steady one, with little change through the years. It basically consisted of: Guy Lombardo, leader; Lebert Lombardo, trumpet; Jim Dillon, trombone; Carmen Lombardo and Larry Owens, clarinets and alto saxes; Fred Higman, tenor sax; Victor Lombardo, baritone sax; Fred Kreitzer, piano; Francis Henry, banjo; Bernard Davis, tuba; and George Gowans, drums.

The band came to New York City in 1929 and had its own radio shows, besides being regularly featured on the Burns and Allen program. The Lombardo band appeared in several movies, notably MANY HAPPY RETURNS (1934), STAGE DOOR CANTEEN (1943), and NO LEAVE, NO LOVE (1946).

This band was the best plug a song could have during the thirties. They made extensive recordings and created more hit songs than any other band. They had unusually long residences at New York's Hotel Roosevelt Grill, and they broadcast New Year's Eve celebrations for over forty years on radio and television. Louis Armstrong was perhaps the band's biggest fan.

MUSICAL THEATRE IN THE THIRTIES

RODGERS AND HART:
"My Funny Valentine"

Richard Charles Rodgers was born in Hammels Station, New York, on June 28, 1902. When he was six years old, he was taken to see THE PIED PIPER, a children's show, composed and written by Manuel Klein and R. H. Burnside. The show was a significant one only because it sparked Rodgers' lifelong fascination with the theatre. Soon after, he was taken to his first Broadway show, LITTLE NEMO, another story for children, based on the cartoon characters of Winsor McCay, with music by Victor Herbert. Although the score has been mercifully forgotten, it so entranced the six-year-old Rodgers that he made up his mind to have something to do with the theatre as his life's work. Very much as the young Kern was taken with Herbert's music, so was Rodgers. In a few short years, it would be Kern's music, especially that from VERY GOOD EDDIE, which would make an indelible impression on Rodgers. Rodgers has said that he went to see EDDIE six times. It was while Rodgers was in high school that the Princess Theatre shows were being produced, and the experience of seeing them—and hearing Kern's music and Wodehouse's lyrics—proved to be the biggest impetus to starting his own career in musical theatre.

Rodgers had composed songs in summer camps and for assemblies in grade school, and when he was in high school, his older brother Mortimer, who was then going to Columbia University, asked him to compose the music for a benefit show that his club was putting on. Rodgers' involvement in ONE MINUTE PLEASE (1917) became a turning point in his life. One member of the club, Philip Leavitt, saw the need for Rodgers to have a lyricist, and he knew of one who happened to need a composer. On a Sunday afternoon in 1918, Leavitt took Rodgers to meet Lorenz Milton Hart (1895–1943) at his home, and the two discovered mutual likes, dislikes and theories about the musical theatre. They both admired the Princess shows and, although Hart was seven years older than Rodgers, they got along famously. As Rodgers later wrote in his autobiography, MUSICAL STAGES, "In one afternoon I acquired a career, a partner, a best friend—and a source of permanent irritation," referring to Hart's erratic work habits.

Within a few weeks of their initial meeting, Rodgers and Hart had turned out fifteen songs, one of which, "Any Old Place with You," was interpolated into A LONELY ROMEO (June 10, 1919), sung by Eve Lynn and Alan Hale. It was the first of their songs to be published, and it was issued by Jerome H. Remick & Company. The show was produced by Lew Fields, formerly of Weber and Fields, and he liked the new team enough to encourage them. He signed them to do the score for his next show, POOR LITTLE RITZ GIRL (July 28, 1920), but had second thoughts during tryouts and hired Sigmund Romberg to add eight numbers, thus reducing the team's contribution to eight. Of the published songs, "Love's Intense in Tents" was the only one to indicate the cleverness of the lyricist. The team met Lew Fields' son, Herbert, who wanted to write librettos for musicals, but had taken such jobs as acting, directing, and choreographing shows as a way of being in the theatre until he could write his own shows. For the next five years, the three created musicals that no one wanted.

GARRICK GAIETIES (May 17, 1925) came about when the junior members of the Theatre Guild wanted a smart revue to raise money to buy tapestries for the Guild's new theatre on Fifty-second Street, then under construction. The revue was also to be used as a showcase for these talented newcomers. The cast included Sterling Holloway, Edith Meiser, Romney Brent, and June Cochrane. When the show opened at the Garrick Theatre (originally scheduled for two performances but running 161 performances), Rodgers and Hart made a name for themselves with two hit songs, "Sentimental Me (and Romantic You)" and "Manhattan." This second song was helped by Paul Whiteman and his Orchestra's recording (Victor 19769). Through the years it has been featured in assorted movies, notably as a recurring theme in Bob Hope's film biography of former New York mayor and Tin Pan Alley lyricist James J. Walker, BEAU JAMES (1957). It was the first in a long line of song classics the team would produce.

THE GIRL FRIEND (March 17, 1926) told the story of a six-day bicycle race. It was written by Herbert Fields and produced by his father, Lew. The show starred Eva Puck and her husband Sammy White, who sang the show's two big hits, "The Blue Room" and "The Girl Friend." The title song, a charleston-inspired number with clever lyrics, hit the spot. It became an instant favorite, with marvelous recordings by Sam Lanin's Troubadours (Banner 1753) and George Olsen's Orchestra (Victor 20029). The two hit songs were recorded back-to-back by the famous piano duo Arden and Ohman (Brunswick 3197).

When the second edition of the GARRICK GAIETIES (May 10, 1926) opened, it contained another Rodgers and Hart hit, "Mountain Greenery."

The team was invited by English producer Charles B. Cochran to create a revue for the London Pavilion. It was to be called ONE DAM THING AFTER ANOTHER (May 20, 1927). Shortly before taking up their duties, the team spent a few days in Paris. On one of those days, while the pair took a taxi ride with two young ladies, they barely escaped colliding with another car. One of the women remarked, "My heart stood still." After Hart said that would make a good song title, Rodgers jotted it down. During their first evening in London, Rodgers found his note, sat down and composed the song, and gave it to Hart, who had forgotten about the incident. He fashioned a lyric and it was put into the revue. Rodgers liked the song so much, he bought the rights back from Cochran to include it in their next Broadway show opening in a few months.

A CONNECTICUT YANKEE (November 3, 1927) was based on Mark Twain's novel and contained not only "My Heart Stood Still" but also the cheery "Thou Swell." "Thou Swell" was introduced in the show by stars William Gaxton and Constance Carpenter, and was given a marvelous recording by Bix Beiderbecke and his Gang (Okeh 41030).

PRESENT ARMS! (April 26, 1928) was a curiosity not only because it imitated the vague plot of Youmans' HIT THE DECK (also written by Herbert Fields), but also because it took that show's star, Charles King, for its star. While the Youmans plot involved the Navy, PRESENT ARMS! was about the Marines. The hit of the show, "You Took Advantage of Me," was not sung by the principals but by Joyce Barbour and Busby Berkeley, who, in addition to being the dance director for the show, was also its second male lead. Rodgers and Hart were very surprised, although gratified, by the song's success, as they had hoped "Do I Hear You Saying (I Love You?)" would be the hit. Indeed, they had practically insured that it would be by placing it in the first scene and again in the third scene. It was also played during intermission and as part of the finale. It was the last music the audience heard as it left the theatre. As Rodgers wrote, "But people forgot it as soon as they reached the sidewalk. Maybe the title was too long, maybe the music was too delicate, maybe maybe maybe."

SPRING IS HERE (March 11, 1929) is notable only for the hit song "With a Song in My Heart." It appeared in the film adaptation of the musical (1930) sung by Alexander Gray and Bernice Claire. It became so identified with singer Jane Froman that her screen biography was named for the song's title. She sang it for Susan Hayward on the soundtrack (1952).

SIMPLE SIMON (February 18, 1930) began the thirties with what should have been a scintillating score. It was a Ziegfeld production to star comedian Ed Wynn and torch singer Ruth Etting. However, when the show was in its Boston tryout, Lee Morse was the female lead and "Ten Cents a Dance" was hurriedly written (in less than an hour) for her. This taxi-dancer's lament was soon given to Etting, who had replaced Morse by the time the song went into rehearsal. It stole the show and became identified with Etting (Columbia 2146-D). It was sung by Doris Day in the Etting film biography, LOVE ME OR LEAVE ME (1955).

AMERICA'S SWEETHEART (February 10, 1931) was the last Broadway show the team would write for five years. They were going, like everyone else, to Hollywood. The show starred Ann Sothern, using her real name (Harriette Lake), and Jack Whiting, who sang the show's only hit, "I've

Got Five Dollars." This became a popular Depression song. It was revived by Jane Russell and Scott Brady in the film GENTLEMEN MARRY BRU-NETTES (1955).

LOVE ME TONIGHT (1932) starred Maurice Chevalier and Jeanette MacDonald. The team created three memorable songs for this film, one solo apiece for the stars and a duet. "Mimi" was for Chevalier. He used it during his entire career, reviving it in the film A NEW KIND OF LOVE (1963). "Lover" was MacDonald's song, and Peggy Lee revived it in the film THE JAZZ SINGER (1953). Her disc sold over a million copies. "Isn't It Romantic" gave us one of Rodgers' indescribably lovely tunes. How-ever, while it was sung by both stars, they didn't sing it together. It was first sung by Chevalier to a customer in a shop, who sang it to a taxi driver, who then sang it to another, until it reached MacDonald, who finally reprised it. It was also featured in the film of the same name (1948). Although never in the hit class, the song has been a standard since its debut.

The team was invited by MGM to write the score for an update of MGM's early film musical, HOLLYWOOD REVUE OF 1929, to be called HOLLYWOOD PARTY (1934). One of the songs they wrote, for Jean Harlow, was "Prayer," but when she couldn't do the film they shelved the song. When asked to contribute a song to MANHATTAN MELO-DRAMA (1934, starring Clark Gable, Myrna Loy and William Powell), Hart merely rewrote the lyrics and called it "The Bad in Every Man." When Rodgers and Hart went to publisher Jack Robbins to discuss publishing the song, he told them that the tune was all right, but the lyrics were not commercial enough. Reportedly, Hart replied, "Commer-cial? I suppose it should be something corny like 'Blue Moon'?" Robbins quickly agreed that that was a good commercial title. Hart then worked on it and Robbins published it as an independent number. It was the largest-selling song Rodgers and Hart had had up to that time, and it was the only song they wrote which wasn't written for a show or film (at least not in its final form). It was featured by Ted Fiorito and sold more than a million copies of sheet music. When Elvis Presley recorded it in 1961, his disc sold more than a million copies. It is said that Hart always hated "Blue Moon."

MISSISSIPPI (1935) gave Bing Crosby "It's Easy to Remember (And So Hard to Forget)" and "Soon." Both made the Hit Parade and can be found today in many cabaret singers' repertoires.

JUMBO (November 16, 1935) brought the team back to Broadway for a Billy Rose production which starred Jimmy Durante, Big Rosie (an elephant), Gloria Grafton, and Paul Whiteman and his Orchestra. The three hits of the show were "My Romance," "Little Girl Blue," and "The Most Beautiful Girl in the World," a lovely waltz introduced by Donald Novis and Gloria Grafton. When JUMBO was filmed in 1962, the third song was sung first by Stephen Boyd, then reprised by Jimmy Durante, twenty-seven years after he appeared in the stage show.

ON YOUR TOES (April 11, 1936) brought together some of the theatre's savviest talents: playwright George Abbott, choreographer George Balanchine, producer Dwight Deere Wiman, and designer Jo Mielziner. It made stars of Ray Bolger and Tamara Geva, who danced the ballet, "Slaughter on Tenth Avenue." This extended number was to achieve an independent life in the concert hall. The hit song was "There's a Small Hotel," originally written for JUMBO but cut during rehearsal. It was introduced by Doris Carson and Ray Bolger. It was later used in the film PAL JOEY (1957), when it was sung by Frank Sinatra. The show was revived twice on Broadway, in 1954 and again in 1982, directed both times by George Abbott. When the last revival took place, Abbott was ninety-five!

BABES IN ARMS (April 14, 1937) provided a score with four hits which became standards, sung by an especially talented cast. "Where or When?" was introduced by Mitzi Green and Ray Heatherton. It was revived in 1960 in a best-selling record by Dion and The Belmonts. "The Lady Is a Tramp" was introduced by Mitzi Green in the show, sung by Judy Garland when it was adapted for a film (1939), and later used in the film version of PAL JOEY, sung by Frank Sinatra. It was also played for a state function when President Gerald Ford gave a dinner for Britain's Queen Elizabeth and asked her for the first dance. "Johnny One Note" was introduced by Wynn Murray. "My Funny Valentine" was introduced by Mitzi Green, but after Judy Garland sang it in the film version, it became one of her specialties. It is a favorite of nightclub singers, especially in February.

The stage musical I MARRIED AN ANGEL (May 11, 1938) was originally conceived in 1933 as a movie project for Jeanette MacDonald, with a book by the team. It wasn't produced until 1938, bringing together the stars of Friml's THE THREE MUSKETEERS (1928), Dennis King and Vivienne Segal. They got to sing the now-standard "Spring Is Here." When the film was finally made in 1942, the song was sung by Nelson Eddy and Jeanette MacDonald, thus taking nine years for MacDonald to star in a project written for her.

THE BOYS FROM SYRACUSE (November 23, 1938) had the finest score

Rodgers and Hart wrote during this decade, fully integrated to the story line, which producer-director-librettist George Abbott adapted from THE COMEDY OF ERRORS (1594) by William Shakespeare. The songs work beautifully within the context of this charming and hilarious musical comedy, and also have had lives independent from the show. "Falling in Love with Love," a lovely waltz, was sung by Muriel Angelus. "Oh, Diogenes!," "Sing for Your Supper," "What Can You Do with a Man?," "Dear Old Syracuse," "The Shortest Day of the Year," and the hauntingly beautiful "You Have Cast Your Shadow on the Sea," as sung by Marcy Westcott and Eddie Albert, have worn exceedingly well. "This Can't Be Love" was also introduced by Westcott and Albert, but was helped on its way to becoming a standard when Benny Goodman and his Orchestra recorded it. When the film was made in 1940, the team added "Who Are You?" to the score. There was a marvelous off-Broadway production in 1963 that demonstrated the show's lasting qualities.

TOO MANY GIRLS (October 18, 1939) included two of Hart's cleverest lyrics, "Give It Back to the Indians" and "I Like to Recognize the Tune." This last was a dig at the swing era's penchant for over-arranging a melody. The hit song was "I Didn't Know What Time It Was," introduced by Marcy Westcott and Dick Kollmar, also used in the film of PAL JOEY.

HIGHER AND HIGHER (April 4, 1940) contained one hit, "It Never Entered My Mind," which was introduced in the show by Shirley Ross.

PAL JOEY (December 25, 1940) was an off-beat musical based on short stories by John O'Hara, having an anti-hero and an aging prostitute as the central figures. The nasty, self-centered "Joey" was played on Broadway by Gene Kelly, with Vivienne Segal as his paramour. "I Could Write a Book" was introduced by Kelly, while "Bewitched, Bothered and Bewildered" was delivered by Segal. The cute "Zip," done by a stripper played by Jean Casto, is a take-off on the literary pretensions of Gypsy Rose Lee. The show had a very successful revival on Broadway in 1952, with Vivienne Segal recreating her original role for her final Broadway appearance.

A CONNECTICUT YANKEE (November 17, 1943) was the last show Rodgers worked on with Lorenz Hart. For this major Broadway revival, produced by Rodgers, the team created three new songs. "To Keep My Love Alive" is one of Hart's best comic lyrics and the last song he wrote. He died five days after the opening of this revival.

Rodgers and Hart's contributions to stage, films and the Alley give them top ranking during this decade. They contributed enormously to the high quality of popular music. While it was often difficult for a show song to stand on its own as a hit or standard, Rodgers and Hart's enduring works are proven exceptions.

COLE PORTER:
"Anything Goes"

Cole Albert Porter was born in Peru, Indiana, on June 9, 1893. He studied violin and piano as a child. He came from wealth and social position, yet he wanted to become part of the Alley. More precisely, he wanted to write musical comedies. His first hit, "Old Fashioned Garden" (1919), was a simple, sentimental song from HITCHY-KOO of 1919, not the smart, sophisticated stuff he had been writing as an undergraduate at Yale. His next hit, "I'm in Love Again," was introduced by the Dolly Sisters in GREENWICH VILLAGE FOLLIES OF 1925. Ben Bernie and his Orchestra helped popularize it.

PARIS (October 8, 1928) was the first real hit show that Porter enjoyed on Broadway, and the principal song of the show was "Let's Do It," introduced by stars Irene Bordoni and Arthur Margetson. With its catalog of the amatory habits of assorted animals, fish and insects, Porter earned his place as a writer of sophisticated lyrics alongside that of Lorenz Hart. When it was interpolated into the film CAN-CAN (1960), it was sung by Frank Sinatra and Shirley MacLaine.

FIFTY MILLION FRENCHMEN (November 27, 1929) sported two hits, "You've Got That Thing," which was sung by Jack Thompson and Betty Compton, and "You Do Something to Me," introduced by stars William Gaxton and Genevieve Tobin. Irving Berlin liked this score so much that he took an ad in newspapers to say that this show had "one of the best collections of song numbers I have ever listened to. It's worth the price of admission to hear Cole Porter's lyrics."

WAKE UP AND DREAM (December 30, 1929) first opened in London (March 27, 1929) with star Jessie Matthews. Frances Shelley introduced the hit song "What Is This Thing Called Love?," which was followed by Tilly Losch's dance to it. Porter was believed to have gotten the basic melody from listening to native music in Marrakesh. It still suits American audiences, often in the repertoire of nightclub singers.

With an ever-growing list of clever and sophisticated songs, Cole Porter divided his time between Broadway and Hollywood from 1930 to 1960. With his successes, Porter joined the ranks of George M. Cohan, Irving Berlin and, sometimes, Walter Donaldson in writing both words and music for his songs. He once described his method of working: "First I think of an idea for a song and then I fit it to a title. Then I go to work on a melody, spotting the title at certain moments in the melody. Then I write the lyric—the end first—that way it has a strong finish. It's terribly important for a song to have a strong finish. I do the lyrics the way I'd do a crossword puzzle. I try to give myself a meter which will make the lyric as easy as possible to write, but without being banal . . . I try to pick for my rhyme words of which there is a long list with the same ending."

THE NEW YORKERS (December 8, 1930) contained "Love for Sale," a song about the world's oldest profession, introduced by the provocative Kathryn Crawford. For years this classic was banned from the radio because of its suggestive lyrics. But there were plenty of customers for Waring's Pennsylvanians' recording, vocal by the Three Waring Girls (Victor 22598).

GAY DIVORCE (November 29, 1932) featured the great "Night and Day," which was introduced by Fred Astaire and Claire Luce. When the film was made (renamed THE GAY DIVORCEE (1934)), Astaire sang it again, in his first film pairing with Ginger Rogers. The song was responsible for keeping alive the show, which was referred to as "The Night and Day Show." Frank Sinatra made a best-selling recording of the song in the forties (Bluebird 11463). As with "What Is This Thing Called Love?," Porter was alleged to have gotten his inspiration for this song from listening to a native tune in Morocco.

"Miss Otis Regrets" (published in 1934) was one of many party songs Porter wrote during the twenties. He wrote it for his friend Monty Woolley, who impersonated a butler and delivered the lines to Porter's accompaniment at Elsa Maxwell's soirees. Wooley sang it for posterity in the Porter screen biography NIGHT AND DAY (1946).

ANYTHING GOES (November 21, 1934) was one of the two greatest scores Porter wrote. "Blow, Gabriel, Blow" and the title song were introduced by star Ethel Merman, who also sang them in the first film adaptation of the musical (1936). Mitzi Gaynor sang them in the second film version (1956). "You're the Top," another of Porter's famous catalog songs, had its genesis in the early twenties when Porter and a Mrs. Mackintosh would amuse themselves after dinner by trying to concoct a list of superlatives that would rhyme. It was introduced by Ethel Merman and leading man William Gaxton. The same couple introduced "I Get a Kick Out of You" early in the show. Thus unorthodox placing of a strong number so early in the show helped the show in this case. Part of the impact of Merman's singing came from the way she split the word "terrifically." She wrote in her autobiography, "I paused in the song after the syllable 'rif.' It was just a way of phrasing, of breaking a word into syllables, and holding on to one syllable longer than I ordinarily would, but for some reason the pause killed the people." She sang it in the first film version with Bing Crosby, while Crosby sang it with Mitzi Gaynor in the second.

JUBILEE (October 12, 1935) contained two Porter gems. "Just One of Those Things," written overnight during the show's tryout, and "Begin the Beguine." Again, Porter's inspiration came from the rhythms of an exotic dance he saw at Kalabahi in the Dutch East Indies. "Begin the Beguine" would likely have remained an obscurity during the thirties if bandleader Artie Shaw hadn't wanted to record it. He had just signed with RCA-Victor's Bluebird label, and the recording director wanted Shaw to do a swing version of Friml's "Indian Love Call." Shaw agreed only if he could record "Begin the Beguine," as arranged by Jerry Gray. The disc sold over two million copies and was the turning point in Shaw's career.

BORN TO DANCE (1936) was Porter's first full-score film. It starred Eleanor Powell and James Stewart. It was Stewart who introduced "Easy to Love," and in spite of his thin singing, the song became popular, even appearing on the Hit Parade, and eventually achieved lasting success. Frances Langford sang it in a reprise. "I've Got You under My Skin" was sung by sultry Virginia Bruce. It was given special treatment on record by Hal Kemp and his Orchestra. In the mid-fifties, Stan Freberg made a devastating parody of it, but by that time it was secure as a classic.

RED, HOT AND BLUE! (October 29, 1936) returned Porter to Broadway. It wasn't much of a show, but it did contain two Porter standards. "Ridin' High" was introduced by Ethel Merman, and she and Bob Hope sang "It's De-Lovely." When the second version of ANYTHING GOES (1956) was filmed, "It's De-Lovely" was sung by Donald O'Connor and Mitzi Gaynor.

ROSALIE (1937) contained two Porter gems and both gave him trouble. While the story was the same as the one for the Broadway show (1928), Porter was hired to write a brand new score, to replace the original songs by George Gershwin and Sigmund Romberg. The title song gave Porter a headache. He composed five tunes before he hit upon the one he liked. When he played it for Louis B. Mayer, head of MGM, Mayer told him it was too highbrow. He advised Porter to go home and "write a honky-tonk song" and forget that it was Nelson Eddy who was to sing it. Porter was peeved, and in exasperation, wrote the corniest song he could think of, using all of the Alley's melodic and lyric cliches for a love song. When it became a hit, Porter was insulted. Irving Berlin finally convinced him to "never hate a song that's sold half a million copies." The other song which became a standard, "In the Still of the Night," was also to be sung by Eddy, but he didn't like its long 72-measure chorus and complained that it wasn't suitable for his voice. Porter went back to Mayer and insisted that it remain and that Eddy sing it. Porter won. Not only did Eddy sing it beautifully in the film, he used it in his concert repertoire for many years.

LEAVE IT TO ME! (November 9, 1938) also contained two Porter standards. "Get Out of Town" belonged to Tamara Geva, and "My Heart Belongs to Daddy" made a star of Mary Martin. It was veteran Sophie Tucker, whose only Broadway book show this was, who advised Martin to sing it in an innocent, baby-like voice. The effect was to elevate Martin to stardom. She sang it again in the Porter film biography NIGHT AND DAY. Marilyn Monroe sang it in the film LET'S MAKE LOVE (1960).

DUBARRY WAS A LADY (December 6, 1939) contained one solid hit and another that would achieve success years later when interpolated into the film HIGH SOCIETY (1956). The second was "Well, Did You Evah?" The solid hit was "Friendship," which was introduced by Ethel Merman and Bert Lahr.

During rehearsals for MEXICAN HAYRIDE (January 28, 1944), Porter talked over a scene with producer Michael Todd. Todd asked him what was the most cliched title in the world. Porter's reply was "I Love You." Todd then bet him that he could take those three words and use only three notes—one for each word—and make a simple tune that would become the hit of the show. Porter accepted the challenge. Bing Crosby made a best-selling recording of it.

HOLLYWOOD CANTEEN (1944) used "Don't Fence Me In," a cowboy number sung by Roy Rogers in this wartime movie. It was originally written for an unproduced film (ADIOS ARGENTINA, 1935). It has been said that Porter paid a real cowboy $150 for the title and lyrics. Roy Rogers liked it so much that he got Porter's permission to use the title for his own western movie (1945) and sing it again. Kate Smith helped to make it a hit by plugging it on her radio program, and Bing Crosby and the Andrews Sisters sold over a million copies of their recording.

KISS ME, KATE (December 30, 1948) is, by general consent, the best and most successful of the Porter shows. It ran 1,077 performances. Based on THE TAMING OF THE SHREW (1603) by William Shakespeare, the show juxtaposed the latest swing ("Too Darn Hot") with Shakespeare ("I've Come To Wive It Wealthily in Padua," and "Where Is the Life That Late I Led?"). The score also contains "Always True to You in My Fashion," "Another Op'nin', Another Show," "Brush Up Your Shakespeare," and "So in Love." This last, in the early fifties, was revived on a best-selling record by Patti Page. Dick Wellstood made a splendid stride piano solo, turning it into the "So in Love Rag." When MGM made the film (1953), the studio added "From This Moment On," which had originally been part of the score of the flop Porter show OUT OF THIS WORLD (1950). In the film it was sung by Ann Miller and Tommy Rall. It was also used for a ballet sequence.

CAN-CAN (May 7, 1953) provided Porter with his last hit Broadway show. "I Love Paris" was inspired by set designer Jo Mielziner's rendering of Parisian rooftops. It was introduced in the show by French star Lilo, making her American debut. In the film (1960), it was sung by Frank Sinatra and Maurice Chevalier. It received a million-selling version by Les Baxter and his Orchestra.

HIGH SOCIETY (1956) was a musical version of Philip Barry's romantic comedy THE PHILADELPHIA STORY (1940). It starred Bing Crosby, Frank Sinatra, and Grace Kelly, with a happy sequence involving Louis Armstrong. The score provided "I Love You, Samantha" for Crosby, while Sinatra got "Mind If I Make Love to You" and "You're Sensational." The title song (a calypso) was sung by Armstrong. Sinatra and Celeste Holm sang "Who Wants to Be a Millionaire?," while Crosby and Armstrong joined forces for "Now You Has Jazz." Interpolating "Well, Did You Evah!," gave Crosby and Sinatra the longed-for duet, with Porter revising his original lyrics for the occasion. "True Love" became Porter's all-time biggest movie song. The soundtrack recording of Crosby and Kelly singing it sold over a million copies.

Cole Porter died in Santa Monica, California, on October 15, 1964.

HAROLD ARLEN:
"Stormy Weather"

Harold Arlen was born Hyman Arluck in Buffalo, New York, on February 15, 1905. He was given piano lessons, and he loved to sing. His main interest was jazz. He once said, "I even ran away from home once to hear the Original Memphis Five, a Dixieland group. They were my heroes." When he began to compose pop songs, it was in the jazz bands that he found his basic inspiration. When he was sixteen, he formed the Snappy Trio to play in Buffalo cafes. The group expanded to become the kind of five-piece jazz band he loved to listen to. Arlen then joined the Buffalodians, an eleven-piece dance band as pianist, arranger and singer. This group came to New York City in 1925 and played the Palace Theatre, where bandleader Arnold Johnson heard Arlen and hired him as arranger, pianist and vocalist for his band. The Arnold Johnson orchestra played in the pit of GEORGE WHITE'S SCANDALS OF 1928. Arlen sang a medley of songs in the pit during the intermission.

In the fall of 1929, Vincent Youmans hired Arlen to sing a song in his upcoming show GREAT DAY, but the number was cut during rehearsal. When the rehearsal pianist took ill, Arlen replaced him. While rehearsing the chorus line in a number, Arlen started fooling around with the introductory vamp, playing it over and over again. Each time, he would improvise a bit of melody, then change the harmony, until Will Marion Cook, the director of the chorus, told him that he ought to polish up the tune and write it down before someone stole it. Arlen took it to his friend Harry Warren, then on the staff at Remick's, who introduced him to lyricist Ted Koehler (1894–1973). Koehler gave the song its lyric and title, "Get Happy." It was put into the NINE-FIFTEEN REVUE (February 11, 1930) and sung by Ruth Etting. Although the revue lasted only seven performances, Remick's published the song. The song became such a hit that Arlen could give up performing and concentrate on songwriting.

Ted Koehler became his fulltime lyricist, and together they got the assignment to write the Cotton Club shows, replacing the team of Jimmy McHugh and Dorothy Fields. Harlem's Cotton Club featured black performers, but catered to an exclusively white clientele. The first revue there for Arlen and Koehler was called RHYTH-MANIA (1931), and for Bill "Bojangles" Robinson they wrote "Between the Devil and the Deep Blue Sea." Also in the score was the production number "I Love a Parade," and a Minnie-the-Moocher song for Cab Calloway, "Kickin' the Gong Around."

EARL CARROLL VANITIES—TENTH EDITION (September 27, 1932) included two Arlen-Koehler songs, "Rockin' in Rhythm" and the classic "I Gotta Right to Sing the Blues." The second became jazz singer-trombonist Jack Teagarden's theme from 1939–1947, when touring with his band.

AMERICANA (October 5, 1932) was a Shubert revue which featured only one Arlen song, "Satan's Li'l Lamb," which marked the first time he worked with both E. Y. "Yip" Harburg (1896–1981) and Johnny Mercer (1909–1976) as lyricists. Arlen was to work with each separately, and most rewardingly, later.

COTTON CLUB PARADE—TWENTY-FIRST EDITION (October 23, 1932) boasted a smash hit in "I've Got the World on a String," sung by Aida Ward in the revue. "Minnie the Moocher's Wedding Day" was tailor-made for Cab Calloway and his Orchestra, who featured it in the show.

COTTON CLUB PARADE—TWENTY-SECOND EDITION (April 6, 1933) was, by all accounts, the most successful of the series, thanks in great measure to Arlen's score, which included "Happy As the Day Is Long," "Raisin' the Rent," and the classic "Stormy Weather," introduced in the show by Ethel Waters. This was her first time to perform before a white audience, and it gave her career a tremendous boost. She made the song hers (until Lena Horne sang it in the 1943 film STORMY WEATHER). It was her superb rendition that prompted Irving Berlin to cast Ethel Waters as a lead in his Broadway revue AS THOUSANDS CHEER later in 1933. George Gershwin remarked on the originality of the structure of the chorus, pointing out that there is no repetition of any phrase from the opening through "keeps rainin' all the time." "Stormy Weather" broke with all the conventions of the popular song. Leo Reisman and his Orchestra had Arlen as the vocalist on the hit recording (Victor 24262).

Next, Arlen produced one of his rare songs not from a show or film score, "Shame on You" had lyrics by Edward Heyman (1907–   ).

CRAZY QUILT OF 1933, for its post-Broadway tour, interpolated "It's Only a Paper Moon," with lyrics by E. Y. Harburg and Billy Rose, into its score. The song was then placed in the film version of TAKE A CHANCE (1933), where it was sung by June Knight and Buddy Rogers. It first appeared, however, as "If You Believed in Me" in the flop play THE GREAT MAGOO (December 2, 1932).

"Let's Fall in Love" (1933) was Arlen's first movie assignment and was written for the film of the same name (1934), in which singer Art Jarrett and actress Ann Sothern introduced the number. It promptly became a success.

COTTON CLUB PARADE—TWENTY-FOURTH EDITION (March 23, 1934) included "Ill Wind," which Aida Ward introduced, and "As Long As I Live," introduced by sixteen-year-old Lena Horne and twenty-four-year-old Avon Long. Benny Goodman and his Orchestra recorded it with a swinging vocal by Jack Teagarden (Columbia 2923-D). It was the last of Arlen's major collaborations with Koehler.

LIFE BEGINS AT 8:40 (August 24, 1934), a title take-off on a popular novel of the day (LIFE BEGINS AT FORTY), was a hit revue with lyrics by Yip Harburg and Ira Gershwin. The score had two hits, "Let's Take a Walk Around the Block," and "You're a Builder Upper," which was introduced by Ray Bolger and Dixie Dunbar.

"Last Night When We Were Young" (1935) was another of the pop songs Arlen wrote without a show or film connection. Lyrics were by Yip Harburg. They wrote it to show appreciation to Lawrence Tibbett, whose house they rented in Hollywood for their first stay. Tibbett recorded the song and it became a standard.

HOORAY FOR WHAT! (December 1, 1937) had lyrics by Harburg and a cast headed by Ed Wynn. It included "Buds Won't Bud," which was to be sung by Hannah Williams (later Mrs. Jack Dempsey), but both she and the song were dropped before the show opened on Broadway. It was later sung by Judy Garland in ANDY HARDY MEETS DEBUTANTE (1940). "Down with Love" was introduced in the show by Jack Whiting, June Clyde and Vivian Vance. "In the Shade of the New Apple Tree" had a fine vocal arrangement by Hugh Martin, who sang it in the show. Martin would be prominent in the forties as a fine composer for films. "Moanin' in the Mornin' " was a feature for Vivian Vance and the "Singing Spies."

THE WIZARD OF OZ (1939) is one of the great musical films of all time. The score by Arlen and Harburg is a masterpiece, with six knockout songs. The most famous of the score, and the only Academy Award-winning song for Arlen, is "Over the Rainbow." As Judy Garland wrote to Arlen's biographer Edward Jablonski, "I have sung it dozens of times and it's still the song that is closest to my heart. It is very gratifying to have a song that is more or less known as my song, or my theme song, and to have had it written by the fantastic Harold Arlen." The other songs, "Ding-Dong! the Witch Is Dead," "If I Only Had a Brain," "The Jitterbug," "The Merry Old Land of Oz," and "We're Off to See the Wizard," are just as memorable and fit perfectly with the film version of the story. An incredible blending of talents created a magnificent whole.

AT THE CIRCUS (1939) starred the Marx Brothers, and Arlen and Harburg wrote "Lydia, the Tattooed Lady" for Groucho. This song became one of his most requested numbers.

"When the Sun Comes Out" (1941) briefly reunited Ted Koehler with Arlen. It was a hit, but was overshadowed by Arlen's next film score later that year.

BLUES IN THE NIGHT (1941) had a score with lyrics by Johnny Mercer.

The four songs are varied, yet all have a high quality. "Hang onto Your Lids, Kids" is a snappy, jive-laden song which perfectly fit the swing era. "Says Who, Says You, Says I!," and "This Time the Dream's on Me" were sung by Priscilla Lane. The title song became a hit almost as soon as the movie was released. Dinah Shore had her first million-selling disc with it, and it has become identified with jazz trombonist-vocalist Jack Teagarden. It has remained a classic.

STAR SPANGLED RHYTHM (1942) was Paramount's wartime tribute in a revue setting using its roster of stars. The most memorable song was "That Old Black Magic," which was sung by Johnny Johnston and then danced by ballerina Vera Zorina. It later became identified with singer Billy Daniels. "Hit the Road to Dreamland" was sung in the film by Mary Martin and Dick Powell, to the counterpoint melody sung by the Golden Gate Quartet.

CABIN IN THE SKY (1943) was the film version of Vernon Duke's Broadway show. For this treatment, MGM called in Arlen and Harburg to add three songs. "Life's Full of Consequence," a duet sung by Eddie "Rochester" Anderson and Lena Horne, and "Happiness Is a Thing Called Joe," an inspiring warm-glow number for Ethel Waters, the two most significant.

BLOOMER GIRL (October 5, 1944) was the first Broadway show Arlen had written since he joined the Hollywood colony. It was a nostalgic look at the Civil War era. The best songs were "Evelina," "The Eagle and Me," and "Right As the Rain."

HERE COME THE WAVES (1944) brought Arlen back to Hollywood. It also gave Bing Crosby the chance to make two of the Arlen-Mercer song hits: "Let's Take the Long Way Home" and "Ac-cent-tchu-ate the Positive." Crosby also reprises "That Old Black Magic" while spoofing his rival, Frank Sinatra, singing it.

OUT OF THIS WORLD (1945) contains another Sinatra spoof, this time involving an absent Crosby. Star Eddie Bracken "sings" the title song, using Crosby's voice on the soundtrack. "June Comes Around Every Year" is a double song, the only one Arlen wrote, and it stands up to those written by Irving Berlin.

ST. LOUIS WOMAN (March 30, 1946) is held by aficionados to be the best Arlen score, some maintaining that it is the best score for a Broadway show ever! Two of the Arlen-Mercer songs did become standards, "Any Place I Hang My Hat Is Home" and "Come Rain or Come Shine." The other songs include "I Had Myself a True Love," "Legalize

My Name," "Cakewalk Your Lady," "I Wonder What Became of Me?,"
"Ridin' on the Moon," and "A Woman's Prerogative," all of which have
entered the standard nightclub repertoire.

CASBAH (1948) contained two fine songs Arlen wrote with Leo Robin,
both sung by star Tony Martin, "For Every Man There's a Woman" and
"Hooray for Love."

THE PETTY GIRL (1950), with lyrics by Mercer, sported "Fancy Free."

A STAR IS BORN (1953) starred Judy Garland and featured a score by
Arlen and Ira Gershwin. Of the charming score, "Gotta Have Me Go
with You," "It's a New World," and "The Man That Got Away" are the
most important. This last song became almost as important to Garland's
career as "Over the Rainbow," and one of her most requested numbers
in her later years.

HOUSE OF FLOWERS (December 30, 1954) starred Pearl Bailey and
Diahann Carroll singing the Arlen songs, with lyrics by Arlen and
Truman Capote. The gems include "A Sleepin' Bee," "House of Flow-
ers," "I Never Has Seen Snow," and "Two Ladies in de Shade of de
Banana Tree."

JAMAICA (October 31, 1957) reunited Arlen with Harburg and gave
Lena Horne two more hits, "Cocoanut Sweet" and "Napoleon."

SARATOGA (December 7, 1959) brought Johnny Mercer back together
with Arlen and resulted in the fine "Goose Never Be a Peacock."

GAY PURR-EE (1962) is an animated cartoon feature, with the voice
of Judy Garland singing "Little Drops of Rain," a great Arlen-Harburg
gem.

As publisher Edwin H. Morris said to Arlen biographer Edward
Jablonski, "Anybody can walk in off the street and give you a hit. That
doesn't make him a great songwriter. Harold has always been a long-pull
composer who expresses himself honestly. His songs last and are, ultimately, more valuable, even financially, than the off-the-street hit."

Harold Arlen died in New York City on April 23, 1986.

VERNON DUKE:
"April in Paris"

Vernon Duke was born Vladimir Dukelsky in Parafianovo, Russia, on
October 10, 1903. After completing his education at the Kiev Conservatory, Duke left Russia and spent time in Europe. He came to the
United States permanently in 1929, composed his first Broadway score
in 1932, and became a citizen in 1938.

WALK A LITTLE FASTER (December 7, 1932) contained Duke's most famous song, "April in Paris." The lyrics were written by E. Y. Harburg. It was introduced by Evelyn Hoey, but didn't attract much attention. It was featured in nightclubs and became a cafe society perennial. Finally, society chanteuse Marian Chase recorded it and established it as a standard. When a film of the same name was made in 1953, Doris Day sang it.

THUMBS UP (December 27, 1934) was another revue, containing only one song by Duke, who wrote both words and music. A follow-up to his previous hit, it was called "Autumn in New York." It was introduced in the show by J. Harold Murray, and, like "April in Paris," which it resembles in no other way, it had to wait a number of years before it became a recognized classic. Louella Hogan made the hit recording of it. It is a brilliantly original conception which is both melodically and harmonically superior to most Alley songs. It truly deserves its permanent fame.

ZIEGFELD FOLLIES OF 1936 (January 30, 1936) had the hit "I Can't Get Started," with lyrics by Ira Gershwin. It was introduced by Bob Hope and Eve Arden. Two Hollywood writers were working on the BIG BROADCAST OF 1936 for Paramount when they saw Hope do the number. They hired him for the film, and his long movie career began. It also established the career of swing trumpeter Bunny Berigan, who made the best-selling recording both singing and playing it. It remained identified with Berigan throughout his career in the big bands. A WNEW-AM listener poll in 1985 named the Berigan record the "best pop recording ever made"!

CABIN IN THE SKY (October 25, 1940) gave Duke his last Broadway hit. "Taking a Chance on Love" had lyrics by John Latouche and Ted Fetter. It was introduced by Ethel Waters in her greatest musical role. She stopped the show regularly, giving half a dozen encores nightly. She also sang it in the film version (1943). When Duke first played the song for Waters, she stopped him after the first eight bars and said, "Mister, our troubles are over."

Vernon Duke died in Santa Monica, California, on January 17, 1969.

ARTHUR SCHWARTZ:

"Dancing in the Dark"

Arthur Schwartz was born in Brooklyn, New York, on November 25, 1900. He studied to be a lawyer, but eventually succumbed to the lure of the Broadway stage. While Ziegfeld made the revue an elaborate, lavish affair, there was a movement, with Schwartz at the vanguard, toward intimate revues that started in the twenties and flourished during the thirties. It took him several years to convince Howard Dietz (1896–1983) that they should team up to write for these smaller revues, but after he did, the team created the best of them. Schwartz began his writing with THE GRAND STREET FOLLIES OF 1926 (June 15, 1926) and convinced Dietz to join him for THE LITTLE SHOW (April 30, 1929), THE SECOND LITTLE SHOW (September 2, 1930), and THREE'S A CROWD (October 15, 1930).

THE BAND WAGON (June 3, 1931) gave the team their first real hits. The revue's sketches were by America's master comic playwright George S. Kaufman, the director was Hassard Short (who had done the MUSIC BOX REVUES and was responsible for the revolving stage, mirrors, and novel lighting effects in THE BAND WAGON), and the cast included Fred and Adele Astaire (their final appearance together), Helen Broderick, Frank Morgan, and dancer Tilly Losch. "I Love Louisa" was staged as a production number in Bavaria, dominated by a merry-go-round. It was the first time a Broadway musical had used a moving turntable. When performed in the movie version (1953), the song was done as a comedy number for Fred Astaire, with support by Oscar Levant. "New Sun in the Sky" was introduced by Fred Astaire as he smartened himself up in front of a mirror. "Dancing in the Dark," one of their most successful numbers, was introduced in the show by John Barker, and then danced to by Tilly Losch. It was written during rehearsals when Schwartz felt they needed "a dark song, somewhat mystical, yet in slow, even rhythm." He had written it by the next morning. Artie Shaw's recording in 1941 sold over a million discs. The title was used for a movie musical (1949), in which the song was sung under the credits, used as a recurring theme throughout, and was featured by Betsy Drake in a production number. In the movie version of THE BAND WAGON, "Dancing in the Dark" became an effective dance sequence with Fred Astaire and Cyd Charisse.

FLYING COLORS (September 15, 1932) had a cast consisting of Clifton Webb, Charles Butterworth, Tamara Geva, and Patsy Kelly. It also contained three Dietz-Schwartz hits. "Alone Together," their follow-up to "Dancing in the Dark," was introduced by Clifton Webb and Tamara Geva. "Louisiana Hayride" was sung by the two in a production number in the first act finale, featuring a night-ride effect. It also provided Webb with one of his famous dance specialties. In the movie version of THE BAND WAGON it was sung by Nanette Fabray. "A Shine on Your Shoes" was introduced on stage by Vilma and Buddy Ebsen, Monette Moore and Larry Adler. In THE BAND WAGON film, it was sung and danced to by Fred Astaire.

REVENGE WITH MUSIC (November 28, 1934) was the team's first book musical, based on the novel THE THREE-CORNERED HAT by Pedro de Alarcon. The stars were Charles Winninger, Libby Holman and Georges Metaxa. The score boasted two hits. "If There Is Someone Lovelier Than You" was introduced by Metaxa. It was originally written for a radio serial, THE GIBSON FAMILY (1933). Of all his songs, this was Schwartz' favorite. "You and the Night and the Music" was introduced by Metaxa and Holman. Al Bowlly made a hit recording initially, and the great ballad was revived in the late forties by Frank Parker.

"That's Entertainment" (1953) was the last hit song the team wrote together. It was for the movie version of THE BAND WAGON and was introduced by Fred Astaire, Nanette Fabray and India Adams (singing for Cyd Charisse). The song became the theme and title of two major film anthologies, THAT'S ENTERTAINMENT (1974) and THAT'S ENTERTAINMENT II (1976), MGM's collections of the best numbers from its musical films of the previous five decades.

Arthur Schwartz died in Kintnersville, Pennsylvania, on September 3, 1984.

THE SINGER OF THE THIRTIES

BING CROSBY:
"Where the Blue of the Night . . ."

Bing Crosby (1904–1977) was born Harry Lillis Crosby in Tacoma, Washington. He was nicknamed "Bing" after a cartoon character whose exploits he followed in a local newspaper. Crosby was one of the greatest entertainers of this century, as he recorded more than two thousand songs, selling a total of over five hundred million copies, with "White Christmas" alone accounting for more than thirty million discs. He was a movie star for over twenty years, appearing in over sixty films. He was in the top ten box office stars for five consecutive years in the forties, and was among the top ten radio personalities for over twenty years.

He and Al Rinker had a vaudeville act when they were hired by Paul Whiteman to join Harry Barris and become The Rhythm Boys in late

1926. After the movie KING OF JAZZ (1930), they left Whiteman to join Gus Arnheim's orchestra at the Cocoanut Grove in Los Angeles.

Crosby began his solo career in 1931 with a nightly radio show. His theme song was "Where the Blue of the Night," which he kept throughout his career. He began to record and to appear in films, the first of which was THE BIG BROADCAST (1932). His first starring role came in his next film COLLEGE HUMOR (1933). He changed from a heavily romantic style of crooning to a lighter, more airy style, helped in great part by John Scott Trotter's arrangements (he was Crosby's musical director for radio and on records). Crosby was greatly influenced in his jazz-tinged style by Bix Beiderbecke and Louis Armstrong. Crosby, Bob Hope and Dorothy Lamour made a series of seven ROAD pictures starting with THE ROAD TO SINGAPORE (1940) and ending with THE ROAD TO HONG KONG (1962).

With his many films, in most of which he introduced several song hits, with his many recordings, and his radio shows, he was the greatest plug a song could have in the thirties. He was one of the most beloved personalities in show business.

OTHER SONG HITS OF THE THIRTIES

1930

"Body and Soul" was composed by John W. Green (1908–89), with lyrics by Edward Heyman, Robert Sour and Frank Eyton. It first appeared in the revue THREE'S A CROWD (1930), where it was sung by Libby Holman and danced to by Clifton Webb and Tamara Geva. Leo Reisman and his Orchestra, featuring Eddy Duchin at the piano, made the first hit recording, followed by tenor saxophonist Coleman Hawkins' 1939 version (Bluebird 10523), which has become a jazz classic.

"Bye Bye Blues" was written by Fred Hamm and Dave Bennett. It was recorded by Hamm in 1925 (Victor 19662), although it was not published until 1930. Bert Lown and pianist Chauncey Gray somehow got their names on the sheet music after they recorded it in July 1930 (Columbia 2258-D). It became the theme song of Bert Lown and his Hotel Biltmore Orchestra.

"Fine and Dandy" was composed by Kay Swift (1905–) and written by her husband Paul James (1896–1969) for the revue FINE AND DANDY. It was introduced by Joe Cook and Alice Boulden.

"Goofus" was composed by bandleader Wayne King (1901–1985) and his violinist William Harold, and written by Gus Kahn. It was made into a novelty hit by Wayne King and his Orchestra (Victor 22600). Phil Harris' recording in 1950 sold another million copies (Victor 20-3968).

"The Peanut Vendor" was composed by Moises Simons, with lyrics by Marion Sunshine and L. Wolfe Gilbert. It was recorded by the orchestras of Abe Lyman, Paul Whiteman, Guy Lombardo, Xavier Cugat and Vincent Lopez. It was revived in the film A STAR IS BORN (1953).

"Please Don't Talk About Me When I'm Gone" was composed by Sam H. Stept, with lyrics by Sidney Clare. It was popularized in vaudeville by Bee Palmer and on radio by Kate Smith.

"Someday I'll Find You" had words and music by Noel Coward (1899–1973) for his play PRIVATE LIVES. It was, appropriately enough, used as the theme song for the radio program MR. KEEN, TRACER OF LOST PERSONS.

1931

"All of Me" was composed by Gerald Marks (1900–   ) and written by Seymour Simons (1896–1949). It was introduced in vaudeville and on radio by Belle Baker. After Frank Sinatra interpolated the song into the film MEET DANNY WILSON (1952), he made a recording that became one of his best-sellers. The song and its title were featured in a 1985 film. It has become one of the best known songs of all time.

"As Time Goes By" was written by Herman Hupfeld (1894–1951) for Frances Williams and Oscar Shaw in EVERYBODY'S WELCOME (1931). Rudy Vallee's recording made the song a moderate success. It was revived in the movie CASABLANCA (1942), where it was a musical theme throughout the film and was sung by Dooley Wilson. The song became so popular that Victor had to re-release the Vallee recording because there was a recording ban by the musician's union at the time. The re-release became a hit.

"Dream a Little Dream of Me" was composed by W. Schwandt and F. Andree, with lyrics by Gus Kahn, and was popularized by Kate Smith on radio and by Wayne King and his Orchestra.

"Good Night, Sweetheart" was written by English bandleader Ray Noble and publishers James Campbell and Reg Connelly. It was introduced in the United States by Rudy Vallee, who made a best-selling record. He later sang it in the film THE PALM BEACH STORY (1942). Ray Noble and his Orchestra performed it in the film THE BIG BROADCAST OF 1936 (1935).

"Got a Date with an Angel" was another English song hit, composed by Jack Waller and Joe Tunbridge and written by Clifford Grey and Sonnie Miller. Hal Kemp and his Orchestra, with vocalist Skinnay Ennis, made the best-selling recording (Brunswick 7319) in 1934.

"Just Friends" was composed by John Klenner (1899–1955), with words by Sam M. Lewis. It was introduced by Red McKenzie.

"Little Girl" was composed by guitarist Francis "Muff" Henry (1905–1953), with lyrics by Madeline Hyde (1907–   ). Henry was the guitarist with Guy Lombardo and his Royal Canadians, who introduced and popularized it. The song was used as the radio theme for Fanny Brice's popular BABY SNOOKS program.

"Marta" was composed by Moises Simons and written by L. Wolfe Gilbert. It was introduced and used as a radio theme by Arthur Tracy, "The Street Singer."

"Out of Nowhere" was composed by John W. Green and written by Edward Heyman (1907–   ). It was featured by Guy Lombardo, but the best-selling disc was made by Bing Crosby, the first of his many hit recordings. It was revived by Helen Forrest in the film YOU CAME ALONG (1945).

"Penthouse Serenade" was composed and written by Will Jason (1910–1970) and Val Burton (1899–1981). It was first recorded by Abe Lyman and later by Harry James. It has been a favorite of jazz pianists.

"Sleepy Time Down South" was written by Clarence Muse (1889–1979), Otis Rene (1898–1970) and Leon Rene (1902–1982). It was featured and used as a theme by Louis Armstrong and his Orchestra.

"That's My Desire" was composed by Helmy Kresa (1904–   ) with lyrics by Carroll Loveday (1898–1955). It was introduced on radio by Lanny Ross and featured by Morton Downey. It made the pop charts when, in 1947, singer Frankie Laine, who had been using the song in his nightclub act, was signed by Mercury Records to record it. His version sold over a million and a half copies, established Laine as a major pop singer, and made Mercury an important company.

1932

"In a Shanty in Old Shanty Town" was written by Little Jack Little (1900–1956), John Siras and Joe Young. It was introduced and featured by pianist Little Jack Little, and revived in 1940 by Johnny Long in a best-selling recording. In the 1950's the song was performed as a honky-tonk piano feature.

"My Silent Love" was composed by Dana Suesse (1911–1987), with lyrics by Edward Heyman. It was adapted from Suesse's instrumental "Jazz Nocturne." The song was revived in the late fifties by both Edie Gorme and Julie London.

"Willow Weep for Me" was composed and written by Ann Ronell, with a dedication to George Gershwin. It was introduced by Irene Taylor and the Paul Whiteman Orchestra, who also recorded it.

1933

"Everything I Have Is Yours" was composed by Burton Lane (1912–), with lyrics by Harold Adamson. It was introduced by Joan Crawford and Art Jarrett in the film DANCING LADY. Billy Eckstine had a hit recording in 1949 (MGM 10259), and it was sung by Monica Lewis in the film of the same name (1952).

"I Cover the Waterfront" was composed by John W. Green and written by Edward Heyman to be used in the film of the same name starring Claudette Colbert and Ben Lyon. However, the movie was completed before the song was written, so it wasn't included on the soundtrack. After Ben Bernie and his Orchestra plugged it on his radio show, the soundtrack was rescored to include the song.

"Stay on the Right Side of the Road" was composed by Rube Bloom (1902–1976), with lyrics by Ted Koehler. It was introduced by Will Osborne and his Orchestra and was also identified with Ruth Etting.

1934

"Cocktails for Two" was composed by Arthur Johnston (1898–1954) and written by Sam Coslow (1902–1982) for the film MURDER AT THE VANITIES. It was a gentle ballad, revived from time to time, until Spike Jones and his City Slickers made their recording in 1944. Their parody sold over two million copies (Victor 20-1628), and the song hasn't been performed straight since.

"I Wanna Be Loved" was composed by John W. Green, with lyrics by Edward Heyman and Billy Rose. It was introduced in Billy Rose's Casino de Paree in New York. It was revived in 1950 on a best-selling record by the Andrews Sisters.

"Love Is Just Around the Corner" was composed by Lewis Gensler (1896–1978), with lyrics by Leo Robin, for Bing Crosby in the film HERE IS MY HEART. Crosby also made the hit recording of it.

"Moonglow" was composed by co-bandleaders Will Hudson (1908–) and Eddie De Lange (1904–1949), with lyrics by Irving Mills. It was introduced by the Hudson-De Lange Orchestra. It was revived in the non-musical film PICNIC (1956), and Morris Stoloff and his Orchestra had the best-selling recording in a medley with the "Theme from Picnic" (Decca 29888).

"The Very Thought of You" was composed and written by Ray Noble. It was introduced by the Casa Loma Orchestra. It was revived by Doris Day in the film YOUNG MAN WITH A HORN (1950).

"What a Diff'rence a Day Made" was a popular Spanish song composed by Maria Grever, with English lyrics by Stanley Adams (1907–). It was revived by a best-selling recording of Dinah Washington's in 1959.

"Winter Wonderland" was composed by Felix Bernard, with lyrics by Dick Smith. It was made popular by Guy Lombardo and his Royal Canadians. A perennial Christmas favorite, it was revived in a best-selling disc by the Andrews Sisters in 1950.

"You Oughta Be in Pictures" was composed by Dana Suesse, with lyrics by Edward Heyman. It was introduced in the ZIEGFELD FOLLIES OF 1934 by Jane Froman. It was revived by Doris Day in the film STARLIFT (1951).

1935

"The Music Goes 'Round and Around" was composed by Ed Farley and Michael Riley, with lyrics by Red Hodgson. The composers were co-bandleaders and introduced this novelty song with Decca Records' newly-formed company. It was Decca's first huge hit (Decca 578). It was revived by Danny Kaye in the film THE FIVE PENNIES (1959).

"Rosetta" was written by Earl Hines and Henri Woode in 1928, but not published until 1935. It was first recorded by Earl Hines and his Orchestra in 1933 (Brunswick 6541). Teddy Wilson made two superb piano solo recordings—one in 1935 (Brunswick 7563) and another in 1941 (Columbia 36632). Hines made his solo in 1939 (Bluebird 10555).

"These Foolish Things Remind Me of You" was composed by Jack Strachey and Harry Link, with lyrics by Holt Marvell. It was introduced by Madge Elliott and Cyril Ritchard in the show SPREAD IT AROUND and was interpolated in the Olsen and Johnson film GHOST CATCHERS (1944).

1936

"Can't We Talk It Over" was composed by Victor Young, with lyrics by Ned Washington. It was made famous by Bing Crosby on radio, and on recordings by Eddy Duchin, Ruth Etting, Vincent Rose and Ben Bernie and his Orchestra.

"In the Chapel in the Moonlight" has words and music by Billy Hill (1899–1940). Shep Fields and his Orchestra made the hit recording. It was revived with a best-selling record in 1954 by Kitty Kallen, and again, in 1967, by Dean Martin.

"Is It True What They Say About Dixie?" was composed by Gerald Marks and Sammy Lerner, with lyrics by Irving Caesar. The team had ambitions for another of their songs with Al Jolson on his radio show, but Jolson wanted another "Dixie" song. As a compromise, they said if he would use their new number on his show, they would write him another "Dixie" song. They then threw this song together in very short order, called Jolson and sang it to him on the phone. He was delighted and promised to include it in his next broadcast. No one remembers what the other song was, but this one was one of his greatest hits. Rudy Vallee helped to secure it as a standard.

"It's a Sin to Tell a Lie" had words and music by Billy Mayhew (1889–1951). It was introduced by Kate Smith on radio and by Guy Lombardo on the dance floor. It was revived in 1955 with a best-selling record by Something Smith and the Redheads (Epic 9093).

"Pennies from Heaven" was composed by Arthur Johnston, with lyrics by Johnny Burke (1908–1964), for Bing Crosby in the film PENNIES FROM HEAVEN. The Crosby recording helped make it a standard. The song was used in the non-musical films FROM HERE TO ETERNITY (1953) and PICNIC (1956). It was further revived in a film of the same name in 1981.

"San Francisco" was composed by Bronislau Kaper (1902–1983), with lyrics by Gus Kahn, for the film of the same name. It was sung by Jeanette MacDonald and others under the credits and was a recurring theme throughout. With such exposure, the song became a hit. The film has been frequently revived and is popular with fans of MacDonald and co-star Clark Gable. Tommy Dorsey and his Orchestra had the hit recording, with a vocal by Edythe Wright.

1937

"The Merry-Go-Round Broke Down" was written by Cliff Friend and Dave Franklin. It was recorded in best-selling editions by Guy Lombardo and by Russ Morgan and his Orchestra. It is still a favorite with vocal groups.

"Once in a While" was composed by Michael Edwards (1893–1962), with words by Bud Green. Edwards is a perfect example of the one-hit composer. But, what a hit! It was first introduced by Tommy Dorsey and his Orchestra, with a vocal by Jack Leonard (Victor 25686).

1938

"I Hadn't Anyone Till You" had words and music by Ray Noble, who introduced it and made the hit recording, with a vocal by Tony Martin (Brunswick 8079). Mel Torme revived it in the late forties. It was also featured in the film IN A LONELY PLACE (1950).

"September Song" was composed by Kurt Weill (1900–1950), with lyrics by playwright Maxwell Anderson (1888–1959), for Walter Huston in the musical play KNICKERBOCKER HOLIDAY (October 19, 1938). After Huston had been cast in the play and before rehearsals started, Weill wanted to know what kind of singing range his leading man had. Huston replied, "No range—no voice." Shortly after, Huston went on a radio program and sang a song to show Weill how he sounded. It was after this broadcast that Weill fashioned the song to suit Huston's style. When the play was made into a film (1944), Nelson Eddy sang it. Bing Crosby revived it in 1946 on a best-selling record. It was also revived in the film SEPTEMBER AFFAIR (1950), when Huston's recording was used on the soundtrack.

"Sunrise Serenade" was composed by bandleader-pianist Frankie Carle (1903–   ), with lyrics by Jack Lawrence (1912–   ). It was introduced and recorded by Frankie Carle and his Orchestra. It was also featured by Glen Gray and The Casa Loma Orchestra. Glenn Miller and his Orchestra sold over a million copies.

1939

"If I Didn't Care" has words and music by Jack Lawrence. It was closely identified with The Ink Spots, a vocal quartet, whose recording sold over a million copies (Decca 2286).

"In the Mood" was composed by Joe Garland (1903–1977), with lyrics by Andy Razaf. It was recorded by Glenn Miller and his Orchestra, not only establishing the band, but also giving Miller his first multi-million selling disc (Bluebird 10416). It was interpolated into the film SUN VALLEY SERENADE (1941) as a feature for Miller and his band. As of 1988, it has been the most valuable copyright of Shapiro, Bernstein & Company.

"The Lady's in Love with You" has music by Burton Lane and words by Frank Loesser. It was written for the Shirley Ross-Bob Hope film SOME LIKE IT HOT. Glenn Miller and his Orchestra made a memorable recording (Bluebird 10229).

"South of the Border, Down Mexico Way" had words and music by Jimmy Kennedy and Michael Carr. It was written for cowboy star Gene Autry for the film SOUTH OF THE BORDER. Autry's recording sold over three million copies in two years.

In the thirties, the movies, a favorite entertainment medium, at long last began to talk. More importantly, they also began to sing and dance, using thousands of songs—both old and new. The major film studios created their own publishing units and bought up several of the largest Tin Pan Alley publishers. The most important composers and lyricists got fat contracts to work in Hollywood either on a picture-by-picture or on a long-term basis. The Big Band era began with Benny Goodman being crowned "King of Swing." Guy Lombardo made it equally big and was named "King of Sweet." Broadway musicals were enriched with works by Rodgers and Hart, Cole Porter, and Harold Arlen. Bing Crosby became the most popular male vocalist of this decade and all of Tin Pan Alley helped people forget the Depression.

THE ALLEY GOES TO WAR
(1940–1949)
The Major Publisher of the Forties

Leeds Music Corporation

The biggest new publishing noise in the Alley was made when Lou Levy (1910–   ) established Leeds Music Corporation in 1939. His motto was "Behind every great song is a greater song publisher." He was the era's most aggressive and, interestingly, best-liked publisher. He expressed his working philosophy this way: "If your competition is putting out blue dresses, you put out red ones." Levy acted upon that philosophy by publishing boogie woogie when the other firms were publishing ballads. When they picked up on boogie, he put out polkas. When they took up polkas, Levy went to calypso. He was not only the first publisher to exploit these different kinds of songs, he was the first to make each type commercially acceptable. His early folios of the works of Pete Johnson and Albert Ammons, for example, contained numbers which previously had been available only on their composers' recordings.

Levy was also the publisher who got more record performances for his songs than any of the other publishers of his time. Recordings generated a substantial income to publishers thanks to the Mechanical Royalty clause in their performance contracts, giving them royalties as the owners of the songs' copyrights. Since the mid-twenties, recording companies had used microphones to reproduce sound, and records were clearer than those made by the old acoustic method of recording directly into a horn. The range of sound became enlarged and more instruments could be heard more fully than ever before. After the end of World War II, when shellac became readily available, recordings started to account for more money in the Alley than did the sales of sheet music. Sheets remained popular and a significant part of the business for another decade, but Levy was the first publisher to take advantage of the sale of records to help fund the exploitation of unrecorded songs in his catalog.

246

As a young man, Levy was a champion dancer at Roseland in New York City, winning many contests to the music of Jimmy Lunceford's band. Later he became the manager of the Andrews Sisters, eventually marrying Maxine. It was at a talent show at a club in Harlem that he first heard "Bei Mir Bist du Schon," sung in Yiddish. Levy was convinced that the number would succeed if it had English lyrics. He persuaded his roommates, Sammy Cahn and Saul Chaplin, to write them, and got the Andrews Sisters to record the song. It became a hit. With the Andrews Sisters as the foundation of what was to become his empire, Levy started Leeds Music to give them a repertoire. He looked for the off-beat song or style and frequently found it. His tremendous energy as a plugger was legendary among his colleagues. He had the knack of employing other successful pluggers, who managed to get the Leeds songs onto the *Sunday Enquirer*'s "Music Sheet List," the *Accurate Report*, and the *Peatman Report*, which listed every plug on radio in the New York metropolitan area, and graded the kinds of plugs, whether played on a local station or on the network, in a medley or alone.

Levy's first hit song was "Undecided." It was followed by "I'll Remember April," "All or Nothing at All," "He's My Guy," "For Sentimental Reasons," "The Gypsy," "Now Is the Hour," and when he took over the publication of "Heartaches," he made it a hit all over again. He loved publishing novelties and began with "She Had to Go and Lose It at the Astor." It was quickly followed by "Dry Bones," "He Plays the Horses," and "Open the Door, Richard!" His boogie woogie hits included: "Beat Me Daddy, Eight to the Bar," "Rhumboogie," "Boogie Woogie Bugle Boy," and such hip numbers as "Well All Right" and " 'Tain't What You Do." He had great hits with such folk songs as "Galway Bay" and "The Foggy, Foggy Dew." Along with the novelties "Woody Woodpecker," and "The Old Piano Roll Blues," Levy popularized radio pianist-comedian Alec Templeton's satiric compositions "Bach Goes to Town," "Mozart Matriculates," and "Undertaker's Toccata."

With such variety of song types Levy exploited, it is startling to learn that his biggest-selling song in sheet music was Stuart Hamblen's (1908–89) religious song of 1950, "It Is No Secret." The same year Levy also had success with Meredith Willson's "May the Good Lord Bless and Keep You."

It is not very often that personal favorites of a publisher dictate a business decision, but when Levy purchased the J. W. Jenkins' Sons company, he did so because they owned his favorite blues number, Richard M. Jones' (1889–1945) "Trouble in Mind" (1937), and the Phil

Baxter (1896–1972) novelty "Piccolo Pete" (1929). Levy continued to confound the Alley and maintained his status as hitmaker when, in 1963, he published "I Want to Hold Your Hand," well before the Beatles were known in this country.

After he had acquired J. W. Jenkins' Sons, Clarence Williams Music, and Olman Music and had created Duchess and Pickwick, Levy sold all of his companies to MCA, Inc., in the early seventies.

MAJOR SONGWRITERS OF THE FORTIES

JIMMY VAN HEUSEN:
"Swinging on a Star"

Jimmy Van Heusen was born Edward Chester Babcock in Syracuse, New York, on January 26, 1913. While still in high school, he had a radio program on a local station, which featured his songs. It was then that he changed his name, taking his surname from the famous shirt manufacturer. He spent four years as a staff pianist in Tin Pan Alley, working for Santly Brothers and Remick's, before he was asked to write his first Broadway show, SWINGIN' THE DREAM (November 29, 1939), based on Shakespeare's A MIDSUMMER NIGHT'S DREAM (1595). From that score, "Darn That Dream," with lyrics by Eddie De Lange, became popular. Benny Goodman, who introduced it in the show, recorded an Eddie Sauter arrangement of it with vocalist Mildred Bailey (Columbia 35331). The following year, Van Heusen teamed with lyricist Johnny Burke to write "Polka Dots and Moonbeams" (1940), which became Frank Sinatra's first hit with the Tommy Dorsey Orchestra.

Van Heusen's teaming with Johnny Burke led him to Hollywood in 1940, when Bing Crosby asked them to write for the ROAD pictures. For THE ROAD TO ZANZIBAR (1941), the team wrote the lovely ballad "It's Always You." Crosby recorded it, and Tommy Dorsey and his Orchestra (with a vocal by Frank Sinatra) also made a hit with their version.

THE ROAD TO MOROCCO (1942) sported two hits by Van Heusen and Burke, "Constantly" and "Moonlight Becomes You."

DIXIE (1943) contained "Sunday, Monday or Always" and "If You Please." The former was sung in the film by Crosby, who also had a hit recording, but his rival Frank Sinatra sold more copies with his recording.

LADY IN THE DARK (1944) included his interpolation "Suddenly It's Spring" (1943) for Ginger Rogers. It was popularized by Eugenie Baird, who sang it on the hit recording by Glen Gray and his Casa Loma Orchestra.

AND THE ANGELS SING (1944) introduced "It Could Happen to You," sung by Dorothy Lamour and Fred MacMurray.

GOING MY WAY (1944) contained "Swinging on a Star," which was written for Crosby and which won for the writers the Oscar for Best Song. It was the first of four Oscars that Van Heusen would win in his career, more than any other composer has won so far.

The same year, Van Heusen, with comedian Phil Silvers as lyricist, wrote "Nancy, with the Laughing Face" for Frank Sinatra's newborn daughter. It was a good omen, as she grew up to become a singing star in the late sixties.

THE ROAD TO UTOPIA (1946) featured Dorothy Lamour singing "Personality," a song which Johnny Mercer recorded for a best-seller.

THE ROAD TO RIO (1947) contained "But Beautiful," which was sung in the film by Bing Crosby.

RIDING HIGH (1950) included "Sunshine Cake" for another Crosby best-seller.

THE TENDER TRAP (1955) starred Frank Sinatra and had a hit title song to start the long, profitable partnership of Van Heusen and lyricist Sammy Cahn (1913–). As a team, they would win three Oscars for their movie songs. As Van Heusen had won a previous Oscar with someone else, so had Cahn ("Three Coins in the Fountain" with Jule Styne). This film also began the new team's successful association with Frank Sinatra.

OUR TOWN (1955) was a television musical adaptation of Thornton Wilder's play (1938). It produced the medium's first original song hit, "Love and Marriage," which Frank Sinatra sang in the show and then recorded on a best-selling disc. It was the first popular song to receive an Emmy. It also received a prestigious Christopher Award for its lyric approach to the song's subject.

THE JOKER IS WILD (1957) was the screen biography of nightclub comedian Joe E. Lewis, played by Frank Sinatra. The only original song in the film was "All the Way," which received the team's first Academy Award for Best Song. Sinatra's recording ensured its success.

SOME CAME RUNNING (1958) gave Sinatra "To Love and Be Loved."

A HOLE IN THE HEAD (1959) was another Sinatra starrer, and the song "High Hopes," hurriedly composed and filmed on the last day of shooting, won Van Heusen and Cahn the second of their three shared Oscars. Again, Sinatra's recording was the best-seller. When Senator

John F. Kennedy was running for President, he asked Cahn to write his campaign song, so Cahn revised "High Hopes." After Kennedy's election, it was agreed that the song had made a significant contribution to the campaign.

The team wrote many title songs for films, including PARDNERS (1956), INDISCREET (1958), THEY CAME TO CORDURA (1959), SAY ONE FOR ME (1959), CAREER (1959), THIS EARTH IS MINE (1959), NIGHT OF THE QUARTER MOON (1959), HOLIDAY FOR LOVERS (1959), WAKE ME WHEN IT'S OVER (1960), WHO WAS THAT LADY? (1960), THE WORLD OF SUZIE WONG (1960), LET'S MAKE LOVE (1960), A POCKETFUL OF MIRACLES (1961), BOYS' NIGHT OUT (1962), THE ROAD TO HONG KONG (1962), COME BLOW YOUR HORN (1963), UNDER THE YUM-YUM TREE (1963), FOUR FOR TEXAS (1963), MY SIX LOVES (1963), JOHNNY COOL (1963), WHERE LOVE HAS GONE (1964), HONEYMOON HOTEL (1964), THE SECOND BEST SECRET AGENT IN THE WHOLE WIDE WORLD (1965), THOROUGHLY MODERN MILLIE (1967), and STAR! (1968).

PAPA'S DELICATE CONDITION (1963) was originally intended to be a starring vehicle for Fred Astaire in 1955, when the team wrote "Call Me Irresponsible." It was seven years later that the film was made, starring television comedian Jackie Gleason. As was the case with several other of the team's film songs, this song was a last-minute inclusion. It won their third Academy Award for Best Song. Among several hit recordings, Frank Sinatra's led the list.

JULE STYNE:
"It's Been a Long, Long Time"

Jule Styne was born Julius Kerwin Stein in London, England, on December 31, 1905. He came to the United States when he was eight years old, and received a thorough training in piano technique at the Chicago Musical College.

"Sunday" (1926) was the first tune Styne created while working as pianist-arranger for Arnold Johnson and his Orchestra in Chicago. It wasn't until he joined Bennie Krueger's orchestra that he took the song to Rocco Vocco, head of Leo Feist's branch office in Chicago. Vocco assigned lyricist Ned Miller (1899–   ) to it and published the result. It became an immediate sensation for Jean Goldkette and his Orchestra, featuring Bix Beiderbecke (Victor 20273). The orchestras of Abe Lyman and Sam Lanin also made successful recordings. Later "Sunday" was used as the radio theme of THE PHIL HARRIS-ALICE FAYE SHOW on NBC. Styne formed his own dance band and played in Chicago hotels and clubs. In 1938 he went to Hollywood to work as an arranger and vocal coach. His first big hit, with lyrics by Frank Loesser, was "I Don't Want to Walk Without You," from the film SWEATER GIRL (1942). The hit recordings came from Harry James and his Orchestra and from Bing Crosby.

In Hollywood, Styne teamed with lyricist Sammy Cahn, and their first hit was "I've Heard That Song Before," introduced by Bob Crosby and his Orchestra in the film YOUTH ON PARADE (1942). Harry James and his Orchestra (with vocal by Helen Forrest) recorded it in 1943 and sold over a million discs.

FOLLOW THE BOYS (1944) contained the only song of Styne and Cahn's to sell over a million copies of sheet music, "I'll Walk Alone," introduced in the film by Dinah Shore, who also had a best-selling record. It was revived by Don Cornell in 1952 with a hit recording.

"It's Been a Long, Long Time" (1945) was an independent song by the team, introduced on radio by bandleader Phil Brito. Harry James and his orchestra (with vocal by Kitty Kallen) made a hit recording.

"Let It Snow! Let It Snow! Let It Snow!" (1945) was another independent song hit for the team. Vaughn Monroe made the million-selling disc.

HIGH BUTTON SHOES (October 9, 1947) was Styne's first Broadway musical. The score, with lyrics by Cahn, included two hit songs, "Papa, Won't You Dance with Me?" and "I Still Get Jealous," both sung by Nanette Fabray in the show.

The film ROMANCE ON THE HIGH SEAS (1948) brought the team's next million-selling hit, "It's Magic," introduced by Doris Day and Jack Carson. Day's recording was a huge success.

GENTLEMEN PREFER BLONDES (December 8, 1949), Styne's second Broadway show, had lyrics by Leo Robin. They came up with two standards, "A Little Girl from Little Rock" and "Diamonds Are a Girl's Best Friend." Both were introduced in the show by Carol Channing, who became a star as a result of her performances of these numbers. When the show was adapted for a film in 1953, Marilyn Monroe and Jane Russell sang these two songs.

Styne's HAZEL FLAGG (February 11, 1953), a Broadway musical with lyrics by Bob Hilliard (1918–1971), had several hits, among them "How Do You Speak to an Angel," "Ev'ry Street's a Boulevard (In Old New York)," and "Money Burns a Hole in My Pocket," which were all used in the film version (retitled LIVING IT UP (1954)), starring Dean Martin and Jerry Lewis.

Styne and Cahn were sitting in their Hollywood office in 1954 when producer Sol C. Siegel came to ask them if they could write a song called "Three Coins in the Fountain." Cahn replied, "We could write a song called 'Eh,' if you want us to." When asked for details, Siegel told them that the studio had just finished a picture in Italy called WE BELIEVE IN LOVE, and that Siegel wanted the title changed. He figured that if a song existed to go with the change, the other studio executives would go along with it. Unfortunately, all prints were being used in editing and the script copies were still in Italy. When the songwriters asked what the film was about, Siegel summarized, "It's about three American girls in Italy who throw coins in a fountain." Styne and Cahn worked it out in an hour and soon had Frank Sinatra's promise to sing it on the soundtrack. His recording sold over a million copies, as did the one by The Four Aces. The song, featured in the film of the same name, also received an Academy Award.

MY SISTER EILEEN (1955) reunited Styne with Leo Robin, and the big hit of the film was "Give Me a Band and My Baby." The biggest recording was by Joe Carr and the Joy Riders (Capitol 3231).

BELLS ARE RINGING (November 29, 1956) had lyrics by Betty Comden (1919–   ) and Adolph Green (1915–   ). The score of this Broadway musical is excellent and contained two enormous hits. "Just in Time" was introduced by Judy Holliday and Sydney Chaplin in the show, and by Dean Martin in the film version (1960). "The Party's Over" was sung in both show and film by Judy Holliday.

GYPSY (May 21, 1959), based on the memoirs of Gypsy Rose Lee, was another hit musical for Styne, with new lyric partner Stephen Sondheim (1930–   ). They had a hit with "Let Me Entertain You" and also scored heavily with "Everything's Coming Up Roses," which Ethel Merman belted to success in the show. When the film version was made (1962), the latter was sung on the soundtrack by Lisa Kirk for Rosalind Russell.

DO RE MI (December 26, 1960) reunited Styne with Comden and Green for one hit, "Make Someone Happy," sung in the show by Nancy Dussault and John Reardon.

FUNNY GIRL (March 26, 1964), with lyrics by Bob Merrill (1921–   ), became Styne's last Broadway show with song successes. "Don't Rain on My Parade," "The Music That Makes Me Dance," and "People" were all introduced by Barbra Streisand, who also sang them in the film (1968).

Her recording of "People" sold over a million copies and received a Grammy Award.

THE DISNEY CARTOON SONGS:
"Whistle While You Work"

Walt Disney created many firsts in animated cartoons and in all of them, songs were central to his ideas. As soon as sound came in, he used songs in most, if not all, of his films, whether one or two reelers or full-length productions. Given the popularity of his cartoons, it was only natural that the songs composed for his films should also be successful. Two of the songs won Oscars. As the films are periodically revived, the songs remain part of our popular music heritage.

"Minnie's Yoo Hoo" (1930) was the Mickey Mouse cartoons' theme song and the first Disney song to become popular. It had words and music by Carl Stalling.

"Who's Afraid of the Big Bad Wolf?" (1933) was composed by Frank E. Churchill (1901–1942), a staff composer for Disney, with words by Ann Ronell. It was featured in the "Silly Symphony" THE THREE LITTLE PIGS.

"The World Owes Me a Living" (1934) was composed by Leigh Harline (1907–1969), with lyrics by Larry Morey (1905–1971), for the "Silly Symphony" THE GRASSHOPPER AND THE ANTS.

SNOW WHITE AND THE SEVEN DWARFS (1937) was Disney's first full-length cartoon feature. It had a brilliant score by Churchill and Morey, including "Heigh-Ho," "Whistle While You Work," "Some Day My Prince Will Come," "I'm Wishing," and "With a Smile and a Song."

PINOCCHIO (1940) had a glorious score by Leigh Harline and Ned Washington. The top songs were "Give a Little Whistle," "Hi-Diddle-Dee-Dee," "Jiminy Cricket," and the first of the two Academy Award Disney songs "When You Wish upon a Star," which was used as the theme song for the Disney television show of the 1950's.

"Der Fuehrer's Face" (1942) had words and music by Oliver Wallace (1887–1963) for the short, DONALD DUCK IN NUTZI LAND. The song proved to be so popular during World War II that the short was retitled to bear the same name as the song. Spike Jones started his reputation as a musical satirist with this number, the only song to become popular by making fun of Hitler. The recording by Spike Jones and his City Slickers sold over a million and a half discs (Bluebird 11586).

"Brazil" (1939) was composed by Ary Barroso, with an American lyric by S. K. Russell. It was included in the score of the film SALUDOS AMIGOS (1942). "Tico-Tico" (1943), composed by Brazilian Zequinha Abreu, with an American lyric by Ervin Drake, was a big feature for Xavier Cugat and his Orchestra. It was also heard in the film.

SONG OF THE SOUTH (1946) was a full-length feature combining live actors with cartoon characters. The score was excellent and included "Uncle Remus Said," by Johnny Lange, Hy Heath and Eliot Daniel. "Everybody Has a Laughing Place" and "Zip-A-Dee-Doo-Dah" were composed by Allie Wrubel (1905–1973), with lyrics by Ray Gilbert (1912–1976). The last was the second Oscar winner (so far) for Disney. While it was sung in the film by James Baskett, it had its hit recording by Johnny Mercer with the Pied Pipers.

SO DEAR TO MY HEART (1948) included the gem "Lavender Blue (Dilly Dilly)," composed by Eliot Daniel, who took the melody from a seventeenth-century English folk song, with lyrics by Larry Morey. It was sung twice in the film, first by Dinah Shore and later by Burl Ives, and was a hit record for Sammy Turner on Big Top Records in 1959.

CINDERELLA (1949) was composed by Jerry Livingston, with lyrics by Mack David and Al Hoffman. The score included "Bibbidi, Bobbidi, Boo," "The Work Song," and "A Dream Is a Wish Your Heart Makes." The last was sung on the soundtrack by Ilene Woods. Perry Como's version was a best-selling record.

ALICE IN WONDERLAND (1949) contained "I'm Late," composed by Sammy Fain, with lyrics by Bob Hilliard.

PETER PAN (1952) had a score by Frank Churchill and Jack Lawrence. The hit was "Never Smile at a Crocodile."

ADVENTURES IN MUSIC (1953) featured "A Toot and a Whistle and a Plunk and a Boom," composed by Sonny Burke, with lyrics by Jack Elliott. Spike Jones and his City Slickers made the hit recording (Victor Y-472).

"Mickey Mouse March" (1955), words and music by Jimmy Dodd, was the theme song of television's MICKEY MOUSE CLUB. Dodd was the leader of the Mouseketeers.

JOHNNY MERCER:
"Blues in the Night"

John Herndon Mercer was born in Savannah, Georgia, on November 18, 1909. While Mercer wrote both words and music, he was primarily known for his lyrics. His major collaborators included Harold Arlen, Hoagy Carmichael, Jerome Kern, Arthur Schwartz, Harry Warren, Jimmy McHugh, Johnny Green, Jimmy Van Heusen, Richard Whiting, Walter Donaldson, Rube Bloom and Vernon Duke. Mercer, who once said, "There are certain writers who have a great feeling for *tunes*, no matter where they come from. I think I'm one of them," was so prolific that it seemed he wrote with practically everybody: performers (Fred Astaire, Bobby Darin, Erroll Garner, Marian McPartland, Trummy Young, Blossom Dearie), bandleaders (Woody Herman, Artie Shaw, Duke Ellington, Benny Carter, Lionel Hampton) composer-arrangers (Gordon Jenkins, Elmer Bernstein, Ralph Burns, Neil Hefti, Paul Weston, David Raksin, Dick Hyman, Bobby Troup, Henry Mancini, Alex North, Michel Legrand, Andre Previn), and even took an idea and a title sent to him by Sadie Vimmerstedt, an Ohio housewife who worked in a cosmetic counter in a department store· in Youngstown. While Mercer wrote the words and music based on her title, "I Wanna Be Around," he shared the royalties with her. Tony Bennett made a hit recording. Vimmerstedt wrote Mercer letters telling him of the changes the song had made in her life. She was getting to be famous. People came into the store asking for her autograph. She was interviewed on Cleveland radio, then in Cincinnati. But when she was asked to go to New York City, she wrote him complaining that, despite her rounds of interviews and busy traveling, she still had to work every day the following week. "I'm tired, Mr. Mercer. I've got to get out of show business!"

Mercer first came to New York with a local Savannah drama company in 1927 and stayed. His first published song, "Out of Breath and Scared to Death of You," was composed by Everett Miller for GARRICK GAIETIES OF 1930 (June 4, 1930). His first real hit was "Lazybones" (1933), with music by Hoagy Carmichael, who was to be a recurring collaborator throughout Mercer's career. "P.S. I Love You." (1934) has a melody by Gordon Jenkins and was revived by the Hilltoppers in the fifties, and is not to be confused with the Beatles hit with the same title in the 1960's.

"I'm an Old Cowhand" (1936) was the first hit to have both words and music by Mercer. It was written for a Bing Crosby film, RHYTHM ON THE RANGE, and Crosby's recording gave it hit status. Roy Rogers revived it in his film KING OF THE COWBOYS (1943). With Matty Malneck, Mercer wrote "Goody Goody" (1936), which Benny Goodman turned into a hit with vocalist Helen Ward.

"Hooray for Hollywood" had music by Richard Whiting and appeared in the film HOLLYWOOD HOTEL (1937). This team scored again with "Too Marvelous for Words" in READY, WILLING AND ABLE (1937).

Harry Warren joined the Mercer bandwagon in 1938 for "Jeepers Creepers" in GOING PLACES, and "You Must Have Been a Beautiful Baby" in HARD TO GET.

Remarkable pianist Rube Bloom joined Mercer for "Day In—Day Out" (1939) and "Fools Rush In" (1940), this last popularized by Tony Martin. Glenn Miller and his Orchestra also made a best-selling recording. Ricky Nelson revived it successfully in 1963.

"And the Angels Sing" (1939) gave Mercer the opportunity to provide lyrics to trumpeter Ziggy Elman's feature with the Benny Goodman Orchestra. The same year, Jimmy Van Heusen wrote a tune for "I Thought About You," one of Mercer's most evocative lyrics.

Although they had written one song together nine years earlier, Mercer joined Harold Arlen in 1941 to write the film score for BLUES IN THE NIGHT. Many fans consider the work they did together to be the most important for each of them. They were both hip-deep in jazz and blues, both were affecting singers, and both were willing to experiment with the standard structure of the popular song. "Blues in the Night," for example, has no verse-chorus organization, but is made of three themes: an A section of twelve measures, a B section of twelve measures, a C section of sixteen measures, and a return to an extended A section of sixteen measures.

"The Waiter and the Porter and the Upstairs Maid" was another song Mercer wrote himself. It was interpolated into the film BIRTH OF THE BLUES (1941). It has the typical Mercer off-the-cuff manner, with a riff-based melody and a delightfully clever rhyming scheme.

1942 was a banner year for Mercer, six hits with collaborators and one hit by himself. His own hit was a novelty called "Strip Polka," which had best-selling recordings by the Andrews Sisters, Kay Kyser and his Orchestra, and by Mercer himself. His film score with Kern, YOU WERE NEVER LOVELIER produced two standards, "Dearly Beloved" and "I'm Old Fashioned." His film score with Arlen, STAR SPANGLED RHYTHM, produced the jazzy "Hit the Road to Dreamland" and another long convention-breaker, "That Old Black Magic." With Carmichael, he wrote the pensive "Skylark," and with film director Victor Schertzinger (1890–1941), he wrote "Tangerine" for THE FLEET'S IN. This song, with its subtle alliteration and internal rhymes, was sung in the film by Helen O'Connell with the Jimmy Dorsey Orchestra.

As if he weren't busy enough writing words, composing tunes, having his own network radio program, and recording other people's songs, he, along with lyricist B. G. DeSylva and record store owner Glenn Wallichs, formed Capitol records in 1942. With a roster of artists that included Nat King Cole, Stan Kenton, Jo Stafford, the Pied Pipers, Ella Mae Morse, Margaret Whiting, and Mercer himself, the company was successful from the start. Mercer's biggest recorded hits came from songs by other writers, such as "Candy" (1944), by Alex Kramer, Joan Whitney and Mack David (Capitol 183) and "My Sugar Is So Refined" (1946) by Sid Lippman and Sylvia Dee (Capitol 268). He made over one hundred recordings in his career including his duets with Bing Crosby, Nat King Cole, Judy Garland, Jo Stafford, Margaret Whiting and Martha Tilton.

"G. I. Jive" (1943) was a song by Mercer alone for the war effort. It combined military jargon with hipster slang. His own recording (Capitol 141) with Paul Weston's Orchestra was a big seller. The same year he and Arlen collaborated on the film score for THE SKY'S THE LIMIT. "My Shining Hour" and "One for My Baby" were both sung by Fred Astaire and turned into hits by him.

HERE COME THE WAVES (1944) produced the swing sermon "Ac-cent-tchu-ate the Positive," with music by Harold Arlen.

"Dream" (1945) was composed and written by Mercer, who used it as the closing theme of his radio program, JOHNNY MERCER'S MUSIC SHOP. Probably his most beautiful melody, "Dream" was first recorded successfully by the Pied Pipers, and was later revived by the Voices of Walter Schumann in a magnificent arrangement (Capitol 1505).

THE HARVEY GIRLS (1945) gave Mercer the first of his four Oscars for "On the Atchison, Topeka and the Santa Fe," with music by Harry Warren. The same year Mercer wrote the lyrics to David Raksin's (1912–) beautiful film theme "Laura." The lyrics were written after the film's release. Woody Herman and his Orchestra had the best-selling recording.

ST. LOUIS WOMAN (March 30, 1946) has a score by Arlen and Mercer, which fans of both think magnificent. It included the classic "Come Rain or Come Shine."

"Autumn Leaves" (1950) has a melody by Frenchman Joseph Kosma and "When the World Was Young" (1950) has a melody by M. Phillipe-Gerard. Both have American lyrics by Mercer.

"In the Cool, Cool, Cool of the Evening" was Mercer's second Oscar winner, with music by Hoagy Carmichael from the film HERE COMES THE GROOM (1951).

TOP BANANA (November 1, 1951) was the first Broadway musical about the remarkable new medium, television, and the first to have a complete score with both words and music by Mercer. The title song, "O.K. For T.V.," and "San Souci" were the show's highlights, along with star Phil Silvers.

Mercer's first all-words-and-music film score was DADDY LONG LEGS (1954), in which Fred Astaire introduced the sizzling, "Something's Gotta Give."

LI'L ABNER (November 15, 1956) was Mercer's most commercially successful Broadway score. The swinging Gene de Paul (1919–1988) music combined with Mercer's Dogpatchese lyrics to provide hits in "If I Had My Druthers," "Jubilation T. Cornpone," and the rhyming extravaganza "The Country's in the Very Best of Hands."

"Satin Doll" (1958) provided Billy Strayhorn and Duke Ellington's melody with Mercer's lyrics.

In "Bilbao Song" (1961) Mercer gave American lyrics to Kurt Weill's music, which scored a tremendous hit as recorded by Bobby Darin.

Mercer's third and fourth Oscars were for songs with music by Henry Mancini (1924–   ), for the non-musical films BREAKFAST AT TIFFANY'S ("Moon River") (1961) and the title song from DAYS OF WINE AND ROSES (1962).

Johnny Mercer died in Los Angeles, California, on July 25, 1976.

LIVINGSTON AND EVANS:
"To Each His Own"

Jay Harold Livingston was born in McDonald, Pennsylvania, on March 28, 1915. He studied piano and came to New York City in 1937 as a pianist and vocal arranger. He and his college roommate Ray Evans (1915–   ) went to Hollywood in 1944 to write for Paramount Pictures. Their first big hit was the title song for the film TO EACH HIS OWN (1946). The best-selling recording came from Eddy Howard. It sold over two million copies. The Ink Spots and Tony Martin each had hit recordings. The song also became a million-seller in sheet music and had a total record sale of three million. In 1961 it was revived by the Platters.

THE PALEFACE (1948) starred Bob Hope and Jane Russell. They sang that year's Academy Award winner, "Buttons and Bows." Dinah Shore's record sold over a million copies.

CAPTAIN CAREY, U.S.A. (1950) gave the team their second Oscar with "Mona Lisa." Nat King Cole's version sold over three million.

THE MAN WHO KNEW TOO MUCH (1956) provided them with their third Oscar. "Whatever Will Be, Will Be (Que Sera, Sera)" was introduced in the Alfred Hitchcock thriller by Doris Day. Her recording sold over a million copies. It was the first time a song was used in a Hitchcock film.

TAMMY AND THE BACHELOR (1957) sported "Tammy," sung in the film by Debbie Reynolds. Her recording sold over a million copies, which was not bad, considering the fact that over one hundred other artists also recorded the song, for a total sale of over ten million records.

OH, CAPTAIN (February 4, 1958) was the Broadway version of the Alec Guinness film CAPTAIN'S PARADISE (1953). "You're So Right for Me" was the hit of Livingston and Evans' charming score.

SID LIPPMAN:
" 'A' You're Adorable"

Sidney Lippman was born in Minneapolis, Minnesota, on March 1, 1914. He came to New York City with a scholarship to Juilliard and became, first, an assistant professional manager at Chappell Music, and then a staff arranger at Irving Berlin, Inc. While there, he met Hal Dickenson, leader of The Modernaires, Glenn Miller's vocal group. Dickenson needed a melody for his lyrics and Lippman supplied it. "These Things You Left Me" (1940) became his first hit. Eddie Sauter made a superb arrangement for Benny Goodman and his Orchestra, with a vocal by Helen Forrest, for a best-selling recording (Columbia 35910). Another popular version was the one by Charlie Barnet and his Orchestra, with a vocal by Bob Carroll (Bluebird 11004).

"I'm Thrilled" (1941) had lyrics by Sylvia Dee (1914–1967) and received a great Bill Finegan arrangement for Glenn Miller's Orchestra (Bluebird 11287). The new team of Lippman and Dee stayed together for sixteen years.

"Chickery Chick" (1945) was the team's successor to "Mairzy Doats." With nonsense syllables taken from an old folk song, it became immediately popular with children. Sammy Kaye and his Orchestra and Gene Krupa and his Orchestra with vocalist Anita O'Day, had two of several hit recordings.

"My Sugar Is So Refined" (1946) came about at a lunch one day when Dee looked at the wrapper on a sugar cube, which read "refined sugar." She remarked to Lippman, "Isn't that a cute idea?" Johnny Mercer thought so too, and he had the hit recording.

BAREFOOT BOY WITH CHEEK (April 3, 1947) was the team's only Broadway show. The hit song was "After Graduation Day."

" 'A' You're Adorable" (1948) had lyrics by Lippman's first collaborators, Buddy Kaye and Fred Wise. The song was written several years before its publication. The three would begin each work session by exchanging jokes, one about a man recommending a friend for a job by listing his qualifications alphabetically: A—he's amiable, B—he's benevolent, etc. From this came the idea for the song. It was a hit for Jo Stafford and Gordon MacRae, and for Perry Como with the Fontane Sisters.

"Too Young" (1951) was the Lippman-Dee collaboration's biggest song. It was introduced by Johnny Desmond, then recorded by Nat King Cole (Capitol 1449), whose disc sold over a million copies. "Too Young" was on the HIT PARADE longer than any other song (twenty seven weeks, and in the number one spot for twelve)! It is a great all-time standard.

WORLD WAR II SONGS

Even though there were more songs written about the First World War, World War II brought home more changes, as our lives were inconvenienced by food (especially sugar) and gas rations, a shellac shortage (limiting the number of records pressed), a paper shortage (limiting the amount of sheet music), and blackouts. It is not surprising that our top songwriters contributed to the war effort by writing songs and, often, donating their revenue to military and civilian agencies. Irving Berlin led off with "Arms for the Love of America" (1941), for the Army Ordinance Department; George M. Cohan wrote "For the Flag, for the Home, for the Family" (1942); Rodgers and Hart wrote "The Bombardier Song" (1942) for the Bomber Crews of the U. S. Army Air Forces; Hoagy Carmichael wrote "The Cranky Old Yank (In a Clanky Old Tank)" (1942); the new team of Rodgers and Hammerstein wrote "The P.T. Boat Song" (1943) for the Motor Torpedo Boats of the Navy; Cole Porter also paid tribute to the Navy with "Sailors of the Sky" (1943); Vernon Duke and Howard Dietz wrote "The Silver Shield" (1943) in honor of the U.S. Coast Guard; Meredith Willson wrote "Fire Up!" (1943), a marching song for the Chemical Warfare Service.

Gerald Marks and Irving Caesar got an early start with "Ev'ry One's a Fighting Son of That Old Gang of Mine" (1940). Willie Lee Duckworth wrote "Sound Off" (1940) as part of "The Cadence System of Teaching Close Order Drill."

J. Fred Coots wrote the hit "Goodbye Mama (I'm Off to Yokohama)" (1941), while Ernie Burnett and Jack Meskill took another vantage point with "Since Kitten's Knittin' Mittens (for the Army)" (1941).

Joe Howard, using an official slogan of the Army, Navy and Marines, wrote his "Keep Mum Chum" (1942), and Sam H. Stept and Ted Koehler wrote "I'm Mighty Proud of That Old Gang of Mine" (1942). "Don't Sit under the Apple Tree" was another great wartime song by Sam Stept, with lyrics by Lew Brown and Charles Tobias. The best-selling records were made by The Andrews Sisters, Kay Kyser and his Orchestra, and Glenn Miller and his Orchestra. "When the Lights Go On Again" was the work of Bennie Benjamin, Eddie Seiler and Sol Marcus, with a best-selling recording by Vaughn Monroe (Victor 27945). The same year Frank Loesser wrote what became the most popular song of World War II, "Praise the Lord and Pass the Ammunition!!"

Johnny Mercer contributed "G.I. Jive"; Kay Swift wrote "Fighting on the Home Front Wins," dedicated to the American housewife; Jimmy McHugh and Harold Adamson wrote one of the best war songs, "Comin' In on a Wing and a Prayer"; and Jule Styne and Sammy Cahn celebrated prematurely with "Vict'ry Polka," all in 1943.

"Bell Bottom Trousers" (1944) was a bawdy sea chantey with new lyrics by Moe Jaffe. Vincent Lopez and his Orchestra popularized it, and Tony Pastor and his Orchestra had a best-selling recording.

While the output of World War II songs was far below the numbers of those written for the First World War, the quality was much better, and the public got behind the ones for the Second World War as a gesture of patriotism.

DANCES OF THE FORTIES

LATIN AMERICAN DANCES:
"Tico-Tico"

While the jitterbug and the fox trot were still very popular, everyone was learning the rhumba and samba, and many Latin songs were given English lyrics. "Green Eyes" (1929, 1941), by Nilo Menendez, with words by E. Rivera and E. Woods, sold over a million discs in the version by Jimmy Dorsey and his Orchestra, with vocals by Helen O'Connell and Bob Eberly. "Frenesi" (1939), composed by Alberto Dominguez and written by Ray Charles and S. K. Russell, was popularized by Artie Shaw and his expanded orchestra in 1940 in a recording which sold over three million copies. These early war years saw the rise of singer Carmen Miranda. Even Walt Disney got into the act with his cartoon SALUDOS AMIGOS (1942), which included "Brazil" and "Tico-Tico."

"Besame Mucho" (1941, 1943) was composed by Consuelo Velazquez, with American lyrics by Sunny Skylar, and made famous by Jimmy Dorsey and his Orchestra. "Miami Beach Rhumba" (1946) was composed by Irving Fields, with lyrics by Albert Gamse. The Fields Trio had the hit recording.

GLENN MILLER:
"In the Mood"

Alton Glenn Miller (1904–1944) led the most popular dance band of all time. He joined Ben Pollack's band in Chicago in 1926 and came to New York City with them. He became a studio musician and arranger. He was a fine trombonist but not an outstanding soloist. He played in several pit bands on Broadway, sometimes led by Red Nichols, Benny Goodman and the Dorsey Brothers. He organized Ray Noble's first American band in 1935, and first formed his own band in 1937. His second band, organized in 1938, clicked the next year when he played that summer at Glen Island Casino in New Rochelle, New York, and made many radio broadcasts. For this band he created what became his famous "reed" sound, with clarinetist Wilbur Schwartz playing over the sax section.

Miller's 1939 summer recordings took the music world by storm. He recorded a double-sided hit with his theme song "Moonlight Serenade" on one side, and "Sunrise Serenade" on the other (Bluebird 10214). Arranger Bill Finegan made a swinging version of "Little Brown Jug" (Bluebird 10286), which was one of the band's most important hits. Still later that summer, the band recorded Joe Garland's "In the Mood," in an arrangement by Miller himself. His other big hits included Erskine Hawkins' "Tuxedo Junction" (Bluebird 10612), Jerry Gray's "Pennsylvania 6-5000" (Bluebird 10754) which was based on a riff from Larry Clinton's "Dipsy Doodle") (Victor 25693, Tommy Dorsey and his Orchestra), Harry Warren's "Chattanooga Choo Choo" (Bluebird 11230), featuring the vocal quartet The Modernaires, and Jerry Gray's "A String of Pearls" (Bluebird 11382).

The personnel for "In the Mood," recorded on August 1, 1939, were:

Clyde Hurley, Lee Knowles and R. McMickle, trumpets; Glenn Miller, Al Mastren, Paul Tanner, trombones; Wilbur Schwartz, clarinet; Hal McIntyre, alto sax; Tex Beneke, Al Klink and Harold Tennyson, tenor saxes; Chummy MacGregor, piano; Richard Fisher, guitar; Rowland Bundock, string bass; and Moe Purtill, drums.

The band starred in the films SUN VALLEY SERENADE (1941) and ORCHESTRA WIVES (1942). The band broke up in September 1942, when Miller enlisted in the Army Air Force as a captain. His plane was lost on a flight from England to France, and Miller was declared dead on December 18, 1944. THE GLENN MILLER STORY (1954) starred Jimmy Stewart in the title role.

XAVIER CUGAT:
"Isle of Capri"

Xavier Cugat (1900 –) was born in Barcelona, Spain, and came to America via Cuba in the mid-twenties. He organized a band specializing in Latin music, and opened at the Coconut Grove in Los Angeles. Besides being the most famous bandleader in this style, Cugat was also a noted caricaturist. His art work often appeared on sheet music covers. He composed a beautiful theme, "My Shawl" (1934), with lyrics by Stanley Adams, (Victor 24508). His other compositions include "Rain in Spain" (1934) (Victor 24387), "Night Must Fall" (1939) (Victor 26074), and "Nightingale" (1942) (Columbia 36559).

From the thirties through the fifties, Cugat made many successful appearances at the Waldorf-Astoria Hotel in New York City. The Cugat band was one of three featured on the now-historic LET'S DANCE program (which brought initial fame to Benny Goodman and his Orchestra). During the forties, Cugat had several radio programs, and appeared as a guest on the shows of others. He was a regular on the Garry Moore-Jimmy Durante Show. He was a favorite on television during the early fifties, when the cha-cha became popular.

Cugat and his orchestra appeared in more films than any other dance band: GO WEST, YOUNG MAN (1937), YOU WERE NEVER LOVELIER (1942), THE HEAT'S ON (1943), STAGE DOOR CANTEEN (1943), BATHING BEAUTY (1944), TWO GIRLS AND A SAILOR (1944), WEEKEND AT THE WALDORF (1945), HOLIDAY IN MEXICO (1946), NO LEAVE NO LOVE (1946), THIS TIME FOR KEEPS (1947), A DATE WITH JUDY (1948), LUXURY LINER (1948), ON AN ISLAND WITH YOU (1948), NEPTUNE'S DAUGHTER (1949), CHICAGO SYNDICATE (1955), and THE PHYNX (1969).

The Cugat band was an important vehicle for the new Latin sounds invading the Alley. A typical personnel included: Phil Hart and Joseph Piana, trumpets; Ruben Moss and Max Nadel, clarinet, alto sax and tenor sax; Xavier Cugat and Max Warnowsky, violins; Nilo Menendez, piano; Billy Hobbs, piano-accordion; Pedro Berrios, guitar; Florence Wightman, harp; Charles Gonzales, string bass; Albert Calderon and Catalino Rolon, drums, maracas, claves; Antonio Lopez, bongos. His vocalists included Carmen Castillo, Lina Romay and Miguelito Valdes.

Among Cugat's many hits were "Isle of Capri" (Victor 24813), "The Lady in Red (Victor 25012), "Begin the Beguine" (Victor 25133), "Say 'Si Si' " (Victor 25407), "Perfidia" (Victor 26334), "The Breeze and I" (Victor 26641), "La Cucaracha" (Columbia 36091), and "Thrill Me" (Columbia 38558).

MUSICAL THEATRE IN THE FORTIES

RODGERS AND HAMMERSTEIN:
"Some Enchanted Evening"

Oscar Hammerstein II was born in New York City on July 12, 1895. He came from a distinguished theatrical family. His grandfather, Oscar I, was a world-famous opera impresario, whose Manhattan Opera Company was bought by the Metropolitan Opera Association. He also built the Victoria Theatre and produced vaudeville shows. The Victoria was managed by William Hammerstein, Oscar's father. His uncle Arthur was a successful producer of Broadway plays and musicals.

Hammerstein started his book and lyric writing while attending Columbia College, writing the varsity show. His first musical comedy, ALWAYS YOU (January 5, 1920), was produced on Broadway by his uncle Arthur. With Otto Harbach, Hammerstein shared the book and lyric writing of the Vincent Youmans show WILDFLOWER (1923). Hammerstein helped make musical history with Jerome Kern when they wrote SHOW BOAT (1927) and MUSIC IN THE AIR (1932). They won an Academy Award for "The Last Time I Saw Paris" (1940), which was interpolated into LADY, BE GOOD! (1941). In addition, Hammerstein wrote book and lyrics for three of the greatest American operettas, Friml's ROSE-MARIE (1924), and Romberg's THE DESERT SONG (1926) and THE NEW MOON (1928).

Richard Rodgers needed a partner after Lorenz Hart turned down the offer to transform Lynn Riggs' play GREEN GROW THE LILACS (1931) into a musical for the Theatre Guild. Hart honestly didn't think it would work. Rodgers, who had known Hammerstein since his own school days at Columbia, invited him to lunch to discuss the project. Hammerstein confided to Rodgers that he had thought of the same project when he was working with Kern, but that Kern, too, had turned it down. Rodgers remembered that first meeting: "Oscar and I hit it off from the day we began discussing the show."

Rodgers' new partnership was in complete contrast to his old one. Whereas Rodgers and Hart lived totally separate lives, and Hart wrote to Rodgers' music, Rodgers and Hammerstein became great friends, shared similar values and lived similar lives. Hammerstein created the lyrics first. As he developed his lyrics, Hammerstein would make up his own dummy tunes. His wife Dorothy once described them as, "Melodies so terrible that they want to make you cry."

The result of Rodgers and Hammerstein's shared passion for "Green Grow the Lilacs" was OKLAHOMA! (March 31, 1943), which refined the musical comedy form when Hammerstein's lyrics, like the dialogue, for the first time advanced the plot. The only exception to their working method in the score was "People Will Say We're in Love." Rodgers composed the music immediately after they had discussed the kind of song it was to be, without waiting for Hammerstein's lyric. While the show was trying out in New Haven, it was titled AWAY WE GO! The musical play had no stars, no chorus girls, no big laughs, and no popular dance routines. The word-of-mouth to Broadway from New Haven was "no girls, no gags, no chance." After its March 31st opening night, the slogan could have been changed to "no girls, no gags, no tickets," as it ran for 2,248 performances. The marvelous score included "All 'Er Nothin'," "I Cain't Say No," "Kansas City," "Many a New Day," "Oh, What a Beautiful Mornin'," "Oklahoma!," "Pore Jud," and "The Surrey with the Fringe on Top." This show was the first to issue an original-cast album recording, a Decca album selling over a million copies, starting the now-standard practice of offering the complete score of a show on a disc featuring the original Broadway cast. The Broadway cast toured for a year, and a second national company toured for ten years. It was to handle this show's music that Rodgers and Hammerstein established their own publishing company, Williamson Music, Inc., named after both their fathers. The film, starring Shirley Jones and Gordon MacRae, was released in 1955.

STATE FAIR (1945) was offered to the team because producer Darryl

F. Zanuck wanted a film that contained the same kind of homespun feeling that OKLAHOMA! engendered. "It's a Grand Night for Singing" was a classic example of a song never coming near the HIT PARADE, yet becoming a standard. "It Might As Well Be Spring" took Hammerstein an agonizing week to work out, but it took Rodgers less than an hour to compose. It also won for them the Academy Award for Best Song, and became one of the team's all-time hits. This one did get on YOUR HIT PARADE, and stayed on for seventeen weeks! STATE FAIR was the team's only original film score, although Hollywood made highly successful film versions of their Broadway musicals. STATE FAIR was remade in 1962, starring Pat Boone and Ann-Margret, with five new songs with words and music by Rodgers alone. Unfortunately, no hits were among them.

CAROUSEL (April 19, 1945) was based on the Theatre Guild's 1921 production of Ferenc Molnar's LILIOM. "If I Loved You" was the hit of the show, introduced by Jan Clayton and John Raitt, while "You'll Never Walk Alone" provided a lasting inspirational number. "June Is Bustin' Out All Over" and "A Real Nice Clambake" lend a gaiety to the score, along with the "Carousel Waltz." The dramatic "Soliloquy" proved to be the longest pop song ever published. It was fifteen pages long (most are printed on three or four pages).

ALLEGRO (October 10, 1947) was an experiment with little or no costumes and scenery and with a Greek chorus commenting on the plot either in speech or in song, which failed with the audiences of its time, although hits were made of "A Fellow Needs a Girl," and "The Gentleman Is a Dope." The last had a successful recording by Jo Stafford.

SOUTH PACIFIC (April 7, 1949) ran for 1,925 performances and won the 1950 Pulitzer Prize for drama. It was based on James Michener's 1948 book TALES OF THE SOUTH PACIFIC (which had been a Pulitzer Prize winner for fiction). Opera star Ezio Pinza negotiated a contract that called for him to sing the equivalent of two operatic performances a week. Therefore, his singing role consisted of only "This Nearly Was Mine" and "Some Enchanted Evening." The latter's recording sold extremely well, and the original cast album sold over a million copies. Two million total copies of sheet music were sold of "Bali Ha'i," "A Cockeyed Optimist," "Dites-Moi," "Happy Talk," "Honey Bun," "I'm Gonna Wash That Man Right Outa My Hair," "There Is Nothin' Like a Dame," "A Wonderful Guy," and "Younger than Springtime," this at a time when sheet music of musical comedy songs never sold very well because they were usually specific to scenes or production numbers. Only the more pop-like songs in a show (if it had any) would become hits

Consequently, the total sales figure for these eleven numbers was very impressive. In addition to earning nine million dollars on Broadway, the show released in its film version in 1958 became one of the highest money-earners in Hollywood history up to that time.

The speed with which Rodgers composed must have dismayed Hammerstein, who labored over his lyrics. Once during dinner, while finishing coffee, Hammerstein gave his partner the lyrics he had carefully worked out for "Bali Ha'i." While conversation was taking place, Rodgers created the melody within five minutes. Later, when Rodgers was sick in bed, Hammerstein sent over his words to "Happy Talk" by messenger. Twenty minutes later, he called Rodgers asking if the lyrics had arrived. Rodgers told him, "I've already written the melody."

THE KING AND I (March 29, 1951) starred Gertrude Lawrence and Yul Brynner, and had a run of 1,246 performances. It was taken from a movie (the first time Broadway had used a film as the basis for a show) ANNA AND THE KING OF SIAM (1946). After Lawrence had seen the movie, she went to Rodgers and Hammerstein and asked if they could make a musical out of it for her. For the first time, Rodgers approached the story through the music in contrast to his approach to OKLAHOMA!, where he and Hammerstein concentrated first on dialogue and lyrics. "Hello, Young Lovers" leads the score, the most popular number of several from the show that have become standards. Others are "Getting to Know You," "I Whistle a Happy Tune," "Shall We Dance?," "We Kiss in a Shadow," and the instrumental "March of the Siamese Children." The film version starred Yul Brynner and Deborah Kerr (1956).

ME AND JULIET (May 28, 1953) was a letdown after the previous two shows. It contained only one popular song, "No Other Love." Perry Como had the best-selling recording. The melody came from the tango section of "Beneath the Southern Cross" from VICTORY AT SEA (1952–53), a television documentary for which Rodgers composed background music for twenty-five hours of film.

FLOWER DRUM SONG (December 1, 1958) gave the team another chance to work in the "Broadway-Oriental vein." The hit of the show was "I Enjoy Being a Girl." Also in the score were "Grant Avenue," "Don't Marry Me," and "Fan Tan Fanny," which was given a super treatment by Joe "Fingers" Carr (Capitol F-4163). The film version starred Nancy Kwan (1961).

THE SOUND OF MUSIC (November 16, 1959) was the last of the team's shows and, with 1,433 performances on Broadway, one of their biggest hits. The main song in this show was "My Favorite Things," introduced by Mary Martin and Patricia Neway. In the film version (1965), the song was sung by Julie Andrews and a children's chorus. "Climb Ev'ry Mountain," "Do-Re-Mi," "Edelweiss," "Sixteen Going on Seventeen," and the title song sold over ten million copies of both the Broadway cast album and the movie soundtrack. THE SOUND OF MUSIC is the biggest-grossing musical film of all time.

Oscar Hammerstein II died in Doylestown, Pennsylvania, on August 23, 1960.

After his partner's death, Rodgers composed five more Broadway musicals, none of great distinction. He and Hart had consistently produced high quality work for the musical theatre, and with Hammerstein, he changed the shape of that theatre for years to come. Richard Rodgers died in New York City on December 30, 1979.

FRANK LOESSER:
"Once in Love with Amy"

Frank Loesser was born in New York City on June 29, 1910. He went to Hollywood in the thirties, where he wrote lyrics, including "Two Sleepy People" and "The Lady's in Love with You." He wrote the most popular Second World War song, "Praise the Lord and Pass the Ammunition." "(I've Got Spurs That) Jingle, Jangle, Jingle" (1942) came from the film THE FOREST RANGERS. The hit recording came from Kay Kyser and his Orchestra, which sold over a million copies. For the film CHRISTMAS HOLIDAY (1944), Loesser wrote both words and music to "Spring Will Be a Little Late This Year." The year 1948 was a banner one, with a top-ranking pop song, "On a Slow Boat to China," (again with Kay Kyser's recording, with a vocal by Harry Babbitt and Gloria Wood) (Columbia 38301), a million-seller. Thereafter, he would write both words and music, as he did for his first Broadway musical WHERE'S CHARLEY? (October 11, 1948). The show was based on Brandon Thomas' 1892 farce, CHARLEY'S AUNT. It starred the remarkable dancer-comedian Ray Bolger, who made "Once in Love with Amy," his own (Decca 40065). In the show, Bolger pretended to forget the lyrics and had the audience sing it along with him. It had been a long time since an Alley writer had planted a "stooge" in the theatre to sing the chorus along with the star, and the gimmick remained a high point of the show. "My Darling, My Darling" was the show's other hit, with Doris Day's recording selling over a million copies. For several weeks, this song rotated with "On a Slow Boat to China" at the top position on YOUR

HIT PARADE. It was for the WHERE'S CHARLEY? songs that Loesser established his own publishing business, Frank Music Corporation.

NEPTUNE'S DAUGHTER (1949) had "Baby, It's Cold Outside" in its score, sung first in the film by Esther Williams and Ricardo Montalban. When it was reprised as a comedy number, Red Skelton and Betty Garrett sang it. It won the Academy Award for Best Song.

GUYS AND DOLLS (November 24, 1950) was based on short stories by Damon Runyon. It was a smashing success, running 1,200 performances. Loesser proved that he could write excellent comedy songs: "Fugue for Tinhorns (I've Got the Horse Right Here)," "Adelaide's Lament," "A Bushel and a Peck," "Luck Be a Lady," "The Oldest Established," "Sit Down, You're Rockin' the Boat," "Take Back Your Mink," and "Guys and Dolls." That he could also turn out impressive ballads was illustrated by "I'll Know," "I've Never Been in Love Before," "More I Cannot Wish You," and "If I Were a Bell." When the film version was made (1955), Loesser added the beautiful "A Woman in Love."

HANS CHRISTIAN ANDERSEN (1952) starred Danny Kaye and had one of the finest original film scores of the fifties. It contained such gems as "I'm Hans Christian Andersen," "Anywhere I Wander," "The Inch Worm," "No Two People," "Thumbelina," and "Wonderful Copenhagen."

THE MOST HAPPY FELLA (May 3, 1956) was an unusual musical, nearly operatic in its scope, based on Sidney Howard's Pulitzer Prize-winning play THEY KNEW WHAT THEY WANTED (1924). "Big D" celebrated Dallas, Texas, while "The Most Happy Fella" and "Happy to Make Your Acquaintance" provided some warmhearted moments. "Standing on the Corner" was the big hit of the show, with the Four Lads making a million-selling recording.

A human dynamo, always in a whirl of excitement and activity, Loesser often worked a sixteen-hour day. It was, therefore, a surprise to friends when he told them the day after THE MOST HAPPY FELLA opened that he was tired and was going to Las Vegas for a "long, long holiday—and this time I mean it. I'll be back in three days."

HOW TO SUCCEED IN BUSINESS WITHOUT REALLY TRYING (October 14, 1961) was Loesser's longest-running show. It saw 1,417 performances in New York and won the Pulitzer Prize for drama. It starred Robert Morse and Rudy Vallee, who also performed their roles in the film version (1967). The song hits were "Brotherhood of Man," "Grand Old Ivy," and the narcissistic "I Believe in You."

Frank Loesser died in New York City on July 28, 1969.

LERNER AND LOEWE:

"Almost Like Being in Love"

Frederick Loewe was born in Vienna, Austria, on June 10, 1904. He composed the European hit "Katrina" when he was fifteen, and by the time he was nineteen, he had graduated the Stern Conservatory in Berlin, where he had studied piano and composition. He wrote the shimmy "Kathrin," with words by R. H. Winter, in 1923. Loewe came to the United States the following year, gave a recital in Town Hall, and began a succession of jobs in and out of music. With scriptwriter Earle Crooker, he composed his first American pop song, "A Waltz Was Born in Vienna," which found success in the show SALUTE TO SPRING, produced in stock by the Municipal Opera of St. Louis, Missouri, in 1937. But it wasn't until he met radio scriptwriter Alan Jay Lerner, that either of them had a career in the musical theatre.

Alan Jay Lerner was born in New York City on August 31, 1918. After graduating from Harvard University in 1940, he came to New York and got a job at the Lord and Thomas advertising agency writing radio scripts, among them the amusing CHAMBER MUSIC SOCIETY OF LOWER BASIN STREET, which featured Henry "Hot Lips" Levine and his Barefooted Philharmonic, and Paul Lavalle and his Woodwindy Ten. Vocalists at different times on the program were Dinah Shore, Linda Keene and Lena Horne. Lerner's meeting with Loewe at the Lamb's Club in 1942 set the stage for one of Broadway's most creative and successful partnerships.

BRIGADOON (March 13, 1947) was the first successful offering of the team. (WHAT'S UP in 1943 and THE DAY BEFORE SPRING in 1945 were flops and produced no memorable songs.) Lerner created the book for the show. The score had delightful songs: "Come to Me, Bend to Me," "Down on MacConnachy Square," "From This Day On," "I'll Go Home with Bonnie Jean," "There But for You Go I," and the two hits, "The Heather on the Hill" and "Almost like Being in Love," the latter sung in the show by David Brooks and Marion Bell. In the film version (1954), it was sung by Gene Kelly. It was the first hit song by the team and received much airplay. Sheet music sales were more than half a million copies. For a show song, this was a remarkable feat.

PAINT YOUR WAGON (November 12, 1951) contained three numbers which survived the show to become standards: "I Talk to the Trees," "Wand'rin' Star," and "They Call the Wind Maria." This last has become popular through the efforts of Robert Goulet, who revived it a decade later on television, in nightclubs and with his recording. (It was the song he had successfully used to audition for the role of Lancelot in CAMELOT.) The film version (1969) retained all three songs.

MY FAIR LADY (March 15, 1956) was based on George Bernard Shaw's play PYGMALION (1912). It broke OKLAHOMA!'s long-run record with 2,717 performances and became one of Broadway's most successful musical comedies. It earned the largest sum any musical had earned until that time, over one hundred million dollars from touring companies, foreign productions (the London run broke all records there, with 2,281 performances), film rights, recordings and sheet music. The original cast recording, released by Columbia Records, sold over five million copies. There were more than twenty cast albums made in more than ten languages. Chappell & Company, who published the sheet music, reported that the show was the biggest thing they'd seen since they entered the business, pointing out that the London branch had been in business for three hundred years! The show starred Rex Harrison, Julie Andrews, and Stanley Holloway. The songs ranged from cockney comedy songs "Wouldn't It Be Loverly?," "Get Me to the Church on Time," and "With a Little Bit of Luck," to the patter songs "Why Can't a Woman Be More like a Man?," "I'm an Ordinary Man," "A Hymn to Him," and the glorious "The Rain in Spain," to the hits of the show, "On the Street Where You Live," "I Could Have Danced All Night," and "I've Grown Accustomed to Her Face." The film version (1964) kept the male stars of the show. Audrey Hepburn (sung by Marni Nixon) replaced Julie Andrews, and the film was a critical and popular hit.

Lerner and Loewe's first original film score GIGI (1958) accented period charm, as did MY FAIR LADY, and starred Leslie Caron, Maurice Chevalier, Louis Jourdan and Hermione Gingold. The score was an especially rich one, yielding many standards, including "I Remember It Well," "I'm Glad I'm Not Young Anymore," "The Night They Invented Champagne," "Thank Heaven for Little Girls," and the title song, which won the Oscar for Best Song. It was popularized in a best-selling recording by Vic Damone.

CAMELOT (December 3, 1960) starred Richard Burton, Julie Andrews, Roddy McDowall and Robert Goulet. It produced the title song, "How to Handle a Woman," "The Lusty Month of May," "What Do the Simple Folk Do?," and the big hit, "If Ever I Would Leave You," which was sung in the show (and on a hit record) by Robert Goulet. Although the show ran for 873 performances and had a huge advance sale ($3,000,000), it was considered disappointing by some of the team devotees, but the only thing wrong with the show was that it followed MY FAIR LADY, an "unfollowable" show. The film version (1967), which starred Richard Harris and Vanessa Redgrave, was a success.

The team broke up after CAMELOT but were reunited briefly to write an original score for the film THE LITTLE PRINCE (1974). Sad to say, there were no hit songs.

Alan Jay Lerner died in New York City on June 14, 1986. Frederick Loewe died in Palm Springs, California, on February 14, 1988.

THE SINGER OF THE FORTIES

FRANK SINATRA:
"All or Nothing at All"

Francis Albert Sinatra (1915–) was born in Hoboken, New Jersey. He was hired as a vocalist by Harry James in mid-1939. Although he recorded "All or Nothing at All" with the James Orchestra (Columbia 35587), it wasn't released until 1943, after he had left James. He joined Tommy Dorsey and his Orchestra in early 1940 and had his first hit "Polka Dots and Moonbeams" (Victor 26539) with the Dorsey band. He also made the films LAS VEGAS NIGHTS (1941) and SHIP AHOY (1942) with the band. He left Dorsey to go on his own in late 1942. In January 1943, he made a sensational appearance at the Paramount Theatre in New York City, where screaming, swooning bobbysoxers proved his popularity.

Sinatra appeared on radio as a regular on YOUR HIT PARADE (the first time during 1944, and again from 1947–1949). Axel Stordahl became his music director and conductor for radio and recordings. The great debate during the forties and fifties was: who is the top male singer, Bing Crosby or Frank Sinatra?

Sinatra starred in the 1944 films HIGHER AND HIGHER and STEP LIVELY, but it was in ANCHORS AWEIGH (1945) that he showed his ability to handle comedy. His film career floundered in the early fifties, but was spectacularly revived when he appeared in a dramatic role in FROM HERE TO ETERNITY (1953), which won him an Oscar for Best Supporting Actor. His million-selling hit record of 1954, "Young at Heart" (Capitol 2703), became the title of a film (1955) starring Sinatra and Doris Day. His musical movie career was revived with the great GUYS AND DOLLS (1955), HIGH SOCIETY (1956), PAL JOEY (1957), and CAN-CAN (1960).

Frank Sinatra has been a headliner for more than forty-five years and is one of the most popular stars of all time.

OTHER SONG HITS OF THE FORTIES

1940

"Blueberry Hill" was composed by Vincent Rose, with lyrics by Al Lewis and Larry Stock. Glenn Miller and his Orchestra (with vocal by Ray Eberle) made the first hit recording. Gene Autry sang it in his film THE SINGING HILL (1941), and when it was revived in 1957 by Fats Domino, it sold over a million discs.

"Dance with a Dolly (with a Hole in Her Stocking)" was composed by pianist Terry Shand (1904–1977), with lyrics by Jimmy Eaton and Mickey Leader. It was made popular by Russ Morgan and his Orchestra.

"How High the Moon" was composed by Morgan Lewis (1906–1968), with lyrics by Nancy Hamilton (1908–1985), for the revue TWO FOR THE SHOW (1940), where it was sung by Frances Comstock and Alfred Drake. It was initially popularized by Benny Goodman and his Orchestra, with a vocal by Helen Forrest. In the early fifties, Les Paul and Mary Ford's recording sold over a million copies (Capitol 1451).

"Johnson Rag" was originally composed by Guy Hall and Henry Kleinkauf as a piano instrumental in 1917. The composers, bandleaders from Wilkes Barre, Pennsylvania, published it themselves. They also issued a song version that same year called "That Lovin' Johnson Rag." In 1940, Miller Music Corp. decided that it needed new lyrics and asked Jack Lawrence to write them. He did, and Guy Lombardo and his Orchestra helped make it a hit.

1941

"Elmer's Tune" was composed by Elmer Albrecht, with lyrics by Sammy Gallop. It was introduced by Dick Jurgens and his Orchestra and made famous by Glenn Miller and his Orchestra. Benny Goodman and his Orchestra (with a vocal by Peggy Lee in her recording debut with Goodman) was also popular.

"How About You?" was composed by Burton Lane, with lyrics by Ralph Freed, for Mickey Rooney and Judy Garland, who introduced it in their film BABES ON BROADWAY. Tommy Dorsey had a successful recording (Victor 27749). It was interpolated into the non-musical film DON'T BOTHER TO KNOCK (1952).

"I Don't Want to Set the World on Fire" was composed by Bennie Benjamin (1907–89) and Eddie Durham (1906–   ) and written by Eddie Seiler (1911–1952) and Sol Marcus (1912–1976). It was introduced by Harlan Leonard and his Rockets and was popularized by the Mills Brothers.

"Moonlight Cocktail" was composed by Luckey Roberts (1887–1968), with lyrics by Kim Gannon (1900–1974). The melody of the chorus was taken from Roberts' instrumental piano rag "Ripples of the Nile" (played by the composer on Circle Records 1028). (Roberts' first publication was his popular "Junk Man Rag" (1913), which had a large sheet music sale, as well as a recording by Fred Van Eps (Columbia A-1417).) Glenn Miller and his Orchestra had a million-seller with "Moonlight Cocktail."

"Racing with the Moon" was composed by Johnny Watson, with lyrics by Vaughn Monroe (1911–1973) and Pauline Pope. Monroe made it his theme song and sold over two million copies of his recording (Bluebird 11070).

1942

"Paper Doll" (written twelve years before it was published) had words and music by Johnny Black, who had composed "Dardanella." The Mills Brothers turned it into a hit with their recording, which sold over a million copies (Decca 18318). Frank Sinatra also helped make it a hit.

"Who Wouldn't Love You?" was composed by Carl Fischer (1912–1954), with lyrics by Bill Carey (1916–   ). It was made famous by Kay Kyser and his Orchestra, with a vocal by Harry Babbitt (Columbia 36526).

1943

"Holiday for Strings" was composed by David Rose (1910–   ), with lyrics added by Sammy Gallop (1915–1971). Rose's own orchestral version made it a hit (Victor 27853). He was the musical director for comedian Red Skelton, who used it as his theme on both radio and television. Rose also composed "Poinciana" and "Dance of the Spanish Onion." In 1962, he composed the instrumental novelty "The Stripper."

"Mairzy Doats" was composed by Jerry Livingston (1909–1987) and Al Hoffman (1902–1960), with lyrics by Milton Drake (1916–). The song was inspired when Drake's four-year-old daughter came home from kindergarten, saying: "Cowzy tweet and sowzy tweet and liddle sharksy doisters." The Merry Macs had the hit record, and the sheet music sold at the rate of thirty thousand copies a day for over a month.

1944

"Sentimental Journey" was written by Ben Homer (1917–1975), bandleader Les Brown (1912–), and Bud Green. It became Brown's theme song after his successful record with vocalist Doris Day. The song was featured in the film of the same name (1946). Television personality Dave Garroway used it as his theme.

"The Trolley Song" was composed by Ralph Blane (1914–), with lyrics by Hugh Martin (1914–), for Judy Garland in the film MEET ME IN ST. LOUIS. Garland further popularized it with her hit recording. The Pied Pipers also enjoyed a best-selling record.

"Twilight Time" was written by Buck Ram (1907–), and the Three Suns (Morty Nevins, Al Nevins and Artie Dunn). The group made the hit recording. Ram also wrote "The Great Pretender" for the Platters in 1955, and that group revived "Twilight Time" in 1958 in a best-selling recording.

1945

"Cruising Down the River (on a Sunday Afternoon)" was written by two British women—music by Nell Tollerton, lyrics by Eily Beadell. Blue Barron and his Orchestra made a best-selling record, as did Russ Morgan and his Orchestra in 1949. The song was used in the film of the same name (1953), starring Dick Haymes and Audrey Totter.

"Day by Day" was composed by Axel Stordahl (1913–1963) and Paul Weston (1912–), with words by Sammy Cahn. Jo Stafford made the hit recording.

"Give Me the Simple Life" was composed by Rube Bloom, with lyrics by Harry Ruby, for the movie WAKE UP AND DREAM. It was made popular by Sammy Kaye and his Orchestra.

"Till the End of Time" was adapted by Ted Mossman from Chopin's *Polonaise* and given words by Buddy Kaye. It sold over a million and a half copies of sheet music, while Perry Como's recording was a million-seller. It was also the title of a movie (1946) which featured its theme.

1946

"Do You Know What It Means to Miss New Orleans?" was composed by Lou Alter, with lyrics by Eddie De Lange. It was introduced in the film NEW ORLEANS by Billie Holiday and Louis Armstrong. It has become a standard with jazz bands and is often heard in clubs in New Orleans.

"(Oh Why, Oh Why, Did I Ever Leave) Wyoming" was a novelty hit with words and music by comedian Morey Amsterdam (1914–).

1947

"(Dance) Ballerina (Dance)" was composed by Carl Sigman (1909–), with words by Bob Russell (1914–1970). Vaughn Monroe made the hit recording, which sold over a million copies. It was successfully revived in 1955 by Nat King Cole.

"How Are Things in Glocca Morra?" was composed by Burton Lane with lyrics by E. Y. Harburg, for the Broadway show FINIAN'S RAINBOW (January 10, 1947). It was introduced by Ella Logan, who starred in the show. The entire score is a gem, with "The Begat," "If This Isn't Love," "Look to the Rainbow," "Necessity," "Old Devil Moon," "That Great Come and Get It Day," "When I'm Not Near the Girl I Love," and "When the Idle Poor Become the Idle Rich."

"Near You" was composed by pianist-bandleader Francis Craig (1900–1966), with words by Kermit Goell (1915–). Craig had the hit recording, but the song got added exposure when Milton Berle chose it as the closing theme of his TEXACO STAR THEATRE television program.

"Smoke Dreams" was written by Lloyd Shaffer (1901–), John Klenner and Ted Steele (1917–) to be the theme song of radio's CHESTERFIELD SUPPER CLUB, starring Perry Como, Jo Stafford, and the Starlighters.

"Tenderly" was composed by pianist Walter Gross (1909–1967), with lyrics by Jack Lawrence. It was popularized by Clark Dennis, and it was revived in 1955 in a hit recording by Rosemary Clooney.

1948

"Enjoy Yourself" was composed by Carl Sigman, with lyrics by Herb Magidson. When Guy Lombardo and his Royal Canadians recorded it in 1950, it became one of the biggest hits of that year.

"Far Away Places" was composed by Alex Kramer (1893–1955), with words by ex-singer Joan Whitney (1914–   ). Two hit recordings made this a standard, one by Bing Crosby and the other by Perry Como.

"Manana" was written by the husband and wife team of guitarist Dave Barbour (1912–1965) and singer Peggy Lee (1920–   ). Peggy Lee's recording sold over a million copies.

"Red Roses for a Blue Lady" was written by the team of Sid Tepper (1918–   ) and Roy Bennett (1918–   ). It was first popularized by Vaughn Monroe, Arthur Godfrey, and Guy Lombardo and his Royal Canadians. It was revived in 1964 by Bert Kaempfert and his Orchestra. Wayne Newton also revived it, as did Vic Dana, to insure its place in the standard repertoire.

1949

"The Hot Canary" was composed by violinist Paul Nero (1917–1958), with lyrics added by Ray Gilbert (1912–1976). It was a showcase number for violin virtuoso Florian Zabach, who made it a hit.

"I Don't Care If the Sun Don't Shine" has words and music by Mack David (1912–   ). It was sung to success by Tony Martin.

"I've Got a Lovely Bunch of Coconuts" has words and music by Fred Heatherton. Danny Kaye had a hit recording, and there was a best-selling disc by Freddy Martin and his Orchestra, with a vocal by Merv Griffin.

"The Old Piano Roll Blues" was composed and written by Cy Coben (1919–   ). Sammy Kaye and his Orchestra, with vocals by Lisa Kirk and Eddie Cantor, made this a hit.

"Rudolph, the Red-Nosed Reindeer" has words and music by Johnny Marks (1909–1985). It was popularized by Gene Autry in a recording that has sold over six million discs (Columbia 38610). According to *Variety*, this is the second best-selling recorded song of all time (the first being "White Christmas"). There have been ninety different arrangements made, total recordings have sold over forty-five million copies, and the sheet music has sold in excess of seven million copies.

"The Third Man Theme" was composed by Anton Karas for the film

THE THIRD MAN. It was recorded on zither by the composer, and this became a best-selling disc.

The hardship on Tin Pan Alley caused by the Second World War, with its critical shortages of paper and shellac, dominated the first half of this decade. Patriotic songs helped to win the war, as did such popular singers as Frank Sinatra, who toured various Armed Services bases, boosting the morale of G.I.'s. Glenn Miller, who had the most popular band, enlisted in the Army and lost his life during the war. It was also a time for the Disney full-length cartoon films and their specially-created songs to help the civilians cope with these years. Latin American music infiltrated the dance, the popular music scene, and films. Rodgers and Hammerstein created the most popular musicals in Broadway history up to that time, while Lerner and Loewe were beginning their careers. Tin Pan Alley recovered from the war years and, unmindful of changing public tastes in pop music developed by and during the war, continued to supply all forms of entertainment with their songs.

THE DEATH OF TIN PAN ALLEY

(1950–1956)

At first, Alley operations at the beginning of the fifties seemed like a continuation of the forties, with songs plugged on radio, movies, records, and the new electronic novelty—television, with the time-honored aim of selling sheet music. And during the early fifties, when the Alley was coming to its untimely end, there appeared on the top charts a greater variety of song types than ever before. Not only were the staples of the Alley, ballads, popular ("My Heart Cries for You"), but there was also success for Latin American songs ("Vaya Con Dios"), syncopated rag songs ("Music! Music! Music!"), hillbilly ("Your Cheatin' Heart"), homespun ("Dearie"), ethnic ("Come on-a My House"), folk ("Goodnight, Irene"), novelty ("Molasses, Molasses"), and polka ("Hop Scotch Polka").

In the established major publishing firms of the Alley, the General Professional Manager bought the songs, directed the pluggers and decided which songs deserved money for advertising. The pluggers, or "contact men," as they were now called, went after bandleaders who had radio programs, solo singers who made recordings and worked the nightclubs, Artist and Repertoire (called "A & R") heads of record companies, and (since the end of the war) announcers of popular music record shows, called disc jockeys (or "deejays").

The most famous of the deejays was Martin Block, of radio station WNEW in New York City, who had started his career by playing records during pauses in the station's live coverage of the Bruno Hauptmann trial in 1935. He created the "Make Believe Ballroom" show, which quickly caught on. Block came to know the publishers, songwriters, A & R men, singers, and pluggers, all of whom he would interview on his program. He was even invited to recording sessions, and his knowledgeable commentary on songs and performers was highly entertaining as well as informative. He drew a large following. As a result, when Block plugged recordings, they became hits.

Al Jarvis, on KLAC in Los Angeles (the first all-deejay station), Eddie Hubbard on WIND (Chicago), Kurt Webster on WBT (Charlotte,

North Carolina), Al "Jazzbo" Collins (a hip, jazz-oriented deejay who worked for several stations in different locations), Bob Horn on WFIL (Philadelphia), Bob Clayton on WHDH (Boston), Eddie Gallagher on WTOP (Washington, D.C.), Ed McKenzie as "Jack the Bellboy" on WJBK (Detroit), and Bill Randle on WERE (Cleveland, Ohio) were among the popular deejays who, individually, made recordings into hits in their regional areas and led to a nationwide airing of their selections. Some, like Bill Randle, discovered singers (Johnny Ray and Tony Bennett) and pushed their discoveries' recordings onto the charts. The deejay became the most important influence in the success of popular recordings. The pluggers, who used to give "professional copies" to bandleaders and singers, now gave sample records to deejays.

The publisher who best recognized the power of the deejay was Howard Richmond (1918–   ), who started what was to become TRO (The Richmond Organization) at the end of 1949. While most publishers were happy to have one or two hits a year, Richmond had six in his first full year of publishing ("Hop Scotch Polka," "Music! Music! Music!," "Goodnight, Irene," "Molasses, Molasses," "Tzena, Tzena, Tzena," and "The Thing"). He accomplished this amazing feat alone, as a one-man operation! Before entering publishing (he was the son of jobber-publisher Maurice Richmond and the nephew of publisher Jack Robbins), he was an assistant to a Broadway publicist. The publicist to whom he was apprenticed started plugging his clients' recordings, and Richmond soon joined his cousin Buddy Robbins in a similar enterprise. By the time Richmond formed his own publishing companies (Cromwell, Hollis and Essex), he knew over three hundred disc jockeys on a first-name basis. He spent a good part of his time on the phone with them, talking up the recordings of his songs, which he airmailed to them. He usually got them to give his records airtime on their shows. His track record at this new kind of plugging was spectacular. His organization became international, and it is now run by his son Larry Richmond (1954–   ).

Plugging methods changed, and recordings at the beginning of the fifties were starting to sound different, too. New electronic gimmickry included overdubbing, echo effects, and multi-track recordings, which resulted in such distinctive approaches as Patti Page's singing a duet with herself in "Tennessee Waltz," Les Paul and Mary Ford creating a sound of many guitars and singers with one guitar and one voice in "How High the Moon," and Ross Bagdasarian's (under the pseudonym of David Seville) "The Chipmunk Song," with his own voice becoming those of the three individualized chipmunks—Alvin, Theodore and Simon—on a record engineered by him as well. It sold two and a half million discs in two weeks.

With these new sounds came a new audience. During the early fifties, nobody in the Alley realized that a shift was taking place in the audience for songs. As Western movies became more popular, country and western songs (formerly known as hillbilly music) became more popular, starting with the Gene Autry and Roy Rogers musical oaters in the early forties. The Aberbach brothers, Jean and Julian, pushed country and western songs using Alley techniques through their companies Hill and Range Songs, Alamo Music, and, finally, Elvis Presley Music.

A new black sound started just after the Second World War, becoming known as rhythm and blues. It was vocal music to be danced to, but the words weren't as important as the beat. Charts in the trade papers showed some top-selling records in these new categories during the late forties, although they hadn't yet had any influence on the pop charts. But, around 1952–53, the songs on these black and country charts started being "covered" by major white pop singers for a growing audience of teenagers, who would soon dominate the popular music scene as the purchasers of pop singles. So, during the early fifties, pop songs didn't reflect the undercurrent of an emerging audience, as publishers ignored the rhythm and blues and country music songs which were captivating the youngsters. Instead the published songs continued to reflect the aspirations of young and middle-aged adults who traditionally had bought sheet music. This stagnation of Tin Pan Alley publishers and songwriters would prove fatal to the Alley.

MAJOR ALLEY HITS (1950–1955)

1950

"Be My Love" was composed by Nicholas Brodszky, with lyrics by Sammy Cahn. It was written for Mario Lanza in the film TOAST OF NEW ORLEANS. Lanza's recording sold over a million copies.

"Dearie" had words and music by Bob Hilliard and Dave Mann (1916–   ). It was an exercise in nostalgia, with a best-selling record by two great Broadway stars, Ray Bolger and Ethel Merman (Decca 24873).

"Frosty the Snowman" was composed by Jack Rollins (1906–1973), with lyrics by Steve Nelson (1907–   ). It was the Christmas hit of Gene Autry, who had had "Rudolph" the previous year. An animated television version of the story is shown every Christmas, keeping this song a standard. The same writers produced "Peter Cottontail," an Easter classic, and "Smokey the Bear," the official song for the U.S. Forestry Department.

"Goodnight, Irene," was adapted by folklorist John Lomax from folksinger Leadbelly's song of the same name. It became popular in a recording by The Weavers, which was on the charts in the number one position for thirteen weeks. It sold more than two million discs. The Weavers were an enormously successful folk-singing quartet (Pete Seeger, Lee Hayes, Fred Hellerman and Ronnie Gilbert), who gave annual concerts at Carnegie Hall. Other million-seller hits by them included "Tzena, Tzena, Tzena," "On Top of Old Smokey," "So Long (It's Been Good to Know Yuh)," and "Kisses Sweeter Than Wine."

"(If I Knew You Were Comin') I'd've Baked a Cake" was written by Al Trace, Bob Merrill and Al Hoffman. Publisher Ben Barton's daughter Eileen had the hit recording.

"Let's Do It Again" was written by Englishmen Desmond O'Connor and Ray Hartley and given a rousing treatment by Margaret Whiting, backed by (then-husband) Joe "Fingers" Carr (Capitol 1132).

"A Marshmallow World" was composed by Peter De Rose, with lyrics by Carl Sigman. It was De Rose's last song hit, made famous by radio-TV personality Arthur Godfrey.

"Music! Music! Music!" had words and music by Mel Glazer, but credit was given to Stephan Weiss and Bernie Baum. It became Teresa Brewer's first million-selling hit recording (London 604). Her perky, syncopated singing blended perfectly with the Jack Pleis Dixieland Band backing her. This rag song coincided with the first major revival of ragtime, sparked by the piano recordings of Joe "Fingers" Carr on Capitol Records.

"My Heart Cries for You" was composed by bandleader Percy Faith (1908–1976), with lyrics by Carl Sigman. Faith adapted the melody from a French tune credited to Marie Antoinette! Dinah Shore, as well as Guy Mitchell, had a hit recording.

1951

"Cry" had words and music by Churchill Kohlman (1906–). Although it was first recorded by Ruth Casey, it wasn't until Johnny Ray recorded it that this song (by a night watchman in a Pittsburgh dry cleaning plant) sold four million copies.

"I Get Ideas" was written by Sanders (a rare example of the one-name composer), with lyrics by Dorcas Cochran. The melody was adapted from an Argentine tango, "Adios Muchachos," and transformed by Tony Martin into a best-selling recording.

"My Truly, Truly Fair" had words and music by Bob Merrill. Guy Mitchell had the hit recording (Columbia 39415).

"Slow Poke" was written by Chilton Price and revised by Pee Wee King and Redd Stewart, who recorded the best-selling disc.

1952

"How Much Is That Doggie in the Window?" had words and music by Bob Merrill. Patti Page made it a three-million seller.

"Lullaby of Birdland" was composed by English jazz pianist George Shearing (1919–   ), with lyrics by B. Y. Forster, for a New York City jazz club. Shearing's own recording was a best seller (MGM 11354).

"Say It with Your Heart" was composed by Norman Kaye (1922–   ), with lyrics by Steve Nelson. Bob Carroll made this a hit with a best-selling recording (Derby 814).

"Till I Waltz Again with You" had words and music by Sidney Prosen. Teresa Brewer made it a million seller (Coral 60873). Incidentally, the song is not a waltz.

1953

"I Need You Now" was written by Jimmie Crane (1910–   ) and Al Jacobs (1903–   ). Eddie Fisher had the million-selling disc.

"The Moon Is Blue" was composed by Herschel Burke Gilbert (1918–   ), with lyrics by Sylvia Fine, for the film of the same name. The best-selling record was by the Sauter-Finegan orchestra, with a vocal by Sally Sweetland.

"Rags to Riches" was composed by Richard Adler (1921–   ), with lyrics by Jerry Ross (1926–1955), as an independent number. It was their first big hit, and it led to their monumental Broadway shows, PAJAMA GAME (1954) and DAMN YANKEES (1955). Tony Bennett sold over two million copies of his hit recording.

1954

"Fly Me to the Moon" was written by Bart Howard (1915–   ). It was introduced by Felicia Sanders. Comedienne Kaye Ballard had a hit recording, and it was revived in 1962 by Joe Harnell.

"If I Give My Heart to You" was written by Jimmie Crane, Al Jacobs, and Jimmy Brewster. Television songster Denise Lor introduced it and made the first recording. The best-selling disc was by Doris Day.

"Miss America" had words and music by Bernie Wayne (1921–). It was for years the official song of the annual Miss America Pageant in Atlantic City, New Jersey. It was sung at the Pageant by emcee Bert Parks.

"Mister Sandman" had words and music by Pat Ballard (1899–1960). The Chordettes had the best-selling disc. It held the number one spot on YOUR HIT PARADE for eight weeks.

"No More" was composed by Leo De John, with lyrics by Julie and Dux De John. It isn't surprising that the De John Sisters had the hit recording.

"Young at Heart" was composed by Johnny Richards, with lyrics by Carolyn Leigh (1926–1983). Frank Sinatra made a disc that sold a million copies. The song was used as the title for a film starring Sinatra and Doris Day (also in 1954).

1955

"Dream Along with Me (I'm on My Way to a Star)" had words and music by Carl Sigman. It became familiar through weekly exposure as Perry Como's television theme.

"Hey, Mr. Banjo" was composed by Freddy Morgan (1910–1970), with lyrics by Norman Malkin. Morgan was the banjoist for Spike Jones and his City Slickers from 1947 to 1958. He formed the Sunnysiders to record his best-selling tune.

"Wake the Town and Tell the People" was composed by Jerry Livingston, with lyrics by Sammy Gallop. Les Baxter and his Orchestra made the best-selling recording.

"Zambezi" was composed by Nico Carstens and Anton De Waal, with lyrics by Bob Hilliard. The best-selling version was made by Lou Busch and his Orchestra (Capitol 3272).

THE ADVENT OF ROCK 'N' ROLL

As we've read in these pages, popular music was originally created for adults, who went to vaudeville shows, theatres, nightclubs, and saloons (and who bought sheet music to sing and play). After World War I, its main market was city dwellers in their twenties and thirties. By the rock era, much popular music was written for teenagers, who now had enough money to purchase records.

Since the Depression, houses and apartment buildings had been built with smaller rooms, making the once ubiquitous piano a luxury. On the farm and in rural areas, the guitar became the instrument of choice. The Armed Forces during the Second World War brought together the city dweller and his country cousin, black and white, to become acquainted with each other's music.

Country and western music, especially with the efforts of the Aberbach brothers, was being recorded in the fifties by Carl Perkins, Buddy Holly and Jerry Lee Lewis, along with rhythm and blues, as performed by Chuck Berry, Little Richard, B. B. King, and vocal groups such as the Penguins and the Platters. These two styles coalesced in the sound and sight of Elvis Presley, the very embodiment and personification of a new pop music, rock 'n' roll.

For years, songwriters had been nurtured by publishers, had learned their craft by playing and plugging the songs of established writers, and had been given the chance to write their own songs and see them in print. The rock revolution changed all that when the spotlight shifted from piano or band to electric guitars, honking tenor saxophones and an insistent drum, when the audience shifted from adults to teenagers, and when the business control shifted from the publishers (who had discovered songwriters, performers, and songs) to the A & R chiefs at record companies (who decided which performers would record which songs).

The growing "underground" music styles were mistaken for mere fads, and it was something of a shock to the veteran Alleymen in 1954 when three songs bringing together these influences appeared on the Top Ten pop charts.

"Sh-Boom" was written by a black vocal quintet, the Chords, who made their rhythm and blues recording for Cat Records (Cat 104). It was immediately covered by a white Canadian quartet, the Crew Cuts, who took their name from the popular hair style of the day, to become one of the first genuine rock and roll million sellers (Mercury 70404). A comforting thought for the Alley was that the song was really a typical

Alley ballad ("Life could be a dream") with vocal rhythmic accents as a gimmick ("Sh-boom, sh-boom, ya-da-da, da-da-da, da-da-da, da"), and its opening verse of nonsense syllables ("Hey nonny ding dong, a-lang, a-lang, a-lang, Boom ba-doh, ba-doo ba-doo").

"Shake Rattle and Roll" had words and music by Charles Calhoun. It was introduced by singer Joe Turner, but it was the recording by Bill Haley and his Comets which launched the song (and the Comets) to dizzying heights and created great interest in rock and roll, a song style they firmly established with their version of "Rock Around the Clock" in the film THE BLACKBOARD JUNGLE (1955). Rock found its ultimate superstar in Elvis Presley.

THE DAY THE ALLEY DIED: APRIL 12, 1954

Symbolically, Tin Pan Alley died on April 12, 1954, when Bill Haley (1925–1981) and his Comets recorded Max Freedman and Jimmy De Knight's "Rock Around the Clock." It had been published a year earlier and would not create a sensation until a year later, but Haley's recording (Decca 29214) would ultimately sell twenty-five million copies worldwide. It became the first international rock 'n' roll best-seller. THE BLACKBOARD JUNGLE soundtrack gave the song and Haley's performance an additional context, so that rebellious teenagers took it as their anthem. The song was such a powerful influence that two other movies were built around the song and its performance, ROCK AROUND THE CLOCK (1956) and DON'T KNOCK THE ROCK (1957). The recording surfaced again in the films AMERICAN GRAFFITI (1973) and SUPERMAN (1978). It was featured in the television series HAPPY DAYS (1974–1984). Bill Haley and his Comets had one more million seller, "See You Later, Alligator" (1956), which they introduced in the film ROCK AROUND THE CLOCK.

ALAN FREED:
The Evangelist For Rock

Rock 'n' roll's greatest promoter and the first to name the music was deejay Alan Freed (1922–1965). He first applied the phrase to the rhythm and blues numbers he was playing on his radio show MOON DOG'S ROCK AND ROLL PARTY in June 1951, on station WJW in Cleveland. He came to radio station WINS in New York City in

September 1954, when he renamed his show ALAN FREED'S ROCK AND ROLL PARTY. He promptly became the genre's premier deejay and promoter. He was the most imitated deejay in town, with others not only copying his personal style, but his format and playlist as well. Freed appeared in the films ROCK AROUND THE CLOCK; ROCK, ROCK, ROCK; and DON'T KNOCK THE ROCK. He produced and hosted many dance parties and rock 'n' roll shows, mostly featuring black performers. The film AMERICAN HOT WAX (1978) traced his career.

ELVIS PRESLEY:

"Heartbreak Hotel"

Elvis Aaron Presley was born in Tupelo, Mississippi, on January 8, 1935. He made his first disc for RCA Victor, "Heartbreak Hotel," in January 1956. From that time on, there was no doubt that Presley was the "King of Rock 'n' Roll," and that the era of Tin Pan Alley was over. For, from this point forward, the list of each year's Top Ten songs would be almost entirely composed of rock and roll numbers which were not sold to any great extent in sheet music form. In his first year of national exposure, 1956, he made two top-grossing films (LOVE ME TENDER and LOVING YOU), had two top-ranking LP's (ELVIS PRESLEY and ELVIS), had five songs in the Top Twenty ("Don't Be Cruel," "Hound Dog," "Heartbreak Hotel," "I Want You, I Need You, I Love You," and "Love Me Tender"), and an incredible twelve more songs on the national pop charts! His double-sided hit recording, "Don't Be Cruel" (composed and written by Otis Blackwell [1932–   ], with co-authorship credited to Presley) and "Hound Dog (composed by Mike Stoller [1933–   ], with lyrics by Jerry Lieber [1933–   ]), sold more than eleven million discs (Victor 47-6604). His soundtrack LP of BLUE HAWAII sold more than five million copies. In his professional lifetime, from his first Sun disc ("That's All Right, Mama" and "Blue Moon of Kentucky"), released in August 1954, to his death in Memphis, Tennessee, on August 16, 1977, Presley earned fifty-five gold singles and twenty-four gold albums. He had more top ten singles and more number one records than any other performer in the history of recorded music. His recordings sold more than six hundred million copies around the world.

THE END OF AN ERA

Until rock and roll, the song and its publication had been the main thrust of the creation and promotion of popular music. With rock and roll, the recorded performance became more important than the written music and words. Publishers were no longer in charge of a song's promotion, and sheet music sales became insignificant to the pop music business. From 1956, rock and roll songs dominated the hit parade and top forty lists. The Alley publishers, who had done so much to develop and promote hit songs for seventy years, could no longer remain as powerful as they had been.

New groups and soloists were writing their own songs, controlling publishing rights, recording their own numbers, and generally writing their own tickets. And while the theatre was still producing musical shows, and film companies still used established songs and newly-created ones, the music business changed so greatly that the Alley and its ways became obsolete.

Long after its demise, on a building at the corner of Twenty-eighth Street and Broadway, Tin Pan Alley was officially recognized for its part in our musical history when a plaque was installed on July 26, 1976, as part of the American Revolution Bicentennial celebration. It read:

"A Landmark of American Music
Tin Pan Alley
28th Street Between Broadway and Sixth Avenues was the Legendary
Tin Pan Alley Where The Business of the American Popular Song
Flourished During the First Decades of the 20th Century."

Tin Pan Alley's legacy is part of our heritage, and with the sheet music and recordings it gave us, it will remain a valuable part of our lives.

Top Ten Pioneer Publishers

The following is a listing of the ten major pioneer publishers of Tin Pan Alley during its period of greatest impact, and their addresses:

M. WITMARK & SONS (1886–1929)

1886–87	402 West 40th Street
1888	32 East 14th Street
1889–93	841 Broadway
1893–98	49-51 West 28th Street
1898–1903	8 West 29th Street
1903–1923	144-46 West 37th Street
1923–29	1650 Broadway (corner 51st and Broadway)
1929–34	1657 Broadway (owned by Warner Bros.)

T. B. HARMS (1875–1929)*

1875–1891	819 Broadway
1892–1904	18 East 22nd Street
1904–1906	126 West 44th Street
1907–1911	1431-33 Broadway (Theatrical Exchange Building)
1912–1933	62 West 45th Street
1933–35	1619 Broadway (owned by Warner Bros.)

*Although the firm was established in 1875, the Harms Brothers did not achieve a major hit until 1892 with the publishing of "The Bowery," featured in Hoyt's A TRIP TO CHINATOWN.

HOWLEY, HAVILAND & COMPANY (1893–1904)

1893	4 East 20th Street (as George T. Worth Company)
1894–98	4 East 20th Street (as Howley, Haviland & Company)
1898–1900	1260-66 Broadway (at 32nd Street)

289

1900–1903	1260-66 Broadway (as Howley, Haviland & Dresser)
1903	1434-1440 Broadway
1904	1440 Broadway (as Howley, Dresser Company)
1905–1907	41 West 28th Street (as P. J. Howley Music Company)
1905–1906	51 West 28th Street (as Paul Dresser Publishing Company)

F. B. HAVILAND PUBLISHING COMPANY (1904–1932)

1904–1913	125 West 37th Street
1914–1916	Broadway and 47th Street (Strand Theatre Building)
1916–1920	128 West 48th Street
1920–1933	114 West 44th Street

JOSEPH W. STERN & COMPANY (1894–1920)

1894	304 East 14th Street
1895–1898	45 East 20th Street
1898–1906	34 East 21st Street (Mark Stern Building)
1907–1920	102-104 West 38th Street

F. A. Mills (1895–1915)

1895–1899	45 West 29th Street
1899–1906	48 West 29th Street
1907–1908	32 West 29th Street
1909–1914	122 West 36th Street
1914–1915	207 West 48th Street

Leo. Feist, Inc. (1897–1935)

1897–1899	1227 Broadway/42 West 30 Street (as Feist & Frankenthaler)
1900–1901	36 West 28th Street
1902	36 West 28th Street (as Leo. Feist, Inc.)
1903–1912	Feist Building, 134 West 37th Street
1913–1916	Feist Building, 231-235 West 40th Street
1917	Feist Building, 240 West 40th Street
1918–1930	Feist Building, 235 West 40th Street
1930–1934	56 Cooper Square

SHAPIRO, BERNSTEIN & COMPANY (1898-present)

1897	229 West 20th Street (as Adelphi Pub. Co.)
1897	10 Union Square (as Consolidated Music Pub.)
1898	48 West 29th Street (as Universal Music Department Co.)
1898–1899	49 and 51 West 28th Street (as William C. Dunn & Company)
1899	45 West 28th Street (as Orphean Music Company)
1900–1901	45 West 28th Street (as Shapiro, Bernstein & Von Tilzer)
1902–03	45 West 28th Street (as Shapiro, Bernstein & Company)
1904	45 West 28th Street (as Shapiro, Remick & Company)
1906–1912	Corner Broadway & 39th Street (Maxine Elliot Theatre) (as Shapiro Music Publisher)
1913–1914	Corner Broadway and 39th Street (as Shapiro, Bernstein & Company)
1914–1918	224 West 47th Street (Strand Theatre Building)
1918–1931	Corner Broadway and 47th Street (Central Theatre Building)
1931–1936	Corner Broadway & 51st Street (Capitol Theatre Building)
1936–1959	1270 Sixth Avenue (RKO Building)
1959–1973	666 Fifth Avenue
1973–	10 East 53rd Street

HARRY VON TILZER MUSIC PUBLISHING COMPANY (1902–1946)

1902–1903	42 West 28th Street
1903–1907	37 West 28th Street
1908–1916	125 West 43rd Street
1916–1920	222 West 46th Street
1921–1923	1658 Broadway (Roseland Building)
1924–1926	1587 Broadway

JEROME H. REMICK & COMPANY (1904–1928)

1905–1908	45 West 28th Street
1908–1911	131 West 41st Street
1912–1931	219-221 West 46th Street
1931–1935	1657 Broadway (Hollywood Building) (owned by Warner Bros.)

TED SNYDER COMPANY (1908–1928)

1908–1911	112 West 38th Street (as Ted Snyder Co.)
1912–1914	112 West 38th Street (as Waterson, Berlin & Snyder, Inc.)
1914–1928	224 West 47th Street (Strand Theatre Building)

"Alexander's Ragtime Band" and Other Favorite Song Hits, 1901–1911. David A. Jasen, ed. New York: Dover, 1987.

American Musician and Art Journal. New York: 1906–1914.

Anderson, Jervis. This Was Harlem, 1900–1950. New York: Farrar Straus Giroux, 1982.

ASCAP Biographical Dictionary. New York: American Society of Composers, Authors and Publishers, 1966.

Atkinson, Brooks. Broadway. New York: Macmillan, 1970.

Baral, Robert. Revue. New York: Fleet, 1962.

Bloom, Ken. American Song: The Complete Musical Theatre Companion, 1900–1984. 2 vols. New York: Facts On File, 1985.

Bloom, Sol. The Autobiography of Sol Bloom. New York: Putnam, 1948.

Boardman, Gerald. American Musical Theatre. New York: Oxford, 1978.

———. Days To Be Happy, Years to Be Sad. New York: Oxford, 1982.

———. Jerome Kern. New York: Oxford, 1980.

Bradford, Perry. Born With the Blues. New York: Oak, 1965.

Brunn, H. O. The Story of the Original Dixieland Jazz Band. Baton Rouge, La.: Louisiana State University Press, 1960.

Burton, Jack. The Blue Book of Broadway Musicals. Watkins Glen, N.Y.: Century House, 1952.

———. The Blue Book of Hollywood Musicals. Watkins Glen, N.Y.: Century House, 1953.

———. The Blue Book of Tin Pan Alley. Watkins Glen, N.Y.: Century House, 1951.

Cahn, Sammy. I Should Care. New York: Arbor House, 1974.

Cantor, Eddie. Take My Life. Garden City, N.Y.: Doubleday, 1957.

Castle, Irene. Castles in the Air. Garden City, N.Y.: Doubleday, 1958.

Chilton, John. Who's Who of Jazz. Philadelphia: Chilton, 1972.

Charters, Ann. Nobody: The Story of Bert Williams. New York: Macmillan, 1970.

Charters, Samuel, and Leonard Kunstadt. Jazz: A History of the New York Scene. Garden City, N.Y.: Doubleday, 1962.

Churchill, Allen. The Great White Way. New York: Dutton, 1962.

Cohan, George M. Twenty Years on Broadway. New York and London: Harper, 1924.

Coslow, Sam. Cocktails for Two. New Rochelle, N.Y.: Arlington House, 1977.

Christensen's Ragtime Review. Axel Christensen, ed. Chicago: 1914–1916.

DeLong, Thomas A. Pops: Paul Whiteman, King of Jazz. Piscataway, N.J.: New Century, 1983.

Dietz, Howard. Dancing in the Dark. New York: Quadrangle, 1974.

Duke, Vernon. Passport to Paris. Boston: Little, Brown, 1955.

Ewen, David. American Popular Songs from the Revolutionary War to the Present. New York: Random House, 1966.

———. Complete Book of the American Musical Theater. New York: Henry Holt, 1958.

———. Great Men of American Popular Song. Rev. and enl. ed. Englewood Cliffs, N.J.: Prentice Hall, 1972.

———. The Life and Death of Tin Pan Alley. New York: Funk and Wagnalls, 1964.

———. Popular American Composers. New York: H. W. Wilson, 1962.

Farnsworth, Marjorie. *The Ziegfeld Follies.* New York: Putnam's, 1956.

Favorite Songs of the Nineties. Robert A. Fremont, ed. New York: Dover, 1973.

Feather, Leonard. *The New Edition of the Encyclopedia of Jazz.* New York: Bonanza, 1960.

Feist, Leonard. *An Introduction to Popular Music Publishing in America.* New York: National Music Publishers' Association, 1980.

Fordin, Hugh. *The Movies' Greatest Musicals.* New York: Ungar, 1984.

Fowler, Gene. *Schnozzola, The Story of Jimmy Durante.* New York: Viking Press, 1951.

Freedland, Michael. *Al Jolson.* New York: Stein & Day, 1972.

———. *Irving Berlin.* New York: Stein & Day, 1974.

Fuld, James J. *American Popular Music, 1875–1950.* Philadelphia: Musical Americana, 1955.

———. *The Book of World Famous Music.* New York: Dover, 1985.

Gershwin, Ira. *Lyrics on Several Occasions.* New York: Knopf, 1959.

Gilbert, L. Wolfe. *Without Rhyme or Reason.* New York: Vantage, 1956.

Goldberg, Isaac. *Tin Pan Alley.* New York: John Day, 1930.

Green, Stanley. *Encyclopedia of the Musical Theatre.* New York: Dodd, Mead, 1976.

———. *Ring Bells! Sing Songs!* New Rochelle, N.Y.: Arlington House, 1971.

———. *Rodgers and Hammerstein Fact Book.* New York: Rodgers and Hammerstein, 1955. Supplement, 1961.

———. *The World of Musical Comedy.* San Diego: A. S. Barnes, 1980.

Hammerstein, Oscar II. *Lyrics.* New York: Simon and Schuster, 1949.

Hammond, John. *John Hammond on Record.* New York: Ridge Press, 1977.

Handy, W. C. *Father of the Blues.* New York: Macmillan, 1941.

Harris, Charles K. *After the Ball.* New York: Frank-Maurice, 1926.

Hart, Dorothy. *Thou Swell, Thou Witty.* New York: Harper & Row, 1976.

Hemming, Roy. *The Melody Lingers On: The Great Songwriters and Their Movie Musicals.* New York: Newmarket Press, 1986.

Isman, Felix. *Weber and Fields.* New York: Boni & Liveright, 1924.

Jablonski, Edward. *Harold Arlen: Happy with the Blues.* Garden City, N.Y.: Doubleday, 1961.

Jasen, David A. *P. G. Wodehouse: A Portrait of a Master.* New York: Continuum, 1981.

———, and Trebor Jay Tichenor. *Rags and Ragtime, A Musical History.* New York: Seabury Press, 1978.

———. *Recorded Ragtime, 1897–1958.* Hamden, Conn.: Archon, 1973.

———. *The Theatre of P. G. Wodehouse.* London: Batsford, 1979.

Jay, Dave. *The Irving Berlin Songography.* New Rochelle, N.Y.: Arlington House, 1969.

Johnson, James Weldon. *Along the Way.* New York: Viking Press, 1933.

———. *Black Manhattan.* New York: Knopf, 1930.

Kahn, E. J., Jr. *The Merry Partners: The Age and Stage of Harrigan and Hart.* New York: Random House, 1955.

Kimball, Robert, and Alfred Simon. *The Gershwins.* New York: Atheneum, 1973.

———, and William Bolcom. *Reminiscing with Sissle and Blake.* New York: Viking Press, 1972.

Kinkle, Roger D. *The Complete Encyclopedia of Popular Music and Jazz, 1900–1950.* 4 vols. New Rochelle, N.Y.: Arlington House, 1974.

Klamkin, Marian. *Old Sheet Music.* New York: Hawthorne, 1975.

Lange, Horst. *The Fabulous Fives.* Chigwell, England: Storyville, 1978.

Levy, Lester S. *Give Me Yesterday: American History in Song, 1890–1920.* Norman, Okla.: University of Oklahoma Press, 1975.

———. *Grace Notes in American History: Popular Sheet Music from 1820–1900.* Norman, Oklahoma: University of Oklahoma Press, 1967.

————. *Picture the Song.* Baltimore and London: The Johns Hopkins University Press, 1976.
Lomax, Alan. *Mister Jelly Roll.* New York: Duell, Sloan, 1950.
Lopez, Vincent. *Lopez Speaking.* New York: Citadel, 1960.
Lord, Tom. *Clarence Williams.* Chigwell, England: Storyville, 1976.
Marks, Edward B. *They All Sang: From Tony Pastor to Rudy Vallee.* New York: Viking Press, 1934.
Marx, Samuel, and Jan Clayton. *Rodgers & Hart: Bewitched Bothered and Bedeviled.* New York: Putnam's, 1976.
McCabe, John. *George M. Cohan: The Man Who Owned Broadway.* Garden City, N.Y.: Doubleday, 1973.
McGuire, Patricia Dubin. *Lullaby of Broadway.* Secaucus, N.J.: Citadel, 1983.
Melody. Boston: 1918–1934.
Music Trade Review. New York: 1899–1933.
Osgood, Henry O. *So This Is Jazz.* Boston: Little, Brown, 1926.
Popular Songs of Nineteenth-Century America. Richard Jackson, ed. New York: Dover, 1976.
Ragtime: 100 Authentic Rags. David A. Jasen, ed. New York: Big 3, 1979.
Ragtime Gems. David A. Jasen, ed. New York: Dover, 1986.
Rice, Edward Le Roy. *Monarchs of Minstrelsy.* New York: Kenny, 1911.
Rodgers, Richard. *Musical Stages.* New York: Random House, 1975.
Rose, Al. *Eubie Blake.* New York: Schirmer Books, 1979.
Rust, Brian. *The American Dance Band Discography, 1917–1942.* 2 vols. New Rochelle, N.Y.: Arlington House, 1975.
————, with Allen G. Debus. *The Complete Entertainment Discography.* New Rochelle, N.Y.: Arlington House, 1973.
————. *Jazz Records, 1897–1942.* 2 vols. New Rochelle, N.Y.: Arlington House, 1978.
Sampson, Henry T. *Blacks in Blackface.* Metuchen, N.J.: Scarecrow, 1980.
Shapiro, Nat. *Popular Music, An Annotated Index of American Popular Songs.* 5 vols. New York: Adrian Press, 1965–1969.
Shaw, Arnold. *The Rockin' 50's.* New York: Hawthorne, 1974.
Show Songs From "The Black Crook" to "The Red Mill." Stanley Applebaum, ed. New York: Dover, 1974.
Simon, George T. *The Big Bands.* New York: Macmillan, 1971.
Song Hits from the Turn of the Century. Paul Charosh and Robert A. Fremont, eds. New York: Dover, 1975.
Southern, Eileen. *Biographical Dictionary of Afro-American and African Musicians.* Westport, Conn.: Greenwood Press, 1982.
————. *The Music of Black Americans: A History.* New York: W. W. Norton, 1983.
Spaeth, Sigmund. *The Facts of Life in Popular Song.* New York: Whittlesey House, 1934.
————. *A History of Popular Music in America.* New York: Random House, 1948.
Stagg, Jerry. *The Brothers Shubert.* New York: Random House, 1968.
Stars of the American Musical Theatre in Historic Photographs. Stanley Applebaum and James Camner, eds. New York: Dover, 1981.
Sudhalter, Richard M., and Philip R. Evans. *Bix: Man & Legend.* New Rochelle, N.Y.: Arlington House, 1974.
Suskin, Steven. *Show Tunes, 1905–1985.* New York: Dodd, Mead, 1986.
"Take Me Out to The Ball Game" and Other Favorite Song Hits, 1906–1908. Lester S. Levy, ed. New York: Dover, 1984.
Taylor, Deems. *Some Enchanted Evenings.* New York: Harper, 1953.

Taylor, Theodore. _Jule: The Story of Composer Jule Styne._ New York: Random House, 1979.

Tucker, Sophie. _Some of These Days._ Garden City, N.Y.: Doubleday, Doran, 1945.

The Tuneful Yankee. Monroe H. Rosenfeld, ed. Boston: 1917.

Tyler, Don. _Hit Parade, 1920–1955._ New York: Quill/Morrow, 1985.

Waller, Maurice, and Anthony Calabrese. _Fats Waller._ New York: Schirmer Books, 1977.

Waters, Ethel, and Charles Samuels. _His Eye Is on The Sparrow._ Garden City, N.Y.: Doubleday, 1951.

Westin, Helen. _Introducing the Song Sheet._ Nashville: Thomas Nelson, 1976.

Whitcomb, Ian. _After the Ball: Pop Music from Rag to Rock._ New York: Simon and Schuster, 1973.

Whiteman, Paul, and Mary Margaret McBride. _Jazz._ New York: J. H. Sears, 1926.

Whiting, Margaret, and Will Holt. _It Might As Well Be Spring._ New York: William Morrow, 1987.

Wilder, Alec. _American Popular Song: The Great Innovators, 1900–1950._ New York: Oxford, 1972.

Wilk, Max. _They're Playing Our Song._ New York: Atheneum, 1973.

Winkler, Max. _A Penny from Heaven._ New York: Appleton-Century-Crofts, 1951.

Witmark, Isidore. _From Ragtime to Swingtime._ New York: Lee Furman, 1939.

Wodehouse, P. G., and Guy Bolton. _Bring On the Girls!_ New York: Simon and Schuster, 1953.

Woll, Allen. _Dictionary of the Black Theatre._ Westport, Conn.: Greenwood Press, 1983.

Woollcott, Alexander. _The Story of Irving Berlin._ New York & London: Putnam's, 1925.

Wright, Laurie. _Mr. Jelly Lord._ Chigwell, England: Storyville, 1980.

Young, Jordan R. _Spike Jones and his City Slickers._ Beverly Hills, Calif.: Disharmony Books, 1984.

Note: Due to space limitations, song titles are not listed.